THE SABOTAGE DIARIES

KATHERINE BARNES

HarperCollins*Publishers*

HarperCollins*Publishers*

First published in Australia in 2015
by HarperCollins*Publishers* Australia Pty Limited
ABN 36 009 913 517
harpercollins.com.au

HarperCollins*Publishers*
Level 13, 201 Elizabeth Street, Sydney NSW 2000, Australia
Unit D1, 63 Apollo Drive, Rosedale, Auckland 0632, New Zealand
A 53, Sector 57, Noida, UP, India
1 London Bridge Street, London, SE1 9GF, United Kingdom
2 Bloor Street East, 20th floor, Toronto, Ontario M4W 1A8, Canada
195 Broadway, New York, NY 10007, USA

National Library of Australia Cataloguing-in-Publication data:

Barnes, Katherine, author.
  The sabotage diaries / Katherine Barnes.
  ISBN: 978 0 7322 9879 1 (paperback)
  ISBN: 978 1 4607 0245 1 (ebook)
  Includes bibliographical references and index.
  Barnes, Cecil Edward, 1907-1952.
  World War, 1939-1945 – Greece – Personal narratives, New Zealand.
  World War, 1939-1945 – Underground movements – Greece.
  World War, 1939-1945 – Engineering and construction.
  Soldiers – New Zealand – Biography.
940.53092

Cover design by HarperCollins Design Studio
Front cover photograph provided with permission from the album of Professor, the
Lord Terrington; background image by shutterstock.com
Back cover: studio portrait of Tom Barnes taken in Cairo in August 1945; background
image shows a map of Greece printed on silk, carried by Tom Barnes during Operation
Harling and photographed by Darren Holt.
Author photograph by Leonie Hong
Typeset in 12/18.5pt Bembo by Kirby Jones
Maps by Laurie Whiddon, Map Illustrations
Index by Michael Wyatt
Printed and bound in Australia by Griffin Press
The papers used by HarperCollins in the manufacture of this book are a natural,
recyclable product made from wood grown in sustainable plantation forests. The fibre
source and manufacturing processes meet recognised international environmental
standards, and carry certification.

For Chris

Contents

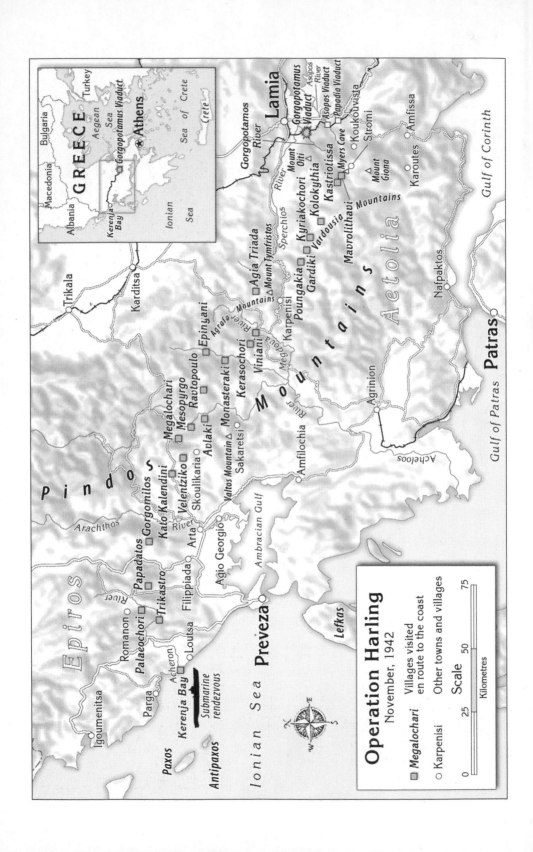

Operation Harling
November, 1942

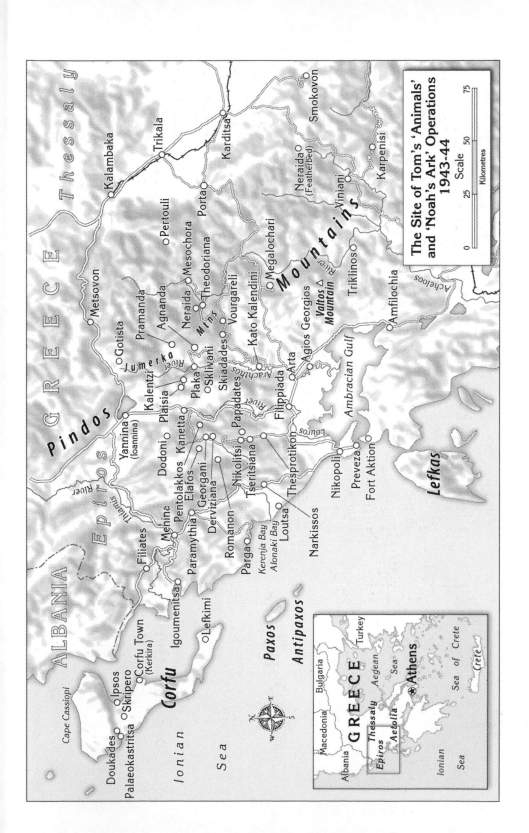

The Site of Tom's 'Animals'
and 'Noah's Ark' Operations
1943-44

A note to the reader

In early 1941, Tom Barnes embarked in the *Nieuw Amsterdam* for service in North Africa with the New Zealand Engineers.

Put to work building fortifications in Egypt, well away from the front, Tom couldn't have imagined that in October 1942 he would find himself parachuting into Nazi-occupied Greece with a small party of Allied special operators. He had accepted a role as a saboteur in the Special Operations Executive's 'Harling' operation. Their task was to demolish a bridge on the Greek railway line that the Germans were using to supply Rommel's army in North Africa. And that was only the beginning of his story.

Some of the techniques used in this book are more commonly employed in fiction than non-fiction.

The narrative is written as though by Tom himself. His voice has been reconstructed from the diaries, reports and letters he left behind at his death. His reflections and thoughts are based on attitudes revealed in those documents.

The dialogue is invented. However, the details mentioned in the dialogue—about the people who speak, their previous service and their families—are real. Their voices have been recreated from their own and others' accounts.

Food, death and family are common preoccupations among those serving in difficult circumstances. Several members of the Harling party published memoirs after the war, in which they noted that food was one of the main subjects they talked about. When members of the Harling party discuss these topics, what they say is imagined but again, any personal details are real. In each case where a conversation is described, evidence from Tom's diaries shows that the people speaking were actually together at that time.

With one exception, all letters are real. Speeches are invented. Notes on chapter sources can be found at the end of the book.

PART I

OPERATION 'HARLING'

ONE

There were twelve of us to begin with. Three engineers, three interpreters, three wireless operators and the three in command: Eddie, Chris and John. Twelve soldiers, under orders to carry out a clandestine operation on the east coast of Greece. Totally dependent on the support of Greek partisans, with the scarce information we'd received from the Special Operations Executive in Cairo—numbers, location, leadership—way off the mark.

After the first operation was over, I found myself with a reputation as a saboteur. One of the best, they said in a newspaper article my mother sent over from New Zealand to my fiancée Beth in Tasmania. I'm not sure where they got that from. I did lead the demolition team for that first, critical act of sabotage— that part's true. For the rest, I'm not so sure.

I had two diaries in 1942, one green, one red. Green for Egypt, red for Greece.

The green one is fat, one day to a page. It came first. The red one is more of a notebook—I had to put in the days and dates myself and keep the writing small. I had no idea when or whether I would be able to get hold of another.

There are no stains on the green diary, although it was stinking hot in Egypt a lot of the time and your shirt stuck to your back. I'd spent the best part of a year building a harbour at Aqaba, that gulf running out to the east from the Red Sea that looks so little on the world map. Dredging, driving piles for the wharf, making roads. Managing D8 bulldozers and Le Tourneau scoops, and the men operating them for No. 3 Section, 21 Mechanical Equipment Company, New Zealand Engineers. I might as well have been back with the Public Works Department in Tasmania, where I'd been before I joined up. Or in Christchurch a few years before that, when I was still in my twenties, for that matter— except for the scenery of the Arabian peninsula, as far from New Zealand or Tasmania as it's possible to imagine.

The red diary is smudged round the edges, small and light so that I could fit it into the haversack I had strapped to my chest when I slipped through the hatch of the B24 Liberator that night at the beginning of October 1942. Some of the pages are so blurry I can hardly make out the words now. Could've been sweat, or melted snow—both at once, maybe, as we struck desperately through the mountains away from the Italians, making for the submarine rendezvous on the west coast of Greece.

September 29 was a Tuesday. That's when the green diary stops. I'd finished up at Aqaba and taken some leave—Palestine, the Lebanon and then Syria—before heading back to Cairo. I'd got a letter from Beth, giving me a blast for not telling her about the trip. Quite right, too. She would have loved Palestine, and among all the beautiful girls I saw in the streets of Beirut she would still have been a standout. I was suffering from desert sores, especially the one on my big toe. It was going to need serious attention now I was back at Maadi, the New Zealand Forces camp outside Cairo.

The camp itself was comfortable enough. It was about nine miles south of Cairo, past the suburb of Maadi, right at the edge of the desert, with wooden huts for sleeping if you were lucky and a view to the pyramids from the nearby slopes. A bit of a home away from home amid the strangeness of Egypt. The canteens were stocked with familiar foods; we even had our very own pie factory.

I was on administrative duties and not enjoying it very much when, quite unexpectedly, a message arrived. *Report immediately to the CRE.*

The Commander, Royal Engineers of 2 New Zealand Division was Lieutenant-Colonel 'Bull' Hanson. I would find him at the Kiwi rest home beside the Nile. Trying to suppress my curiosity, I walked in, past injured soldiers returned from the front, who were resting in wicker armchairs, or heading off to the pool with towels over their shoulders. Ladies from Cairo and the surrounding suburbs, who staffed the club as their contribution to the war effort, were hovering solicitously over the convalescents.

Hanson had just got back from Headquarters NZ Engineers in the Western Desert. A civil engineer by training, in the first war he'd served in the Wellington Regiment. More importantly, he'd been on the winning New Zealand army side in the 1919 Empire rugby tournament.

While we'd been in Aqaba doing construction work, the front had seemed a long way off, and news had come through in a dribble. We knew the New Zealand Division had been in the thick of it around El Alamein since early July, and we were jealous. We felt we were missing out on the action. That's when I had started trying to get into the Division as a sapper—a military engineer—and that's what had brought me back to Cairo.

'Tom,' said Hanson, getting up as I walked in. 'Good to see you again.' The sun shining through the window was lightly touching the short, tight curls that sat close to his head; they looked rather like the curly fleece of a carpet sheep.

We'd met already, at the Engineers' dinner the previous week, and talked about roads and harbours—the sort of conversation only engineers can enjoy, I suppose. He'd built a road from Alamein to Kaponga without any heavy machinery. I'd dredged the harbour at Aqaba without a dredge. We'd had plenty to talk about.

'Your story about the harbour,' he said now, 'I was impressed. Real ingenuity.' Instead of the dredge we didn't have, we'd used a drag bucket and a hoist rope to dig out the basin for the lighters, those shallow-draft barges that would ferry supplies and passengers between moored ships and the wharf.

Hanson stopped to wipe the sweat off his wrists with his handkerchief. 'That's why we thought of you. For another job entirely.'

He paused. I waited.

'We're looking for a couple of Kiwis,' he said, 'to join other sappers on a special job for the Commander in Chief.' Why Kiwis, I wondered. Later I decided it must have been because they thought we were all particularly tough due to our colonial upbringing—but no one ever really explained that.

'Yes, General Alexander himself. Not with the Division—I know that's what you've been after—but plenty of excitement. And danger. We thought you might be up for it. Working behind enemy lines.'

'Really?' I was astonished—and intrigued.

'This is not an assignment,' he said. 'It's entirely voluntary and top secret. I'm afraid I can't tell you anything else at all unless you decide to take it on.'

I swallowed. What a decision to make in a hurry. But then I realised it might fit the bill—the action I'd been after, all that time in Aqaba. So I replied, after not too embarrassing a pause while my mind churned through the possibilities, 'Yes, Boss. Yes. I'm up for it.'

New Zealanders didn't call superior officers 'sir'. It made us uncomfortable. With 'Boss', everyone knew where they stood.

'All right, then. You may know I was in the show in Greece last year. The topography there is incredible—those mountains rise thousands of feet sheer from the coast. There's only a single railway line linking Salonika in the north with Piraeus—the port of Athens.'

He explained that Rommel's supply line ran along that railway—up to forty-eight trains a day, transporting goods through Greece to the Mediterranean, where they were unloaded onto ships bound for Africa.

'Now that they hold Crete and the Dodecanese Islands, they can make that crossing pretty much with impunity,' Hanson said. 'If we can disrupt the supply line on the Greek mainland, our position here in the North African theatre will be far stronger. The Hun will be forced to take a longer journey from Salonika to Crete and some of it will have to be by daylight. That will give our subs the chance to have a shot at his supply ships.

'The mission you'll be involved in is code-named "Harling". We're dropping a party into the Greek mountains to blow up one of the railway bridges on the Salonika–Piraeus line.'

Three bridges had been earmarked, he told me; it would be up to the party to determine which one would be most feasible.

'When you say "dropping", what do you mean exactly?' I asked.

'Well, by parachute, of course,' he replied. 'You'll get some basic training tomorrow. The Special Operations Executive has a handful of Liberators for purposes like this. You'll be jumping from one of them.'

I'd never heard of the SOE. If I'd known then what I knew later, I might've tried to cry off right then and there. But it sounded exciting—glamorous, even—when Hanson told me that 'the Firm', as SOE were known, were running the show from the brown block of flats in Garden City that the taxi drivers called 'the spy house'—Rustum Buildings.

'The Firm is a special Churchill initiative,' Hanson explained, 'to get our people behind enemy lines in occupied Europe, building resistance armies for when they're needed. There's been a bit going on in Yugoslavia already, supply drops and so on. We'll send a submarine to take you off when it's all over—except that some of the party are going to stay in Greece to work with the resistance.'

'In and out pretty quickly, then. How long altogether?' I was thinking of how long I'd be out of contact with Beth—and my parents, too, of course.

'The timing is critical. Our plans for the Western Desert mean that we need the line cut before mid-October. The sub will arrive off the west coast near Paramythia at Christmas.'

'So I'll be signing on for about three months. That sounds all right.'

'Good, then. You'll sleep at Maadi tonight. Tomorrow you'll get a full briefing. We have three Kiwis lined up at present in case something untoward happens—only two of you will go. The party will be leaving virtually straight away.'

As I walked away, I couldn't believe my good luck. At last my engineering qualifications were bringing dividends. In all my efforts to get into the Div, the most I'd been hoping for was laying and clearing mines with the other sappers. This would be far more satisfying.

I wondered who the other two Kiwis were, and ran through possibilities in my mind. What had made them think of me, and would I be one of the chosen two? I had plenty of experience with explosives from road building, especially around Aqaba, but this was different. How could I make certain I wasn't the one left behind?

I had some reservations, too, once I'd calmed down a bit. This sounded like a job for a commando unit, not for sappers like us who hadn't even had full infantry training. Commandos were a new idea. We'd heard the odd rumour about them, and the rest we imagined—training out in the wilds, Scotland or somewhere like that, learning the best way to kill silently and then disappear. They had a training school at Haifa, I'd heard.

In the afternoon I went into town and hung around for a while with an old mate, trying to quell my excitement and focus on practicalities. There was something I wanted to buy. By the sound of things I'd be sleeping rough in Greece for quite some time—even Maadi would seem civilised, no doubt, though we'd had to bivouac in the sand the night we marched in. I'd heard about a type of rubberised bed that you inflated at night and could roll up and carry with you the next day (minus the air, of course). I thought it was a great idea. I was determined to get hold of one in Cairo if I could.

Egypt was not at war. Under the terms of their treaty with Britain they were not obliged to be. They had handed over the strategic areas to the Brits—and the desert, for what it was worth—but for the rest it was business as usual. The shops in Cairo were thriving and it was amazing what you could buy.

With a bit of perseverance, I managed to locate what I was after in one of the larger stores. It was called a 'Li-Lo'.

I had to wait till I got back to camp to try it out. When I arrived there I found Noel Brady packing for the Greek job as well. Noel had been with the Division in the desert around Mersa Matruh and Bir Rhirba so it made a lot of sense that he had been picked.

We packed up as much of our gear as we could. Fortunately I had posted quite a lot of things to Beth just a couple of days earlier: a length of camel-hair cloth, some things in filigree silver—sugar tongs and six Armenian serviette rings—and three cushion covers from Aleppo. I was collecting things for our home after we married, things that would remind me of the places I'd been. I wrote her a letter that night—number eighty-two—but couldn't tell her anything.

Then I laid out the Li–Lo on the floor. I thought I might get some respite from the bed bugs. Rumour had it 18 Battalion had imported the critters to Maadi Camp from Kasr-el-Nil barracks back in the early days of the camp, but in fact I'd had bugs in my bed since Aqaba.

Blowing up the Li–Lo was surprisingly hard work. I was looking forward to a good night's sleep, but unfortunately the bed bugs had no trouble making the short journey to my new bed. And the Li–Lo went down overnight.

We could smell sausages cooking as we strolled into the wooden mess hut for breakfast next morning. Noel and I were struck with the same thought—better eat as much as possible while we could. The food was bound to be worse in Greece, and far less certain, whereas there was lots to eat at Maadi and it was pretty good.

'You blokes missed another balls-up at Shafto's last night,' one of the others said as we sat down to eat. Shafto's was the camp cinema, where for three piastres or 'ackers' you had the privilege of sitting on hard wooden seats and watching while the reels were screened in the wrong order, or the sound reverberated so much that you couldn't make out the words, or the projector broke down. The building was so flimsy that one night when the troops were particularly angry about the dodgy film and had started hurling chairs around, the roof had fallen in. Everyone had been fined to pay for the repairs.

'What went wrong this time?' said Noel. 'On second thoughts, don't tell me—I can guess. The projector broke down and when they fixed it you couldn't hear the rest of the film for boos and whistles.'

'You guessed it, old man, near enough. Not that the film was that good anyway—some old British thing. If it'd been a Jimmy Cagney, now …'

At breakfast we found out who the third Kiwi sapper was— Arthur Edmonds. He had been with 6 Field Company at

Ruweisat Ridge and then at Alamein laying and clearing mines. Again, it made sense for them to pick him. I still wondered about myself. I hoped Hanson hadn't overrated my ingenuity.

After breakfast Noel and I were summoned up 'Bludgers' Hill' to Headquarters NZ Division for a meeting with Brigadier Stevens, the commander of Maadi camp. Stevens was about fifty, with receding hair. His bushy eyebrows were like my own— if I didn't have them trimmed, everyone laughed about them. He had been a New Zealand army regular since the First World War and was said to be an extremely able man, in spite of the diffidence in his manner.

The last time I had talked to him I had come away disappointed. Back in January I had been to see Lady Freyberg, wife of the Commander of the NZ Expeditionary Force, to discuss my chances of getting into the Division. She'd sent me to talk to her husband, General Freyberg himself. Both of them seemed keen and I thought I was as good as in. But then I went to discuss it with Stevens and he knocked it on the head—at least I'd thought so. When I'd returned to Cairo from Aqaba, he had put me on administrative duties. It was supposed to be the quickest way into the Division, so I had gone along with it. Now, as he sat upright at his paper-cluttered desk, he seemed pleased that I would be seeing some action at last.

'It's my duty to inform you two of the risks involved in this undertaking,' he began. 'You'll be dropped into occupied Greece. Certain areas of the country are primarily under the control of the Italians, others of the Germans, including Athens, of course. And then there are the Albanians.

'It appears that there are bands of resistance fighters operating in the mountains. They will light signal fires to guide your aircraft in for the drop. After that you may expect some help from them, but basically you will need to subsist off the country until such time as the operation takes place.'

The Brigadier was playing with a pencil on his desk as he spoke, flipping it one way and then another between his fingers.

'Our information is that the people of Greece hate the occupying forces and are likely to help a British operation. We have no detailed intelligence about enemy operations in the mountains but you will have to take every precaution to ensure that the enemy doesn't hear of your presence or, worse still, of your mission.

'You must preserve absolute secrecy about this operation before you leave the country. You won't be able to tell your families where you are or what you will be doing.'

We nodded. We hadn't expected anything else.

'It's early days for the SOE—but certain principles have been established for operations they've been carrying out in Yugoslavia and elsewhere. You'll be in uniform. That way if you're captured, you will fall under the Geneva Convention and can't be shot as a spy—theoretically, at least. But just in case, everyone will be issued with what they call a "suicide pill". If you think you're likely to be tortured, use it. That way you can't reveal anything of use to the enemy before you die—as you will anyway; it'll just be a question of how quickly.

'We'll make every effort to take you off after the operation, but we can't promise anything. If for some reason the submarine can't make it, you will have to stay in Greece until another opportunity arises, and that could be a long time, perhaps not until liberation. For all that time you would be in hiding, having to live off your wits, never able to let down your guard or to trust anyone absolutely. You could be killed or captured, taken off to Germany or Italy to a POW camp, perhaps for years.

'These are beyond the risks that soldiers are expected to sign up for. I'm giving you another opportunity now—if you feel that you don't want to take it on, you can still pull out.'

Noel and I interrupted each other in our eagerness to assure him that we were up for it, risks and all. Neither of us wanted to appear less than enthusiastic.

'Then finish your packing. This afternoon the three of you will be taken into Cairo for further briefing. That's you two, plus Edmonds. You won't be coming back here to Maadi camp. I wish you some excitement—but not too much—and a successful operation.'

'Thank you, Boss.'

'And don't go calling the British officers "Boss". They won't like it.'

Something to get my teeth into at last. Perhaps this time people would be jealous of me, rather than the other way round. That's if they ever got to hear about it. But I was determined about one thing. No matter what the danger, I was going to come out alive. I was going to go home to Beth, just as I'd promised her when I joined up. We would get married and live happily ever after. And hopefully, if it all went to plan, I'd have quite a story to tell our children.

We were expecting to be picked up a bit after two but we were a little early. After a few minutes, Arthur Edmonds joined us.

Arthur was bigger than me, but he wasn't throwing his weight around. I was ready to be intimidated by his experience, but he had other things on his mind that afternoon.

'What a nightmare,' he said. 'Packing up to leave.'

I was surprised but didn't say anything. Packing seemed the least of our worries.

'Three months in the desert,' he went on. 'Three months laying minefields every day in the sweltering heat. My stomach packs it in, and in the middle of getting over it they ask me to join this little party.'

'You don't want to go?' Noel looked immediately brighter.

'In my condition?' said Arthur. 'Of course not. But what can you do?'

You could say no, I thought. It was supposed to be voluntary, after all. As it was, one of us would have to stay behind. Why not him?

At 2.15 sharp a British staff officer, Major Derek Lange, arrived in a Buick. We were impressed. Normally we tried to get hold of a one-ton truck or a Norton motorcycle for our trips to Cairo. Otherwise, we were stuck with the train.

'Hot as blazes, isn't it, sir?' Noel said to Major Lange as the camp disappeared behind us. There were three miles of desert to cross before we got to the suburb of Maadi.

'This is nothing to Aqaba,' I said. 'Hotter than the hobs of hell there—at the right time of year.' Or the wrong time, depending how you thought of it. 'One day we were driving up Wadi Itm and the car boiled all the way up—we had to stop and put water in it every couple of miles. It was hard to breathe, it was so hot— and the air was full of that fine dust—you know what I mean.'

'Yes, I know all about that dust,' said Lange. 'Well, by the sound of things you fellows won't be seeing too much more of the hot weather. You might find the mountains of Greece quite a bit colder. I believe the forecast is for rain and snow.'

'I hope they give us plenty of warm clothes,' I said. The cold was hard to imagine.

'Don't worry, you'll get a chance to pick out everything you think you'll need—weapons and equipment, too. I think you'll find some of the gear they've been developing for special operations rather interesting.'

We headed north through Maadi on our way to Cairo. Maadi was near Cairo, but it wasn't Cairo—that was why the wealthy wanted to live there. Hot purple and pink hibiscus lit up the green as we drove smoothly through the streets. The soft jacaranda blues of early summer were gone, the carpets of blossom on the ground long ago turned to brown mush, which had in turn disappeared rapidly in the heat. Only a few big, crackly seed pods remained on the ground as a reminder. The houses had lawns and flowerbeds—it always seemed like a miracle after coming in from the desert.

As we drove past Maadi station, a two-carriage passenger train was just departing. Nearby was 'The Tent', set up by generous Maadi residents to make the life of the Kiwi soldiers easier with cups of tea and sandwiches. You could play table tennis there, or mini golf if you fancied it. I can't say I did.

It was impossible to make the trip to Cairo without being held up by multiple obstructions. First you had to manoeuvre around all the other vehicles on the road—donkey carts and watermelon carts, not to mention the famous 'bint carts', with a platform that carried perhaps half a dozen black-covered women to the fields and back again, a single man walking alongside to look after the donkey that was pulling the whole affair. Everyone with a camera seemed to have a photo of one. Then there were the animals, a flock of sheep perhaps, with black and white lambs, or a herd of goats. Camels, too, and water-buffalo being led out to pasture with their calves. Men walking in long robes with turbans or red fezes; children often in nothing at all.

We headed for Garden City and pulled up outside the Rustum Buildings. Immediately the everyday Cairo street racket enveloped us: trams, street vendors, horse-drawn gharries, and the screech of carts with steel tyres. There was the usual stink of sweat and garlic and rotten vegetables. A small horde of beggars demanded *baksheesh*—alms—as we got out of the car.

I felt elated as I climbed one flight of stairs after another behind Major Lange's sweat-stained back. Soon we would meet the other members of our party. I couldn't wait to hear about those three bridges.

TWO

'Brigadier,' said Lange, 'the three New Zealand sappers for the Harling party: Captain Tom Barnes, Captain Arthur Edmonds, and Lieutenant Noel Brady.'

Brigadier Keble seemed to be dressed for the weather rather than his rank, with nothing but a sweaty vest on top and shorts below. As I found out later, he reported to Lord Glenconner, the head of SOE, who was rarely seen in person and therefore known as 'God'. Keble's own nickname was 'Bolo'.

'Ah, welcome, welcome,' said Keble. 'Yes, the Harling operation. Top priority with the C in C. Keep Rommel from Cairo and the rest of the Delta by cutting his supply line through Greece. Risky, quite risky. But they believe it can be done—the Greeks, I mean. I hear you're all very keen to take part—unfortunately we can only take two of you. As you know.

'The bridges we're looking at are all in the Brallos Pass area, near Thermopylae. Asopos would be best. That's my view. Inaccessible gorge. Hard to rebuild—take a long time.'

We crowded in to get a glimpse of the maps, but the Brigadier was already moving on. 'Well, I believe Colonel Hanson has already given you a preliminary briefing. You'll get a full briefing later from Colonel "Eddie". He'll be in charge on the ground. He'll decide which of the bridges to go for, in consultation with the resistance fighters of course. And with "Chris", who'll be his second in command. The very best of luck to you.'

He shook hands with each of us, and then Major Lange ushered us out of the room and down the corridor to a meeting with Colonel Hanson.

'Good to see Kiwi sappers in the thick of it,' Hanson said. 'The most urgent thing now is your parachute training. You're due at the training centre at Kibrit later today. It's usually two weeks, but there isn't time for that. You'll be getting two days instead. Then there are fittings for parachutes and harnesses, and you'll need to select all your gear, too, especially the explosives.'

'How will that travel, the explosives and so on?' Noel's voice sounded thick, and he tried hurriedly to clear his throat. Like me, he was probably wondering whether we would have to drop with explosives strapped to our backs. No wonder he was sweating.

'In special canisters. They'll be dropped with you from the aircraft.'

'I see,' said Noel. I could hear his relief.

'The most important thing,' Hanson went on, 'is to meet the rest of your team. They're due here later this afternoon. For security reasons, you won't know each other's full names. In general, you will be known by your first names, unless you already go by a nickname—like you, Tom.' Although my first name is Cecil, I've been called Tom—from Tom Thumb—ever since I was a child.

The Major took us downstairs and knocked on an open door. 'Chris' was standing on the far side of a table full of maps. He looked up, took the salute, and then came around the table to shake each of us by the hand.

He had reddish fair hair. In Australia, they'd have called him 'Bluey'. That's if they dared, because Chris was upper-crust English, with an accent to match. He was also disconcertingly tall. They would've had to do it behind his back.

He was very young to be second in command of our operation, I thought. He couldn't have been past his mid-twenties. As a major, he outranked all of us, but being in command of people who are much older than you isn't easy. You have to win their respect. He had a job ahead of him.

Major Lange had told us that Chris had served as an intelligence officer in the Greek campaign, and had worked for the SOE for six months in Crete after it fell to the Germans, living off the land. He spoke Greek fluently. Later, I would learn that Chris was really Christopher Montague Woodhouse, usually known as 'Monty'. His father had a title. But Chris wasn't the kind of person to shove that in your face. It only came out a long time afterwards.

I began to wonder if perhaps, at thirty-five, I was too old for this job. Would I be the oldest in the team? This was the first time I'd ever thought about being overtaken by a younger, stronger generation—and I didn't like it. I hastily pushed it out of my mind.

Chris had been a trainer at the SOE school in Haifa, he told us now. On the brink of joining the SAS, he'd been approached about the Harling mission instead. He seemed reserved at first—we both were, I suppose—but later I got to know him very well indeed.

The others weren't coming that afternoon after all, it turned out, so we wouldn't be going to Kibrit just yet. Chris's briefing would be just for us.

The contour maps and blueprints I'd been looking forward to were laid out on a central table. Arthur, Noel and I pulled up chairs, sweating as usual. My chair was wooden and cane-bottomed—at least I wouldn't have to peel myself off it when I got up.

Now the real work began.

'These three bridges,' Chris started, 'our three targets—are all on the slopes of Mount Oiti.' When he said 'our', a shiver slid up my spine.

'Look, this is the town of Lamia,' Chris went on, 'north of Athens. Mount Oiti is to the south of Lamia—seven thousand feet up. Look at the contour lines.'

Those Greek mountains again—first Hanson, now Chris. They must be really something, I thought.

'Obviously any approach would have to be from above. You've got blueprints for two of the bridges there in front of you, Gorgopotamos and Papadia. We're expecting the Asopos one to arrive at any minute—I hope it'll be in time. In the meantime we have to rely on this magazine photo from 1909. Ludicrous, isn't it? Anyway Colonel Eddie is preparing demolition plans for all three targets.'

I picked up the Gorgopotamos blueprint and studied it carefully, wondering what the cross-section was, where we'd have to lay the explosives—if that was the target Eddie selected.

When the British forces withdrew from Greece in 1941, Chris told us, they had left a wireless set in Athens with some friendly officers. Cairo was in touch with our chief agent there, 'Prometheus', via a relay station in Turkey. SOE had cabled him early in September to ask if an attack on the railway line between Salonika and Athens was feasible. His reply was definite. Yes, they could do it, but they'd need British help—at least two explosives experts and a party to support the mountain resistance fighters in the operation. Along with the explosives, of course. Timing was very tight—the party would have to be dropped between 28 September and 3 October in order to carry out the mission in time.

'Who will the explosives experts be?' asked Noel.

Chris stared at him. 'Well, you, of course. Whichever two it turns out to be. And a third for the other plane.'

'Oh,' said Noel. 'Of course.' I was glad Noel had asked that particular question and not me.

'How will we recognise the location for the drop?' asked Arthur. 'Will someone meet us?'

'A resistance leader called Seferiades. He's a lawyer. Prometheus has sent him from Athens to meet us when we drop. He'll arrange to have a ring of twelve bonfires lit and to set off flares to indicate the dropping ground in the Mount Giona region near the village of Koukouvista. By the way, the Greeks call resistance fighters *andartes*. Best remember that.'

'*Andartes*,' we repeated dutifully. Our first Greek word.

Of the members of the Harling party who would remain after the operation, one was 'Themis', the only Greek; a second lieutenant, he was on secondment to the British army with the rank of captain. The others were two wireless operators and Chris himself.

'And the aircraft we'll be using for the drop?' asked Arthur.

'We have three B24 Liberator aircraft at our disposal,' Chris replied.

'The new American bombers,' said Arthur. 'We saw a film about them at the Maadi cinema. Three quarters of a million each. But supposed to have a very good range.'

'That's correct,' said Chris. 'None of the other aircraft we use would be suitable for that very reason.'

We would be split into three parties for the landing in Greece, each with a leader, a sapper, an interpreter and a wireless operator— and each with enough explosives to carry out the operation. That way if something went wrong, the mission could still go ahead.

'It looks as though it'll be tomorrow before you head out to Kibrit,' said Chris. 'You'll meet the others there. In the meantime, the Firm are putting you up tonight on a houseboat on the Nile. You can have dinner there, and afterwards you're free to have a good time. Could be the last chance for a while, so make the most of it.'

Houseboats on the Nile—there were a lot of them. There was even a nightclub on one. Before the war, they had taken tourists up to Aswan and Luxor in luxury. Now soldiers had taken their place, but the boats remained. The Firm had stocked one for us with plenty of beer and a bottle of whisky, too. We parked ourselves on padded benches around the open whisky bottle, and talked everything over, an ashtray filling rapidly as we lit one cigarette after another.

After dinner Noel and I went out on the town—the Dolls and the Trocadero—a final blowout. Back at the houseboat, we slumped down to sleep it off.

It wasn't easy to get up in the morning. Leaving the houseboat to its aroma of beer bottles and stale cigarette butts, we stumbled across the gangway to Major Lange and the waiting Buick, trying to smarten ourselves up as we went.

With the freshness of the morning diminishing minute by minute, we drove out to the SOE depot to collect some of our gear. The major who met us—his name escapes me now—had a harassed air about him. Perhaps he had an objection to handing over his precious toys in such a hurry.

'Well, let's see,' he said. 'You're all down for the same things. A revolver and ammunition—Lugers all round. A commando knife each, the Fairbairn/Sykes Mark 3. Have you used one of these before?'

We hadn't.

He looked pleased. We were a captive audience.

The knife had a hand-finished seven-inch blade sharpened from the point all the way to the oval cross-guard, a cross-hatched grip and a neat leather scabbard. The blade was blued so that it wouldn't glint and give you away to the enemy.

'I understand you're going in uniform,' said the major, 'so perhaps you will manage without the usual training for spies. SOE seem to be a bloody disorganised bunch and you're not the first we've sent off somewhere in a rush.

'Anyway, you need to know that it's harder than you think to kill silently with this knife. Always strike upwards: that's the first thing. Hold the victim's mouth and nose shut. You'll silence his first cry but it's next to impossible to silence his dying gasps. There will be a lot of blood. And keep away from other orifices as much as possible—if you take my meaning, gentlemen.'

He handed each of us a leather belt for gold sovereigns, which would finance the operation. We each wore one when we jumped. Heavy with coins, they were liable to slip around under your webbing when you were hanging from your parachute harness and you couldn't do anything about it.

Next came a tin of hard rations, a torch, several flares in different colours, some Benzedrine tablets and the suicide pill Brigadier Stevens had mentioned the day before. It was concealed in a button. I hoped I would have the right button to hand if I ever needed it.

Finally, we were each given some tiny buttons that unscrewed to reveal even smaller compasses inside, and several maps of Greece to different scales, printed on silk to be sewn into our clothes. That way if we were patted down in a routine search, they wouldn't be found.

'Who dreams these up?' Arthur asked, trying to use his fingers delicately to unscrew the button cap.

'I believe they've got a whole establishment working on them back in England, in Hertfordshire,' the major replied. 'The Frythe, I think it's called. There are more things coming in all the time. There are guns disguised as pens, and explosives disguised as animal droppings—cow pats and mule dung. Look here—this is the Enpen. It takes a.22 round but it looks like an ordinary pen that no one would bother to steal.'

He was rapidly warming to his subject, but Major Lange gave us the nod that it was time to go.

'You'll have the chance later to collect all the personal gear you need—uniform, boots, messing gear, et cetera.'

The Buick took us back to the SOE offices for yet another briefing. I didn't record who gave it and now I can't remember. My diary says we were taken further into confidence. Let me say at once that any confidence we put in that briefing was misplaced. In fact you could say that that Thursday afternoon was the start of all our troubles.

They told us there were guerrilla bands at Mount Giona and Mount Tymfristos. Seferiades controlled the first lot, between two and three hundred. A Colonel Zervas commanded the group at Mount Tymfristos, perhaps as many as twelve hundred. The location of his headquarters had been corrupted in the signal, but they believed it was at Pera Kapsi, near Karpenisi. Seferiades' group might 'owe fealty' to Zervas. Later, in Greece, lounging around the table after an outdoor summer meal or huddled up in greatcoats as rain bucketed down outside and the wind threatened to tear the tiles off the roof, Chris and I laughed together as we remembered this bizarre medieval terminology. But at the time, it seemed romantic and exciting.

A third resistance leader we were to look out for was called Karalivanos. He was supposed to be associated with Seferiades. The Giona band, possibly supplemented by a detachment from the Tymfristos band, would support our operation, they thought.

Colonel Eddie was under orders to choose the bridge that would sever railway communications for the longest time. There was to be an alternative plan in case the first attempt failed—to be carried out hard on the heels of the first, to get the element of surprise. No one would be expecting the guerrillas to have the stamina for a second try.

After the briefing a truck took us to the parachute school at Kibrit, in the Suez Canal Zone south of Moascar and Ismailia—a four-hour drive. Chris came with us. As we neared our destination we passed one RAF installation after another, until, as the light faded, we could barely make out the planes.

* * *

At last we met the other officers in the Harling party. They were, to put it mildly, an odd assortment.

Denys must have been born complaining about something. The milk, perhaps, or the sleeping arrangements. Since then, he'd made a habit of it—you could tell by his sardonic eyebrows. He was commando-trained, as were Nat and John, but it beat me how he coped with the conditions, given his predilection for comfort and good food. Most recently he'd been organising a commando squadron in Syria, and was unimpressed that he'd been called away from it.

Denys knew the whole region well, having worked for the Ottoman Bank for a long time before the war. He spoke Greek fluently, and a number of other languages, too. He was older than some of the others—around thirty, five years younger than me—and balding. To comfort himself for the inadequacy of the world as he found it, he smoked a pipe.

Themis was along as an interpreter. Chris knew him already— they'd been instructors together at the commando training school in Haifa. Good-looking, dark-haired, Themis spoke English quite well. For someone in his early twenties he'd already seen a lot of action, first against the Italians in Albania, before the Nazis moved into Greece, and later in Crete, where he'd been taken prisoner by the Hun, escaping to join the resistance in the Cretan mountains.

I was surprised that Themis wasn't in Greek uniform. Apparently the Greeks had asked for only British personnel, so the Firm had decided to put Themis in a British uniform and hope for the best. What we didn't know—and what those who were briefing us should have known but didn't—was that to some of the Greek resistance fighters, Greek officers working directly for the British were traitors. Cairo probably imagined it would be unimportant, but Themis was to stay behind in Greece, and in the long run it mattered a lot.

John was third in command. He was of a similar height and age to Chris, well built and quite handsome, but surprisingly unsure of himself for a person with those natural advantages. He lacked Chris's rapport with the men, and looked a little ill at ease in his new rank of major.

Nat had managed a stud farm in Thessaly, the rich farming plateau to the east of the central mountain range of Greece. Like Denys, he spoke Greek fluently and was along as an interpreter, in addition to his commando expertise. Unlike Denys, he had a full head of hair; it made him look younger than his thirty-two years. Compared to Denys, he was relatively uneducated. Denys had read classics at Cambridge and never let us forget it.

Inder looked like a baby. He must have been barely twenty, and a good two inches shorter than me. His father was a Sikh, his mother Scottish, and he'd been raised mostly in Edinburgh. He'd come direct from the Royal Engineers Training Depot in Ismailia. An officer from GHQ Cairo, he told us, had appeared out of nowhere and announced they were looking for officers for a parachuting operation. Inder had volunteered. As he put it himself—'Why not?'

And then there was Colonel Eddie, just a few months older than me. He was a career soldier with a lot of experience who had seen service with the 7th Armoured Division in the Western Desert. He had a high forehead, accentuated by a receding hairline, and a thinnish face. Like Denys, he smoked a pipe.

Eddie was already a parachutist. He'd learnt to jump in his spare time while he was a senior army instructor at the Combined Operations School on the Suez Canal. As he explained it, he'd wanted to draw attention to the fact—which no one had yet realised—that airborne troops could have a role supporting seaborne troops in an assault landing. He did one jump to prove his point, and then decided he might as well finish the training. Now he seemed like an old hand.

Of the three signallers, two were rather quiet. Mike Chittis, a Roumanian from Palestine with unruly brown hair, didn't speak English at all well. Doug Phillips, with a longish face and hair parted in the middle, was quiet and dependable.

Len Wilmott, however, was an entirely different story. He had an unusual face, with a square chin and high cheekbones that became more prominent as he got thinner. As a sergeant, he was theoretically subordinate to all the officers, but he took a shine to Arthur and me and we saw what he hid behind his compliant exterior. He had a colourful turn of phrase that could make the most boring story diverting—not that his stories were ever boring. His gift for a good yarn was second to none. He wasn't much more than twenty but he'd started work on a fishing boat at thirteen, before enlisting as a boy soldier. One way or another, he'd already seen more of the foibles of humankind than many people see in their lifetime.

At first, we were all scrupulous about our nicknames, worrying that we might accidentally betray somebody's surname, or his real first name, once we'd learnt them. But as we got to know each other, we inevitably began to let our guard down.

We would have one day's training before our first jump. As we loped out to join our instructor, the Little Bitter Lake to the south, and the much bigger Great Bitter Lake to the north, lay blue and calm in the early light.

We discovered another Kiwi already there, enrolled in the regular parachuting course—Bill Jordan, whom we knew from Maadi camp. He was Irish by background and a journalist by training. Like Len, he told a good yarn. One of his best was about the time he'd volunteered to become a human torpedo. The op had been cancelled in the end, when he'd already almost completed the training. Parachuting behind enemy lines was to be his next escapade—pretty tame after the torpedo stunt, I would imagine—but he was getting longer to prepare than we were.

In the evening we went to get our harnesses fitted. Over our uniform we could wear either a camouflage jump suit, fastened with zippers and equipped with a number of pockets for storing our gear, or a padded flying suit. The parachute harness had to fit over the top of everything else. I hoped we would fit through the hatch—I didn't want to get stuck thousands of feet above those mountains we kept hearing so much about.

'Ready for the big moment, Tom?' asked Arthur as we struggled out of bed before dawn the next morning. 'Did your Li-Lo stay up?'

'No, it seems to have gone down again,' I said, pretending not to notice his glee. 'Oh, look, the plug came out. That's easily fixed.'

We were jumping from a 'Wimpy'—a Wellington bomber—at dawn. The exit was a hole in the floor. As we took off, I silently rehearsed the drill. Feet together, roll forward. Feet together, roll forward. The dispatcher fixed the static lines of our parachutes to the 'strong points' in the fuselage of the plane. As we jumped, the static lines would snap, jerking the parachutes open above our heads.

'Action stations! Go, go!'

I landed well and the instructor praised my exit, too. It was a great experience, but certainly not thrilling—there didn't seem to be anything to it. But I had officially become the first member of the 2 NZ Expeditionary Force to jump by parachute, beating Noel Brady by two seconds.

Perhaps it was a pity that Noel didn't make the first jump. At 2.30 the following morning we did our first night jump, and became professional parachutists. But shortly afterwards, Eddie told us that Noel had drawn the short straw. Arthur and I would be going to Greece; Noel would be staying behind. He must have been terribly disappointed. I was relieved that the suspense was over and excited that I had won my place in the team, even though my apprehensions weren't entirely extinguished.

And then it was Sunday—only one day to go. We got a free run of the depot for uniforms, haversacks, rations, mess tins and so forth.

Chris pulled us over to the stacks of boots. 'These ones have leather soles,' he said, 'and metal studs. We'll need them for the mountains. I suggest everyone takes a pair. And make sure they fit properly. You'll be sorry if they don't.'

'I'm OK for boots,' said Denys. 'I've just had a pair made to order in Alexandria. Good timing, eh?'

'Are they as strong as these?' Chris asked.

'Better,' said Denys. 'The soles are crepe rubber. I know the Greek mountains and I know they'll be good.'

'What about razors?' asked Nat.

'I'm not taking one,' said Denys. 'I use a cut-throat. But we won't be shaving, anyway. How would we get hold of hot water in the mountains?'

Not shaving! Several of us were horrified. We would look like a rabble—very un-British. But as it turned out, Denys was right. Shaving was far too difficult and we all grew prolific beards in Greece.

Before we left the Canal Zone, we went to the airfield to look over a Liberator aircraft. The flight crew were Kiwis—all good scouts, all keen to explain to me, as the engineer of our party, the special features of their plane: the double tail (developed from a flying boat), the Davis wing (fuselage-mounted with a high aspect ratio for better fuel efficiency), the range (2,100 miles or 1,800 nautical miles at maximum). We would be flying more than 620 nautical miles each way.

We entered the plane from the rear. It was designed to accommodate twin bomb bays, each the same size and capacity as in the Yanks' Flying Fortress. Over a short range the Liberator could carry up to 8,000 pounds of bombs. Less over a very long range, of course, but still a lot—2,700 pounds. But on our expedition, those bomb bays would be carrying our canisters. Each bay was divided into a front and rear compartment, with a narrow catwalk between. The crew showed us how the bomb bay doors retracted into the fuselage to reduce drag and keep up speed over the target area.

Denys had been up in a Liberator before. Unlike the Wimpy, the Liberator had not been designed for parachutes and ours had been modified to provide the 'strong point'—the point of attachment for our harnesses. Our lives depended on this strong point, for if it gave way our chutes would not open. A member of the crew—the 'dispatcher'—would fit our harness, attach it to the strong point at the right moment, and tell us when to drop, in communication with the pilot.

Denys asked if all was well with the modifications.

'See for yourself,' said the dispatcher. 'Nothing to worry about.' It certainly looked all right, and Denys seemed happy enough.

As the plane had no proper parachute hatch, we would jump through the emergency exit. It looked tight, but we had a few goes and it seemed OK—just. With our flying suits on, we were going to be very bulky.

By the afternoon we were back in Cairo. We had an hour of signals training in the evening, learning the codes we'd need to keep in touch via the wireless. After that we were free.

Inder and Themis looked very much the worse for wear in the morning. They'd hit the town in a big way, and had decided to drive themselves home, inebriated, in a rented car. Inder had insisted on driving but soon hit the footpath, taking out a tyre. The tyre changed, they were off again, this time with Themis at the wheel and Inder urging him on to faster and faster speeds.

Suddenly, headlights had come right at them. Themis swerved just in time. Curiously, the lights had come from a train—they'd been driving along the railway line without noticing. To everyone's surprise, they had managed to make it back in one piece. But they badly needed a hangover remedy, and headed off as soon as they could to Shepheard's Hotel to get one.

After a briefing from Eddie and Chris, we had some time to write letters home—probably our last chance to do so for a while. I wrote to Mother first, then tackled the one to Beth. It was hard to know what to say. 'I'm on a new posting but I can't tell you what it is'? Or perhaps, 'You won't hear from me again for a few months but everything is fine'? I usually write letters easily, but this one was hard, and it was a relief to get to the end. 'Goodbye for now, darling. Your very own Tom.'

They gave us a pile of Letter Mail Telegram forms, too—they would go off once a fortnight, so our families would know we were OK. And I picked out a New Year's card for 1943, just in case the submarine was late. When I came home I found it among Beth's things—'Honest I ain't a lion! I'm just a little friendly puss wishing you a purrfectly grand New Year.' Funny to think she kept it all that time. It seems to belong to another era, when things were simpler and we could still play a little at being children, even while the world was at war.

Only a few hours to go now. We drove out to Fayid airfield together and had dinner in the officers' mess. I happened to sit next to the pilot of Arthur's team.

'Malcolm Rolph-Smith,' he said, 'from Auckland. AKA "Golf Ball".'

'Tom Barnes, from Wellington. Nice to meet you. Is this your first time with the SOE?'

'Not at all. We've been at it a while, me and Jacko and Hatch here. First time to Greece, though.'

'Where else have you been?'

'Yugoslavia. Dropping British agents and their supplies. First we did survey flights over the Balkans to find good dropping places. The first flight I made to Yugoslavia was more than fifteen hours. That was back in March. Aeons ago.' He laughed.

'What's it like there? Is it as mountainous as Greece?'

'Not quite. I think Greece would have to take the cake for packing in the most mountains per square mile—and the highest. Terrible storms over Yugoslavia, though. I can't tell you how many missions we had to abort.'

'That must've been frustrating for the parachutists,' I said. 'Getting all keyed up for nothing.'

'You'd be surprised how often it happens,' he replied. 'But if it goes well, we see the fires spring up suddenly and we signal down to the partisans. We drop the men first, then the supplies, so that they land close—within 200 yards. Then the partisans put their fires out in a big hurry and we leave them to it.'

I hoped everything would be that simple for us.

After dinner the twelve of us made our final walk to the planes. Our battledress, flying suits and harnesses were almost unbearable in the heat. Once on board, we had to crowd together in the cockpit to keep the weight forward for takeoff. Plastic explosive and guns—twelve cylinders of them in all, each one containing three canisters—were weighing down the plane.

We were first into the air, just on sunset. We headed to the east of Crete to avoid flak from the German guns. After takeoff we edged back along the gangway, past the cylinders stacked in the bomb bays, shed all our gear and settled in: it would be four or five hours before we were over Greece. They had given us coffee in a thermos, sandwiches and rum. There were no seats but plenty of blankets, which we needed as the temperature gradually dropped. I dozed off.

At some point I was awakened by unfamiliar bursts of sound. Flak was coming up from an island on our flank. We seemed to be turning sharply. As quickly as it had started, the disturbance stopped and I went back to sleep.

Eddie woke us at about one o'clock. We would be over the dropping ground in about twenty minutes.

Now I was scared. I struggled into my flying suit and harness, my fingers stiff and unwilling to do up the clasps.

I was to jump behind Eddie. The dispatcher attached Eddie's static line to the strong point. We seemed to be circling and circling again. Eddie was wearing headphones so that he could communicate with the pilot, and after a few minutes he was called up to the cockpit. The dispatcher had to unhook him.

He seemed to be gone forever. Finally, he reappeared.

'We can't find the signal,' he said. 'No fires in a circle, no flares. We're going to have to abort.'

We were so tense with anticipation that we found it hard to believe it wasn't going to happen. At the same time we were immensely, stupidly relieved.

'We'll have to try again another night. Take off your gear and go back to sleep.'

We crossed back into Egypt at dawn and landed about eleven hours after takeoff. I felt a little silly as we disembarked and walked back across the tarmac.

The planes needed to be serviced before they could take off again. Our next opportunity would be in two days' time, on the night of 30 September. If we didn't go then, it would be three long weeks before the moonlight was suitable again—and that would be too late.

We were going to jump on the 30th no matter what. Eddie and Chris had decided, and the rest of us were glad. None of us could face the thought of another abortive trip. If there were no signals, John Cook's party would drop first and they would set off flares to guide the rest of us down. That's if the location was safe.

When we reported at the airfield again two nights later, I asked Chris what he had been doing to pass the time.

'Denys and I did a lot of swimming in the pool at the Gezira Club,' he replied. The Gezira Club was a sporting club on Gezira Island in Cairo. It had polo fields and a golf course, even a race course. 'And I spent a lot of time lying in bed reading. I'm halfway through a book—Dostoevsky's *The Idiot*. I can't take it with me, so God knows when I'll finish it.'

'The pool at Maadi was good enough for us,' said Themis. Maadi camp had its own pool and every Kiwi soldier knew the story behind it. Our General Freyberg was a former swimming champion, famous for having swum the Bosphorus in the lead-up to the Gallipoli campaign, and he wanted our soldiers to be able to cool off in the heat. The Maadi scouts organisation had let us use their land right on the edge of Maadi proper, so that we would have palm trees as a backdrop instead of just desert. The pool had been completed in five weeks, chlorine plant and all.

We climbed back into the planes, with a different crew this time. The novelty had well and truly worn off. Themis and Nat had changed planes so that Themis was now with John.

At about 1 am, the dispatcher woke us abruptly. We struggled into our suits and harnesses. We were over the target area, but couldn't see anything through the windows. Whatever was out there, we were all determined to jump.

'Seen this lot before, haven't we?' shouted Len over the noise of the engine.

'Where are the red flares?' That was Denys. 'Those buggers haven't sent them up. Why not?'

Then we spotted something—red lights way down there on the ground. Three fires in a sort of triangle. Not twelve fires in a circle, but something.

Eddie spoke to the captain over the intercom.

'Someone's down there,' he said. 'Let's go and find out who it is.'

THREE

Crack! The static lines struck the tail of the Liberator as they snapped, releasing my parachute.

The cold hit my face. I looked up through the shroud lines to comfort myself with the sight of my parachute opening above me. Then I could look down. From 13,000 feet the contours of the mountains and valleys below were clearly visible in the moonlight, the tops of the ridges whitish-grey and gleaming. That was a surprise. Had it snowed already?

I had jumped immediately after Eddie. His chute suddenly sprang into view below me, illuminated by something—his torch, I suppose. But he was moving rapidly away across the landscape, already too far to make contact. I saw a few other parachutes dropping more slowly—they must have been our containers.

The cold had already penetrated my flying suit. It was hard to believe I was above the Greek mountains, with winter coming on. Two weeks ago in the heat of Maadi camp this would all have seemed incredible—like something out of a novel. But my whole year in New Guinea in 1938, surveying for the Papua Oil Development Company, had been like that. This new experience would be tough, I knew, but I'd been wanting a challenge after all.

And where was John's party? I couldn't understand why they hadn't set off the flares to guide us down. Those fires that we'd seen from the air—they might be nothing at all to do with us. Who could tell what danger we might be dropping into?

I was a few hundred feet up and looking out for a landing place when the wind caught me and blew me away from the fires, over the top of a ridge. The bushes coming towards me were growing bigger by the minute—fir trees, a massive forest of them, and no safe dropping place in sight. The fires had vanished.

Suddenly branches swept my face. A few feet more and I jerked to a stop. My parachute had caught in a fir tree. Luckily the branches had stopped me colliding with the trunk, while my helmet and flying suit had protected my face and body, more or less.

It was hard to disentangle myself from the harness with the rucksack on my back, but impossible to take it off before I had done so. After struggling for perhaps ten or fifteen minutes I succeeded, and managed to get the chute down. I folded it up and left it beside a rock. I couldn't imagine there would be enemy soldiers roaming around in this precipitous landscape.

Alone. Apart from the rasp of the plane's engines, rapidly attenuating to nothing, there was no sound but the wind in the trees. No English voices, no matter how carefully I listened. Nothing but dark forest all around me and the scent of rotting wood underfoot. No guide, no interpreter, no leader, no wireless operator. And I spoke no Greek.

I knew I was on the far side of a valley, the wrong side. My rucksack on my back, I started to scramble down the cliff face. In spite of my efforts to take it steadily and avoid a sprained ankle, loose stones rolled and bounced ahead of me. Soon I was panting and sweaty in spite of the sharp coldness of the air.

As the ground levelled out, the fir trees thinned and I was able to see further. On the other side of the valley, the ground sloped up steeply to another ridge, the trees on its top black against the sky.

Soon the moonlight would wane. In New Guinea I had spent hours outside in the muggy heat, learning the stars so that I could determine latitude for the survey I was working on. Different stars here, I thought as I looked up, and the dark shapes above me obscured much of the sky. It would be foolish to go any further tonight. I lay down under a tree to wait for dawn.

Thoughts whirred in my head. Tomorrow—at least there would be daylight. The others must be beyond the next ridge, the one I'd been blown across. I would use the dawn light to orient myself and cross the valley to find them.

Beth—I wished I could look at the photo of her that I kept in my wallet—small and neat and pretty with her wavy brown hair, in the dark blue dress with white spots. Every night before I went to bed, ever since I'd left New Zealand, I looked at that photo.

Next day was difficult going. There were no tracks that I could see, just thick vegetation and stony ground. Soon I started climbing again. As I went I could picture Colonel Hanson, sitting in that room at the Kiwi rest home with the sun shining on his curly hair. His voice repeated over and over in my head the same few words—'Those mountains rise thousands of feet sheer from the coast'—like a wireless program I couldn't turn off.

It wasn't until around midday that I reached the top of the ridge. Another cliff, another valley lay before me. There were no fires to be seen now, of course. This valley was huge, and even more thickly vegetated than the last. As I started down through the trees, I wondered how we would ever find one another.

Then I heard a voice. 'Who's that?' it said, and then, 'Captain Tom, is that you?'

It was Len. I clasped his arm in relief. He pointed upwards.

'Look at this, sir,' he said. 'Look at my parachute.' It was tangled in the branches of a fir tree above our heads, a package of wireless batteries dangling beneath. The wireless itself had been

Eddie's responsibility. 'I've been trying for hours to get it down, since dawn.'

'Heard anything of Eddie and Denys?'

'Nothing.'

'Look, you stay here and keep trying,' I said. 'The others can't be far away. I'll find them and bring them back here. And by the way, Kiwis aren't great sticklers for hierarchy. We're all in this together—just call me Tom.'

'OK,' he said, still not using my name. 'I'll be glad of a breather. But don't be too long. I was getting the wind up all alone here.'

I continued down the slope. There were more sounds, an intermittent tinkling and then something that sounded like animals bleating—sheep or goats. There must be shepherds around somewhere, I thought with relief; further down in the valley, perhaps. From what we'd been told, they would most likely be friendly. As long as there were no soldiers around, Italian or German …

Suddenly I glimpsed a man with his back to me. Was that British battledress? What was he up to? Then I realised what he was doing: pinning a note to a tree. There were two men with him, both wearing hooded capes. I froze for a moment, concealed by the trees.

When I was sure it was Eddie, I stepped out from my hiding place.

'Eddie, thank God. Len's back up the ridge, too. He's been trying to get his chute down.'

Eddie gave an audible sigh of relief. The two men looked from him to me and then back again.

'Have you seen Denys?' asked Eddie.

'No sign of him,' I replied.

'We've got to find him. I've got these two shepherds here but my two words of Greek don't go very far.' We'd all been taught two words of Greek: *eimai Englezos*, I'm English. At least for Eddie it was the truth. I hoped his two companions had understood.

Eddie had lost his rucksack. When he'd landed, he'd left it and gone looking for help. When he returned with the two shepherds, having spent the night at their fire, it was gone. That was what his note was for—in case one of us had found it.

I took one of the shepherds with me to help Len get his parachute down, while Eddie and the other shepherd went to look for Denys. Without any interpreter, we were stuck.

A couple of hours later, Len and I were sitting at the rendezvous when we heard Eddie coming back. We had brought our packs and Len's parachute down the hillside with us. The Greek had gone off to find my chute and bring it back.

'No Denys?' I asked Eddie.

'No Denys,' he replied. 'I met another Greek, though. Seemed to be looking for something—what we dropped, I suppose. I sent him off with the other fellow to find Denys.'

Around midday, we heard voices coming through the trees towards us—Denys with a couple of locals. He'd landed in a tree, dived through it and slammed into the rocks below. He had a couple of broken ribs and his chute was still up the tree. He couldn't draw breath without wincing, but he'd found out quite a lot.

We were about ten miles south of where we should have been. The nearest village was called Karoutes, and there were no Italians or Germans there—fortunately, the nearest garrison town was about an hour away. The man offered to fetch an ex-army officer who lived in the village, to come up and help us.

'Ask him to bring us some food,' said Eddie. Denys, Len and I still had our rucksacks and were able to share some chocolate with him, but Eddie's pack hadn't turned up. He'd had nothing to eat but a few olives the Greeks had given him. And so far there was no sign of the canisters containing all our other provisions.

By the time we heard our Greek returning through the trees we were all very hungry, and Denys was in increasing pain.

The man was carrying a bag. He brought out some bread and goat's cheese, and then a bottle of local wine. The bread was round, yellow and rather dry. It was hard to swallow, but we washed it down with the wine. The cheese was strongly flavoured but delicious. We wished there was more of everything.

The ex-army officer, when he appeared, was surprisingly young. He recommended moving to a safe hiding place nearer the village, where they could bring us food more easily. He led us down to the spot in the valley where Eddie had met the two shepherds—flatter and more comfortable than further up—and left us there while he went back to the village for more food. We didn't dare light a fire for fear of giving ourselves away.

'Olives for breakfast, olives for lunch, and now olives for supper,' said Eddie as we sat in the dark, eating what the young officer had brought us. 'It's a good thing I like olives.'

'You'll either love them or hate them by the time you leave,' said Denys. 'I'm used to them, of course. I've spent so many years around the Mediterranean that they're a staple for me. You people might find it harder.'

Well, good for you, Denys, I thought. But Eddie didn't react. 'Did you speak Greek before you lived here?' he asked.

'Well, I read Classics at Cambridge,' Denys replied. 'But to speak modern Greek you need to spend time in the country. Otherwise you sound like something out of a book.' He went to flick an olive pit into the darkness, then thought better of it.

'I wonder how long it will be before we meet the resistance fighters,' said Eddie.

'And get those canisters,' I added. I was thinking of my Li-Lo.

'Not long, I hope,' said Denys. 'Broken ribs, nowhere to sleep—this trip's not going to be a picnic.'

The young officer returned next morning with several villagers, mostly women. Together we carried our gear—including the heavy wireless equipment—down to the valley floor, across the road, and up a steep path on the other side. We wondered where the men were—we didn't yet know that in the mountain villages it was the women who carried the heavy loads, not the men.

Suddenly, turning a corner, we came upon a bizarre figure blocking the track. Two bandoliers of ammunition were slung across his chest, crossing in the middle. A third circled his waist. He held a rifle at the ready, and several knives with decorative handles were stuck into his belt. He wore a version of the Greek national costume with black pleated skirt and pompoms on the shoes. At least, I used to think it was the Greek national costume. As I quickly found out, it is the uniform of the *Evzones*, who are—or were, before the occupation—elite light infantry or mountain troops in the Greek army. This man, however, was not clean and well presented as you would expect a soldier to be. He looked rough.

But he was armed. He was no shepherd. I looked across to Eddie to see how he would react.

The man gestured for us to follow him off the path. There we found four others, similarly dressed and accoutred. Each wore a string of trinkets around his neck that jingled when he moved. Trophies from Italians they had killed, it turned out.

Thank God for Denys. He quickly found out who they were. The man who had confronted us on the path was Karalivanos, and these were his men. At last, one of the *andartiko* leaders we'd been told about in Cairo. But he didn't exactly look promising.

'Denys, explain that we've just arrived by plane,' said Eddie. 'We're here on a special mission and we need to get in touch with the *andarte* bands around here. Ask him where the rest of his men are.'

'He says this is all he has—five altogether.'

We exchanged glances. According to the intelligence from Cairo, Karalivanos was a regular army major leading a band of one thousand guerrillas.

'Ask him if they can help us to collect our canisters,' said Eddie. 'Explain that they'll be scattered over the slopes, back the way we came. They've probably rolled down the mountainsides and got stuck in hollows or crevices in the rocks.'

Karalivanos was most obliging. He would mobilise the villagers to look for our canisters and show us to a place where we could establish ourselves while we waited for our next move. I couldn't help wondering what he thought would be in it for him.

He led us to a small plateau with a good view of the valley and the approaches from below. It looked straight across to the slopes of the mountain we had come from, where our stores must still be lying. There was good cover, so we would be able to light a fire. We got ourselves set up while he organised a search for our stores.

The most pressing question on our minds—apart from recovering our canisters—was the whereabouts of the other two parties. We knew they couldn't be too far away, but judging from the terrain we'd already encountered, a few miles might mean hours or even days descending precipitous slopes and crossing ravines.

We needed radio contact urgently. If we could get through to Cairo, they could help us locate the others. But we had no luck at all getting the wireless set going. It must have been damaged in the drop. We would have to wait for the spare parts from the canisters.

We were sheltering from the biting wind next morning when a single mule bearing two canisters emerged from the forest, followed shortly afterwards by a whole train.

The joy on the others' faces must have matched my own. Relieved to have something to do, we started unpacking immediately, pulling out Sten guns and ammunition, and looking forward to finding our personal kit. But while we unpacked, Denys questioned Karalivanos, and the story he told filled us with alarm.

The villagers had been making off with the canisters as fast as they could find them. Some had tried to eat the cellophane-wrapped packages of plastic high explosive—we felt sick just thinking about it.

Karalivanos boasted that he'd made them hand over their booty—but the tally was worrying. We had just enough explosive left for the demolition—the villagers had ultimately found it unpalatable. But there was none of our own food or kit, only a few greatcoats belonging to one of the other parties.

None of the canisters could be identified as having definitely come from our plane. I was very glad I'd had the foresight to put my precious camera in my rucksack. Otherwise, no doubt, it would have been gracing one of the village houses by now. I wondered what they had made of the Li-Lo.

There was more news when we had finished unpacking. A messenger arrived from the village to say that two battalions of Italian mountain troops were on their way up, about two and a half hours' distance. We would have to move.

I felt a sudden thrill of fear and pushed it down. There was work to be done: packing the gear we'd just unpacked, and hiding what we couldn't take with us.

By 2.30 am we were off, heading towards the north-west with four mules. At 4 am we stopped and slept for a few hours, then trudged on again in a bitterly cold wind with a few spots of rain. By 10.30 we'd made it to Karalivanos's den.

When we saw it, everything became clear. Karalivanos was a simple horse-thief. He and his few men, accompanied by a woman apiece, were the thousand-strong guerrilla force we'd been hoping to find.

This was bad. First we'd missed Seferiades, who was supposed to light the circle of fires for us. Now Karalivanos was no good, either. We'd have to pin our hopes on Zervas. But what if he turned out to be a horse-thief as well? We were four men alone in the Greek mountains, with just enough explosives, some Sten guns and little else. How could we carry out the operation on our own?

I rigged up my parachute as a tent or mai-mai. My anger against Cairo was mounting, and I let it grow. Better anger than fear.

Len had started working on the wireless. When I'd finished with my mai-mai, I squatted down next to him. Without a functioning transmitter, we were in deep trouble.

'See this notice that came with the set?' Len said to me.

'"Insert crystals here",' I read. 'That seems clear enough. Where are the crystals?'

'Can you see them?'

I looked around carefully.

'No. Don't you have them, Len?'

'No, I bloody well don't. Of all the damned stupid things, Cairo must've packed them in a stores container. And we don't have the container. Either it's been lost or someone has swiped them. Perhaps they thought they were diamonds.'

'What are they for?' I asked.

'The crystals are on pre-set frequencies. Without them it's just trial and error—you'd have to stumble upon the right frequency when they happen to be transmitting. You might be lucky—but it's like pissing into the wind.'

'Let's get the batteries hooked up at least,' I suggested. 'Perhaps we can listen across the band of frequencies.'

He agreed. At least it was something to do.

We chatted about this and that. I wondered if he had a girlfriend. He didn't look old enough to have a wife and family— although you can never be sure.

There was a girl, as it turned out: Connie. She worked with his sister, Yvonne, in London.

Len's parents had met in France, he told me, during the first war. His father was English, and his mother half-French. She had been a despatch rider—using horses from her father's haulage business, under fire sometimes.

'Must've been an exciting life,' I said.

'She was young then,' he replied. 'Not so exciting after she married my father. He gives her one hell of a time.'

'And Connie?'

'We saw a bit of each other,' said Len with a grin. 'I was posted to the London Area Signals Regiment for a year. Twelve-hour shifts in an underground bunker. Boring as hell. That was until I got called in to see some crew called the Inter-Services Research Bureau. They gave me a posting to the Middle East.'

He was talking about the SOE.

'And a promotion to sergeant. I was only nineteen, so I was really chuffed. But I couldn't tell Connie where I was going, even when she was sewing my chevrons onto my uniform.'

'Do you keep in touch?'

'When I can. Some day I might do something more than that. What about you?'

'I'm engaged to an Australian girl, Beth. From Tasmania.'

'Where's that?'

'Ever looked at a map of Australia? It's the big island down the bottom.'

'How did you meet her?'

'She came across to New Zealand. Her father gave her the trip as a present for her twenty-first birthday. I met her then.'

'Pretty good present,' said Len. 'They must be well heeled.'

'Her father ran a shop, selling clothes and so on. Furniture, too. But he died suddenly in '38. Beth found herself having to manage the business.'

'You've got something solid to look forward to, then. Better stay alive.'

'I'm doing my best.'

We had no luck with the wireless. We were hanging around doing nothing much when one of Karalivanos's men turned up with a live sheep slung over his shoulders. We couldn't help wondering who he'd nicked it from, but that didn't stop us watching him kill it and ready it for the fire with interest. It seemed to take no time at all.

While the sheep was roasting, they chopped up the kidneys, liver and heart and stuffed them into the intestines like a sausage, which they wound around a stick and cooked over the fire.

'Looks OK,' I said. 'I ate a lot worse at Aqaba. Sheep's eyes, for a start. Sour camel's milk, too—that nearly made me sick.'

'What were you doing at Aqaba?' asked Denys. 'That's the wrong direction for the fighting, isn't it? I thought you New Zealanders were in the Western Desert.'

'Well, I wasn't—although I wished I had been. We were building a harbour in case the Hun took Cairo. Speaking of camels, we had this diesel hammer for driving the piles for the wharf—Leaping Lena we called her.'

'What's that got to do with camels?' Denys interrupted.

'I'm coming to that. The Arabs wanted to celebrate driving the first pile by killing a camel for luck. So they brought out one of their camels—the oldest and most decrepit one they had—and made it kneel down right there on the wharf. There they were with the knife poised, waiting, and at the very instant Lena dropped the weight on the pile they slit its throat. Then they cut it up and shared it around the villagers. Blood and entrails all over the place.'

'Sounds as though you were having more fun than we were.' Always thinking other people were getting out of things—Denys was already annoying me, and I was relieved when it was time to turn in under my mai-mai.

Len and I worked on the wireless again the next day. We desperately needed to make contact with the other two parties.

The batteries were flat, so we rummaged through canisters looking for the jars of battery acid, until Len let out a curse. 'I've found what's left of them. All smashed, every last one. Not packed properly. Bloody Cairo.'

'What about a charging engine?' I asked. 'Surely we have one of those?'

After a few minutes' rummaging, Len fished out a heavy case. 'This must be it.'

'You hold and I'll pull,' I suggested. 'It seems to be well and truly stuck.'

'Damn them to hell,' said Len after a few minutes. 'It's rusted solid.'

I couldn't help wondering whether they had any brains at all in Cairo. They'd sent us to Greece with completely unusable equipment, knowing full well we'd be totally dependent on it for survival. What did they think they were doing?

There was a rumour of another British party on the other side of the nearest mountain. Denys and Len left with Karalivanos and his second in command to check it out while we continued south of Mount Giona.

After we'd settled for the night, Denys and the others returned with Arthur and Mike, the wireless operator from Chris's party of four. They'd been as cosy as anything in a cave spacious enough to stow all their gear as well as themselves. Chris was away at a nearby village, and they'd left Nat at the cave.

Arthur had had a perilous landing, he told us, narrowly missing jagged rocks and landing in the only clear space for six feet around—just a hundred yards south of a thousand-foot drop. One of the straps had broken on Nat's parachute—probably damaged by battery acid from the batteries attached to his harness—and he'd had to hang on for dear life to the other one, all the way down. But they'd been lucky enough to land right near one of the fires. Upon landing, the party had found two escaped prisoners of war who had been there since the Allied withdrawal, Turkish Cypriots called Yannis and Panayiotis.

At least now we had two of the three parties—with the two Cypriots, that made ten. That just left John's lot. And Len and Mike were hopeful that between the two damaged wireless sets they could concoct one working model. At least Mike's crystals had arrived intact.

I told Arthur that none of our food or personal kit had turned up.

'What about your precious Li-Lo?' he asked with a grin.

'Gone AWOL.'

'Bad luck,' said Arthur. 'Our gear dropped pretty well on top of us. It's all accounted for.'

'Any luck with your wireless?' Len asked.

'No. Most of the equipment got smashed in the drop. We were hoping you might have made contact with Cairo.'

'Our batteries are flat,' I said. 'Our charging engine is only slightly damaged, though. We're still hoping to get it going.'

'And I assume you haven't heard anything of John's party?' asked Eddie.

'Correct,' said Arthur. 'We never saw the flares they were meant to let off. Did you?'

'No. We can't understand what happened to them.'

'Got cold feet, perhaps, up there at thirty thousand feet.'

Arthur was more suspicious of John than I was—I wondered if he had reason. I had been imagining them injured in the drop and unable to get help. After all, Denys had cracked his ribs, and Arthur had only escaped injury by a stroke of luck.

We woke next morning to a pleasant day, the first we'd had—windless, clear and warm. The Italians seemed to be enjoying it, too—their planes were overhead for about an hour, circling. We hoped this was just routine surveillance, but sent a message to the village to find out what they knew. We heard nothing back.

We had still had no definitive contact with the real *andartes*. Karalivanos had some kind of informal arrangement with the local leader, a certain Aris Velouchiotis, and we'd sent messages to him, but heard nothing. Chris had made a couple of contacts in Amfissa, too, but nothing reliable.

Soon we were summoned to join the others—except for Chris, who was still away—at their cave. We were delighted to find that Golf Ball, our Kiwi mate from Cairo, had made a pre-arranged drop of explosive to Chris's party—they knew it was him because he'd signalled his identity—and now we had plenty of explosive to do the job.

Karalivanos and his gang, it now appeared, had regarded their help as an investment: they were expecting to share in the goodies from the drop. When they didn't get anything, they took themselves off in disgust.

'Shall we share a tent tonight?' Denys asked me.

'Sorry, Denys,' I replied. 'Arthur and I are going to rig up a mai-mai together. We're planning to have a comfortable night—isn't that right, Arthur?'

Arthur glanced over his shoulder at Denys. 'Right. Sorry, old man.'

It was a bit of a toss-up between Denys and Arthur, what with Denys's complaints and Arthur's teasing about the Li-Lo. I would have been just as happy for them both to leave me alone. But Arthur and I were fellow Kiwis as well as fellow sappers, and that counted for something.

The day deteriorated. We were eating miserably in the rain, trying to keep the drips out of our dinner, when an oldish Greek man appeared. He had a large moustache that drooped a little on one side, giving him a lopsided look, and was unshaven and grubby, with holes in his country shoes.

His name was Nikolaos Beis. 'How are you, OK?' he said in a slight American accent. As we soon found out, his spoken English didn't extend much beyond this greeting, although he'd lived and worked in America and understood a lot. But his smile as he greeted us lit up his whole face, and I felt immediately inclined to like and trust him.

Beis brought some important intelligence. He had been in Koukouvista, the village where we should have dropped, had the flares been there to guide us. The day before we arrived the Italians had turned up, rounded up all the villagers in the square, and marched away every male over the age of sixteen. No one knew where they'd taken them, and the women were in despair. Among them had been the lawyer Seferiades, the agent of Prometheus who was supposed to link us up with the *andartes*.

No wonder there hadn't been any signal fires.

'So those Italian planes overhead ...' said Denys.

'Looking for us, apparently,' said Eddie. 'Seems we've been betrayed.'

Beis was talking rapidly to Chris and Denys.

'He says we should move,' Chris said to Eddie. 'As soon as possible. He knows another cave, more remote but closer to our targets. And it's larger. There's a village below, Stromi, but it's not too close—about two hours away. They'll look after us.'

Chris himself was sceptical about the panic. In Crete there had always been rumours flying about—that the Germans knew where they were, and were coming after them. The events in Koukouvista might have had nothing whatsoever to do with us, and the villagers probably wouldn't mind separating us from our stores.

But Eddie decided we couldn't take the chance. We would do what Beis said, but we would take our stores with us so the Italians couldn't find them.

This was the second time we'd had to run from the Italians, and this time we were lumbered with more stores—several hundred pounds of plastic explosive more, in particular. Not to mention the personal kit that Chris's group had been lucky enough to recover

Denys and I, Nat, Len and Mike headed off first. The track was steep, and rapidly got steeper. It wasn't long before we emerged beyond the treeline. Above us were massive slabs of whitish rock.

Denys was a little way behind me.

'Hey, Denys,' I called out, turning round. 'I remember seeing rocks like this when I was dropping from the plane. I thought it was snow. But there wasn't any snow when we got down. I couldn't work it out.'

Denys grunted. His broken ribs were still giving him trouble. Soon my energy for talking evaporated too, as the donkeys trudged on with their loads, stumbling every now and then on the stony track.

We stopped for the night in what seemed like the only level spot on the whole mountain. Setting out again the next morning in the rain, my pack bit into my shoulders and I could feel every step I had taken the day before. After a while one of the mules collapsed. I knew how he felt.

When we got to our new camp, utterly exhausted, two men were standing waiting for us. One was a villager. The other was dressed as a second lieutenant.

'Mirhail Shibli Khouri, Palestinian Regiment,' the latter said, coming forward eagerly.

Khouri was really a private. The Germans had got him after the retreat, and he'd jumped off a train to escape. Since then he'd been on the run, and had promoted himself because he thought he would get better treatment from the locals. His strategy had paid off—he'd got himself a girl in Stromi village. Eddie now promoted him to unpaid lance-corporal, to save his honour.

Somehow he found himself some stripes for his new rank—God knows where from.

Khouri, Beis and the villager were soon deep in conversation, and Nat and Denys went over to join them. All Len, Mike and I could do was stand and watch.

After a few minutes the villager turned to us and pointed up the hill. '*I spelia*,' he said. '*I spelia*'.

I had expected some Greek words to be familiar from English, but until now I hadn't managed to catch any. Now I thought of 'speleologist' and realised he must be pointing to the cave. We considered going to have a look, but it turned out to be an hour and a half's climb up the mountain. And our lunch was underway—a whole sheep roasting on a spit over the fire— and we were exhausted. Instead we went down to the stream, which seemed to bubble right out of the rock, for a drink. Then Denys and I put up our mai-mais, using fir branches as well as the parachutes—a definite improvement.

As the afternoon wore on a thick mist came down, cutting visibility to a few feet. Suddenly a loaded mule materialised right in front of us. A muleteer followed, and then Arthur. He brought disquieting news. The Italians had raided Karoutes, the village where we had landed.

'I bet they found some of our things in the houses,' said Nat.

'Yes, Tom's Li-Lo bed would have been a dead giveaway,' said Arthur. 'I wonder how they explained that.'

FOUR

Still no word of John's party. Still no useful contact with the *andartes*—you couldn't count Karalivanos, and Eddie's messages to Aris seemed to have gone unheard. Still no wireless contact with Cairo. And time was passing.

After our meal, we made our way to the cave that was to be our home, high on the northernmost spur of Mount Giona, bounded by deep valleys to the north, east and west. Although the slopes opposite looked close enough to touch, anyone trying to reach us would have to go down and then up again, and that would be slow. There was no snow, although elsewhere in the mountains the first snow had already fallen; the cave faced the wrong way for it. This was welcome news.

Overhanging rocks partially shielded the entrance. I ducked to get in—and nearly bumped my head on the stalactites hanging from the roof.

'A real palace,' said Arthur, following me in. 'The floor could be a bit flatter, but apart from that …'

'It stinks of sheep,' said Denys. 'Damp, too.'

'We'll be warm, at least,' I said. The villagers had brought us bedding, and an axe for chopping firewood.

'In dirty blankets,' said Denys.

'At least they're not wet blankets, Denys,' I said. 'If John Cook's party ever turns up, I doubt if we'll all be able to lie down at the same time. But Beis here—sorry, Barba Niko—will see us right.' Beis had insisted that everyone call him 'Barba Niko'. 'Barba' means 'uncle'—something a younger person might call an older one in an informal and friendly way.

We unpacked our gear and assessed our stores. Four hundred pounds of plastic explosive and 112 of gelignite. And a cauldron for cooking, parked just inside the entrance to the cave. Wherever Barba Niko went, the cauldron went with him.

We soon received a delegation from Stromi village. First came a tall and imposing priest with a long grey beard, Papa Andreas Pistolis. Next were Yannis Pistolis and his cousin Kostas Pistolis—all good friends of Barba Niko. Close behind was the village president—another Pistolis. They'd brought up wonderful, welcome food.

We sat down in a circle and passed around mess tins heaped with roast mutton, onions and potatoes. When we'd cleared our plates and wiped our hands on our trousers, we turned our attention to a basket of big green apples. The scent was glorious, tempting you to take that first perfect bite, crisp and juicy in your mouth.

The priest made a short speech, and Nat translated. He was glad we had come to help fight the Germans, he said. God himself must have dropped us through the clouds.

'Could've picked a level spot to drop us in,' said Arthur, wiping his chin with his sleeve. 'He can't have had his mind on the job.'

'Distracted by the Western Desert, perhaps,' I offered.

'Or the Russian front,' said Arthur.

'Well, now, that would be a bit of a dilemma,' I said. 'Should God help the Reds or not?'

'Shut up, you two,' said Nat. 'Papa Andreas says that one day this cave will be famous and there will be a sign here with our names on it.'

'Only if we blow one of the bridges,' I said. 'Otherwise only God will remember us.'

'And it won't be one of his better memories,' said Arthur.

For all our jokes, it was a huge relief to have found people who wanted to help us, especially after our experience in Karoutes. The operation became a real possibility again. There were kisses all round when the Stromi clan finally departed.

Eddie called an officers' meeting on the grassy flat outside the cave. We sat or squatted, glad to get off our feet.

'If we don't find the *andartes* soon,' said Eddie, 'we'll have to attempt the operation with volunteers from around here. That will mean arming and training them.'

'We don't have enough Stens,' said Nat.

'We'd have to get another drop,' said Eddie. 'Assuming we can get the wireless going. Or send a message via Prometheus.' Prometheus was still our only means of communication with the outside world.

Eddie put me in command of the demolition party, with Arthur and Nat. Nat was officially an interpreter, but in the absence of Inder, he was needed with us. It was an odd set-up: three captains—Arthur, Nat and me—with no men. Len and Mike answered directly to Chris and Eddie, who were senior to all of us. But my team were all of the same rank as I was. It would be a challenge to manage it.

A messenger arrived from Prometheus. Cairo had reported that we'd dropped, and the messenger had been sent to see if we needed anything.

'Boots,' we all said. 'Socks. Get them to send a planeload.'

Eddie gave the messenger some gold sovereigns to buy boots and socks on the black market. When he returned to Athens they would signal Cairo to find out where Cook and his party were.

We were cosy in the cave after dinner. Someone had managed to rustle up some dry tobacco from one of the villagers—crumbly stuff, but better than nothing. Denys lent me his spare pipe. Others rolled cigarettes with scraps of paper, anything they could find.

'Remember that meal at the officers' mess?' said Arthur. 'At Kibrit, the night we were leaving?'

'When we didn't end up leaving after all,' I said.

'With Golf Ball and so on,' said Arthur. 'Roast beef and Yorkshire pudding.'

'With lots of gravy, and roast vegetables,' said Nat. 'Crispy brown potatoes and green beans.'

'And trifle. Don't forget that,' said Eddie. 'Sherry trifle with nuts on top.'

'And decent cigarettes,' said Chris.

'What about that steel gantry we had to jump off?' said Arthur. 'Standing up there watching other people land, hoping you wouldn't be the one to hurt yourself.'

'And the sand so much harder than it looked,' said Chris.

'And jumping off that twenty-foot wall,' said Nat. 'That wasn't much fun, either.'

Later, Chris told me he'd had a bad landing on his second real jump, hitting the ground with his legs straight and then misjudging which direction to roll. He'd hurt his back and been winded so badly he couldn't speak. He'd worried Eddie might decide he was unfit to go, so he'd taken his time gathering up the parachute while he waited to get his breath back. But by the time he told me that, we were friends, and a little readier to admit to our own weaknesses.

'That fellow whose parachute had twisted,' Chris said now. 'You remember? Fell like a bomb, and our instructor was just contemptuous.

'Old Bill Jordan was trying to frighten us with a lot of stories, too,' I said.

'Who?' Eddie asked.

'The Kiwi journalist,' I replied, 'in one of the other groups. The one who'd been training to be a human torpedo.'

'I don't recall,' said Eddie.

'Well, we knew him already,' said Arthur. 'From Maadi camp. He was quite a character.'

'I'll tell you a funny story,' said Chris. 'I was once arrested for being a German parachutist.'

'Where on earth was that?' asked Nat.

Chris laughed. 'In Northumberland,' he said. 'I'd been on an intelligence training course at Swanage. We had this rotund little major, couldn't wait to shoot someone. Keble, his name was. I couldn't believe it when I came across him again in the SOE offices in Cairo as a brigadier. I think I briefed some of you straight after you'd been in to see him.'

'Guy in the sweaty singlet,' said Arthur.

'That's the one. Anyway, I got sent up to a Corps headquarters in north Yorkshire. We had to look for possible landing places for the Germans. I was on the beach one day when a coastguard noticed me and asked to see my papers.'

'Thought you looked like a German, did he?' I said.

'Apparently. There was a woman there egging him on. She kept saying, "Arrest this man, coastguard. Arrest this man."

'"I'm checking his papers, ma'am," he said. "Don't worry."

'"It's no good looking at his papers, coastguard. I am a Justice of the Peace and I know this man is a German parachutist." She knew all German parachutists had forged documents, you see.'

'So what happened?' asked Arthur.

'It took some time. But eventually I got the coastguard away from the JP woman and managed to convince him I was in intelligence.'

'Well, now you are a parachutist and you do have forged documents,' I said.

'Funny, isn't it?'

We slept in the cave that night for the first time. After some experimentation, we found that we could all fit if we arranged ourselves in rows of four. Barba Niko slept across the entrance, with his cauldron close by. During the night we each collected a few legs and arms in the face, but nothing could keep us from sleep for more than a few moments.

It was wonderful to wake next morning to the sound of bells tinkling, and the sight, as we came out of the cave, of sheep and goats grazing on the slopes below. The sun was picking out the white walls of houses in a village across the valley to the west, some distance away but clearly visible. It all seemed very peaceful after our two close calls with the Italians. I suddenly felt at home.

'What's that village over there, Barba Niko?' I asked.

'Black Rock,' he replied. 'Black Rock village. Mavrolithari.'

'All the rocks around here seem to be white,' I said. 'Why is it called Black Rock?'

'You'll have to ask them.'

We started on the task of moulding explosives for the bridge—although we still didn't know which bridge it would be. Len hadn't had any luck charging the batteries for the transmitter, so he joined us. Arthur carefully explained to him that we were making the explosive up into blocks.

'So here we are,' I said to Arthur. 'You and me, the resident demolitions experts. You seem pretty confident.'

'We used explosives to blow tree stumps out of the ground back home,' he replied. 'And I've got a bit of demolitions training—we all did in the Field Companies. I don't suppose you got that, Tom, in your outfit?'

'We used explosives to build our roads out at Aqaba and Naqb Shtar. And we touched on plastic explosives in a bomb disposal course I did last year. We didn't get any to handle, though.

Didn't realise it would look so much like green plasticine. And that smell—I can't quite think what it reminds me of.'

'Almonds,' said Len.

'Of course,' I said. 'That's what it is. It's no wonder those children back at Karoutes wanted to eat it. Either that or play with it. And I've been meaning to ask you something, Len. I got the impression in the plane that you'd parachuted before. Not a novice like us. But you didn't say anything last night when we were talking about Kibrit.'

'You won't believe this,' Len said, 'but I was actually at Kibrit as an instructor.'

'Why didn't you say something?' said Arthur.

'Officers,' he replied shortly. 'They don't talk to the likes of me. Except for you two Kiwis. You're different.'

I hadn't thought about it before, but I could see what he meant. The signallers weren't exactly excluded, but they weren't included, either.

'How did you come to be an instructor?' asked Arthur. 'Had you had a lot of experience?'

Len laughed. 'A bit like your experience with explosives, by the sound of things. I'd jumped off the wing of a bi-plane a few times—well, eight times, actually.'

'A bi-plane? You've got to be joking. When was this? The Great War?' said Arthur.

'Might as well have been,' said Len. 'Held together with strings, more or less. No proper exit, no static lines, no nothing. Just one trainee on each wing, scared shitless. I was paired with this officer called Templer because we were about the same weight. The first time, when I was hanging onto my wing for dear life, he said to me, "Don't you hold back when the time comes. Otherwise it's curtains for you, boy, nothing surer."'

'And that was it for training?' I asked.

'I did some more at Kibrit. Jumping from 500 feet. Saw a few things. One day I'd done a couple of jumps from a Bombay and I was watching the others go. The dispatcher was a sergeant. Just as he yelled "Go", he saw the strong point break, leaving nothing to anchor the static line. Too late. The guy had gone. The second guy was right behind. He went too. Then the sergeant screamed out "Stop!" and managed to grab the third guy. Otherwise he would've been a goner, too.'

What could you say to that? It made our little course seem like a piece of cake.

Four days later we got more bad news. Three hundred Italians were at Koukouvista, three hours away, looking for us. Just when we were starting to get comfortable.

The village president warned us to move. The Italians had come this way before, believing the villagers had been feeding the *andartes*, and had smashed the president's teeth with rifle butts—he opened his mouth to show us. The villagers were afraid of being taken hostage, so all the able-bodied men were taking to the mountains.

Both the Italians and the Germans had taken to using hostages as a means of subduing the locals. One particularly nasty tactic was to attach a cage filled with hostages to the front of their trains. That way the hostages would be sure to cop it if the line was sabotaged.

As soon as the president had gone, Eddie and Chris gathered us together for a briefing.

'We've decided to wait and see what happens tomorrow. It'll take the Italians a while to move up all these men. If it looks as though we're in danger, we'll take off. We'll still be ahead of them'.

I was pleased. I was in no hurry to clear out for a third time.

Next morning, everything seemed quiet. But towards late afternoon, Khouri the Palestinian came running back from sentry duty, binoculars in hand.

'Campfires across the valley! I see smoke!'

'Let's have a look,' said Eddie. 'Yes, I can see them moving around, putting up their tents. Someone count the fires.'

'Quite a lot,' said Nat. 'More than ten fires. Maybe twenty or more.'

'I've counted thirty,' said Chris quietly.

I looked through the glasses. The Italians were clustered around the fires, cooking their dinners. There seemed to be about ten around each fire. That made about three hundred soldiers. The intelligence from Stromi had been correct.

Barba Niko thought we would be safe for another night. The soldiers were about a mile and a half away. Getting down the mountain and then up again would take them some time. We would move in the morning; he knew a place where we would be safe, on the western side of the spur.

About midnight, another runner arrived from Athens. He brought a warning from Prometheus. The Italians were scouring Mount Giona, terrorising the villagers. Somebody might betray us.

Eddie sent the runner back with a letter, asking Prometheus for details of Zervas's location and instructions how to get there. Zervas looked like being our only hope—as long as he had a real band of guerrillas under him, not a few braves like Karalivanos.

A little later, the president made the steep trip up the hillside with a further warning. Another column of Italians was moving up from the west. They were camped in a village only half an hour from Mavrolithari, the Black Rock village.

There was no denying it this time—we had to clear out. We packed up and cached the gear we couldn't take with us. Then we combed the area, trying to remove anything that would let the Italians know the cave had been in use, and scattering sticks and grass on the paths leading up to the cave. The Italians would take it out on the villagers if they thought they had been looking after us. As we worked, we could see the Italians on the opposite slope, just a few hundred yards away. They looked like they were searching for someone—us.

'Look,' said Nat, pointing towards Mavrolithari. 'Something's going on over there.'

'More Italians,' said Arthur. 'And a whole lot of mules. We're not moving a moment too soon.'

I decided to take all my gear—a hell of a load. We trekked for three hours around the mountain, then came back to get more gear, constantly on high alert. We were completely done up by the time we'd finished. But it was worth it.

Our new camp was a broad grassy ledge about two-thirds of the way up the mountain. Sheep were grazing peacefully among the broad-branched cedars.

'Hey, Tom, come over here,' called Arthur. 'Look at this.'

The shepherds had built a series of water troughs for the sheep out of hollow logs. Each one was placed slightly below the one before, the water cascading down from the top.

'Great idea,' I said. 'Barba Niko, this is a real haven.'

He looked pleased. 'Is good, this place. Plenty of wood. Food ready soon. Us safe here.'

'Beans and bread again,' Denys muttered as we sat down on the grass to eat. 'This vegetarian food is really hard on my stomach. Even when we get a goat or a sheep it's always a stringy old beast. My gums are hurting and I seem to have diarrhoea most of the time.'

'You've got to chew the beans well,' said Arthur. 'I've been having trouble with my stomach, too, but I reckon chewing is the secret.'

'Running out of toilet paper certainly hasn't helped,' I said.

For once I couldn't blame Denys for complaining. I thought the food was OK, perhaps because I was so hungry, but it was minimal and monotonous. I was pretty sure I was losing weight, although without a mirror it was hard to tell.

'The boki is the worst,' said Denys. 'Boki' was our shortened form of *kalamboki*. We thought at the time that this was what the local corn bread was called, although as we found out later, it actually referred to the cornmeal rather than the bread itself, which was called *bobota*. It was harder to chew than wheat bread, and harder to digest.

We finished off the meal with what Barba Niko called 'mountain tea'. He made it for us from chamomile that he gathered on the slopes and it was bright yellow. Our sugar rations had run out very early on, so we usually drank the tea unsweetened, except when the villagers had brought us some Stromi honey.

Barba Niko was a real trump. His clothes were falling apart, he had no socks, and one of his shoes had barely any sole. Yet he managed to wangle things out of the villagers that we would never have been able to get for ourselves. As far as I am concerned, he saved our lives. When Chris asked him why he was going out of his way to look after us, he answered, 'I heard that God had sent Englishmen from heaven to help us. It's my duty to look after you.'

While we were waiting for the runner to come back from Prometheus, Eddie went off to reconnoitre the three bridges. Yannis Pistolis—who had worked on the railway line—had volunteered to act as guide, and Denys went along as interpreter. They would be travelling mostly at night.

We had given nicknames to the three bridges, so that the locals wouldn't have any information to reveal if they were caught. The Asopos viaduct was always 'The Soapy One', Papadia was 'The Priest One' and Gorgopotamos was 'The George One'. We were all hoping to do the 'Soapy One'—it looked the most exciting.

Meanwhile, Len and Mike were still struggling with the wireless. They had found a ruined shepherd's hut on a rocky outcrop and set up their gear. There was barely any petrol left for the charging engine and although we went back to the cave to look for some, we couldn't find it.

'I know how to give batteries a great big fuck,' said Barba Niko suddenly. 'Big machine in the water—will do it for sure.'

'Where?' asked Chris.

'Not far, not far. I take Len.'

He went off to get a donkey. He and Len loaded the batteries onto its pack saddle, one on each side, and disappeared over the edge of the plateau.

They were gone a long time. In the meantime, we heard—and then saw—a few Italian fighters overhead. Barba Niko had assured us we had good cover from above. We hoped he was right.

When Len and Barba Niko came back, Len was optimistic.

'What on earth was the big machine in the water?' Chris asked.

'A water-mill,' Len replied. 'The wheel drove an electric plant.'

They took the charged batteries up to their station. But we still had no petrol to run the charging engine

By the time Eddie and Denys came back from their recce, we had already returned to our cave—except for Len, Mike and Panayiotis the Cypriot, who were staying up the mountain with the wireless gear. There was no food, but we made a fresh brew of mountain tea.

'Well, what is it to be?' asked Arthur, blowing on his tea. 'The Soapy One or the Priest One? It's one of those two, right?'

'We went to the Priest One first,' said Eddie. 'Yannis went off to the railway station to find out the garrison strength. We got a good look at it. We could see the guard-posts easily.'

'What about cover?' I asked.

'Nowhere near enough. Rolling hills, not many trees at all.'

'And from other directions?' asked Arthur.

'All covered by guard-posts. Swarming with Ities.'

'No go, then?' asked Arthur. 'What did Yannis find out?'

'Well, his intel confirmed it. Two to three hundred guards. They only finished rebuilding it last spring, after we destroyed it during the withdrawal. They're keeping a good eye on it.'

'The Soapy One, then?' said Arthur.

'We found a good spot above it, looking down. It's a really precipitous gorge—you have to see it to realise how steep. The blueprints don't give you a good idea of it at all. We went a little way down the gorge and came to a big waterfall—maybe a fifty or sixty foot drop. You couldn't possibly get a big group of *andartes* down that way. The approach at the other end would be through a flat valley—but we already knew that.'

'So no go there, either?' asked Arthur.

'It would be too risky. We have to have a good chance of success.'

'And the George One?' said Nat.

'We were in a thicket. We couldn't get a really good view and it was too dangerous to get closer. As it was, there was a path through the thicket and a few people came past, very close to us. We could see the guards on the bridge, but we couldn't see the guard-posts at either end.'

'Did you get a good look at the piers?'

'Through binoculars,' said Denys. 'We couldn't get any closer.'

'Most of them are masonry, so they're no use as a target,' said Eddie. 'The two at the northern end are steel, though.'

'What's the cross-section?' I asked. To save time at the operation itself, we would need to pre-shape the explosive to fit the cross-section of whichever bridge we chose.

'L-shaped, I believe,' said Eddie. 'As far as I could see without going any closer.'

'What about Yannis? Did he find out anything useful?' said Nat.

'He came back in a state. The Italians had got hold of him and questioned him. When they found out he wasn't a local, they told him to get back to his own village quickly. He was scared they would send out a party to follow him. He insisted that we move right away.'

They had cleared off up the mountain in the dark, thousands of feet up, until they found a spot where they thought they would be safe. Yannis had managed to get them a little food and they had slept outdoors in the bitter cold. Then, coming back, they had got lost.

'Yannis was a hopeless guide,' said Denys. 'Absolutely hopeless.'

'Poor Yannis,' said Eddie. 'He was doing his best. He was terrified, and he'd had virtually no sleep for forty-eight hours.'

Eddie had offered Yannis a gold sovereign for his trouble. Yannis had been offended at first. But when Eddie assured him it was meant as a memento, rather than pay, he'd reconsidered.

'He took it in the end,' said Eddie. 'Then finally we got to a village. Yannis went in and after a while came back with some villagers. They brought us masses of food. Denys ate five eggs, one after another.'

Eddie was hoping to go in for the op at Gorgopotamos in a couple of weeks. But we needed more information about the garrison. Yannis's cousin in Lamia had a friend who lived right near the viaduct and he was going to come and see us, to give us what information he had. He could be a liability, but it was a risk we would have to take.

We passed a day or two peacefully at the cave, moulding explosive and playing bridge. Barba Niko was teaching us some words of Greek. Arthur was his best pupil—he would get up early so that he could follow Barba Niko about as he prepared breakfast. Eddie and I were learning a little too and we practised around the camp. *Kalimera*—good morning.

On the last day of October, Kostas Pistolis came up from Lamia. Eddie explained what we needed to know—how big the garrison was, where the emplacements were and what they were like, where there was barbed wire. Kostas promised to find out what he could.

The next day the runner from Prometheus returned from Athens.

'*Kalimera. Ti kaneis.* How are you?' Arthur greeted him. '*Kalimera*,' came the reply. The runner tipped the contents of his bag onto the ground. Boots and socks tumbled out.

Arthur, Eddie and I were elated at understanding the greeting, but were at a loss for the rest of the conversation, and had to rely on our Greek-speaking colleagues as usual.

The news was bad.

'We've landed in the wrong place,' said Chris. 'Zervas's HQ is at Sakaretsi in Epiros. That's sixty miles to the north-west. That's where Zervas was expecting us.'

'So Pera Kapsi was ...' said Denys.

'Wrong,' said Chris.

'Well, they've certainly landed us in it,' said Nat. 'A real cock-up. Thanks a million, Cairo. Thanks, Bolo Keble. Your vest isn't the only thing that stinks.'

FIVE

Without radio contact with Cairo, the villagers were still our only source of information. They brought us the news that the battle for El Alamein had already started. If we didn't hurry up, our operation would be too late.

Now that we knew that Zervas was away to the north-west, Eddie sent Chris to make contact with him, taking Barba Niko as his guide. We had still heard nothing from the local leader, Aris, so without the support of Zervas we would be on our own except for any volunteers we trained ourselves.

Eddie had given Chris a deadline of midnight on 17 November. If they brought it off, it would be a miracle. Just sixteen days to cross the mountain ranges of central Greece, find Zervas and bring him back with enough troops to do the job. Ten miles a day as the crow flies—in precipitous mountain country, without allowing for detours to avoid Italian patrols from the big towns, Karpenisi and Agrinion over to the west.

If anyone could succeed, it would be Chris. We'd realised by now how incredibly tough he was—and he was a tireless walker, with a loping, seemingly effortless stride, honed no doubt in the mountains of Crete.

As we waited for him to return, we took bets on his success. But the real stakes were far higher. We knew the Italians were looking for us. We'd had three close calls already. Another attempt could come at any time.

Len and Mike were moulding explosives with Arthur and me on the grassy patch in front of the cave. I'd cut down a big fir tree and sunshine was streaming through the gap. An old woman from the village was washing our clothes in the creek and singing to herself.

The quarter-pound bars of explosive hardened in the cold. Before we could shape them, we had to unwrap each bar and warm it between our legs or in our hands. When it was soft enough, we added Vaseline and moulded it into blocks.

'Len,' I said, 'you've handled explosives before, haven't you?'

'In Poland,' he said.

'When were you in Poland?' Arthur asked, surprised.

'The day Germany invaded, as it turned out. The Firm sent me—at least I suppose it was the Firm. No one told me anything at the time.'

'The usual story,' I said. We were no longer starry-eyed about clandestine operations—far from it, after they'd dropped us sixty miles out of our way on the wrong side of the mountains. Not to mention Karalivanos turning out to be nothing but a brigand.

'They couldn't have planned it worse if they'd tried,' Len said. 'I was supposed to make for Munich—someone would meet me at the station there. That was all I knew. I had three haversacks of wireless gear I was lugging around, and I had to make sure it travelled in the guard's van, not with me. I was bloody glad I didn't have it with me in the compartment, because the German police went through everyone's luggage at the border.'

A man had met Len at Munich as arranged, with the correct password, and taken him to a small hotel. There Len waited for about ten days, until suddenly the hotelier had rushed into his room and delivered a message that Len was to go to the British embassy in Warsaw. He didn't even know where Warsaw was, except that it was in Poland.

He made it as far as Prague, which was under German occupation, and then got on the night express to Warsaw. It was full of Hun soldiers. At the border the train suddenly stopped. Luckily, the conductor spoke English. Germany had invaded Poland and the train wasn't proceeding. Len managed to push through the crowds to the guard's van to get his bags, then found a corner of the railway station and went to sleep.

'It took me two days to get onto another train,' Len went on. 'It was a stopping train. It stopped with unbelievable frequency. We eventually got a fair way like that but then it stopped for good. One of the railway people told me that Warsaw was being bombed and the driver and guard had absented themselves. We were fifty miles from Warsaw. I stashed the haversacks in a culvert and walked along the railway line until I got to the city.'

The embassy staff had already gone. Len spoke no Polish and had no contacts, so he had no way of getting anything to eat. Luckily for him, a Polish girl who spoke English took him home and fed him. Then her family passed him over to the resistance. He was moved on, then moved on again. They helped him to get his wireless gear back but he had no frequencies or callsigns, having missed his rendezvous at the embassy, so he never raised London, and after a while the set was left behind.

It sounded like a complete stuff-up. It hardly gave you confidence in the organisational ability of the SOE. And it was all so depressingly familiar—the lack of proper planning, the failure to provide the basic information people would need to survive in the country. Now it was happening to us.

One day Len had gone with the resistance to an old mine, where they had an entire arsenal of weapons and explosives, plus a lot of German and Russian uniforms. They wore the German ones when they were attacking the Russians and vice versa. That's where he had his first experience with explosives, sabotaging the railway yards around Warsaw.

'I learnt the first principles of sabotage pretty quickly,' he said. 'Remove a part that's difficult to replace. Or take the same part from every engine, so they'll have no spares.'

At last Len got a message via the underground to return to England. When he finally made it to Gibraltar, he was carted off for interrogation by British military personnel. They didn't believe his story.

'So that was that,' said Len. 'Back to England on a destroyer. When I got back, all they said was, "If anyone asks where you've been, say you've been to Scotland."'

It was good to know that Len was full of ingenuity and hidden talents. It was not so good to know that the organisation we were working for was incompetent. In the midst of all the uncertainty, it just added to our worries.

The woman had finished the washing and spread our clothes over bushes to dry.

'*Efcharistoume*,' we said as she was leaving. Thank you.

She smiled. '*Parakalo*.' You're welcome.

Eddie had sent Bafas, the only one of Karalivanos's men who seemed trustworthy, to Karoutes to get the stores we'd cached there on our first flight from the Italians—in particular, our extra explosives. He'd been gone so long we'd given up on him, but now he turned up unexpectedly.

He'd been bringing our stores on a train of mules, he told us, when he'd run into Italians—a couple of the villagers from Karoutes had worded them up. He'd had to cut the loaded mules loose and scatter them, hoping they'd wander home. And then when he got to our stores dump on Mount Giona, he found the Italians had been there before him. He barely got away.

This was bad. Without the extra stores, we had barely enough explosive to do the job.

Early in November, Kostas Pistolis came up from Lamia with the information we needed about Gorgopotamos. The Italians were there in strength, well fortified in concrete pillboxes behind barbed-wire entanglements.

'We'll need forty to fifty *andartes* to do the job,' said Eddie. 'Let's hope Chris's mission to Zervas comes off. And we'll have to redouble our efforts to get hold of Aris. But Gorgopotamos is the one. Definitely.'

'Ask Kostas about the cross-section, Nat,' I said.

'He doesn't know,' said Nat. 'He'll send us up a farmer who lives near the bridge. He should know.'

Whenever we got news, it seemed, it was bad. We would see someone trudging up from the village, and we would start speculating gloomily about what it would be this time. But suddenly two pieces of good news arrived, one on top of the other.

First the village priest came up to tell us that Chris had run into some British officers on his journey to the west, and they were now on their way to us. It had to be John and the others—at last. Then Khouri the Palestinian ran down from the signallers' little eyrie higher up—they couldn't transmit from the cave because the mountain was in the way—in great excitement, just ahead of Len and Mike. They'd listened at the scheduled time the previous night, as they'd been doing ever since they got the batteries going, and they had just made out Cairo. It lasted a little while, very weak, and then faded away, and they hadn't been able to get a signal through. But it was something.

Our food supply was down to zero. Denys took me down to the village to eat at Yannis Pistolis's house.

'*Kalispera*, Yanni,' I said as we arrived. I'd been sufficiently coached in Greek grammar to drop the 's' from a man's name when I talked to him.

'*Kalispera*,' he replied. Good evening.

He introduced me to his wife. They had already entertained Denys and Eddie, who had eaten with them on their way to the recce with Yannis.

The cottage was full of simple but beautiful things. I admired the linen that Yannis's wife had embroidered, and asked Denys to tell her about the things I had been sending back to Beth for our own home after the war—whenever that was. Via Denys she and I carried on quite a conversation in the small room where we were sitting.

'Is she beautiful, your fiancée?'

'Of course,' I replied. 'She has dark hair and eyes. And she is quite small.'

'And she lives with her parents?'

'Her father died just before the war. She lives with her mother in Australia.'

'In Australia? But you are from New Zealand, I heard? How did you meet a girl from Australia? Is it a long way?'

'Not very far. A few hours on a flying boat. I met Beth when she came to New Zealand for a holiday.'

'And then you asked her to marry you?'

'No, I went off to a job in New Guinea. While I was there I decided I wanted to marry her, but I was waiting until my contract was finished. We wrote to each other every now and again. One day a letter came saying she had got engaged to someone else.'

'Exchanging letters and not engaged to be married!' she said.

'We were friends. That's how we'd left it. So I took leave from my job and got on a plane to Australia. She lives in Tasmania— that's a big island in the south.'

'Ah, an island. We have many beautiful islands here in Greece. So I hear. But I haven't seen them.'

'Greece reminds me of Tasmania. It has big mountains, too, although Tasmania is very green, much greener than here.'

'Our mountain is bare and our soil is thin. What happened in Tasmania?'

'When I saw Beth I managed to persuade her somehow. It wasn't as hard as I'd expected.'

'But to break an engagement! To shame yourself and your family—and above all, the man.'

'Better to break the engagement than to live unhappily with someone you don't really love.'

'Better to decide well and then stick to it. Love can come later.' She exchanged a glance with Yannis as she spoke. I could see that she disapproved of Beth.

'What's the news of the war?' Denys asked Yannis. I was grateful to him for turning the subject so deftly.

'Good. Very good,' he replied. 'The advance in the Western Desert has got as far as Daba. The Greeks are to the south. Tom's New Zealanders were mentioned—they are doing well.'

'What about the Eastern Front?' said Denys. 'And Japan?'

'Russia is doing well too,' he said, 'and the Japanese are retreating in New Guinea.'

Fighting in New Guinea would be a nightmare, I thought, in those dense jungles. You could get flash floods when the rivers rose with virtually no warning. I knew there were very steep mountains up in the north, although I hadn't been there. Perhaps it would be a bit like fighting in the Greek mountains—for us, that came later, much later. But in New Guinea it was so steamy, and you had to watch out for tropical ulcers—they could be a killer.

'We hope the liberation of Greece is not too far away,' said Yannis. 'The Germans have taken everything we have, even our olive oil. At least here in the mountains we have our goats and our vegetables—we've heard that many people in Athens have starved to death. Everyone in Greece is longing for the Allies to come and free us. And while we wait, we look to the *andartes*.'

We asked about Aris. Yannis told us he was a strong leader and a good fighter, although some people said he controlled his *andartes* through fear—there was a rumour that he had shot one of his own people for stealing a chicken. They didn't know exactly where Aris was, but he was around. Yannis didn't know why he hadn't responded to our messages. He must have had his reasons.

It was time to leave. We had a long, steep climb in the dark ahead of us.

'*Andio*,' we said. '*Efcharistoume*.' Goodbye. Thank you.

'*Sto kalo na pate*.' All the best.

Barba Niko returned by himself with a hangdog look and three days' stubble. His dirty toes were protruding from even bigger holes in his shoes than when he and Chris had set off. His army greatcoat was even more tattered.

'Chris walk fast,' he said. 'Very fast. Too fast for me.'

We hadn't really expected him to stick it out for the whole trip, so we weren't too disheartened. We were counting down the days until Chris's return, imagining the moment when we would see the first of Zervas's *andartes* coming along the path to the cave. And before that, with any luck, John's party would arrive. Meanwhile we were training Khouri and the two Cypriots for the demolition party.

We were lounging round the fire the night of Barba Niko's return, warm in our parachute overalls, when Barba Niko suddenly burst out with, 'Tonight we have examination. We see whose Greeks is better—Arthur's Greeks or Tom's Greeks. Or maybe Eddie's Greeks.' I knew by now that the word for the Greek language, *Ellinika*, was plural. 'How you say, "We will go to Gorgopotamos bridge?"'

I was immediately struck dumb. I never seemed to be able to think of the right words in a hurry. But Eddie and Arthur were getting there.

'Bridge is *yefira*,' said Arthur. 'And "we will go" is *tha pame*.'

'*Tha pame yefira Gorgopotamos*?' said Eddie.

'We've got to say "to the" as well,' said Arthur. 'Bridge is feminine, isn't it?' He appealed to Barba Niko, who refused to help them out. 'I think it is. So "to the" is *stin*. *Tha pame stin yefira*. Then we have to say "of Gorgopotamos". So *Tha pame stin yefira Gorgopotamou*.'

'Arthur wins!' said Barba Niko. 'He has the best Greeks. He interpret soon—not need Denys or Nat anymore.' We all laughed and cheered.

'Don't go flaunting your Greek—or should I say your Greeks—anywhere near the Italians,' said Eddie. 'Not if that's all you can say.'

Barba Niko took off again to make contact with John's party. Meanwhile Yannis Pistolis and some others came up from the village with a story to tell. Karalivanos had been going around the villages demanding food, supposedly on our behalf. And the previous night, two Greek gendarmes in the pay of the Italians had come to Stromi, wanting potatoes for the garrison. Karalivanos and a couple of his men picked them up and took them out into the countryside. They beat the gendarmes up, threatened them with worse and then let them go in their underwear. Now people would associate Karalivanos's ruffianly acts with us.

This was dangerous. The Italians might start targeting Stromi in their search for us. Eddie went down to the village with Arthur and Khouri to meet with Karalivanos and warn him off. Nat, who had supplanted Denys as Eddie's favourite interpreter after Chris, went too, although he wasn't feeling well. Denys said he didn't mind about being supplanted, but I didn't believe that for a minute.

Denys, Yannis and I were left alone in the camp. I wasn't feeling well, either. When I mentioned it to Denys, he told me he had a terrible headache.

'I think it's the explosive,' he said.

'But it's supposed to be safe to mould by hand.'

'Yes, but it gets under our fingernails,' said Denys. 'And we eat with our fingers.' It was true. We had no cutlery except our knives. We must have been transferring it into our mouths. We'd have to be more careful.

The others arrived back next day rather the worse for ouzo and honey but with a good yarn. Eddie had told Karalivanos that Chris was on his way back with a strong force of *andartes*, and threatened to have him shot for betraying our presence to the Italians if he didn't do what he was told. Karalivanos fell for it. He got the two policemen re-clothed and calmed them down. They got their potatoes and went on their way. We all hoped it would be enough.

Denys and I had another dinner in Stromi the next day. Yannis told us a message had come through to say that John's party would be arriving the next evening with a band of Aris's men. Great news!

We slept at Yannis's place that night, in beds with sheets and pillowcases—unimaginable comfort. I slid under the sheets like a little fish slipping into the water after the fisherman has let him go.

Next day Denys and Khouri took off to meet John's party.

Suddenly they were with us, a burst of men talking and talking in English and Greek.

'Who's this?' said Nat. 'It can't be Themis, can it, behind that beard?'

'Our beards are bigger,' I said. 'We've been here longer.'

'Let me introduce Nikiforos,' said Themis. 'That's the name he goes by, at least.'

'*Kalispera, Nikifore,*' I replied.

Nikiforos looked young—early twenties at most. He was armed with a German automatic, with bandoliers crossed over his chest and a little cap embroidered with four letters: ELAS. He had brought about twenty-five men with him, but they'd already gone up the mountainside to stay with Len and Mike—there wasn't room for them at the cave.

'If it wasn't for Aris's men,' said John, 'we'd have been prisoners of the Italians long ago.'

'Why? What happened?' said Eddie. 'They've been after us more or less since we dropped, but so far we've been able to keep out of their clutches.'

'We dropped practically on top of an Italian garrison town,' said Themis. 'Karpenisi.' This was close to Pera Kapsi, where Cairo had mistakenly believed Zervas's HQ was located. 'They were firing on us as we were coming down. Automatic weapons, then heavy machine-gun fire. There were mortars landing around us as we hit the ground.'

'When was this?' I asked. 'When did you drop?'

'Two weeks ago. We left Cairo on the night of the 27th.'

'You mean to say you didn't drop when we did?' I asked. 'What happened?'

'Not suitable,' said John. 'There were no signals. It wasn't safe to drop so we went back to Cairo.'

Themis raised his eyebrows. Later, he would tell me that he believed sheer cowardice had prevented John from jumping. As a result of John's reluctance, Cairo had appointed Themis leader of the group until they joined up with the other parties, with the acting rank of major.

Doug had been lucky. He landed right inside the town, and the locals took him into hiding straight away. But the others had no idea where he was. Themis found Inder first, and then John. They were only a hundred yards from the Italian outposts, but in thick bushes where they couldn't be seen, in spite of all the flares the Italians had let off. One of the wireless sets had dropped close by but they couldn't retrieve it under fire.

When no one came to help them, they took off towards the hills. Inder and Themis still had their haversacks but all their documents, including the information and photos of bridges, were in John's personal bag, and it was left behind in the confusion of the attack. Bad news for all of us if the Italians figured out what the photos were for.

A village priest had offered to shelter them. Then Nikiforos happened to pass by with his band and asked them to meet his men, who were stationed in a school.

'The men were all wearing caps with ELAS embroidered on them,' Themis said. 'I thought they must have meant *Ellas*, Greece. They were a mixed bunch and I thought perhaps they hadn't learnt to spell very well. They told us they'd seen the plane, but not the parachutes.'

Themis told the *andartes* that they were part of a British mission. Another party had parachuted into Greece somewhere around Mount Giona a month earlier and they needed help to find them. The *andartes* promised to take them to their leader, Aris, in the forest at Velouchi the following day.

'You met Aris?' said Eddie. 'So he does exist? What's he like?'

'To look at, do you mean?' asked Inder.

'Well, yes,' said Eddie. 'To begin with.'

'Short,' said Inder. 'Big black beard, but that doesn't tell you anything—most of them have beards. Wears a khaki tunic, but no badges. Crossed bandoliers like the others. Black fur hat— Cossack-style—his inner circle, too.'

'He wasn't exactly welcoming,' said Themis. 'He said we might be German spies and he couldn't afford to take the chance. I think he was particularly suspicious of me—a Greek in British uniform. He told his men to lock us up until our identity could be proved. As they were leading us away, Nikiforos was trying to persuade him—telling him we couldn't possibly be spies because they'd seen us arrive by plane, and that treating a British mission like this wasn't good policy.'

After they'd been locked up a while, Aris suddenly seemed to decide to believe them after all. Themis thought perhaps it was because so many people knew they were there—and how they'd arrived. Otherwise they might have been shot straight away as spies.

'Aris isn't in sole command,' said John. 'There are three of them—a kind of triumvirate in theory, although it appears not in practice. Aris is the "*kapetanios*", the leader. Nikiforos is the military leader. There's also a political adviser. In practice Nikiforos answers to Aris, but Aris himself reports to a central command in Athens, whom Nikiforos has never met—he doesn't even know their names.'

John, Themis and Inder had accompanied the *andartes* for a long time. Eventually another group of ELAS guerrillas arrived—and they had Doug with them. Then, just a few days ago, the priest of a nearby village had sent through two notes from Chris. One was for Aris, telling him Chris was going to meet Zervas. The other was for John's group, telling them the location of our cave. Aris had sent them off to us straight away.

No doubt everyone but me had a rollicking night of it. I wasn't there to see—I got the job of fetching three of the leaders of Aris's band up to our cave, in the dark both ways, through light rain and then heavy fog: one hell of a trip.

The next morning, more guerrillas turned up. Not all were as well equipped as Nikiforos. There was an odd assortment of uniforms, some Italian, some German, some belonging to the Greek Gendarmerie, and now and then a faded Greek military uniform. A few lucky ones had Italian boots. Others wore slippers made from undressed goatskin—or even slices of rubber tyre fastened with wire. Some were barefooted. They all lived in hope of killing an Italian and getting his boots and his machine gun. A useful proportion already had Breda light machine guns, the ammunition to go with them slung in bandoliers across their chests. Others had rifles—Mausers, Mannlichers, Lee Enfields. The not-so-lucky ones had obsolete Turkish rifles.

We'd ordered timber from a local sawmiller to build the framing for the explosive. We showed the *andartes* the dummy bridge pier we'd built to practise on. Nikiforos promised us full support. Now it was just a matter of waiting for Chris.

The camp was full of cheerful activity as those not in the demolition party trained the *andartes* in the use of the Stens we had brought for them. By the sound of things they were having a lot of fun. We gave ELAS half the Stens and half our hand grenades, too. And to our delight Nikiforos, seeing Denys eyeing off one of the sheep the *andartes* had brought with them, promised us half.

For those of us in the demolition party, completing the frames for the charges was the top priority. Each bar of moulded explosive was laid between two pieces of wood and secured with parachute cord. We'd be using primers and Cordtex fuse cable to initiate the explosion—two methods, to make doubly sure. We would carry everything on our shoulders to the bridge, and then use more parachute cord to tie the explosives in place. Nikiforos agreed to supply a few extra men for our demolition party, and to help transport the explosives to the target.

We were as prepared as we could be—but Eddie was worried about Chris.

'God knows whether he's had any success with Zervas,' he said. 'We've got Nikiforos's lot, but it's not really enough. And Chris is going to arrive back absolutely exhausted. He'll probably need a bit of time to recuperate.'

'He'll be OK,' I said. 'He's tough.'

'Yes, and young,' said Eddie. 'That's in his favour.'

'Very strong, Chris,' said Barba Niko. 'He—how you say it?— leave me lying dead.'

'I think you mean he left you for dead,' said John.

Just at that moment, we heard someone coming. It was the priest from Stromi village. His news was good—the best. Chris had sent a runner. He would be back the next day. And he had with him both Aris and Zervas, along with a large force—over a hundred *andartes*.

The operation was on.

After everything that had gone wrong—the Italians constantly after us, the loss of our explosives, the mysterious non-appearance of John's party—at last we had something definite ahead of us. Daunting, now that it was so close—but definite.

SIX

We didn't know it yet, but the arrival of Aris and Zervas would propel us right into the midst of Greek resistance politics and the various groups around which opposition to the occupying forces was consolidating. As we began to understand the ideologies, the rivalries, the complications, we felt more than ever how much Cairo had let us down in their initial briefing—all of us, but especially those on whose shoulders the responsibility for diplomacy would rest: Eddie and Chris.

Zervas, a former army colonel, had been one of the founders of the Greek National Republican Organisation—generally known by its Greek initials, EDES—in late 1941, the same year in which the dictator Metaxas had died. The titular leader of EDES, General Plastiris, in exile in unoccupied France, was represented in Greece by Zervas's second-in-command, Komninos Pyromaglou. The constitution of the organisation included a commitment to oppose the return of the Greek king, except by the will of the people.

Zervas had left Athens for north-west Greece in July 1942 to lead the EDES resistance in the mountains; his base was in his home district around Jumerka. What held EDES together, as much as anything, was Zervas's own personal leadership.

The group of which Aris was 'kapetanios' was on the political left. The National Popular Liberation Army, known by its initials ELAS, had been founded in Athens in April 1942 as the military arm of a pre-existing organisation, the National Workers' Liberation Front (EAM); EAM itself had been founded in September 1941 by the Greek communist party, the KKE. But that didn't mean that all the members of ELAS were communists, not by any means.

Aris came from the city of Lamia, which made him more or less a local in the area of the three bridges. He had set himself up in the region of Mount Tymfristos, traditionally known as Velouchi—hence his *nom de guerre*, 'Aris Velouchiotis'. His real name was Athanasios Klaras.

What we eventually knew about these organisations came in scraps and shreds of information, picked up here and there as we struggled to understand who they were and where they stood politically. The size and allegiances of both groups were fluid. And it took a long time before we understood the complicated relationship between ELAS and the communist party. But once we understood the significance of those two sets of initials, ELAS and EDES, they were constantly on our tongues, along with the names of their respective leaders, Aris and Zervas.

We completed the charges, alert to every sound that might herald Chris's return.

'*Chionizi*,' called out Barba Niko suddenly. '*Chionizi*. It snow.'

Through the lightly falling flakes a figure appeared. Not Chris. A messenger. Someone had betrayed our location.

'We should be used to this by now,' said Arthur. 'We just get nicely settled in one place and then the same old bad news arrives.'

'Well, we would've been moving anyway,' said Eddie. 'But we'll get everything ready in case we need to clear off in a big hurry. With any luck they'll arrive well after we've left.'

It was 17 November. Chris's time would be up at midnight. He wasn't back by 10 pm so we settled down for the night. Voices woke us at a quarter past twelve.

'Fifteen minutes late,' said Chris, 'as Eddie has already kindly pointed out.'

We wriggled out of our dirty blankets and sat up.

Chris had no intention of apologising. 'Zervas is at Mavrolithari village now with fifty *andartes*,' he announced, 'and there are more than a hundred of Aris's men there too. I came on ahead with Zervas's adjutant here so that I wouldn't be late.'

'We won't court-martial you on account of fifteen minutes,' said Eddie. 'And that's wonderful news. We've been expecting you—we got your message yesterday.'

'We've been taking bets on whether you'd make it before the deadline,' called out Nat.

'This is Captain Michalis Myridakis,' said Chris, introducing the tall, dark man who was standing with him. 'He's Zervas's personal adjutant.'

'*Yia sou*,' we said. Hello.

'*Yia sou*,' he replied. '*Chairo poly.*' Nice to meet you.

'Chris wasn't late,' said Myridakis. 'The clock has changed to winter time. It's still 11.15.'

Everyone clapped.

Zervas, when he appeared, turned out to be a short, round man with dark greying hair and a neat khaki uniform. He looked about fifty but it was hard to tell behind the jutting beard. He seemed jovial and bright-eyed about our operation.

The senior officers—Eddie, Chris, Nikiforos and Zervas—retired to a smaller cave nearby for a conference, with Themis and Chris translating. When they emerged, Eddie announced that he had offered his services to Zervas as chief of staff. It was a surprising move—but a shrewd one.

Our last night in the cave, our last yarning around the fire. We all wanted to hear Chris's story.

'After I sent Barba Niko back,' he told us, 'I stopped at a woodcutter's hut. I didn't want to go into a village by myself. The woodcutter was full of questions. Where was I from and where was I going? He went through a whole lot of countries, trying to place me. The last one was Russia. I felt bad that I kept on disappointing him so I said I knew Russia. That was a mistake.'

'What happened?' asked Eddie.

'He asked me what towns I knew in Russia. I suggested Omsk. That was my second mistake.'

'Why?' said Nat. 'Had he been there?'

'He was born there! In the tavern by the church in the main square. I steered the conversation away from Russia after that. A couple of nights later I met an old woman on the edge of a village, just as dusk was falling. She was washing clothes at the village spring. I took a chance and told her I was a guerrilla. She wanted to know where I was from. I took another chance and named the village I'd just passed through, twenty minutes down the road.'

'Your third mistake?' asked Nat.

'Not at all. She said she knew I was a foreigner. But she put me up for the night. Turned out her son was in the merchant navy and had been to London, but she didn't have much idea where it was.'

'I was covering fifteen miles a day on foot,' he went on, 'and it should have been fast enough, but after a while I realised that everyone I asked for directions was more concerned about keeping me away from the Italians than getting me where I was going. I was moving too far to the west.'

But in the end it worked out well. Chris stopped to chat to a priest and heard that another party of parachutists had landed— just a week before, and practically on top of the Italians. Aris had rescued the parachutists from the Italians. Then he had taken them with him to the south-west.

'So you wrote some letters,' said John.

Chris nodded. 'I take it that's how you came to be here.'

'Yes,' said John. 'Your letters put the wind up Aris. He sent us on with Nikiforos. I think he was worried that Zervas might get all the glory for blowing the bridge.'

Finally Chris had made it to Zervas's HQ at Sakaretsi. That's where he had met Myridakis, Zervas's adjutant. They had a lot in common because Myridakis was a Cretan, and Chris had been in Crete, of course. The next morning they set off to meet Zervas, who was in action against the Italians.

'Do you know what Zervas said when he saw me?' Chris said. '"*Kalos ton evangelon.*" That means, "Welcome to the angel of good news." I formally offered myself as his liaison officer with GHQ in Cairo. Then I explained our mission. He agreed at once to come back with me to join Eddie. He would bring most of his force with him. The plan was to leave a rearguard so that the Italians wouldn't realise Zervas had decamped.

'Zervas needed twenty-four hours to sort things out at his end. We left on the 12th. That gave us six days to make the deadline. Zervas thought that if we took a more direct route we would make it. Then we got to Viniani village and heard that Aris was just a few hours away. We stayed with an ex-emigrant to America—the only person in the village with a bath, actually.'

'A bath!' exclaimed Nat and Arthur at once. 'Did you have one?'

'No, we didn't. So don't be jealous. But our host was shocked when I said I wanted to meet Aris. Said Aris and his lot were communists and that communists were terrible people. And Zervas was worried that Aris would attack us. But I sent another note to Aris to ask him to join us.'

Aris arrived the following morning, and they all gathered at the house of the American, who didn't take it too kindly. Zervas and Aris had never met, but they made an effort to get on. Zervas was in Aris's territory so was disposed to be conciliatory. And Aris didn't want to miss out on the propaganda benefits of being involved in a successful strike with the British. He agreed to join the mission, and to put his force under Zervas's command for the operation.

They left a rearguard at Viniani—mostly Zervas's men—to create a diversion, as the Italians were bound to notice their movements when they passed near Karpenisi. Aris stopped at Gardiki village to meet representatives of his central command, while Zervas and Chris travelled on to Mavrolithari. Conscious of his deadline, Chris had pressed on with Myridakis.

No one but Chris could have done it—I was sure of that. When I first met him I'd wondered about his capacity, being so young, to carry off his role. Now I saw how lucky we were to have him. Someone ten years older might have had the endurance for the trip Chris had just completed, but not the speed. And Chris had the diplomatic skills required—that was clear. He'd been able to make both Aris and Zervas see the operation in terms of their own advantage. Political skills—I knew I didn't have them. If anyone could make things work in Greece after the rest of us had departed, it would be Chris.

We'd met Zervas—now we couldn't wait to meet Aris. He'd eluded us for so long that we'd wondered if he even existed. Now we knew he did. But what could we expect from him, and would he be the ally we needed?

Six weeks living in the cave, if you didn't count the brief interlude at Barba Niko's camp. Now it was time to leave.

'I can't help feeling a bit nostalgic,' Denys said to Eddie and me as we were packing up.

'I know what you mean,' I said. 'It's like deserting an old friend, isn't it? There'll be no one to yarn around the fire in the evenings, no one coming up from the village with a sheep over their shoulder.'

'No one coming down from the wireless camp to say the equipment's broken down again,' said Eddie. 'No one waiting for news of the *andartes* that never comes.'

It was two o'clock in the afternoon before we were ready. We marched down in the snow through Stromi towards Mavrolithari with our train of mules, feeling rather strange to be travelling openly by day. People came out of their houses to greet us and offer us glasses of wine and *tsipouro*, a home-made brew that packed a punch. We were considerably warmer and much more cheerful by the time we left the village.

Coming round a corner on the track to Mavrolithari, we saw someone waiting by the side of the road—Karalivanos. Eddie, in front, ignored his salute, remembering the incident of the gendarmes and the potatoes. The rest of us did the same as we passed.

We found Mavrolithari already full of *andartes*, cooking their evening meal over open fires. Denys went off to the school to arrange some accommodation for us.

'I've met the fabled Aris,' he told us when he finally reappeared.

'What's he like?' asked Nat.

'He tried to push past me in the school, so I told him to shove off. Then he told me who he was so I introduced myself. He wasn't exactly friendly. Just said, "My officer here will fix you up," and brushed past me again. A hard and cold man, I would say.'

Mavrolithari was quite a large village, and we scored a room above a stable on the outskirts of the village. There were two goats and a cow in the stable below; a single chair was the only furniture. We got an enormous meal, though, from the *andartes*, so were happy enough to spread our blankets out on the wooden floor.

Then we noticed something else in the room—a large demijohn.

'I wonder what's in there,' said Inder.

'Only one way to find out,' said Denys.

'We're in luck,' said Inder, tasting it. 'It's *tsipouro*.'

'What about the old woman who owns the place?' said Arthur. 'Imagine what she's going to say if we drink all her *tsipouro*.'

'That's tomorrow's problem,' said Denys.

The evening improved dramatically.

In the morning, Denys sent Nat to ask the old woman to milk the cow for breakfast. After a while she appeared at the top of the ladder and announced grumpily that the cow had no milk at this time of the year. When she realised that we'd been consuming her *tsipouro*, she wasn't pleased. The Greek-speakers had to do some quick negotiating and hand over some money.

We went out to the square to see what was happening. On one side, a group of old men were sitting with their sticks, surveying the scene with a keen eye and chatting animatedly. They were shaded by a plane tree with a massive girth of trunk. Nat asked the old men how old it was. Six hundred years at least, they said.

We were surprised to find Karalivanos at the school, where everyone was assembling. We had all assumed that Aris would punish him when he arrived, for terrorising the neighbouring villages. But there he was, as large as life, accompanied by some of his gang. A weeping girl drooped in the midst of them, a lot of strange purple markings on her forehead.

Karalivanos had captured the girl a couple of weeks before and had kept her to bring before Aris. He said she'd been collaborating with the Italians. It was pretty clear he was using her as a pass back into Aris's good graces.

The girl must have been about twenty. She appealed to Nat to put in a good word for her—she must have liked the look of him and could see he spoke Greek. She said Karalivanos's gang had punched her with a rubber stamp with the Greek letter Π—'p' for *poutana*, the Greek word for whore—and twisted her arms to get her to confess. Nat was sympathetic but there was nothing we could do and they took her away. We heard later that they had shot her out at the village cemetery. I tried not to think about her body slumping to the ground, the marks still on her forehead.

Eddie held a conference later that day with Aris and Zervas. He had modified his plans in order to make full use of the extra *andarte* forces that were now available. The moon was nearly full, so the attack would have to be soon. We would aim for 25 November. Five days away.

Aris and Zervas sent off a recce party to the bridge through the lightly falling snow. Then, in what turned out to be a habit of his, Aris disappeared.

Meanwhile, Arthur and I had the job of briefing and training the *andartes* who'd been assigned to our demolition team. Both Zervas and Aris had lent us some men—supposedly their best. We hoped they would prove to be so.

'What *is* the plan, Tom?' Len asked me as we prepared to meet with them for the first time.

'Why, haven't Eddie and Chris briefed you?'

'Not a bloody word,' he said. 'Those two are too high and mighty to talk to us plebs.'

Together Arthur and I told him what was going on. Two small parties would cut the railway line north and south so as to delay any reinforcements, while two larger parties would attack the bridge at each end. There were concrete fortifications— pillboxes and so on—at both ends. Once these attacks were all underway, the demolition party would make a separate approach to the bridge.

'Can I join your party, Tom?' said Len. 'You know I can handle explosives.'

'Sounds good to me,' I replied. 'If they haven't given you another role, I can't see why not.'

In the morning we all left for the nearby village of Kastriotissa, which would give us easier access to the bridge. This was the second—and last—day of training for our new *andartes*. They were very keen, but there was little ammunition for practice rounds on the Stens and no grenades to spare for training.

The officers met in conference next morning in the Kastriotissa schoolroom, a cloud of cigarette smoke hanging in the air. The children's benches had been dragged haphazardly around a contour map spread on a low table. A stove in one corner took the chill off the air.

Zervas leant forward to speak. 'The rear rendezvous is at Mount Oiti—at a deserted sawmill about 13,000 feet above the bridge. There are a few huts and so on that we can shelter in.'

On the map, the contour lines were practically on top of one another—it would be extremely steep. 'We will move to the sawmill in two days' time, on the 24th. We can travel there safely in daylight. After dark we will leave to take up our positions.'

Zervas, Aris and Eddie discussed the best time for the attack to commence. At 10 pm the Italian garrison would still be active. They agreed on 11 pm.

The assault would start simultaneously at both ends of the bridge. The plan allowed for two demolitions, an hour or so apart, to be sure of bringing down the two steel piers. The eight remaining masonry piers we could do nothing about. There were ten spans altogether—the bridge was about 650 feet in length—and we were determined to bring down three of the spans.

We would have two hours to lay the charges. Having the explosive already prepared to fit the cross-section of the piers would be an immense help. Based on the evidence we had, we'd prepared for an L-shaped cross-section.

'Four hours altogether,' said Aris. 'We should be out by 3 am. What external communications do the Italians have?'

'Telephone and telegraph contact with nearby garrisons,' said Eddie. 'The telephone wires run across the bridge. At one minute to zero hour the groups going to the north and south of the bridge will cut the lines.'

'But the battle will still be heard,' said Aris. 'So we'll be expecting Italian reinforcements.'

It was likely the reinforcements would arrive within two hours, by train or road. The other parties would deal with them as well.

Aris stubbed out his cigarette in one of the ashtrays that were starting to spill their contents onto the map beneath. 'The timing must be coordinated exactly. The attack must start simultaneously from the north and south ends at zero hour.'

'Captain Myridakis, would you go over the arrangements for those two attacks?' asked Zervas. The Cretan stood up.

'The group to attack the northern end comprises twenty-three men from EDES under Second Lieutenant Papachristou. The other group is larger—around sixty men including officers—because the command post and barracks are situated at that end of the bridge. This is a combined group of ELAS and EDES, including Karalivanos and four of his men.'

'Any questions for Captain Myridakis?' asked Zervas

'How will we know when it's time for us to go in?' I asked.

'I will fire a red flare when both ends are cleared. That will be your signal,' said Myridakis.

'The third group, now,' said Zervas. 'Major John.' The *andartes* still knew us only by our nicknames.

John stood up, rather red in the face. 'A small group of British and ELAS men will move south through the tunnel. Our task is to cut the telephone and telegraph wires and blow the railway line. We will also take care of any reinforcements that may come along from that direction.'

'Captain Themis?' said Zervas.

Themis was in command of the fourth group of ELAS, about the same size as Cook's. 'We have a similar mission for the northern end of the bridge,' he reported. 'After cutting the communications lines we will mine the track to derail the next train that comes along from the direction of Lamia, and then engage the occupants. This should block the bridge and stop reinforcements getting to the garrisons.'

'The fifth group is all ELAS,' said Aris. 'Heraklis will be in command.'

'We will occupy the bridge over the river Sperchios on the Lamia–Frantzi road and engage reinforcements coming by road,' said Heraklis.

'Two and a half miles away,' said Eddie.

'Yes,' said Heraklis. 'If need be, we will burn the bridge.'

'The sixth group is the demolition group,' said Zervas. 'Captain Tom?'

'We will be transporting a large volume of explosives to the bridge,' I said. 'On the signal we will go in and begin to attach the explosives. I will blow a whistle to warn people to take shelter.' To cover our party, we had Bafas with his Tommy gun, plus armed *andartes* from ELAS and EDES. And four mules to carry the explosives.

'The command post,' said Zervas. 'Four from ELAS and four from EDES plus my two bodyguards. Eddie and Chris from the British mission. And a reserve of thirty men to deal with any contingencies.'

Zervas and Aris would carry out a final reconnaissance with Eddie and Chris and a few others, leaving on the 24th.

'There will be reprisals for our attack,' said Aris. 'You know that, don't you?'

'We have had warnings,' said Eddie. 'But I have my orders. I have to follow them.'

* * *

'What do you think it feels like to die?' asked Inder that night.

We were sitting on the floor with blankets around us, drinking *tsipouro*. Inder had now taken Nat's place in our demolition party, as originally intended.

'Quickly or slowly?' asked Arthur.

'Well, either. You don't know how it might happen, do you?'

'I saw plenty of people die in the desert,' said Arthur. 'The lucky ones go quickly with a mortar—or a mine, if they're right on top of it. One minute they're there—the next you're looking at the bits. Gut-wrenching for you, but they're out of it. Dying slowly—that's harder.'

'Yes, but how does it feel to be them, I wonder? Is there a moment when you realise you're done for? How much pain do you feel, or are you somehow anaesthetised to it? What do you think, Tom?'

'I'm no expert,' I said. 'You all know this is my first real engagement.'

I had been in a few sticky situations in New Guinea, it was true. Once I'd had to fix an outboard engine under water in a river infested with crocodiles. That wasn't fun. I couldn't help imagining jaws suddenly closing on my legs or torso, wondering how much it would hurt and how quickly I would go. But I had never been under fire.

'That's all right, Tom,' said Inder. 'We trust you.'

'Anyway, we shouldn't be under attack,' said Arthur. 'If everything goes according to plan, the garrisons will have been wiped out before we go in.'

'If everything goes according to plan,' repeated Denys. 'Anyway, I always think of death like this: we practise for it every day.'

'How's that?' asked Arthur.

'Every day we go to sleep at night. We give up on everything—our thoughts, our plans, our problems, and just slide away. So when our time comes to die we will have had lots of practice.'

'Maybe you're right,' said Inder. 'If you go and look at tombstones they often say "Fell asleep on such and such a date", don't they? "Rest in peace."'

'That's just to make it easier for the people left behind,' Nat scoffed. 'They can't bear to admit that the dead person doesn't exist anymore, so they kid themselves that they will wake up again in a better place.'

'In the conference today, Zervas said we were helping Greece,' I said. 'What do you think, Themis? Are we?'

'We were sent here to help the Allied war effort,' said Themis. 'That's the beginning and end of it, really. As Eddie said, we're under orders.'

'If you're going to die,' said Inder, 'you would like to think it was worth it.'

'Politicians always want soldiers to think that,' said Nat. 'That's why they have war memorials and remembrance days. Otherwise who would they get to fight?'

'Well, I'm tired,' said Arthur. 'And tomorrow's a big day. I'm going to lie down in my blanket and practise dying.'

As we left Kastriotissa next morning it was raining heavily. The rain turned to snow as we climbed the mountain, water rushing away in runnels under our feet. At the summit the snow became a blizzard.

We arrived at the abandoned Hondroyannis sawmill, six hours from the bridge, in the early afternoon—a hundred and fifty men and twenty heavily laden mules. The snow was a foot deep. The recce group departed soon after for the forward rendezvous, a terrace called Plakoto on the edge of the forest. Some of the other parties needed explosives to use on the railway tracks, and we prepared those as well as some of our own. Food was not plentiful but the *andartes* built big fires with the timber lying around. At least we were warm.

Our party was allocated to a wooden shed with the ELAS leaders, but they preferred to doss with their men. Some of the *andartes* made shelters in the mill itself, which was open at the sides. Others leant planks up against the timber piles and built a fire at the entrance to keep warm. Some of them had *tsipouro* with them, while others were drinking wine.

We built a fire inside our shed. The smoke gradually made its way up to the ceiling and hung there, dispersing only slowly, but at least we were able to take off our sodden socks and dry them. Only a few of us had boots suitable for walking through deep snow.

At midnight, we woke suddenly. There was a strange, reddish light and people were shouting. We were into our boots and out of the shed in no time. One of the large wooden piles was well ablaze and had set fire to the fir trees above.

'The explosives! The explosives!' yelled Arthur. The explosives had been unloaded from the mules and stacked inside the mill to keep dry. They were some distance from the fire, but not far enough. If the wooden roof of the mill caught fire, the whole operation would be over before it had begun.

The *andartes* were as close to the fire as they could get, attacking it with snow and axes. We worked on the nearby stacks, breaking them up so that they wouldn't be engulfed if there were a sudden conflagration.

'What if they see us from down below?' asked Inder as we worked frantically. 'They'll come looking for us.'

'I think we might be in luck,' said Nat. 'This low cloud is our best friend.'

'This position isn't visible from the bridge, either,' said Eddie.

At last the fire was under control. A close call.

Next morning we were off at 9 am for Plakoto, the whole gang and the mules. After all those weeks of waiting and planning, it was hard to believe we were so close at last.

'I wonder what Zervas and Aris and so on have found out,' said Arthur as we trudged through the snow, cold, wet and muddy. 'No nasty surprises, I hope.'

'I wonder what they'll have for us to eat when we get there,' said Inder. 'I'm starving already.'

'Well, they won't be lighting a whole lot of cooking fires down there, that's for sure,' said Denys.

'We'll probably get cold beans,' I said.

'Again,' said Denys. 'I don't know if my gut will survive until the sub comes to take us off.'

'It's better than having the opposite problem,' I said.

'You reckon?' said Arthur. 'It's diarrhoea that gives me the shits. So to speak.'

'Sometimes having the shits can be better,' I said. 'I'll tell you what happened to my batman in Egypt. He was a real cracker. He started out with me in Gianaclis and came with me to Aqaba. Used to fix everything up nicely for me wherever we were.'

'I could have done with one like that,' said Denys. 'Mine was no bloody good at all.'

'Anyway, he got piles. The food was terrible at Aqaba to begin with, until we got in with the Tommies' mess. We were all constipated. But he was the worst. Blood everywhere every time he took a shit. We got the doc to examine him. Thought he would be OK.'

'And was he?' said Arthur.

'No. The doc said it was so serious he would have to go home. First he went off to the hospital in Cairo. We kept in touch— used to write every week. Then he got shipped off back to New Zealand and that was the end of it.'

'That's hilarious,' said Denys. 'What a story.'

'Yes, unless it happens to you,' I said. 'Or someone you like.'

We were still cold and hungry by the time we got to Plakoto. We found the others already assembled, waiting for a final briefing. Both Zervas and Aris made spirited speeches to the men.

There were two new huts at the northern end of the railway line, according to the intel gathered by the reconnaissance party. This meant the Italian guard had been increased. The area had also been fenced with barbed wire but not, as far as we knew, electrified.

We went through the duties of each detachment of *andartes* one by one, rehearsing exactly what each party had to do.

'I have three flare pistols here,' said Eddie. 'Lieutenant Papachristou, this one is for the northern end. You have a white flare. Fire it when resistance has been neutralised. Captain Myridakis, you have a white and a red flare. Fire the white under the same conditions as Papachristou—when you have neutralised the resistance. Fire the red flare when both ends are clear. This will be the signal for the demolition party to go in. General Zervas, this is your pistol, with a green flare. This will be the signal that the operation is finished.'

At last it was time to eat—a lump of boiled mutton on the bone for each of us and a hunk of bread.

'Cold,' said Denys. 'Not much, either. And no beans. Beans would've filled our stomachs at least.'

'Just a snack, really,' said Arthur.

We would have to go in hungry.

SEVEN

It was dark as pitch and the going was bloody. The slope was steep and slippery and there was no track. Five groups had gone down ahead of us in the drizzling rain and now the mud was liquefying under our boots and the hooves of the heavily laden mules. We were blind and deaf in the darkness, using our hands to keep contact with the man in front.

Two thoughts fought in my head as we descended. One was quiet satisfaction. At last I was doing what I had come to do— useful professional work. This thought brought a spreading warmth to my belly and chest. The other thought, if you could call it that, was crude fear. Each time this lurched to the surface, the pit of my stomach went cold.

The two feelings were still fighting it out when we arrived at the meeting place at the source of the Gorgopotamos River.

The moon was up now, but low cloud diffused its light. Our HQ were directly behind us. They seemed to be conducting a whispered debate. After a minute or two they took up position on the north bank. Then came an urgent call: 'Len, where's Len?' He went to see what they wanted and didn't come back.

The four parties for the north and south headed for their positions.

Now it was just us. The demolition party, Denys and his team of guards, and our guide, Yannis Pistolis. Three soldiers—the two Turkish Cypriots, Yannis and Panayiotis, and Khouri the Palestinian—one each to assist the three sappers. Four EDES *andartes* and four from ELAS, including Bafas from Karalivanos's gang. Four mules and 400 pounds of plastic high explosive. And the river to cross.

There was a bridge of sorts—a single narrow plank laid from one bank to the other. Getting the overloaded mules across—and in silence—was hell. Every second they threatened to topple off the plank into the river, taking their load with them.

Everyone safely across, we offloaded the mules. Each man took his forty-pound load on his shoulders.

Yannis Pistolis guided us through thick scrub, past the reservoir whose waters we could see tumbling down an iron conduit to the small power house maybe a hundred feet below, and over countless small tributaries. Our heavy packs impeded us and we had to fight our way along. Now the power house was below us, the bridge to the north, the piers that were our target around the hill out of sight.

As we walked, a rhythmical sound forced itself into my consciousness above the noise of rushing water. The sound came from the south and was getting louder and louder. The unmistakable galumphing noise of a train. We exchanged surprised glances. We had checked the timetable. No train was due.

The train took a minute or two to cross the bridge and then disappeared to the north.

Yanni signalled a steep descent. We slipped and slid to the bottom with our loads. Ahead of us a small path led to the bridge, about two hundred yards away.

From here the bridge soared above us against the milky clouds—ten spans, eight masonry piers, and the two steel piers that were our target, 100 feet high.

We were late to our positions but as all was still silent the others must have been too. Everyone was at a high pitch, watching for the battle to begin.

At 11.15 the racket broke out, sudden and shocking.

'*Aera! Aera!*' The war cries came across the river from HQ, over the din of the water.

Our Stens clattered. We could clearly see the yellow flashes of our Mills grenades at both ends of the bridge. Almost instantly we heard a deeper sound. Heavy machine guns. The Italians must have been expecting us after all. We'll give the *andartes* until one o'clock, I thought.

The battle continued at full spate. A brief lull, then another fierce volley of gunfire. Another lull, another volley. Bullets spat around us. Our single heavy machine gun broke out, down below HQ.

We were staring at the luminous faces of our watches. Fifteen minutes. Thirty minutes, forty. It was after one o'clock. How much longer would the ammunition last? We were getting colder by the minute.

Denys was chewing on his empty pipe. He knew we couldn't afford to risk giving our position away to those still fighting above us.

There had been no Verey signals. None at all, although we strained our eyes looking for them.

Finally, at 1.15, there was a dull explosion from the south. The railway line blown. At last.

Then a flashlight from across the river. Eddie was shouting above the noise of the river and the battle.

'Go in, Tom. Go in!'

'Come on,' I said. 'Load up.'

We had to slide down the slope to the power house. A few lights were still on. I sent a couple of the *andartes* to warn the Greek engineers to stay inside out of the way.

As we came around the corner we heard a machine gun open up, much too close for comfort. We dived off to one side of the path. But almost immediately, we realised it was our own Bafas.

'Ask him what the hell he's doing, Denys,' I whispered.

'He says he thought he saw an Iti.'

'Tell him to calm down. He might give us away. Let's get on—quickly.'

The road to the bridge stretched ahead and we raced along it. More mud. In the near distance a low stone culvert appeared. We could shelter behind it when we blew the charges.

Now we had to leave the path and clamber up the bank. I'd been expecting barbed wire and now we were on top of it. The bolt cutters were ready in my hand.

Yannis signalled again.

'Look out for mines,' mouthed Denys.

There was a strong chance there would be anti-personnel mines, we knew. It wasn't something our reconnaissance parties had been able to check.

There was only one way to find out. I cut the wire and kicked the pieces away. The others came through the gap behind me. Another fence was just ahead. It got the same treatment. We ran to the first steel pier. No explosions, no problems—therefore no mines. We were in luck.

The pier was huge above us. We had studied the blueprints so many times it should have felt familiar, but the reality was bigger and more daunting than I had ever imagined. At the base, four massive steel feet were deeply embedded in concrete.

I was looking for the cross-section. Something was wrong. The girders weren't L-shaped at all. They were more like a square U. We had got it wrong. Disaster!

But I was thinking fast, recalculating in my head. We hadn't known how thick the steel legs of the pier would be, so we had calculated for twice as much explosives as we thought we were likely to need. Six main charges, sixteen small. A picture flashed through my mind—sitting outside the cave, making up the charges, yarning in the sunlight day after day. I dismissed it.

'We'll have to redo everything. Take the charges to pieces, stuff the explosives into the leg of the girder, wedge them in with the wooden frames, then connect the fuses. Let's get cracking.'

'How long's this going to take you, Tom?' said Denys. 'Surely it's impossible.'

'We have to do it,' I answered quietly. 'That's all there is to it.' Fortunately the moonlight was stronger now and we could see to work.

Above us the shooting continued—machine guns, Tommy guns and grenades were going off all around. The curve of the bridge put us in the line of fire. We could hear the clang of bullets hitting the girders above us. Others pocked the ground behind.

Arthur and Inder took one pier leg each. The other two were mine. I was sweating like a pig. After weeks in the mountains, it was a shock to be back at sea level.

Denys had his guards stationed in a rough circle about twenty yards across. Every now and again they fired at something—God knows what.

After a while things seemed a little quieter directly overhead. At the northern end, however, the shooting just kept going.

We were laying the charges on the cross members when out of the blue came a big explosion near Denys. Stones and splinters crashed into the bridge.

Denys went over and shouted up at the *andartes* on the bridge. I could imagine what he was saying. If they hit the explosives, we would all be gone.

Silence. They seemed to have got the message. But then came another crash, another explosion. More projectiles flying up from the ground around us. Were our *andartes* lobbing grenades?

Denys marched up the slope a bit and again called up to the bridge. Someone yelled back and there was a shouted exchange.

Then we heard a voice from over the river. It was Chris.

'How much longer?'

'Ten minutes,' I said to Denys, and he relayed my answer back to Chris. It had taken us nearly an hour to lay the charges.

Arthur and I finished at the same moment, and I went across to check his work and Inder's. We had fixed detonators and fuses in two places. Now we were ready to light the fuses.

'It's all set,' I said. 'Denys, send the others back to the power house.'

I got out my whistle. Just at that moment, a white flare soared into the air from the northern end of the bridge. Then almost simultaneously, a red flare from the south. Our signal to go in. A bit late! We all booed.

Arthur and I struck our fuse caps and made sure they were burning properly. Then I blew the signal to take cover—three blasts on the whistle. We took off at a run for the culvert. Arthur stayed outside below the bank.

There was water in the culvert. We waited, shivering, in the cold and wet. The entrance faced away from the bridge so we had no line of sight.

Dead silence. I was looking at my watch. Two minutes up. Two minutes thirty. Two minutes forty-five. Three minutes. We exchanged glances.

Three minutes five. Three minutes ten. Three minutes fifteen.

A blinding white flash and a terrific bang. So close it was like a direct blow to our ears. You could hear it echo right back up the gorge.

Inder went to run out immediately but I held him back. 'Can't you hear that clanging noise? That's bits of the pier hitting the metal spans. Just wait a minute.'

We went back together to inspect our handiwork. Arthur was already there.

Two spans were damaged. One of them was rendered useless, lying half in the river and half on the bank. The other was hanging by a few bent girders. The pier was still standing, but it was twisted and leaning and about ten feet shorter than it had been.

There were cheers from HQ. Amid the din I could clearly distinguish Chris's voice shouting 'Hooray!'

By now most of our *andarte* helpers had cleared off.

'We've got a job to finish here,' I said, 'and we're on our own. I want it to take the bastards six weeks to repair the bridge. We'll lay charges on the front of the damaged pier and on the other metal one. And we'll finish off the other span as well.'

We raced back to our stash of explosives on the path by the culvert and lugged it back to the bridge. As we got to work, Eddie came running along the bridge from the north. He shone his flashlight down when he got to the gap.

'Congratulations!' he shouted. 'Now you've got to hurry up. Zervas wants to withdraw his men.'

We were still twenty minutes off finishing the job.

'Do you hear that?' asked Arthur. It was that galumphing noise again. 'Ities.'

'From Lamia,' said Inder.

'Nothing we can do about it,' I said. 'It's up to Themis and his lot now.'

A flash and the crash of an explosion. I heard the train stop, then start again. We could hear our two machine guns rattling away.

Denys came over and told us what was happening. Ities were pouring out of the carriages and our lot were engaging them.

We thought we'd been going as fast as we could. Now we went even faster. Our machine gun went silent for a few minutes, then started up again.

In ten minutes, we were ready. The battle to the north seemed to have quietened down but we had no idea who had won it. Perhaps even now Ities were creeping down to surround us.

I blew my whistle again. Inder took one fuse and I took the other. Inder's was no bloody good—I had carried it inside my battledress and it was soaked in sweat. I tried twice but it wouldn't light. We lit the other and sprinted back to cover.

Another satisfactory explosion. At almost the same moment, a green flare went up from HQ, then another and another. It was 2.15.

As soon as the metal stopped flying, we went to inspect our work. Both spans were down. One steel pier had been completely destroyed. It would be six weeks' work at least to repair the bridge.

Time to get out. We rushed back to the power house, where several of our helpers were skulking.

Denys asked them angrily why they hadn't come out to help with the second explosion. He wasn't impressed by their answer.

'They say they didn't know they were needed. One of them got injured in the explosion: Yorgos Kokkinos. Didn't bother to take cover. They've carted him off.'

I knew the man. We called him *Kokkinos*, 'Red', because he had a red beard. We didn't know his real surname. There was no time to find out how he was.

'Let's go, Yanni.'

Yannis led us back up the slope, to where we had left the mules above the reservoir. We rounded up three of the animals but the fourth had strayed. The muleteer was nowhere to be seen.

'Pistoli!' called Denys

Yannis hushed him urgently.

'What's his problem?' I asked.

'He says we mustn't use his last name. If the Italians overhear, his family will be for it.'

'Fair enough. But we can't afford any more time to look for the mule.'

We trudged up past the falls with the three mules in tow. A hell of a climb. But wonderful conditions—rain and heavy fog all the way. Good luck to the Italians trying to locate us. Everything had gone wonderfully, in spite of the delay taking the bridge. I felt as though we were leading a charmed life.

When we got to the forward rendezvous at Plakoto, the other groups were still coming in.

'Any casualties, Tom?' asked Eddie. His voice was flat and tired.

I told him Yorgos Kokkinos had collected some metal in the arm. Chris was there, too. 'What about casualties on the other side?' I asked him.

'All killed, according to the reports I've heard so far.'

'A bit unlikely?' I said.

'We'll see. Oh, and the *andartes* took a prisoner. Against orders.'

'Where is he?'

'Over there.'

A young fellow in a greyish vest and bare feet was surrounded by some of Aris's *andartes*. His face was the colour of his vest.

I saw Denys talking to them, and then I saw someone strike the Italian on the head with the crook he was carrying. Denys tried to intervene.

'What's going on, Denys?' I asked. 'What are they saying?'

'They're saying they want to have some fun with him. He's a southern Italian. Name of Giovanni. A swine—like all of them.'

'What, do you speak Italian, too, Denys?'

'A bit. Enough.'

We set off back towards the timber camp, the Italian trudging along in his bare feet. An ascent of over 3,000 feet lay ahead of us. Every now and then we heard the noise of a plane above the clouds. They must have been spotting for us. What a godsend the weather was.

'Tom, I've got to sit down for a minute,' said Arthur. As he spoke, his legs seemed to fold underneath him and he sank down beside the path in the snow. Apart from exhaustion, we were all desperately hungry.

I left him sharing his emergency ration with Bafas and another of the *andartes*. I knew I would be in the same predicament if I broke my stride. And above us, rocks and trees were starting to take shape in the very first light of dawn.

Four and a half hours through deep snow to get back to the rear rendezvous. Arthur didn't catch up with us until we were nearly there. He seemed to have got a second wind.

'I had to keep stopping and resting,' he said. 'And the Colonel had to hitch a ride on a donkey. He was all in.'

No wonder. By the time we reached the timber yard at 9.15 am, we had been on our feet for twenty-six hours.

The *andartes* straggled in, having done the whole operation, most of them, with nothing but strips of goatskin between their feet and the rocks and snow. Their endurance was astonishing.

Barba Niko was waiting for us in the shed.

'You do it!' he said. 'I hear the bang from here, I see the sky light up. You get those Iti bastards in the balls!'

By now we were too exhausted to share his elation. But Zervas sought me out and shook my hand.

'*Syncharitiria, syncharitiria,*' he said. Congratulations.

'*Parakalo,*' I replied. Don't mention it.

'What are we getting, do you think?' asked Inder as we lined up for food. 'Something substantial, I hope.'

'You might be out of luck, Inder,' said Arthur, looking at what others were carrying. A chunk of meat, most likely boiled goat, and another of boki.

We ate quickly, then threw ourselves down and slept like the dead.

We woke to thick fog. More luck. But we would have to move off quickly. The Italians would be on the hunt and now they would be determined to get us.

'Six weeks, Barba Niko,' I said as we set off together. 'Six weeks at least before they can repair it, I reckon.'

'Six months for sure,' he replied. 'They stupid, those Ities. Six years, even.' It was a relief to joke around with him again—and with Len, who had finally showed up.

'Where did you get to last night, Len?' I asked.

'That bastard Eddie,' he said. 'He sent me back up here in the dark to call Cairo.'

'On your own?'

'No, he gave me two *andartes*. But they didn't speak English and you know what my Greek's like.'

Len had had to keep Cairo on listening watch, and report to them when the signals went up for success. If the mission had failed, he was supposed to report what he could and then clear off back to Mavrolithari. He had his failure message already coded.

'I was waiting for the fighting to start at eleven o'clock,' he told me. 'Nothing. More time went by—more nothing. It must have been nearly 11.15, wasn't it?'

'About that,' I said. The details of the night before were blurring.

'Finally I saw the white Verey light. But still no explosion. I was urging you on in my head. And cursing Eddie because I wasn't there with you.'

'How much could you see?' I asked him. 'The explosion, I mean.'

'It was amazing. The whole sky lit up. Then a massive roar came rolling right up the valley. It shook the sawmill here, didn't it, Barba Niko?'

'Like what you call it—an earthshake,' said Barba Niko.

'Earthquake,' said Len. 'I wouldn't be needing that failure message. Then I got on the set. Of course the bloody thing chose that moment to stop working. Then when the Colonel got here in the morning, do you know what he said?'

'What?'

'"Not through to Cairo yet? Why not, man?" Then he said, "It's too late now. Get that set packed up. And hurry up." But I could see he was exhausted. So I held my tongue.'

Back to Mavrolithari. Rain was pelting down, stripping the last few leaves from the big plane tree in the square, but it looked like the whole village had turned out to welcome us. Waving their walking sticks in excitement, old men watched keenly as we marched up in the midst of the *andartes*. Aris and Zervas dismounted, and we were besieged by village men and women offering small glasses of *tsipouro*. Children darted about in the rain, excited by the novelty of it all but not quite understanding what was going on.

Everything was suddenly worthwhile—the drop into such precipitous country, the weeks spent ducking and weaving, the perils of the demolition under fire. I think we all felt a bit larger than life.

The Italian captive was nowhere to be seen. I caught up with Denys.

'What's happened to the prisoner?' I asked.

'Eddie told me to interrogate him quickly because the Greeks were going to shoot him.'

Eddie and Chris hadn't been able to stop it. When Denys got there they were still arguing with Aris, but Denys thought they'd already decided it was inevitable.

All Denys got out of him was the name of his lieutenant. He said there had been about eighty men guarding the bridge but quite a few had cleared off when the battle started.

'He seemed to be past it already,' Denys said. 'I told him what was going to happen and asked if there was anything I could do for him but he didn't respond.'

'So they shot him?'

'No. It was much worse than that. Aris's men had been arguing about who was going to do the job. Then they pulled forward a young lad, whom they called Atromitos—"Fearless"—and gave him a short sword. He only looked about sixteen. He wasn't too keen but apparently it was a tradition—to blood him. I hoped the blade was good and sharp. He took the sword and they urged him on. They were all laughing. They took the prisoner further away, stripped him, and made him kneel in the snow. Then they said, "One blow, lad. Make it just one blow."'

'And did he?'

'No. Maybe the blade was blunt. The men just laughed. Three more blows it took.'

'Denys!' I said.

'And that was it. They just left him there.'

I felt sorry for Denys for having witnessed it. It would be stuck in his memory now.

In Mavrolithari that evening there was a big debrief in the schoolhouse—the leaders of the three cooperating groups and their staffs.

First up was Myridakis. 'At the northern end the force was stronger than we anticipated. They must have heard us cutting the wire—they opened fire straight away. Either that or they knew we were coming.' The plans in John's bag, I thought suddenly.

'The recce party had missed a concrete pillbox,' Myridakis went on. 'They had more and heavier weapons than us, and the barbed wire trapped us directly in front of them.'

'They couldn't get away from there, right?' said Eddie.

'That's correct,' said Myridakis.

'When we knew the attack had been driven back,' said Eddie, 'we decided to send in the reserve. It was a good thing we were all on the north side. Chris and I went forward with them. Our machine guns covered the charge to the post, and our men took it with a grenade attack.'

'So that's why it took so long,' I muttered to Denys beside me. 'I couldn't understand it.'

'To the south I had to change the order of battle,' said Myridakis. 'Those in command of a couple of the sectors felt they were too dangerous. I took over those sectors with the support of Karalivanos and his men. There was some reluctance to advance—those rumours that the fence was electrified didn't help. But Karalivanos was exceptional. We took all four Italian defence posts. Then we started mopping up. And we mounted a guard for the demolition party.'

'Thank you, Myridakis,' said General Zervas.

'Now the demolition party,' said Aris.

'We went in at 1.15,' I said, 'cutting two double-apron wire fences. We blew a steel pier, bringing down two spans. We cut the spans with a second lot of charges to prevent them being re-used and damaged a second pier. We used all 400 pounds of explosives except for two tins of gun cotton. We withdrew on the signal after the second explosion.'

'You haven't mentioned the cross-section of the bridge,' said Chris.

'It was a different shape,' I said. 'We had to disassemble all the charges and pack them into the girders by hand. Because of this it took us an hour to lay the first lot of charges.'

'I saw those two spans jump up into the air and crash down into the gorge,' said Eddie. 'A wonderful sight. A great job, Tom. Convey our congratulations to the demolition party.'

'How long do you expect it will take them to repair the bridge?' asked Aris.

'Six weeks at least,' I said, 'depending on the scale of repairs. A temporary repair would be quicker. They may try to build wooden trestles. I wish them luck with that.'

John Cook was next. His party at the bridge had not seen any action but had blown up the line anyway before returning.

Then it was Themis's turn.

'It was difficult to climb the pole to cut the telephone wires,' he said. 'Lambros from ELAS and I both tried. So we chopped down the pole first, and then cut the wires. We had laid our device on the track. When the bridge blew we thought we would be withdrawing, so I went down and removed the device, so that it wouldn't fall into enemy hands. Then Lambros reported that there would be a further explosion, so I quickly put it back.

'Then we heard a train coming, but quite slowly. That was probably why it wasn't derailed when the device exploded. There were two carriages full of Italian soldiers. One had lights on, which made it an excellent target, but we only had rifles and two light machine guns and no grenades were thrown. The Italians jumped out of the train quickly and scattered. Fortunately the green Verey signal came not long after that and we were able to withdraw. We wouldn't have been able to hold them off much longer.'

Attention then turned to the question of reprisals against the local villagers.

'We have asked GHQ Middle East to drop leaflets over the area in the event of a successful attack,' said Eddie. 'The leaflets will say that the operation was conducted by British commandos, and that reprisals will be considered a war crime for which counter reprisals will be taken by bombing Italian villages.'

'Let's hope it works,' said Chris.

'Well, heartiest congratulations to all of you,' said Eddie. 'The mission we were sent here to accomplish has been a resounding success, thanks to the cooperation of ELAS and EDES. Aris,

Zervas, I will recommend to GHQ Middle East that you both receive the OBE for your efforts.'

Aris got quickly to his feet.

'I am not interested in decorations,' he said. 'What good are your British decorations to me? What I need is equipment for my men.'

Eddie was hefting a couple of bags of coins. 'I am authorised to give you these gold sovereigns,' he said to Aris and Zervas, 'for expenses you have incurred in carrying out the operation.'

'Don't try to buy me,' said Aris. 'We in ELAS will continue to direct our operations in the best interests of the liberty of Greece. That will be our only consideration. Is that understood?'

'Understood,' said Eddie.

'In that case, I am happy to accept the money on behalf of my men.'

'In addition,' said Eddie, 'I would like to offer each of you a small gift. What would you like? I will advise Cairo what to drop for you.'

'Boots for my men,' said Aris at once. 'They have carried out this entire mission without them. Now I want them to be properly equipped.'

'Boots it is,' said Eddie. 'Zervas?'

'Let me take it under consideration,' said Zervas. 'I will let you know tomorrow.'

'GHQ hopes very much that this successful mission will be the beginning of a continuing and fruitful cooperation between the *andarte* groups in opposing the occupiers,' said Eddie. 'As you know, several of our team are staying in Greece. Chris, Themis and two wireless operators will be posted to General Zervas's headquarters in Valtos, where they will receive fresh instructions from Cairo.'

'I would like a British liaison officer with me as well,' said Aris immediately.

'Unfortunately that cannot happen at present,' said Eddie. 'All the remaining members of the party will be leaving Greece in December. But I will advise Cairo of your request.'

That night the village put on a real feast for us. Sheep spit-roasted with herbs and lemon, potatoes and onions, and plenty of wine. Nat and Denys got all the details of the battle from the *andartes*— the things that hadn't been reported in the debrief—and passed them on to us.

Everyone had been waiting, looking at their watches, as zero hour passed and nothing happened. Then an ELAS *andarte* on the south side of the river had got himself stuck in the mud, and his commander shouted at him. The Italians on the south side opened fire, which tipped off their counterparts to the north. Chaos broke out on both sides of the bridge.

It only took the *andartes* twenty-three minutes to take the south side. They cut through the barbed-wire entanglements and mounted a grenade attack on the fortified posts. The Italians took off in a hurry. Our side captured a Fiat heavy machine gun— the *andartes* tried to cart it off without disassembling it because they didn't know how, but it was too heavy and they ended up throwing it into a gully.

The north was another story. Our side had lost the element of surprise; having been forewarned, even by only a few seconds, the Italians opened up immediately with rapid heavy fire and a grenade attack. Lieutenant Papachristou tried to approach three times and each time he was repulsed. So he decided to go in from the left, a bushy area that formed a natural barrier, protecting the Italians. This was a break with the plan.

Papachristou sent a messenger to tell General Zervas at HQ the reason for the delay, but the messenger was so confused that he got things completely wrong—he told Zervas that Italian reinforcements had arrived and driven our side back. Fortunately Zervas didn't believe him. He knew the calibre of his men, especially Papachristou, who had been decorated in Albania, and he knew no reinforcements had arrived. HQ were worried, however, as the fire from our side was by now only sporadic—quite a lot of the *andartes* had cleared off and only a few were left.

The Italians had a pillbox we needed to take. One shot from it had almost taken out one of the EDES *andartes*, Stergios Voulgaris—it had struck the ground so close behind him, the dirt it kicked up struck the back of his head. Now General Zervas sent a message down to Papachristou, instructing him to take the pillbox no matter what.

At the same time they had another tough decision to make, Aris and Zervas and Eddie. The delay meant that if we waited until the north end was taken, the Italian reinforcements would cross the bridge before we'd had time to complete the demolition. We would have to call off the whole operation. So they decided to send us in before the north was taken.

Eddie was worried, but Aris and Zervas convinced him that we would be safe—the south was clear, and the masonry piers would protect us from the fighting to the north. But when Zervas shouted the command to fire the white flare, our signal to go in, Myridakis couldn't hear him above the gunfire. So Eddie went to the riverbank and called out to us, stepping on one of the *andartes* in the process. That explained why there'd been no white flare, and why the red flare to show the north was clear didn't come until so late.

Aris had been magnificent. Nat and Denys heard the same thing from both ELAS and EDES. And our explosion had shaken Mount Oiti.

We had an excellent billet this time around.

'I can just imagine the Germans now,' said Denys. 'I know what the Balkan railway system's like. There'll be no end of trouble—delays everywhere. And on the Athens side, too.'

'Good,' I said. 'The more trouble they have, the better pleased I'll be.'

'I'll just be happy to get on that submarine,' said Arthur.

'Back to sticky old Cairo,' I said. 'I can't wait.'

'That's all very well for you lot,' said Themis. 'I'm staying. Not that I'm not proud to be staying. But we've been through a lot together. Everything will be different now.'

'The war seems to be going better at last,' said Inder. 'Maybe it won't go on much longer. Then we can come to Greece and be tourists instead. Maybe we can visit you.'

'Any time,' said Themis. 'We'll show you some real Greek hospitality.'

The village was still in a state of excitement the next morning in spite of falling rain. Everyone had turned out in the square, ready to drink our health all over again.

Zervas and Aris were talking to Eddie and Chris.

'Can you tell what they're talking about?' I asked Arthur beside me.

'Only a word here and there. I'm not really sure.'

Then Denys came over. 'What was that about, Denys?' said Arthur. 'I couldn't really catch it.'

'They were deciding on boundaries between the two bands. We have to go through some of Aris's territory on our way to the coast. Zervas promised not to try to recruit there.'

'It seemed like an amicable discussion.'

'Very amicable.'

Soon the meeting broke up. After Aris and Chris had wandered off, I saw Zervas take Eddie aside and speak with him, briefly, alone.

It was already past eleven o'clock and we were in a hurry. Our small Harling party clustered around Barba Niko. Eddie had a speech to deliver.

'Barba Niko,' he said, 'for two months you have looked after us. Our food, our mules, everything we needed. I don't know how you did it.' Barba Niko couldn't speak. Tears were rolling down his face, mingling with the rainwater that ran off his cap.

'You never once failed us,' Eddie went on. 'Above all, our mission owes its success to you.'

Barba Niko kissed each of us in turn, pressing his customary stubble against our bearded cheeks.

'Goodbye,' I said. 'I'll come and find you after the war.'

'Safe journey,' he said. 'May you return to your homes in peace.'

Zervas had arranged a courier, who was waiting in the square. He was to take a message to Prometheus in Athens, who would send a report of the mission's success to Cairo and name the spot on the west coast where we would wait for the submarine. Eddie also ordered a sortie to deliver clothing and weapons to Zervas's dropping ground near Valtos, between the 12th and the 18th of December.

Our parting from Aris's men was warm and friendly. We were all still on a high. Those who could chatted with the villagers— others, like me, tried out our few words of Greek.

'Watch out for the Italians,' warned Nikiforos as we finally prepared to go. 'Don't think you've seen the last of them. They'll be after you more than ever now. The Germans, too—and they know how to fight!'

Reluctantly, grudgingly, I realised he was right. The Italians and Germans—both—would already be turning their thoughts to reprisals against the villagers. And they would be after us like never before. Getting up the mountain and away after Gorgopotamos would be just the beginning. The hard part was still to come.

EIGHT

I found myself directly behind Eddie as we walked. Laden mules filed ahead of us in the rain, churning up the path. Zervas was up towards the front on a horse. My thighs were stinging, irritated by the dirty wet wool next to my skin, but it was not clear where our next wash was coming from.

It was now 28 November. The submarine was due the week before Christmas. We had a bit over three weeks to get all the way across Greece, crossing the Vardousia mountains and the Pindos range—known as the 'spine' of Greece because it separated Thessaly to the east from Epiros to the west—to Zervas's current HQ in Megalochari village in the Valtos region, in the south of the Pindos mountains. We would leave Chris and Themis there with Len and Doug, and Zervas would give the rest of us an escort to the coast—the remaining members of the Harling party, plus Khouri the Palestinian and the two Turko-Cypriots, Yannis and Panayiotis.

Eddie turned to speak to me. 'Guess what Zervas asked for as his gift.'

'No idea. Weapons for his men?'

'A case of whisky.'

'Is that what he was talking to you about after the meeting this morning?'

'Yes. I think he was embarrassed to say it in front of Aris yesterday.'

'So are we dropping that in? I hope it arrives in one piece.'

Setting out to the west across the Vardousia mountains that first day, we were seven hours on the track. Towards the end we hit a steep descent, an hour in the slush down to the village of Kolokythia. A small village nestled among fir trees and mountains—not much of a place to stay and lousy food, but out of the wind and rain at least.

Next was Kyriakochori. Coming along the winding road into the village at lunchtime the following day, we heard one peal after another from the church bell. As we neared the village, we spied the belfry thrusting up among the trees a little below us.

'What do you reckon has happened?' Arthur asked.

'A birth, perhaps?' I said. 'Sounds too happy for a death.'

'It must be someone important,' he said. 'The mayor's family or something.'

As we entered the village there seemed to be a lot of people about, lining the streets and cheering. The church bell was still ringing.

'It's for us,' said Inder. 'Isn't it?'

He was right. As we passed along the narrow, winding street, everyone wanted to shake our hands. Many had tears in their eyes. When we got to the village square we found a wonderful spread laid out for us—boiled and roasted chestnuts, raisins, almonds and eggs. The whole town was waiting to celebrate with us, pressing food on us, more and more. Even when we were full—and I'd wondered if I would ever be full again—they were still offering us more.

One of the villagers brought me a glass.

'*Tsipouro,*' he said. '*Yia sas!*' Cheers!

'*Yia sas!*' I replied.

He asked me what role I'd played in the mission. When Nat explained that I was in charge of the demolition, the man shook my hand fiercely.

'You have come here to help Greece,' he said. 'Thank you. We will never forget.'

Our time in Kyriakochori was short, but we managed to do quite a lot of drinking. We parted reluctantly from our new friends.

Gardiki village was next. Chris was a fast and tireless walker and had arrived well ahead of us.

As we approached we could hear the villagers singing. I assumed they were singing a Greek song, but gradually the words became clearer. '*It's a long, long way to Tipperary ...*'

Cheering broke out—they had seen us coming. Chris stepped from his informal podium to meet us.

'What was the singing all about?' said Arthur.

'Well,' said Chris, 'they wanted the British national anthem. But "God Save the King" isn't what you would call lively, and seeing most of them think Tipperary is the national anthem anyway, I thought, why not?'

He had already taken the opportunity to make a speech. Now it was Zervas's turn. When he'd finished, round after round of cheering broke out, followed by more speeches from the priest, the mayor and the doctor. People started to argue over who would put us up for the night.

We looked at one another with a single thought between us—beds! Real beds with proper mattresses. Sheets and pillowcases, too, if we were lucky.

A band was tuning up on the far edge of the square. There were drums and pipes, and several instruments that looked like long guitars, beautifully inlaid and polished. I asked the woman beside me what they were. '*Bouzouki*,' she answered. '*Bouzoukia.*'

It was the first time I had seen or heard one. When the musician plucked the strings, it made a metallic kind of sound.

The mayor was on his feet, arms outstretched, feet stamping. For a minute or two he danced alone as everyone watched. Then another man joined in, linking arms with the mayor. One person after another joined the line, always at the same end.

Then they came after us, pulling us forward. We linked ourselves onto the line and tried to follow the steps. At first it was confusing but I got the hang of it pretty quickly. More people joined in, women as well as men. The pace sped up and soon our battledress was soaked in sweat back and front.

Eventually the dance broke up. By then we needed a drink.

'*Pou einai ta Maori*?' somebody called.

'Maori?' My ears pricked up. 'Denys, what did they say? What's going on?'

'They know some of the party are New Zealanders and they've heard of the Maori battalion.' The Maori battalion had fought on the Greek mainland and Crete the previous year, and the villagers had heard about their breakout in the Western Desert. When Zervas had told them there were New Zealanders in the British party, they got excited.

'I wouldn't like to disappoint them,' I said. 'Come on, Arthur.'

I pulled him forward to do a *haka* for the villagers. They gathered in a big circle around us. We put on our best grimaces and our most blood-curdling shouts. When it was over, they clapped and cheered so long, we gave a repeat performance.

Then they started to pull us towards a large house across the square.

'It's the doctor's house,' said Denys. 'A real house, too.' It had a proper front door, with steps leading up to it.

Inside, pretty girls in prints and polka-dots crowded the room, along with their mothers, fathers and brothers.

I must have looked more like a caveman than someone who belonged in this civilised house. But they seemed to be giving us admiring looks nonetheless.

'They're treating us like heroes,' I muttered to Arthur.

'I could get used to it,' he answered.

General Zervas was ensconced in the sole armchair, closely surrounded by men from the village, with a few women squeezed in around the edges. He seemed to be regaling them with stories—he was a great raconteur—and everyone was laughing.

Inder soon became the focus of a group of older ladies, who unsuccessfully pressed drinks on him. As a Sikh, Inder didn't drink at all, but they seemed to be taking the rejection well. Perhaps that was because he was trying to talk to them in Greek. His attempts were received with much hilarity.

Suddenly I was the centre of a crowd of admirers myself. I called Arthur and Denys over and Denys agreed to translate— although his nose was a little out of joint because they were mainly interested in us New Zealanders.

'Did the Italians put up much of a fight?' a man in a brown jacket asked us. 'We think they are cowards.'

'We thought our men would overpower the garrison in twenty minutes,' said Arthur. 'But they were better armed than us. We were waiting near the bridge, ready to go in. We waited for an hour, then an hour and a half. In the end we went in under fire. As we were working two mortars landed nearby. We were lucky not to be hit.'

'We were even luckier that the mortars didn't strike our dump of explosives,' I added. 'Otherwise the mission would have been done for.'

'We hope the British will come soon to liberate Greece,' said the man. 'Here in Greece we still remember Lord Byron with honour. With his own money he brought a force here to liberate us from the Turks.' This was the first time I had heard the Greeks mention Byron. It wouldn't be the last.

Arthur had drifted away from our group and was chatting to one of the girls in a corner. There was some laughter and head-shaking from her; then I saw them head for the door. Immediately a young man detached himself from another group and joined them. They weren't going to be allowed to leave the room.

The priest had won the honour of billeting Denys, Arthur and me. His son took us to a little café on the square for dinner. The mayor, it turned out, was also the proprietor.

'I wonder what we're going to get,' I said to Arthur.

'Chicken,' he said confidently.

'What makes you think that?'

'Didn't you hear the racket when we arrived? Sounded like all hell had broken loose in the poultry yard.'

Sure enough, the mayor's wife appeared, carrying large plates of chicken with a kind of macaroni, and olive bread.

'*Oriste*,' she said. Here you are.

I risked my Greek for the first time. '*Ti einai*?' What is it?

She clapped her hands. '*Heliopita*,' she answered.

'*Heliopita*,' I said. '*Einai kala!*' It's good!

Being so new at Greek, I had taken her to mean the whole dish. Actually *heliopita* was the olive bread.

Anything would have tasted good after two months of beans and boki. But the food was delicious, and there was plenty of it. I was really enjoying myself.

In our room at the priest's house there was one bed, a suspicious-looking divan, and the floor. We threw for it. I got the floor.

'How did you sleep, Arthur?' I asked next morning. He had got the bed.

'It was very dirty,' he said. 'Not quite the comfort I was looking forward to.'

'What about the divan?' I asked Denys.

'Not too bad. And the floor?'

'Hard, you bastard, hard. What do you think?' I looked for something to throw at him.

First thing after breakfast, Denys and I went to a service in the big church on the square. I'd never been in an Orthodox church and I wanted to be able to tell Beth all about it.

'We buy a candle each,' said Denys as we went in. 'We light it here, and then we stick it in that stand over there.'

Denys made the sign of the cross three times. I tried to copy him. It's not so easy the first time you try.

We found our way to a pew and, imitating the other worshippers, stayed standing. Between us and the altar was a screen decorated with icons of the saints. Little doors let us glimpse the altar on the other side.

'The *iconostasis*,' Denys whispered. It seemed to glow in the darkness.

A chant started up, and a lighted candle on an ornate stand and a silver-bound Bible were borne forward in a procession that moved slowly from the back of the church. Much of the action seemed to take place behind the screen, visible only through the little doors.

As we left the church, Denys paused to chat to the villagers. I wandered back into the square and found Chris sitting by himself in the little café.

'Can I join you?'

'Of course,' he said. 'You like Greek coffee? I'll get you one.'

'I learnt to like Greek coffee when I was working at Gianaclis last year.'

'Never been there,' said Chris. 'I've heard of it, though—more or less a Greek colony, isn't it, in the Nile Delta?'

'Yes, south of Alexandria. Big grape-growing estate run by Greeks; about 1200 acres. I believe the wine is quite famous— that's what they told me, anyway. Very pleasant place.'

'What were you doing there?'

'Building fortifications. Nests of pillboxes and so forth. Working with McCormack dozers and D6 Caterpillars. They're no end of trouble. There was a three-and-a-half cubic yard scoop that we got up there just after we started. Ditched itself in the canal. We managed to get it out, though.'

'You speak about those machines with such enthusiasm. The names mean nothing to me.'

'Working with machines all day is a bit like working with people,' I said. 'You get to know their idiosyncrasies. Some men have the patience to work with them. Others pit themselves against them as though they're the enemy. They're the men who are always bringing their machines into the workshops because they're always breaking down.'

My coffee arrived. 'In Gianaclis I made friends with a man called Pierrakis,' I said. 'He owned the estate. He used to invite us over for parties. He wanted some of our men to come back and work for him after the war, levelling the ground for him and so on. When I left he was really upset. Asked me to keep in touch.'

'You must have been sorry to leave.'

'Well, I was excited about going to Aqaba to build the harbour. I didn't know then that I'd be coming here, of course.'

'You know,' said Chris, 'I came through this village on my way to find Zervas. I sneaked through, hoping no one would see me and give me away. Then on the way back to the cave, with Aris and Zervas, it was like a triumphal procession. Lots of speeches—Aris, Zervas and myself. Everything was patriotic and everyone loved us.'

'They seem to be pretty pro-British. Tipperary and so on.'

'They can afford to be. They probably see us as a ticket back to prosperity. Elsewhere things are harder and Aris in particular has more luck recruiting.'

'What do you think of him? Aris I mean,' I asked. 'He and Zervas are so different.'

'They're more alike than different,' said Chris. 'That's my view.'

'What makes you say that? Zervas asking for whisky and Aris for boots for his men. That says something about them. But Aris can be cruel, I think. I heard he whipped someone within an inch of his life for stealing a sheep and then shot him when he confessed. Zervas seems a more convivial man.'

'Aris has a sadistic streak, there's no doubt about that. And Zervas loves good living and gold. But they're both born adventurers. They have a similar sense of humour, too—I saw them lying side by side in a straw hut at the sawmill, with their legs sticking out, exchanging stories and laughing their heads off. In other circumstances they could be allies—if they weren't coming at things in opposite ways.'

I could see what he meant. He was astute, that was certain. Remarkably astute for someone so young. Just as well, I thought—seeing he's staying on here. He'll have to make sense of what's going on between these two groups of guerrillas. It was clear even to me that they didn't exactly trust one another. And who were they really, Aris and Zervas?

'So Aris is on the left?' I asked. 'I've heard people say that he's a communist.' I knew being a communist had been illegal before the war, when Metaxas was still in power. Plenty of people had been imprisoned for it. It wasn't necessarily something you shouted from the rooftops.

'It depends who you talk to. What I know for sure is that the organisation that sits behind ELAS—EAM—appears to be a grouping of left and centre parties. Zervas says they're controlled by the Communist Party. That's why he refuses to join them. But there's a lot more I need to understand if I'm going to be of any use here. I might have to go to Athens somehow to get a truer picture.'

'You'd better be careful there. You'll stand out like a sore thumb.'

I spotted Arthur crossing the square and called him over to join us. He sat down and leant back in his chair, his legs thrust out in front.

'I could do with more of this,' he said. 'Feted everywhere we go. Good food, plenty to drink. Lots of admiring girls.'

'I wouldn't get used to it,' said Chris. 'This is the last wealthy village. By the time we get near Valtos you'll see real poverty.'

It was time to go. Themis had arrived to summon us to an officers' meeting at the house where Eddie was staying. Eddie got the armchair and the rest of us squatted or stood.

'The message we sent to Cairo by runner when we left Mavrolithari wasn't only about the gifts for Aris and Zervas,' Eddie said. 'I've recommended two of you for immediate awards—Chris and Tom. I've also recommended Zervas and Aris for OBEs. And Barba Niko for the British Empire Medal. Everyone else will get a mention.'

There was much cheering and clapping.

'You deserve it, Tom,' said Arthur generously.

'It could just as well have been you leading the party,' I said. 'But thanks.' If I had been in his shoes, I would have been jealous—if he was, he hid it well. But at least I had acquitted myself with honour.

'One other thing,' said Eddie. 'Don't mention the submarine to anyone. That information must on no account get through to the enemy. Even Zervas doesn't know where the rendezvous is. For your information alone, the location is a bay at the mouth of the Acheron River, south of the town of Parga.'

'When?' asked Denys.

'Four nights. Four consecutive nights just before Christmas. We'll signal each of those nights until the submarine signals back. We have barely enough time. We're going to have to push it along. I want everyone to be prepared for a hard trek. It won't be easy on any of us.'

Especially on you, Eddie, I thought to myself. I was full of respect for Eddie's leadership. He'd seen us through the trying events that had dogged our operation. But his temporary collapse after the op had shown that he wasn't likely to stand up too well to a massive mountain trek.

Now that our work was done, I couldn't wait to get out of the place. I had been out of touch with home for two months. No letters from Beth, no news from my mother or my brothers and sisters. They would have received the cards I'd written before we left, but by now they must be wondering what was going on.

My life in Aqaba seemed like peacetime in comparison. Mail coming regularly, sometimes three or four letters at once. Parcels from time to time with useful things from home: cakes; flea powder for the bed bugs; tinned fruit. I could just taste those pears I'd opened one night in my comfortable tent.

It had been fun in the cave, if you didn't think too much about the constant threat of discovery, the worry about the *andartes* not showing up, the sudden alarms and excursions. The demolition job had been satisfying, although I wouldn't like to have to repeat it. But now I was completely focused on that submarine. I could see us there on the headland, signalling. I could see the flash of the signal coming back to us, hear the swish of the oars as the boat came through the water. I could smell the bacon and eggs they would have ready for us on board.

On to the village of Poungakia. Rain dripped from beautiful wooden balconies as we walked past the village houses to the square. Another turnout to welcome us, *tsipouro* to drink. Another pretty girl to take Arthur's eye, a lass in a blue dress with white flowers.

At 10 pm we finally got our dinner: boiled eggs and apples.

'They keep a good eye on their girls,' said Arthur. 'Mum and Dad seem to be watching all the time, even when they're doing something else. But that's a lovely girl, that one I was talking to.'

'What's her name?' asked Inder.

'Maria.'

'Nothing unusual there,' I said. 'Every second girl seems to be called Maria.'

'They're a devout lot,' said Denys. 'And it's traditional. They have to use either saints' names or classical names.'

'Like what?'

'Well, Antigone or Elektra. That kind of thing.'

'What about the boys?'

'Haven't you met a Sofoklis yet?'

'No, I can't say that I have.'

Our hosts had kindly washed our socks for us and we were drying them by the fire in our bare room.

'We'll be off at 2 am when the moon's up,' said Denys. 'It's nearly eleven now. I'm going to sleep while I can.'

Suddenly around me people were feeling for their things, pulling on their boots. I looked at the dial of my watch. Three hours' sleep. I felt terrible.

We had slept in our dirty clothes as usual, so getting dressed didn't take very long.

'Clean socks,' whispered Inder.

'Dry, too,' replied Arthur. It was amazing what such a small thing could do for our morale.

We crept downstairs and out the door. The moon was up as anticipated but a fog was down; it seemed to muffle sound like the felt dampers on the strings of Beth's piano.

The cold struck straight through our clothes. We hurried to the square, where the others were already gathered. Zervas and his men were rubbing their hands and stamping their feet.

'The mules,' whispered Eddie. 'The mules haven't arrived yet.'

We stood around shivering. I looked at my boots and wondered how they were going to stand up to the trek. Denys was always crowing about his wonderful made-to-measure boots with the crepe rubber soles. Perhaps the rest of us would be reduced to strips of goatskin like the Greeks.

'Where the bloody hell are they?' said Eddie after a while. 'We're losing time.' We had to get across the Lamia–Karpenisi road before daylight. There was a lot of Italian troop movement on that road, and they would be on the lookout for us.

I looked at my watch. Three am. An hour of sleep lost for nothing.

At last we heard the clop of the mules on the paving stones. It was 3.45.

'Great,' said Denys. 'We'll be two hours late crossing the road.'

The mules set off on the track leading up the col behind the village. Zervas and his personal officers went next, Zervas on a mule with Myridakis following close behind. Then Chris and Eddie. We were just ahead of the rearguard.

As we passed through the back gardens of the last few wooden houses, fir trees loomed above us. The moon shone milky through the fog. We could see a little in the forest, enough to keep from stumbling as the ground went up and up ahead. A rich, spicy smell rose up from the rotting material on the ground as our feet disturbed it.

Over the ridge, down the other side to a gully with a small creek, small enough to spring across without getting our feet wet. A track branched off to our right. The word came back along the line—not that way.

Up again through the forest. Down across another gully. Then steeply up.

The trees were getting further apart and shorter. Then we were out of the forest into low scrub. White patches lay on the ground directly ahead.

I turned to Arthur behind me. 'Rock or snow?' I whispered. 'What do you think?'

'We'll soon find out.'

We passed a few more tracks. There was white rock—and then there was snow. We continued to climb. Soon the snow was deep.

We bunched together. The fog was very low now. At least there was no danger of enemy troops chancing on us up here. They never came this far into the mountains. Not then. Not until the Germans brought in their elite mountain troops.

'What would you like to be doing right now?' I asked Inder. 'If you didn't have to be here, trying to get out of Greece with the Italians after us?'

He gave it some consideration. 'I would like to be back in Edinburgh,' he said after a while. 'I would like the war to be over so that I could be back at university, finishing my engineering degree.'

Inder had been nineteen years old—eighteen months into his degree—when everyone around him started to join up. He got himself into the Black Watch, the famous Royal Highland Regiment, as a private.

'You're one of the youngest of us, and I'm one of the oldest,' I said. 'I didn't join up until the very end of 1940, when they set up the New Zealand Engineers. Well, that's not entirely true. I joined the Australian army first, a few months earlier. But I was already thirty-three. You're not the youngest to join up, though. Did you know Len was a boy soldier?'

'No, I didn't.'

'He was fifteen. He joined a Boys' Company as an apprentice wireless operator. I didn't know they had such things.'

Lt-Col Tom Barnes, DSO, MC.

Beth Harris, Sydney, September 1940. 'This is a beauty no mistake. Don't you like my girl?'

World War II soldiers, New Zealand Forces Club, Cairo, Egypt. New Zealand Department of Internal Affairs. War History Branch: Photographs relating to World War 1914–1918, World War 1939–1945, occupation of Japan, Korean War, and Malayan Emergency. *Ref: DA-01299-F. Alexander Turnbull Library, Wellington, New Zealand. http://natlib.govt.nz/records/22552517*

Monty ('Chris') Woodhouse, bearded.

A map of Greece printed on silk, a button compass and two of Tom's diaries.

Barba Niko.

Group photo of the Harling party at Megalochari. Back row, left to right: Themis Marinos, Denys Hamson, Nat Barlow, Chris Woodhouse, Inder Gill, Eddie Myers, John Cook, Arthur Edmonds and Tom Barnes. Front row: Len Willmott, Mike Chittis and Doug Phillips. Looking on are Dr Papachristou and his family. The Italians burned the family's house a few weeks after the photo was taken.

General Zervas, Plaisia.

Aris Velouchiotis.

Georgios Agoros and Tom Barnes.

Toula.

Frank Hernen and Len Wilmott.

'A break and a smoke': John Cook, Dennis Nicholson and Aristidis ('Boulis') Metaxas on the retreat to Thessaly, November 1943.

Epirus 3/40 regiment on the trail from Plaisia to Sklivani.
Toula is at front left.

Mule driver and mule,
November 1943.

Tom wearing a 3/40
EOEA regiment cap,
Plaisia, December 1943.

Chris Woodhouse
decorating Zervas,
Plaisia, March 1944.

Agoros, Zervas, Voula and Tom at Lakka Souli, Plaisa, probably March 1944.

Crossing Acheron stream.

Captain Peter Musson at HQ, Derviziana, 1944.

Deciphering messages from Cairo and outstations, Romanon Monastery, September 1944.

Boulis Metaxas feeding the Mission's pet mule, Skiadades.

Andartes de-lousing their clothes. Standing is Major Yannis Katsadimas, Commander III Battalion, 3/40 Regiment.

Captain Dennis Nicholson balancing the monthly sovereign account, Derviziana. Each bag contained 12,000 sovereigns.

Women carrying
ammunition to
a forward dump,
Derviziana.

Lola, EDES nurse from the General Hospital, Derviziana.

Boxes of ammunition and mules, Anolaki Bay.

The first practice shoot with a 75 mm mountain pack gun. Brought in by sea in July 1944, the gun had a range of 8000 yards.

Sylvia Apostolidou, Athens,
November 1944.

ABOVE AND LEFT
Crowds at an EDES
parade in Yannina
after the German
withdrawal.

Wedding at Doukades, Corfu, February 1945.

Sylvia Apostolidou at the pyramids.

Studio photo of Tom given to Sylvia Apostolidou, August 1945.

Tom and Beth, date and photographer unknown.

'I didn't either,' said Inder.

'So what was it like in the Black Watch?'

'I didn't fit in. Not at all. They used to kill themselves laughing when I got into my pyjamas to go to bed at night. None of them had pyjamas.'

'Really?'

'No, and they used to pinch bits of my uniform.'

'What for?'

'So I wouldn't have them on parade the next morning. I had to pay to get them back. They thought I was a rich boy. I suppose I was, compared to them. There was probably a lot of poverty in Edinburgh but I hadn't seen any of it growing up. My family were comfortably off.'

'How did the regiment cope with you being half Indian? And a Sikh, too?'

'Not well. The funny thing was, we used to have Church Parade every Sunday. This was after I'd been promoted to lance-corporal. There were a few of us who weren't Presbyterians—one or two Jews and so on. We had to fall out and it was my job to march us into town. As soon as we got out of sight, we headed for the pub. I was the only NCO, you see.'

'Did you ever get caught?'

'Never. After a few minutes the Presbyterians would turn up too, having marched straight through the church and out the other side.'

'Presbyterians, eh? Same in Deloraine, where my fiancée lives. Lots of Presbyterians there—all Scots originally, I imagine. Her last name is Harris.'

'In … Tasmania? Is that the right name? Seems hard to imagine.'

'Beth's father had a big store in Deloraine, in the north of Tasmania. Good business from the local farming community. And a travelling store, in a van—used to go all over the place to people who couldn't get in to do their own shopping. Right up to the coast.'

'Had? What happened to the shop?'

'Nothing, it's still going. But Beth's father dropped off the twig just before the war. Beth runs it herself now.'

'I imagine you can think of better things than being in the cold and fog on top of a mountain range.'

'Well, yes. It's good to have done something real in the war now, though. I can go back and hold my head up. Before that I felt I was wasting my time.'

'Do you think you will take over the business from Beth?'

'Not on your life. I couldn't think of anything worse. And I hope I can persuade her to give it up too, when we're married. She's always thinking about it, even when we're doing something else entirely. They can put in a manager, as far as I'm concerned.'

We started to drop down again off the ridge, going faster now. Back below the treeline, trying to move noiselessly through the forest. Heading north-west, keeping to the fringes of forest wherever we could. It would soon be dawn.

Light rain was swirling through the fog as we crouched at the edge of the road. It was nearly sunrise. Zervas's scouts gave us the all-clear.

The road was poorly metalled but obviously well used. Up and over we went, hoping none of the mules would stumble in a hole. A few moments of complete exposure and then we were across, heading for the cover of sparsely clustered trees a few hundred yards away.

We had barely made it when we heard the sound of vehicles. We exchanged looks of horror. Trucks were coming along the road from Karpenisi not far to the west, making a racket with their diesel exhausts. Italians.

One truck after another roared down the road. As each one passed we felt more and more exposed; I could hear the sound of brakes in my head, imagining soldiers leaping off and coming for us. We hoped to hell the mules were safely out of sight.

After a few minutes there were no more trucks. No one had stopped. No one had seen us.

'If we'd been just two minutes later!' whispered Themis under his breath.

There was no time to lose. Another convoy could come along at any moment. We had to get on, swiftly—and without a sound.

Once we were safely away from the road, Zervas's men picked up a local guide. He managed to waste an hour of the precious night scouting around for the track before they sent him off with his tail between his legs. Then we were off up the mountains again, heading for Mount Tymfristos.

'More snow,' said Denys. 'At least my boots are standing up well.'

'Good for you, Denys,' said Arthur. 'Aren't you the lucky one?'

After a while we stopped climbing. Thick cloud was down so it was hard to see what was around us, but we seemed to be following a saddle. We had to pick our route carefully to keep out of the deeper pockets of snow at the foot of the rocky outcrops.

A call to halt.

'What's the matter, Chris?' I called.

'Seems like we're lost,' he replied. 'Got off the track by mistake, and now they can't find it again in the snow.'

We stood around waiting, the warmth of our bodies leaking away into the mist. Soon we were shaking with cold.

At last we set off again.

'Thank God,' said Arthur. 'I was wondering if we were going to freeze to death while we were waiting.'

'Instead of being shot by the Italians,' I said. 'One way or another we'd be dead.'

'Which is better, really?' said Inder.

'Neither,' said Arthur briskly. 'Neither is better. We're off now, anyway. Think about warm beds tonight. You never know, we might get lucky this time.'

The red roofs of a village appeared as we descended the mountain. Every now and again one of us would slide into a snowdrift and have to struggle our way out.

'Agia Triada,' said Themis. 'That means "Holy Trinity".' He looked at his watch. 'Let's see. It's late noon now.'

'What do you mean, late noon?' said Arthur. 'It's nearly three in the afternoon. What are you talking about?'

'No, it's late noon. Until around three—around now. Then it's afternoon.'

'Noon is a point in time,' I said. 'Right on midday. As soon as it's past, it's afternoon. Even one minute past twelve is afternoon already.'

'Not in Greece it isn't,' said Themis.

'But by three o'clock the afternoon's half over,' said Arthur.

'Especially at this time of year,' I said. 'The day is closing in already. Soon it will be evening.'

'It won't be evening until it gets dark,' said Themis. 'That's how it works here. In summer you eat dinner in the afternoon.'

'Well, judging by how long it takes them to get us something to eat, this is going to be a particularly long afternoon,' I said. 'Maybe it won't finish until ten or eleven o'clock.'

Ten and a half hours of walking on three hours' sleep. The village looked wonderful as we trudged in—solid, well-built houses, a cut above any we had seen elsewhere. They even put the doctor's house at Gardiki in the shade.

But something was missing—the crowds that had welcomed us in previous villages.

When we reached the square, Zervas was already giving a truncated version of his usual speech, emphasising the contribution of all three parties. His audience was sparse.

'Aren't those Aris's men over there?' said Arthur. 'I thought we left them all back at Mavrolithari.'

'We're on Aris's turf here near Karpenisi,' said Chris. 'It might be wise to be a bit circumspect. I'm off to find the village squire. That's who I stayed with on my way through. Eddie, are you coming?'

They went off with Zervas and Myridakis.

After a while Chris came back to get us.

'They're holding a "people's court" in the village today,' he said. 'They've invited us to go and have a look. I think they're very proud of it. Want to come?'

We followed him to the schoolhouse.

On a raised platform at the front of the room, half a dozen people were sitting around a table. The local priest seemed to be taking notes. Everyone else was standing below the dais, completely engrossed in the proceedings. From what I could make out the dispute was between two village men.

After a while I left them to it. The language was fast and furious and I couldn't keep up with it. When I caught Denys afterwards, I asked him what it was all about. I thought I could rely on him for a good cynical account. But I got a bit of a surprise.

'Boundary dispute,' he said. 'They didn't seem to have too much trouble agreeing on the outcome. Actually they're pretty interesting, these people's courts. I was talking to one of Aris's men afterwards and he said it's a new thing. Before, people had to take their legal matters to Karpenisi. There are no roads, so they had to go on foot, and it was too expensive for most of them anyway. Let alone getting behind with their planting or whatever. Aris took it into his head to abolish the gendarmerie around here.'

'A bit of social engineering?' I asked.

'I'm not sure it was that thought out, really. But there were precedents in other villages.'

Denys, Arthur and I were billeted together as ususal. When we entered the house we'd been allotted to, we could see at once that it was superior to the village homes we'd stayed in elsewhere. There was a small, cramped hall furnished for everyday living, and we glimpsed a grand living room with fancy furniture beyond. In the bedroom were real spring beds—one each. But the meal was late and meagre.

I was too tired to care. I went to bed and slept like the dead. Later, when I understood more about how things were in some of those villages, I regretted judging them so harshly for not feeding us better. Food was scarce, and the *andartes* who came through demanding to be fed were a heavy burden, whether they paid or not. And those villagers who'd worked in America—with the more elaborate houses and decent beds—had had no remittances of money since the occupation started.

One hour out of Agia Triada, up beyond the treeline, we heard planes overhead. German Junkers—what else could they be? Spotting for us, no doubt.

We were well past Mount Tymfristos by now, heading for the Pindos range. It was early December. Another three weeks of dodging Italians—I wondered how we could keep it up.

We dropped down towards the River Megdova in the late afternoon. We'd been told to be on the lookout for an old stone bridge, just before the village of Viniani.

Suddenly there it was: a single span, curving high over the river in its stony bed. There looked to be no mortar holding it all together—just precision cutting and laying.

'Look at the stonework,' said John. 'I wonder how old it is.'

Zervas's scouts looked about carefully before we started up and over. All clear. First the mules, then Zervas, mounted on a horse again today. The rest of us following in file over the cobblestones. How many decades had it taken to wear them down like this?

Foot and mule traffic only, it must have been—it was surely too narrow for a cart.

Chris was just behind me on the bridge and as we came off it he caught up.

'This is where we all met for the first time, Aris and Zervas and I. Remember I told you about the American with the bath? That was here.'

'You'll be able to see him again,' I said.

'I hope we might stay in his house again. He has the best house in the village. You can pick it by the low stone wall right around the front. And this time I wouldn't mind a bath.'

As we arrived in the village, Zervas was already assembling his troops for his usual speech. The bridge, the British, cooperation with Aris, victory. We knew the script by now. Denys and I stood by, muttering 'bullshit' from time to time through our beards. It broke the monotony.

I liked that about Denys. I too was a bit of a cynic when it came to lofty expressions of sentiment, especially when made in public in front of an admiring audience. A new fellow-feeling was developing between us. It certainly made things more bearable—more fun, even.

With Arthur, I had a different kind of understanding. Now that the Li-Lo was a distant memory, he no longer made me the butt of his jokes. He'd been like a rock at Gorgopotamos, and he'd had the grace to commend me on my leadership; he'd said he liked the way I always said 'we' rather than 'I'. We got along pretty well now, mostly.

We arrived at Kerasochori village the following day in brilliant sunshine. More speeches. A good lunch at the priest's house, served by his pretty daughters. They were certainly easier on the eye than our gang. We all looked like bandits by now.

After lunch Chris came to find us.

'Did you get your bath last night?' I asked. 'We were all jealous.'

'The bath was broken,' he said shortly. 'But come on. Officers' meeting right away. In the house across the way.'

Once we were all gathered, Eddie came straight to the point.

'Zervas's scouts have picked up news of Italian movements. They're trying to cut us off. They're coming down from Yannina and across from Arta. We're going to have to change our route.'

We couldn't afford even a small encounter with the Italians, I knew. We had scarcely three rounds of ammunition apiece.

'So what do we do?' asked Denys. 'Where can we go?'

'We'll go due north,' said Eddie. 'To the Agrafa Mountains. No one will follow us there.'

'Agrafa?' said Arthur, blinking.

'Uncharted,' said Chris. '*Agrafa* means uncharted. In other words, wilderness.'

NINE

I didn't like the sound of that. We'd be going out of our way, deeper into the Pindos range to the north than we'd been expecting—which meant more time on the run. More time for the Italians to get ahead of us and cut us off, I couldn't help thinking.

If ever you have to travel through an uncharted mountain wilderness, you'd probably want to go by day. At least then you'd have some hope of seeing the dangers ahead of you—and of doing something about them.

We started out by day—3 pm—and the good track held out for a while. The path was overgrown and we had to fight our way along, but that didn't worry us by now. Up and over a few steep hills, nothing to it, trying not to think about what might lie ahead.

I was walking directly behind Len. I hadn't seen much of him since we'd left Mavrolithari. The three sergeants were always billeted together, never with us.

'How do you feel about staying in Greece, Len?' I asked quietly.

'Well, you and Arthur are leaving me behind,' he said. 'I'm not sure who Doug and I are going to talk to.'

'You'll have to learn some more Greek,' I said. 'There are plenty of likely Greek girls around. Tell them you did Gorgopotamos. They'll be all over you like a rash.'

'With their chaperones,' he sighed. 'I've noticed they don't let them out on their own. With any luck I might find someone without a family in tow.'

'If your friend Connie doesn't mind.'

'Well, we're not engaged—yet. But I've got a plan. We have a bit of a secret code going, us signallers.'

'Of course. There have to be some perks to the job, right?'

'Right. One day I'm going to get Cairo to transmit a message to London—they won't know anything about it. Ask Connie to marry me. Not yet though. I'm going to wait for her twentieth birthday.'

'When's that?'

'Next October. Less than a year now.'

'Well, good luck. Will she be able to answer?'

'You bet!'

The daylight was long gone when our route turned steeply upwards, and there was no moon. Now it was hardly a path, more of an endless stumble; we heaved our bodies up one step and then another, rocks dislodging themselves under our feet to tumble away below.

I was conscious of a vast empty space beside me. I felt cautiously with my foot to the left. Nothing. Never mind, I consoled myself. This must be a narrow bit. Soon it'll widen out and we'll be able to hug the rock wall.

I started to think idly about the word *Agrafa*. Uncharted—like a river no one had been along, or a sea no one had ventured into. Pathless …

There always seemed to be paths of some kind in Greece. There were plenty of villages that didn't have roads, but they all had paths. Mule tracks, mostly, with every now and then one of those high arching stone bridges over a gravelly river bed that would flood in the thaw.

The path didn't widen out. It got narrower—soon it was nothing but a ledge, a foot wide if that, going on forever.

Creeping forward, I kept my right hand against the rough solidity of the rock wall for comfort. Now I knew what was beside me—the empty air above a river far below. I could hear the water.

Nat was in front of me now. Suddenly he stopped.

'What's going on, Nat?'

'How the hell would I know?'

Stock-still on a ledge only fractionally wider than my two feet, trying desperately not to move or even to sway. In the dark, I had no real way to judge the position of my own body. Without warning, pain shot through my thighs and knees, running down to my shins. My hands were sweaty.

It was terror: absolute terror.

I thought about the others. Inder had youth on his side, and was small and light. But John? He had a lot more weight to carry than I did and he wasn't a powerful man. Eddie hadn't had the strength to haul himself up the mountain after Gorgopotamos.

It was entirely possible that someone would slip.

Five minutes went by, more. It was hard to tell how long.

Then, with a surge, we were moving again.

Another sudden stop.

'What's up this time?' I whispered to Nat. 'We've barely made ten feet.'

No one knew.

Waiting, moving forward a few feet, stopping again for perhaps fifteen minutes. None of us with any idea what was happening. I tried to ignore the pains in my legs, and to keep my body upright and still.

Finally a whispered word came back.

'Ities. In our way.'

So much for being safe in the uncharted mountains.

I imagined us jumping off the cliff like they do in adventure stories, letting the river carry us away. But what if it were shallow? I couldn't see it so I didn't know. They would find our bodies smashed at the bottom—maybe with the bones picked clean by vultures. Did they have vultures here? I didn't need that picture in my head.

Hours and hours went by. The sudden impetus as we took off, the jerk as we halted, never knowing for how long, always listening for the cry of someone succumbing to terror or fatigue and slipping over the edge—the cry that, fortunately, never came.

At last I sensed a descent. The depth of air to our left, down to the river, seemed to lessen.

'Crossing ahead. Boots and socks off,' the word came back. I wondered how cold the water would be—no, I knew.

We paused briefly on the other side to put our boots and socks back on. Then up, along a ridge, and down again. Another crossing. Boots off again, our toes cold as frogs' feet, then on again on the other side.

Eventually we found ourselves on a flat, rocky space.

'Bridge,' was the word now. 'Girder bridge across the river.'

I couldn't see it in the dark but I followed Nat over. I could hear the river below—a few rapids, by the sound of it, but not a real torrent.

Over and up again. More climbing. Half an hour after midnight, we reached the next village, Monasteraki, looking forward to our dinner, but we got a poor welcome. There was no food for us here. Seven to a room, we went to sleep on empty stomachs after nearly fourteen hours on our feet.

'I'm fed up to the back teeth with this place,' I said to Denys as we got up the next morning. 'And if we don't get breakfast, I'll be ropable.'

'Don't worry,' said Khouri. 'I find something. Come on, Denys!'

They disappeared downstairs.

Denys came back first. 'No luck with mine host,' he said. 'No breakfast. But I hope Khouri might have something up his sleeve. Of course it's not customary to eat breakfast.'

We'd just started a game of cards when Khouri came back. He'd crept into the larder while Denys was talking to the host and filched a few pounds of filthy goat's milk butter.

We tossed the cards aside and fell on it, breaking pieces off with our fingers, ignoring the stench. It took us only a few minutes to eat the lot.

Sated, we went out into the village and immediately ran into Chris.

'What sort of billet have you got, Chris? Enough to eat?' asked Arthur nonchalantly.

'Poor and grudging,' he replied. 'And no.'

'Ours too,' said Arthur. 'But we've just knocked off a couple of pounds of butter between us. Rancid, unfortunately.'

'I didn't like to say so,' said Chris, 'but I can smell it on you. Is that what you were served up for breakfast?'

'Not exactly,' said Denys.

'What news of the Ities?' asked Inder.

'All around, according to Zervas's scouts. And his family are here—his brother and sister and a young nephew. Apparently they were the only ones who managed to escape with him from Athens when he came to the mountains.'

'Out of the frying pan, into the fire,' said Arthur. 'For them, I mean.'

'I hope not,' said Chris. 'We're heading more or less due north from here, further into the mountains. No one will expect us to go that way. We'll be travelling mainly by night. And we'll need to carry our essential stuff ourselves, so get your gear off the mules.'

'What time are we leaving?' asked Inder.

'Whenever we're told.'

After we'd sorted our things, we got the cards out again and settled down to some serious bridge. Around three o'clock, we heard a hum overhead.

'Sounds like planes,' said Denys.

'I'll go and have a look,' said John.

'What a bloody stupid idea,' said Denys, pulling him back. 'They'll see you. What do you think they're here for?'

'Oh, yes. Well …' John quickly sat down again.

'They sound quite low,' said Arthur.

'Yes, too low,' said Denys. 'I don't like it.'

After a while the noise died away.

'Given up?' said Arthur.

'Or gone for reinforcements,' said Denys. 'I hope no one else was stupid enough to think of going out for a look.'

'Lay off, Denys,' said John.

Inder was sitting out of our card game. Arthur sent him off to find out whether we'd be leaving before dinner.

He returned after a few minutes.

'We're probably staying another night,' he said.

'Great,' said Arthur. 'In this miserable hole.'

Every day we stayed put made me more anxious about our rendezvous. That submarine was calling to me. What if it came the first day, the 22nd, and we weren't there to see the signal? What if they couldn't get close to shore the second night, or the third night? We were losing time in Agrafa and I was itching to be moving.

Next morning there was again no sign of breakfast.

'Come on, Tom,' said Denys. 'Let's see what we can bludgeon out of that bastard today.'

We caught our wonderful host before he went off to work his fields. Denys interrogated him about his pantry.

'Honey,' said Denys. 'He's got honey.'

Honey! We had money for that.

After a swift negotiation, we brought it back to our room in triumph. A pound pot. We passed the pot from hand to hand, scooping the honey out with our fingers and licking it off. Nothing had ever tasted as wonderful.

Then it was out to the village spring or *vrisi* to wash our sticky hands and faces—it wasn't much fun having honey in your beard—feeling a little sick but with more energy in our legs than we'd had for days. And not a moment too soon. At eleven we got the word to leave.

We headed north-east, back towards the river. Now we could see what we'd been up against the night before. Range after range of mountains disappeared to the north. High, snowy ridges to the west and east. It was just as well we hadn't been able to see anything on the way in.

Our path led us above a gorge and we paused to have a look.

Water was slipping quietly over the edge, curtaining the mossy boulders below in fine vertical sheets. Crowding into the narrow space, the waters of the river jostled below us. For a moment, the sight lifted our hearts beyond plain grinding endurance.

We couldn't stop for long. The sun was already disappearing behind the ranges. By the time we got to the next village, it was dark. The village, Epinyani, was small and poor but Zervas's speech about our exploits was warmly received.

'Welcome, welcome,' said the host when we got to our billet.

English again. It was indeed welcome.

The hall was dark and thickly populated with goats. We climbed up the stairs and into the room above, where a dog, a cat and another goat had taken up residence. We had *trachanas* for dinner, that cross between porridge and soup, made with oats, that we called 'truck'.

Before I fell asleep I thought about that gorge we'd seen earlier in the day, with its rocky sides filmed in water. For a long moment I felt myself back in that tranquil place.

We woke after a good sleep to a glorious day. It soon became clear that this was not going to be a breakfast-free establishment. As soon as we opened our eyes, our host arrived with a cloth, which he spread on the floor ready for our meal. 'Good morning, good morning,' we cried.

The house was filled with the smell of fresh bread. Usually Greek families seemed to keep their bread for days. It was always dry and rather tough.

'You must have got up very early to bake for us,' said Nat, helping to arrange the cloth. 'I hope you didn't stay up all night.'

Our host didn't reply but disappeared to get our food.

'I think they did stay up all night,' said Inder.

The host returned shortly with his wife. Between them they had brought bread, honey, cheese and tea. A feast.

'Stay and eat with us,' said Arthur.

They looked a little embarrassed. 'We eat already, down in the hall,' said our host. 'This is for you. Soon you cross the mountains. Very high, very tough. Need strength.'

'Thank you.'

'I bet they didn't eat downstairs,' said Inder as we headed out into the sunshine to find the others. 'I bet they had a handful of olives and gave us what they were going to have for dinner.' Truth be told, what they gave us would have fed them for a week, maybe more. How generous they were, how hospitable and kind, with the little they had.

For some time now, stories of Italian troops searching for our little band had been meeting us at every village. Now, a runner arrived. Aris and his men had run into a thousand Italians on our trail and had sent them off with a flea in their ear. Aris offered to send some of his men to accompany us further.

'Zervas thinks we'll be OK,' Chris told us. 'Once we're over the Acheloos River we'll be in his territory. Tomorrow we'll cross the mountains to the west to Ravtopoulo, and then we're only a few days away.'

I couldn't wait.

We got a good welcome in Ravtopoulo, although we'd had to climb up and slide down some of the worst mountains we had seen.

Moving west the next afternoon, we gained the top of a ridge and held to it until we dropped down into a broad river valley.

'I wonder if this is the Acheloos,' said Denys. 'I'll ask.'

He overtook a few people and then disappeared. When we came down to a fine stone bridge, he was waiting for us.

'I was right,' he said. 'The Acheloos. Zervas's territory on the other side.'

'I'd better take a photo, then,' I said, 'if this is it. And it's a wonderful bridge.'

Not far to Avlaki village now. I wondered if we would get a poor village and a good feed, or a good village and a bad feed. It turned out to be the latter. We should have been inured to it by then, but our empty stomachs always kept our hopes up.

Nat went to ask our host how old the bridge was.

'Built in 1907,' he told us when he came back.

'Like me,' I said. 'The year I was born.'

'Before my time,' said Nat.

'1910, wasn't it?' I said. 'When you were born?'

'Well, yes.'

'Three years, then,' I replied. 'I'm three years up on you.'

'Still, chances are I'll still be alive when you're dead,' he said.

'Chances?' I said. 'Don't count on it.'

'Just look at this,' said Arthur as we sat on the floor around the customary cloth in the next village, Mesopyrgo. 'Beans, onions, fried potatoes, cheese …' He bit into an olive.

'And bonzer brown bread,' I said.

'What do you mean, "bonzer"?' said Denys. 'What kind of word is that?'

'It means "good", doesn't it, Arthur?'

'Of course. What's wrong with it?'

'Sometimes you fellows sound so terribly colonial,' Denys replied.

'Do you realise we've finally hit the jackpot?' said Arthur, leaning back contentedly with his arms behind his head. 'It's always been one or the other—good meal or good house, never both at once.'

'Sheets on the beds, too,' I said.

'Really?' said Arthur, going immediately to check. 'Bliss!'

On 12 December we arrived at Megalochari, which I now understood to mean 'Great Grace'. It turned out to be more a scattering of houses than a village. Zervas had his headquarters here, hidden in the foothills of snow-covered mountains. We clustered around his radio to hear the news broadcast.

'This is the BBC. The Eighth Army is pursuing its advance in Libya. Rommel's Afrika Korps are taking a beating around El Agheila ...'

'Things seem to be looking up,' said Eddie. 'And I hear that the BBC announced on Monday that guerrillas had blown up a bridge in Greece. A hundred and fifty killed and prisoners taken, it seems.'

'Really? Did we kill 150?' said Arthur.

'If the BBC said it, it must be true,' said Eddie.

Next morning, as we unwillingly complied with the custom of no breakfast, we got the order to repack our kit. 'Minimum gear, only what you can carry. No mules from here on.' The land was unproductive and we might get little to eat. We couldn't afford to waste any energy.

What could we jettison? We still had a change of underwear each. We'd managed to get hold of some rough woollen stockings to replace our worn-out socks. Blanket and groundsheet, torch, maps—we needed those. Anything we could afford to leave behind went off to Zervas's house.

'Tom, how much do you reckon you've got?' said Arthur.

'Forty to forty-five pounds,' I replied. 'Probably closer to forty-five.'

'Me too, I reckon,' he said.

'I've got less,' said Denys. 'Probably only fifteen to twenty. But I'm not sure I can manage even that much.'

'I'm thinking the same thing about mine,' I said.

'Well, if you're worried, I should be more worried,' said Denys. 'You're the toughest of all of us.'

We assembled in the street in the late afternoon. Our party would be twenty-four. Zervas had entrusted us to the care of Captain Myridakis the Cretan, and we knew we would be in good hands. As we prepared to set off, we were all conscious that these were our last hours together as a group. Not far beyond this village, Chris, Themis, Len and Mike would leave us for the dropping ground. Khouri and the two Cypriots, Yannis and Panayiotis, would continue on with us: they'd been offered the chance to escape on the sub and had accepted gladly. A small group of Zervas's men would escort us to the coast.

We posed for some photos. The local doctor, Dr Papachristou, took one of our party, officers in the rear and NCOs squatting in front—rather like a school sports team, except for our beards and the beehives in the background.

We moved on beyond the village to the point where we were to part. Now that it was time to say our goodbyes to Zervas, Chris and co., I wasn't prepared for the sudden rush of regret. I felt huge admiration and a growing affection for Chris—but realistically, I wasn't likely to run into him again.

'Hope to hear how you're going some time,' I said. 'All the best—I know you've got what it takes.'

'Thanks,' he said. 'See you in the Long Bar at Shepheard's Hotel one of these days. When you're next in Cairo. I'll leave a message with "Saint" Joe, at the bar. "If you see Tom Barnes, tell him I'm in town." You do the same for me.'

He wanted to keep in touch—I was delighted.

As the commander of our operation, Zervas could have been remote and unapproachable to someone of my rank. But he hadn't been, and he wasn't now. We kissed warmly on both cheeks.

'*Efcharisto poly*,' I said. Thanks very much.

'*Efcharisto poly*, Tom,' he replied. '*Andio.*'

Len's turn next. I shook his hand and he wrung mine back. I wished him luck with Connie. I would miss his sharp tongue and his capacity to extract endless entertainment from the pettinesses of those he was subordinate to.

This looked like being the most exposed part of our trip, and the most dangerous. Once we'd gone beyond the Valtos Mountain below the South Pindos range, we'd be out of Zervas's territory. And near the coast, there'd be no mountains to conceal us.

We would travel mostly by night, hiding during the day and keeping away from villages as much as possible—with no substantial resistance presence in the area, the villagers were justifiably nervous of the enemy, and likely to betray us for the sake of their own safety.

We had ten days left to make the rendezvous.

We crossed the range in the dark. When we struggled into the village of Velentziko late that night, there was no reception party waiting for us. But at 10 pm we heard the Liberator over the dropping ground where we'd left the others.

We were on a wider than usual track the next day, so Denys and I could walk side by side. As usual, hunger pangs were pulling at our stomachs.

'What would you eat?' I asked. 'If you could have anything you wanted.'

'Well … let's say we're in the Grill Room at Shepheard's,' said Denys. 'We've come in up the steps past the terrace. A whole lot of off-duty officers are lounging about in those wicker chairs, drinking coffee and keeping an eye on the hullabaloo in the street. We cross that mosaic floor to the bar. We order something from Saint Joe—what'll it be, Tom?'

'A "suffering bastard".'

'Make that two, Joe. Two suffering bastards. But go easy on the ginger ale.'

'We take our time in the bar, chatting.'

'But we're pretty hungry, so we don't stay *too* long. We head to the Grill Room and order steaks with potatoes and onions.'

'Tomatoes, too. Grilled tomatoes. And what about mushrooms?'

'Definitely, if they can get them,' said Denys. 'And asparagus. Long, thick, juicy stalks of it.'

'I've only ever eaten asparagus out of a tin,' I said, 'rolled up in those fancy sandwiches. But I'll give it a go. What about some bacon with our steaks?'

Denys looked disapproving. 'You don't eat bacon with steaks. What kind of a palate have you New Zealanders got? Bacon? Certainly not.'

'I'm trying the asparagus,' I said. 'Why don't you try the bacon?'

'That's different,' he said. 'It's good for you colonials to learn how to eat properly. But if I ate bacon with my steak I'd be encouraging you in bad habits.'

'Thanks, Denys. I appreciate your solicitude. When I go back to Australia I'll be able to show off my new-found gastronomic expertise in the local café. I can watch everyone else eat bacon with their steak and eggs and feel superior.'

'Do the Australians do it too?' he said. 'Oh dear!'

'Anyway,' I exclaimed, 'you do eat bacon with steak! What about filet mignon with bacon wrapped around?'

'Well, yes. That's true, I suppose.'

'One of those Nubian waiters brings the steaks,' I went on. 'Two big plates. What will you go for first?'

'The potatoes. Fried potatoes with onions.'

'But we get those here—sometimes. I'm going for the steak first. Not sheep, not goat, but beautiful beef. Juicy and pink in the middle.'

'We watch the traffic on the river,' said Denys. 'See what's happening on the houseboats.'

'Do you want to come back to the New Zealand Club with me after?' I said. 'I'll sign you in.'

The day went on. Just before dark, we made the Arachthos River, effectively the western boundary of the Valtos—but not before the fool guide had managed to get us lost several times.

Once we'd reached the river, we had to struggle downstream—there was a good girder bridge, but we didn't dare use it. The moon was in its first quarter and the going was hard. Finally we stopped. A boat was heading towards us, getting closer with each jerk of the oars—a crazy little ferry.

'Just as well we've lost so much weight,' I said. 'Otherwise I reckon even two of us would sink it.'

'Yes,' said Denys. 'Arthur, you and Tom had better not go together. You've got the heaviest kit. You don't want to end up in the drink.'

It took an hour to get us all across. An hour of standing around hungry and cold, first on one side of the river and then on the other. By the time we arrived at that night's village it was 11 pm. All of us bedded down in the same house, with only 'truck' for supper. We'd been walking for over fourteen hours on six hours' sleep. We collapsed onto the floor in full rig.

The next day, we woke at 6.30 am and walked until just before noon. After that we lay low until dark in a valley well away from any villages.

As soon as we'd dropped our kits, Nat pulled off his shirt.

'Seeing we'll be staying here for a while,' he said, 'I'm going to look at my bites. I'm ready to swear it's not just fleas from those village blankets.'

Arthur pulled up his own shirt and inspected his chest. 'You're right, Nat. It's lice. They're biting me too, as if there's no tomorrow.'

Soon each of us was stripped to the waist and all hands were busy catching lice and fleas. The fleas were quick, while the lice had to be hunted down in the seams of our clothing. It passed the time, at least.

'Lawrence of Arabia had a theory about lice,' said Eddie.

'Oh yes? What's that?' said Arthur.

'Well, you keep turning your vest inside out—or your shirt, whatever's next to your skin. You turn it one way and then the other. The lice keep finding themselves on the wrong side.'

'So what?' said Arthur. 'You reckon they get fed up and leave?'

'That's the theory,' said Eddie.

'Pardon my scepticism,' said Arthur. 'Lice are smart. They're not easily fooled.'

The popping of lice between fingers and thumbs continued.

'Tell me,' said Inder after a few silent moments. 'If you were going to die, say in three days' time, would you prefer to know or not to know?'

'What sort of a morbid question is that?' said Arthur.

'No, but really. I want to know what you think.'

'Well,' said Arthur, 'it depends. Would we all be dying, or just one of us?'

'Would it make a difference?'

'Well, yes,' said Arthur. 'If it was only one person—say the Italians knew we were in a certain village and they came in the night and all but one of us got away. If you knew, you could make some arrangements ahead of time. You could send messages to your family. You could write a letter. No point doing that if we were all for it, though.'

'If you owed someone some money, say, you could pay them back,' I said.

'What about if you owed them something else?' said Nat. 'What if they'd had it coming to them for weeks and you knew you were running out of chances?'

'Well, yes,' said Arthur dubiously. 'Maybe.'

'I think it's better not to know,' said Denys. 'Live as if there's no tomorrow. Otherwise you'd be shit-scared and useless, to yourself and everyone else.'

'I think you're right, Denys,' I said. 'How would we be able to keep going if we knew we weren't going to make it? As it is, it's only the thought of our "guest" waiting outside that bay that keeps us going.'

We always referred to the submarine as our 'guest'. Eddie had impressed upon us that none of the Greeks must hear the word 'submarine'. But the *andartes* all knew. We were sure of it.

'That and the sunshine,' said Inder. 'We've been so lucky with the weather. When it's sunny you can't help feeling buoyant, even if you're weak from hunger and your boots keep breaking.'

'What if our guest doesn't show up?' said Nat. 'What then?'

'It doesn't bear thinking about,' said Arthur.

'If we're playing what-ifs,' said Eddie, 'tell me this. If you only had time to write one letter, who would you write it to?'

'Do you mean your parents or your wife?'

'Yes, or your children. If you have any. After all, they'd have to grow up without you. You might like to pass on something, some advice—something like that.'

'You mean, "Don't volunteer for secret missions behind enemy lines"?' said John.

'That would be a good, practical piece of advice,' said Eddie.

'Especially coming from you, John,' said Nat.

'Now then,' said Eddie. 'Inder, you're the youngest. Who would you write to?'

'My mother,' said Inder. 'And my sisters. And my father. One letter for all of them.'

'And what would you say? Come on, Inder,' said Arthur.

'Well, I'd say … I don't know. It would be so hard. I'd say I'd been looking forward to the end of the war. I'd say I would have liked to finish my engineering degree. I'd say I loved them. What else could you say?'

'What about you, Eddie?' said Denys. 'You're the oldest. You have to go next.'

'Well, I'm not married, of course. I wish I was. Seven years in the Middle East, though—the options are limited. I don't even have a girlfriend. So I suppose I would write to my parents.'

'What would you say?'

'I'd say I've had a pretty good life as a soldier and I don't have too many regrets. Goodbye and all that, I suppose. I'm not one for airing my feelings in public, really.'

'What about you people with sweethearts?' said Denys. 'Tom?'

'I had to fight for Beth,' I said. 'I hot-footed it down from New Guinea when she told me she'd got engaged to someone else. It would be hard to say goodbye. But I wouldn't want her grieving for me all her life. And anyway, it wouldn't happen. They'd be after her like bees around a honey pot.'

'You do realise there won't be too many bees left, don't you?' said Denys. 'Like after the Great War. There'll be no one left for them to marry. All those single women, getting on with their lives because they can't find anyone to settle down with.'

'All the more for us,' said Nat.

'Yes,' said Eddie. 'I might find someone.'

A few nights later we stayed in a kind of shanty town of brushwood huts.

'Who are these people, Nat?' asked Inder. 'They look like Gypsies to me.'

Nat had been chatting with the *andartes* about them. 'They're refugees from Albania, apparently.'

'Do they speak Greek?' I asked.

'Well, yes,' said Nat. 'They're not actually Albanians. They're Greeks. But they're nomads. They travel with their flocks, and live on milk and cheese mostly. Meat now and again.'

The Gypsies were extremely generous. Nat, Inder and I basked in the warmth of our hut.

Suddenly came the sound that had been echoing in my imagination all the way along the trek—gunshots.

Italians! Our hosts bolted up the mountainside. We followed more cautiously, ducking behind whatever cover we could find.

It was a false alarm. Nothing but sheep-thieves. One of the Gypsies had fired a shot to scare them away. We reassembled in the cold and the wet.

The next morning we retraced our steps. In the end we'd made better time than expected—it was only 19 December and we were practically at the coast. Captain Myridakis didn't want to arrive too early as it was going to be difficult to lie low and hide there.

Nat had negotiated the purchase of a goat from the Gypsies for one gold sovereign, and the *andartes* had brought it with them. It was already on the fire when we trailed in at noon. We were seriously weakened by now from poor and inadequate food.

'Smells like goat,' said Nat.

'You smell like goat,' Denys shot back.

'They say you smell like what you eat,' said Nat.

'Then we should smell of truck and beans,' Denys retorted. 'Not much goat on the menu since we left Gardiki.'

The meat was delicious, but one goat didn't go very far among all of us and we got very little each. John wanted to buy another goat from the Gypsies for the next day.

'They're too poor,' said Eddie. 'They need their animals for breeding. That's what they told Captain Myridakis. It's hard for them to get new ones.'

'Oh,' said John. Like the rest of us, he was looking thin, and his clothes were hanging off him. His shoulders sagged as he walked, and he kept to himself quite a bit.

But we were almost there. One more night with the Gypsies, one more 3.30 am start. Then just an exposed plain lay between us and that submarine.

Two hours after setting out the next morning, we reached a mountain ridge. It was still dark, but as the sun came up behind us we found ourselves about 1500 feet up, looking across to the sea and the islands beyond. We had crossed Greece from east to west.

It was 21 December.

We'd made it. We'd made it on time. The Italians hadn't got us, and that submarine would be here in just a few days. Just as well: we were at the end of our strength.

The Captain was pointing out the islands offshore. Nat was translating but I suddenly found I could understand whole sentences. Even in my weakened state, I felt a thrill of elation.

'That island is Paxos,' said the Captain. 'And Antipaxos there. And we can see the bottom of Corfu as well, to the north. And see up to the north near the coast—that's Paramythia airfield. German-occupied, of course. And Parga down there.'

'Well, with any luck we'll be passing them soon,' said Inder. 'Under water.'

'Let's hope so,' said Denys. 'Imagine making it all this way and then getting taken out by a U-boat.'

We looked down to the valley below, the valley we now had to cross. A river crept slowly to the sea, spreading out into swampy flats that were a vivid, unlikely green. The Acheron.

'Do you know what the Romans called the Acheron?' said Denys.

'No. What?'

'The Styx. It was one of the five rivers of the underworld in Greek mythology. Zeus is supposed to have turned the original Acheron—the person—into a river because he gave the Titans a drink while Zeus was fighting them.'

'You can see why the legend runs like that,' I said. 'It's a real valley of death down there.'

'Well, I hope it's not our valley of death,' said Denys. 'We're a bit short of six hundred, and we're no Light Brigade. I want to get out of Greece in one piece.'

It was bitterly cold and windy on the ridge that day. We crouched behind some low stone walls that formed a rough sheep pen, taking it in turns in the small brushwood igloo that the shepherds used. Only a couple of us could fit in at a time. The food situation was grim, as usual.

Suddenly, we all tensed. We could sense someone looking at us. A young lad was standing there. A shepherd, by the look of him. We had been seen, in daylight—and by someone we knew we couldn't rely on.

'*Baba*! *Baba*!' he called. Dad, Dad. Then he said something I couldn't understand.

'"Strangers",' whispered Nat. 'He's telling his father he's found a whole bunch of strangers up on the mountainside where they shouldn't be. And some of them look like soldiers.'

A man appeared around the side of the mountain, then shrank back as the *andartes*, knives unsheathed, quickly moved in on him and the boy.

'What are the *andartes* saying to them, Nat?' I asked. 'I can't hear.'

'I can't make it out either.'

'Do you think they'll kill them?' whispered Inder.

'They may have to,' said Denys.

After much fierce talk and gesticulation, however, the *andartes* allowed the boy and his father to depart. We hoped the pair wouldn't betray us. Apparently the *andartes* had threatened them with all kinds of horrible deaths if they did.

After a day spent on that exposed ridge we were in worse shape than ever. And the latest news was that the Ities were on our trail again, ten hours behind us. We were relieved to get moving again.

Down on the plain, the swamp spread out endlessly in front of us. In the moonlight the tall scrub cast deep, confusing shadows. We tried to move silently, but it was hard not to react when our feet slipped into the icy water. Every now and then a duck would take off with a thump of its wings, giving us a start. More to the point, it would betray our presence to anyone who might be listening.

We had a rendezvous with a guide. We waited for him for two hours in absolute silence, knowing our lives depended on it. We couldn't proceed without him—he knew where the gendarme posts were located.

It was just before dawn on 22 December when we finally reached the rendezvous point for the submarine. I was jubilant, but had no energy left to show it. We lay on a low hill, sleeping and dozing in the sun for most of the day, each in our own patch of scrub. The Captain would not allow his men to make any demands for food at the nearest village, in case the villagers betrayed us. I comforted myself with thoughts of bacon and eggs on the submarine—fried bread, too, with any luck.

After nightfall, once it was completely dark, we made our way down to the bay. As we approached, a boat slid silently into shore. We moved quickly back into the scrub.

A man climbed out of the boat and started unloading heavy tins. A smuggler. Olive oil from Cyprus, probably. We left him to it.

We crept around to a likely headland and fired up our torches. The batteries had long since given up, but Arthur and I had been humping along two heavy accumulators since we left Megalochari, with hoods we'd concocted to direct the light straight out to sea.

We took it in turns to flash the code, two men working at a time. The code was 'AR', flashed at three-minute intervals. Denys and Inder went first, then Arthur and I. Arthur flashed the torch while I watched, straining to see anything breaking the waters, listening for the sound of oars or a boat scraping the gravelly shore.

When our time was up we surrendered the equipment to Nat and John.

'Good luck,' we whispered.

At 4 am we called a halt. Nothing doing that night.

'Tomorrow,' said Inder. 'Tomorrow we'll see that shape breaking the waves, and then we'll hear the boat coming. We'll jump in and off we'll go.'

'You can go in the first load, Inder,' said Arthur. 'I don't mind waiting for the second.'

We trekked back to the hill, tired, hungry and thirsty. We slept, or dozed at least. That submarine had better come—I knew we couldn't stand up to another long march.

* * *

Eventually a meal arrived from somewhere. Meat, boki, and rice cooked in the broth of the meat. Very little each, but it was good.

There was a full moon that night, and it was not so cold. Denys and Arthur were on watch. Around midnight, Denys gave a soft, excited call.

'It's come! I saw it surface! Just a few hundred yards off. Then it went around the headland and disappeared. Tell Eddie!'

We all rushed to see the great sight. We strained our eyes and ears. But there was nothing there.

Denys had been the most sceptical of all of us about the submarine. But as he shuffled back to his post, it was clear the old pessimist had nurtured his own secret hopes.

We slept through the day until a heavy shower woke us in the afternoon. More food arrived—a meal that gave new meaning to the term 'light lunch'. It was Christmas Eve—our last chance. If the submarine didn't come tonight, it wasn't coming at all.

When we gathered on the headland at 11 pm, everyone was cranky. It was as cold as hell and then it started to sleet.

Midnight came and went. Christmas Day—Beth's birthday.

As I took my turn on the signalling with Arthur, I tried to figure out what time it would be in Tasmania. She would have been to church—they always celebrated Christmas in the morning and had a birthday tea for Beth in the afternoon. I wished I could have sent her a present. I comforted myself by thinking of the things I'd sent from Cairo. Would they have arrived yet? It was hard to know. I thought of Beth and her mother eating turkey and ham and Christmas pudding. Potatoes, too, and green peas fresh from the garden. They would have shelled them together, Beth and her mother.

Her last letter had arrived on 14 September. Letter number 58. I'd asked her to number them, so that I could tell what order they should be in. Sometimes a whole batch would arrive together, and sometimes they arrived out of order.

I thought about the last time we'd danced together. It was in Launceston, just after we'd got engaged. I was in civvies—it was before I joined up. It was odd to think of it now—my uniform seemed like part of me.

She was in a white dress with a full skirt. The dance floor was crowded with people getting in a good time while they could. We loved to do the quickstep together and I tried to steer us around the edge of the floor; the centre was full of people doing the swing and it was getting a bit dangerous. But when we spotted a small space, we pushed our way into the middle to join them. Her skirt spun out as she twirled out under my arm and back again, rock step and out again.

After a few songs we got hot and went for a drink. Then we heard the band start up 'When Irish Eyes Are Smiling'—our favourite for the Viennese waltz. We ditched our drinks.

'I feel like I'm flying,' she said. 'I'm so lucky you're a good dancer. You realise I couldn't have married you if you weren't?'

'You're easy to lead,' I said. 'You stand up straight. So many girls slouch, and then you can't do anything with them.'

A slow waltz was next. She moved in closer. My leg was against her thigh. She rested her head on my shoulder, the shoulder she always called hers.

'I can't wait until we're married,' I said.

She blushed and pulled away a little. But not for long.

John and Nat arrived to take over the watch.

'Anything doing?' said John.

'Nothing,' I replied.

And that was it. The last night went past just like the others—this time without even any false alarms. It looked like being the worst Christmas Day on record.

The prospects for food were poor to non-existent as we huddled in our scrubby shelters for the last time. But then Eddie gave the Captain some money, and one of the men took off to try to buy us something.

'Isn't that rather dangerous?' I said to Denys.

'Well, we'll be moving on after tonight,' he said. 'Security can't be quite so important.'

About four in the afternoon, some pork arrived. The *andartes* had killed a pig and cooked it on the spot for us. We couldn't get enough of it. Later, we all got the runs.

It was getting dark again. A runner arrived from Zervas with a message from Cairo. We all crowded around. We could see from Eddie's face that something was wrong.

'They've changed their minds,' he said. 'The submarine's not coming. We're staying.'

'What, all of us?' said Denys.

'All of us.'

PART II

OPERATION 'ANIMALS'

TEN

No eggs and bacon for us. No fried bread, either.

I felt my strength and courage draining away. We'd humped our loads for three weeks on rations that wouldn't have kept a cat alive. Only the hope of the submarine, and the elaborate fantasies we'd constructed around it, had given us the endurance to take the next detour, to struggle up the next mountain, to drag ourselves out of a few hours' sleep for yet another dark and bitter start, only ever an hour or two—it seemed—ahead of the enemy.

Now we would have to do it all over again, just to get back to the village we'd started from. And then what?

All we wanted to do was to get out of Greece. We'd signed up for the one op, we'd done it, it was over. They'd promised to get us away afterwards. Now they'd broken their promise.

Maybe they'd never expected us pull it off. Maybe they never thought we would get out alive. But we did, and we had. We should have been able to count on them to keep their side of the bargain. It wasn't fair.

All of us felt it—all of us said it over and over again as we set off that evening yet again after just a few hours' sleep, until the talk petered out in utter exhaustion and we were left with our own whirling thoughts.

Beth—I'd been looking forward to the stack of letters waiting for me in Cairo, and more to come. I'd been looking forward to telling her something—even the smallest hint—of what I'd been up to. My elation at the success of Gorgopotamos—I wouldn't be able to tell her any details, where or when, but at least she would have known that I'd been involved in an op, and that I'd done well.

How would she even know where I was now? She would get my New Year's card in a week's time—but after that, nothing. She would worry. All I wanted now was to get back to Cairo, back into regular communication, until the war was over and I could go back to her.

It was too dangerous to go back the way we'd come. The Italians from Parga, just north of the rendezvous point, were out looking for us. We had to cut away to the north.

The weather broke. It was raining and windy and cold as blazes.

Up in the middle of the night to travel after a few hours of sleep, slipping down mountain paths in the dark, struggling to manage the loads on our backs. Eating badly and never enough.

We got a bit of a respite at Romanon monastery for a day or so, and Denys managed to put the hard word on the abbot to feed us properly. Apart from that it was pure misery and we took it out on each other.

It was early January when we got back to Megalochari.

Themis came out with the villagers in bucketing rain and hail to meet us. He could see what state we were in, and quickly got us into a cottage. We stripped to our underwear and collapsed. Some kind person took the heap of wet, stinking clothes away to dry.

'There's someone here who wants to see you,' Themis told us.

'We don't want to see anyone,' I said. 'Just get us something to eat, will you? And then leave us alone.'

Someone opened the door and came in. I looked up. It was Bill Jordan, the Kiwi journalist and would-be human torpedo whom we'd last seen at Kibrit.

'What on earth are you doing here, you old bastard?' said Arthur. We were too knackered to get to our feet to greet him.

'Who's this taking my name in vain?' said Bill. 'You don't seem to have had a shave since you left Cairo. Or a wash, for that matter. And you should be ashamed, the state your clothes and boots are in. I'll have to have a word to your commanding officer about that.'

'How did you get here?' said Arthur.

'Same way as you. I dropped in. Not long before Christmas.'

'That makes you the unlucky thirteenth,' said Nat. 'But you look a bit knocked around.' Bill had broken his arm and some ribs when he landed.

'Bill,' I said. 'Go and see what's holding Themis up. He's supposed to be getting us something to eat.'

'Nothing doing here,' said Bill. 'No food at all. Oh, except for some bully beef that came in my drop.'

'Bully beef?' we all shouted. 'Wonderful!'

'You've got to be joking,' said Bill. 'What's happened to you?'

'You don't want to know, Bill,' I said. 'Just go and fetch the bully, will you?'

Bill and Themis came back together. We got one tin of bully each. It was delicious. But one tin wasn't enough.

Bill also produced a thick envelope—instructions for Eddie from Cairo. Reluctantly, Eddie disappeared to study the new plans. We wondered what they would mean for us.

Bill explained that the Firm had sent him to take charge of the signals. They'd got the wind up because they hadn't been hearing from us. He was to get regular communications up and running.

'You won't believe this, boys,' said Bill, 'but the charging engine Cairo gave me was all rusted up. And they didn't pack it properly, either. It got smashed up when it landed.'

'Of course we'll believe it,' said Nat. 'We'd be surprised if they didn't make a balls-up of everything.'

'Now the wireless has broken down because the battery in the charging engine's flat,' said Bill. 'We sent it over to a mechanic in another village. He reckoned he could fix it. A woman carried it here on her back.'

'Oh, yes,' said Denys. '"It's too heavy for a mule—get a woman to carry it."'

'That's exactly what the husband said. This woman looked half-starved. And it was the heaviest engine of the lot, with the cast-iron casing. I couldn't believe it.'

'I bet they didn't fix it, either,' I said.

After Captain Myridakis's desperate but successful efforts to keep us away from the enemy all the way to the coast and back, we were dismayed to hear from Bill that we'd landed in a hornet's nest. The Italians were after Zervas. While we were away, they had moved against Skoulikaria village, across the Valtos Mountain west of Megalochari, and then towards Megalochari itself. Then suddenly, while Zervas was at Skoulikaria for a flanking strike, they had checked their advance. No one knew why. But from now on our safety, it seemed, would be intextricably entangled with Zervas's success in keeping the enemy at bay.

To make things worse than they already were, it snowed during the night. The cold slid gleefully under our greatcoats next morning as we walked to the officers' meeting Eddie had called at his billet, wondering what arrangements Cairo had thought up for us now.

Chris wasn't there—he was away touring with Zervas—but everyone else was, all anxious to find out what was happening.

'I'm delighted to convey Mr Churchill's warmest congratulations to all of you,' Eddie began. 'They are extremely pleased with the outcome of the mission.'

'So they should be,' said Denys.

'That's the good news,' said Eddie. 'The bad news is that policy towards the *andartes* seems to have changed.'

'Oh yes?' said Denys. 'That sounds ominous. So was the non-appearance of the submarine a change in policy too?'

'Partly,' said Eddie. 'From what I can read between the lines. But it was also a practical decision.'

'That's right,' Bill broke in. 'The C-in-C had just lost a submarine on a similar mission. They couldn't risk losing another one.'

Instead, Cairo had had a bright idea. A new British mission would build the *andartes* into what would effectively be an internal army in Greece, able to undertake large-scale operations against the occupying forces. Eddie would be in command. Bill Jordan was the first of many British personnel to be dropped in as liaison officers between the *andartes* and Cairo, answering to Eddie as commander in the field.

Six Greek army officers in Athens—the so-called Six Colonels—would lead the *andartes* remotely, far away from the mountains where the resistance groups operated. Chris was to move to Athens to be Eddie's liaison officer with them. Everyone would be under the Anglo-Greek Committee, the executive arm of the Greek government in exile, which had been based in Cairo since the beginning of the German occupation.

'What about us?' said Denys. 'How are they going to get us away?' We were all hanging on the answer.

'Well, that's the thing,' said Eddie. 'They've asked us all to stay on. To work with the new mission.'

'What?' said Denys. 'There's no way I'm going to stay here. We volunteered for one operation. Now it's over, we're going home.' There was an angry chorus of agreement.

'Yes, well, they're very pleased about the mission,' said Eddie.

'Too pleased,' I said.

'Perhaps,' said Eddie. 'Now what I want to know is this—do any of you have any inclination to stay on? If so, I want to hear from you in the next day or so. For the rest, I'll try my best to get you off. I know you were all volunteers, and I don't want any man to remain here against his will.'

'What have you got in mind?' asked Denys.

'A seaplane,' replied Eddie. 'I'll signal Cairo with that suggestion as soon as we can get the gear up and running. We'll talk to Captain Myridakis about a suitable rendezvous.'

For the first time, our capacity to communicate with Cairo coincided directly with my own interests. I determined to get one of the generators going so that we could send the signal. I went off to find Len, but first I had to get permission from Bill to visit the signallers' cottage. He'd put his foot down about discipline. Apart from the signals staff, only Eddie and Chris were allowed in—but I got a special dispensation because I was good at fixing things.

It was good but strange to see Len again after our farewell only a few weeks before. Mike Chittis was there too. Together we looked at the engines.

'That Greek engineer really buggered this one up,' said Len. 'And then it got a bang when his wife collapsed under the weight.'

'Can't have done it any good,' I said.

We were working companionably on one of the Chore Horse generators when I got a summons to see Eddie in the cottage where he was billeted.

'Tom, I've just had John in,' Eddie said as soon as I walked in. 'I had something to discuss with him that affects you as well.'

'What's that, sir?' I asked.

'John's role as 2IC on our abortive trek didn't contribute much,' Eddie replied. 'He doesn't seem to command the respect of the men.'

'I believe that's true, sir, unfortunately. He got off on the wrong foot before he even got here. Themis says he was too scared to jump when the rest of us did. That's why they shifted the command to Themis next time around. John doesn't seem to have been able to put that behind him.'

'On the other hand, you inspire confidence in the men,' said Eddie. 'You did it at Gorgopotamos. It wasn't just your technical achievement—although I suspect very few engineers in the British army could have done what you did—it was the way you stayed cool and in control. And on the trek—I noticed how you kept everyone going. I think your own stamina and bravery encouraged them.'

I was embarrassed. I don't suppose anyone finds personal praise particularly easy to hear.

'Thank you, sir.'

'I have told John that I'm demoting him to captain, and promoting you to major,' Eddie went on.

'How did he take that, sir? If you don't mind me asking.'

'He took it well,' said Eddie. 'So you'd better go away and put up another pip.'

'If you think it will help things.'

'I think it will. Congratulations, Tom. This will make you third in command. And another appointment you should know about—Themis is now my aide-de-camp.'

'I'm delighted to hear that,' I said. 'From what I've seen of Themis, I'm sure he will be absolutely responsible and completely reliable.'

'Oh, and Tom,' Eddie said as I went to leave, 'I'm moving my HQ to Skoulikaria village.'

'Where the Italians attacked Zervas?'

'Unfortunately, yes. But we need to join Zervas. I've sent a message to Chris, telling him to meet me there, too. I'm leaving you in charge here. Nat will go with me, and Khouri.'

I went back to the signallers' hut and told Len and Mike my news. They both shook my hand and slapped me on the back.

'You deserve it,' said Len. 'Major Tom.'

After some days' work, we managed to get one of the generators going. Bill finally got through to Cairo, to everyone's great excitement. Now surely we would get confirmation of where and when the flying boat would pick us up. But we heard nothing.

We were relieved when a message came from Eddie to bring the W/T—our wireless transmitter equipment—to his new HQ in Skoulikaria. Bill and Len came with us, leaving Doug and Themis at Megalochari.

We trailed up and over Valtos Mountain with our mules through fifteen inches of snow, the cold and wet striking through our decrepit boots. Coming down we were soon among fir trees, every branch bowed under a burden it was keen to offload onto any unsuspecting person who might brush past. The village, when we reached it, was also deeply encumbered with snow.

The signals team began working long hours, composing and coding signals to Cairo and decoding signals from Cairo to us. Meanwhile, Bill and I started work on the generators. I put a new cylinder head gasket into one, which got it going again. And we finally identified the problem with the second—a warped commutator. Naturally there was no metal-working lathe available—all we had was emery paper. But with the motor running, I thought that might do the trick. I was right. At last I got the engine giving a charge.

EDES now had a long-range wireless transmitter of their own as well, a massive one. Colonel Mimis Bardopoulos, an important associate of Zervas and co-worker with Prometheus, had lugged it all the way from Athens and stayed on to help us.

Nat had volunteered to stay in Greece. His fluent Greek would make him useful to Eddie, who accepted his offer gratefully.

John Cook also volunteered, but as he had no Greek there was no suitable job for him. He was knocked back.

The others, however, had nothing much to do. Eddie couldn't assign them to anything long-term, as no one knew when we might be evacuated. A lot of energy seemed to be going into arrangements for the purchase of a pig, Denys being the prime mover in the venture.

'Do you know what I just heard?' said Arthur as he dealt the cards one evening.

'What?'

'Gorgopotamos. It's being repaired. How do you feel about that, Tom?'

'What's today?' I said. 'January 13. So about six weeks. That's what I thought. Although Barba Niko was a bit more optimistic.'

'Apparently they're repairing it with wood,' said Arthur. 'Wooden trestles.'

'Really?' I said. 'They'll have to carry a lot of weight. A lot of movement, too, with all those trains coming and going. I hope they collapse.'

'Pity we couldn't do Asopos, too,' said Arthur. 'Now that would be a repair job.'

'Too hard,' I said.

'Yes,' said Arthur. 'But if you could bring it off ...'

For a week we heard nothing from Eddie—no word about his meetings with Zervas and Chris. Finally he arrived back on a mule, too sick to walk. He had been soaked through by pouring rain. Even once he was dry he was still shivering. Nevertheless he insisted on filling us in.

Cairo had roundly rejected the seaplane idea. Impracticable, they said. Not exactly the news we wanted to hear. And Eddie asked us to reconsider whether we would stay in Greece to help with the new mission. Given the circumstances, we were under stronger pressure to agree.

Back at our billet that night, we talked over the renewed offer.

'You speak Greek, Denys,' said Inder. 'Would you think of staying?'

'Not on your life,' said Denys. 'The minute I can get out of Greece I will. Cairo deceived us. I refuse to volunteer for anything else.'

'I want to get out too,' said Inder. 'What about you, Arthur?'

'I'm in two minds, actually,' he said. 'Might be a good opportunity.'

'For what? You won't find those Greek girls an easy lay,' said Denys. 'Not the ones you meet in the villages.'

Arthur was offended. 'I'm going to sleep,' he said. 'You bastards can do as you like. And no doubt you will.' Off he went to enjoy his spring bed.

At least things were proceeding satisfactorily with the purchase of the pig. Bill and the signallers were in on it now and so was I. We did our research carefully and selected our investment with all the science at our disposal. A hundred thousand drachmas down, the balance to be paid off later. We'd commandeered some white flour from a parachute drop, and Denys had arranged for the old lady we were staying with to make up enough dough for a couple of big loaves.

We were standing around watching as our pig gasped out its final moments, and looking forward to a big blowout meal, when Themis appeared. He had been with Eddie. He didn't quite seem to share our enthusiasm for the pig.

'Eddie's really ill,' he said. 'His temperature's 105.'

'Well, serves him right,' said Denys. 'Remember when we were at Romanon monastery on the way back, and it was raining like blazes? Captain Myridakis asked if we'd like to stay and rest for another day, and Eddie said no, we'd keep going. "We can take it," he said. It's an act of God, this illness.'

Themis turned away. If he was too worried to react to Denys's callousness, we knew it must be serious.

Eddie was in a house on the far side of the village. Dr Theophanis Kosmas, the local doctor, came to examine him and said he had pneumonia. The doctor had no medicines for it, and neither did we—all we had was aspirin and quinine. But as soon as Zervas heard about Eddie's condition, he sent Dr Papachristou from Megalochari to help.

Dr Papachristou confirmed bronchial pneumonia. Eddie mustn't be moved. His condition was critical.

Just after Dr Papachristou had delivered his verdict, more bad news arrived. The Italians had renewed their drive against Skoulikaria. Their fires had been sighted four hours away, and they were heading in our direction.

Suddenly we were in a flat spin. Bill was expecting a new wireless operator, Stan Smith, to drop. We couldn't let him fall straight into the hands of the Italians. Bill insisted that he and Len should stay in Skoulikaria until they could warn Cairo to hold off on the drop. Bill sent Doug off with one set of wireless equipment, which he was to hide outside the village.

Would the Italians move up in the dark? That was the big question. Unlikely, we thought. First thing next morning would be time enough. We settled down for the night.

We awakened some hours later to find Themis and Mimis frantically searching around us as we lay on the floor. The Italians had crept up under cover of darkness. They were in the outskirts of the village already. We had nearly been caught napping.

Mimis grabbed a tent and a couple of pieces of wood—the makings of a makeshift stretcher. Then he and Themis cleared out at a run. They were going to get Eddie away.

ELEVEN

It was Eddie's only hope. The Italians were hardly likely to leave him undisturbed. They might move him—that was the best we could hope for. If they did, it would probably kill him. More likely, they would shoot him on the spot.

Eddie knew the Italians were coming. He had his commando knife ready. If we left him behind, he was going to kill himself before the Italians could get him. Themis tried to take the knife away from him—gently—but Eddie wasn't having any of it. How he thought he would use it in his weakened state I had no idea. His suicide pill would have given him an easier way out— but perhaps he had lost it on the way to the coast.

Mimis and Themis hoisted Eddie's stretcher onto a donkey. Yannis and Panayiotis, the two Cypriots, helped to steady the sick man between them and they set off into the darkness as fast as they safely could, Dr Papachristou bringing up the rear.

The villagers were off, too. They'd already hidden their most precious belongings—as had we. As the convoys departed, the panniers of the mules heavily laden, hens squawked and sleepy little boys and girls trailed behind.

By now there was barely a mule to be found. Denys could only rustle up two, and one of those was a dud. We took off at speed after Themis and the others, managing to get hold of another mule en route.

By some miracle, Eddie survived the journey. Themis stowed him away in a warm and comfortable house well off the beaten track, and a runner arrived from Zervas with M&B tablets.

We were on the road again the next day. We passed group after group of *andartes*, all heading in the opposite direction, towards Skoulikaria. There was going to be one hell of a battle. We were itching to join in—but apparently we were too precious, and no one had any time to stop and tell us what was going on.

When we reached Mesopyrgo, our host from last time was waiting for us.

'The jackpot house, remember?' said Denys.

'How could we forget?' said Arthur. 'Good food and sheets on the beds.'

'And bonzer brown bread,' said Denys.

'You're learning, Denys,' said Arthur. 'You'll be a colonial yourself before you know it.'

How our circumstances had changed since that last visit. The grim news came that the Italians had torched Skoulikaria in reprisal for harbouring the two HQs, Zervas's and ours. It was hard to imagine flames leaping from the comfortable houses we'd slept in just a couple of days before, the villagers' homely furniture still inside.

'Just think what would have happened to Eddie if we'd left him there,' I said. 'Thank God Themis insisted on moving him.'

'And the villagers,' said Arthur. 'There'll be no houses for them to come back to. They'll be refugees.'

'And it's winter,' said Inder. 'We know they've got food in that cache in the forest, but what about shelter from the snow? What about the children and the babies?'

'The *andartes* will have to look after them,' said Denys.

'Yes,' said Inder, 'but how will they look after little children? They can't keep them on the move all the time.'

'People from other villages will surely take them in,' said Denys. 'The Greeks are extraordinarily hospitable when people are in trouble. They'd give their right arm to help them.'

'Yes, but they're very isolated around here,' said Arthur. 'The people from the next village over are like foreigners to them. Remember the lady Chris met on his way to find Zervas? He told her he came from the next village and she swallowed it.'

Suddenly Denys jumped up and swore. Then it hit me too— the pig! We'd left our half stowed in the roof of our billet in Skoulikaria.

'Roast pork,' said Arthur. 'Barbecued pork!' And suddenly we were all whooping with laughter, tears streaming down our faces, our legs collapsing under us. A wake for the unfortunate pig, destined to undergo its final apotheosis untasted.

The *andartes* hadn't been able to protect the town, but they'd made the Italians scarper. There were reports of five hundred casualties, killed and wounded. Later we learnt to be suspicious of figures like this, which could be wildly inflated. But at the time, we had no way of knowing what was—or might be—true.

Eddie turned the corner. He'd survived the threat of the Italian drive, the difficult move, the days in isolation, and was on the mend. Although he was still very weak, we decided it was time for a small celebration in the village pub. Ouzo all round, on us. The local men could always be counted on to lend their support to a celebration.

Soon enough, Eddie was issuing orders again. He summoned Arthur to his room. Some time later Arthur arrived back, full of importance. He had been appointed officer in charge of stores. He had volunteered to stay on in Greece—not much of a surprise to any of us.

The rest of us were instructed to prepare for regular drops of supplies. We arranged a dropping ground above the village and were put on collection duty—everyone but Arthur.

This was a junior NCO's job, nothing more, and I hated it. Roused from sleep by a message from the signallers, racing up to the dropping ground through the snow in the dark, trying to get the fires lit before the Liberator came over. If we were lucky, we would be in time and the canisters would come down. They might land right on top of the fires; they might land a mile away. If we missed the plane's first pass, we might catch it on the second. Often we didn't get sufficient notice of the drops, and we wouldn't get the fires lit in time. I took to sleeping in a thatched cottage full of goats, nearer to the dropping ground.

If the stores fell close we could collect them straight away, working through the small hours. If they didn't, we might have to hunt all day, trying to get to them before someone else did. One night, fifty-one pairs of boots ended up in the river.

It certainly didn't make us more enthusiastic about staying in Greece. All we wanted was to resume what now seemed like normal life back in our units. But still no one had proposed a constructive plan to get us out. If there'd been a real job on offer in Greece, it might have been a different story entirely. I knew that, and I imagined others felt the same.

After we had been in Mesopyrgo about ten days, General Zervas came to see us. He invited us to dinner with his officers, and treated us to lamb and potatoes cooked with mountain herbs. I watched to see how he would manage his beard as he ate. We had all discovered the problem of stale food caught in our beards.

'So,' he said affably to me as the wine was poured, with Denys translating. 'You've had a frustrating trip to the coast and back again. What now?'

'Arthur has taken up the offer to stay,' I said, 'and you probably know that Nat has been sent to Gardiki to be liaison officer for Aris. The rest of us are still hoping to be taken off.'

'*Po, po, po,*' he said. 'That won't be easy.'

'If we had some worthwhile work to do,' said Denys, 'it might be different. At the moment we feel as though we're marking time.'

'Of course there is a lot of marking time in war,' he said. 'Waiting for the mines to be cleared. Waiting for the order to attack.'

'Yes,' I said. 'But at least those are proper jobs. For officers, I mean.'

'We're seeing plenty of action with the Italians,' Zervas told us. 'And we have many army officers with a depth of experience in regular warfare. But we try to avoid being drawn into pitched battles. It's not what guerrilla fighters are best at.'

'No,' said Denys. 'You'll be going for the unexpected attack and the quick getaway.'

'Like an ambush?' I asked.

'Exactly,' Zervas replied. 'We've done scores of them. You get an Italian convoy that covers the same route every day at the same time. You choose a good spot—a narrow defile, for example, with a river on one side and cliffs on the other, just past a bridge. You lay the mines the day before—you would enjoy that, Tom—and explosives under the bridge. Saw halfway through the telephone poles so they can be pulled down quickly. The convoy comes along. A few big explosions ahead and behind, and they're stuck like rats in a trap. You're there waiting with the machine guns trained on the spot. You lob in some hand grenades and a whole lot of rocks, and follow in to finish them off. Road blocks to deal with reinforcements.'

'Knowing the area well gives you a big advantage, then,' I said.

'Of course,' said Zervas. 'You can get good intelligence quickly, and you have local support for your men. A highly mobile striking force and good communications—that's what you need. And that's what we have.' He emptied his glass and reached for the bottle.

Now that we had crossed the mountains from east to west, I could see how the terrain would lend itself to the kind of fighting Zervas was describing. In fact, the mountains had to be the guerrillas' greatest asset, especially because the Italians weren't trained or equipped for them. At that point there were no elite German mountain troops to worry about.

As the evening wore on, talk turned to other things. Whisky flowed freely and the General started to sing. After a few minutes, everyone joined in. Not all of us were as tuneful as Zervas.

Each song seemed to have slow verses and a fast chorus. It wasn't long before a few *andartes* were dancing.

'What are these songs?' I asked Denys. They didn't sound like modern popular songs.

'*Kleftika tragoudia*,' he said. 'Klephtic ballads. I don't know much about them but Chris might.' Chris was away on his mission to Athens, meeting with the 'Six Colonels' and the *politikos* who controlled ELAS.

I sat transfixed, watching the Greeks dance. Good dancing requires good music, and they had it down to a fine art. The slow verses kept you on tenterhooks. Then, suddenly, they would ratchet up the pace until everyone was singing at full speed, and more and more dancers joined the line. Soon they were skipping the slow verses and singing the choruses over and over again.

They know how to enjoy themselves here, I thought. They know how to let go. And, I suddenly realised, I loved it.

The next day Eddie and Themis joined us in Mesopyrgo for an officers' meeting. Eddie was often away, looking after his new wider responsibilities; as his ADC, Themis naturally went with him.

There had been reprisals for Gorgopotamos. The Italians had picked up seventeen people, mostly from Ypati village, to the north-west of the demolished bridge. They had taken them down to the viaduct and shot them.

'Who?' asked Arthur quickly.

'I'm afraid one of them was our schoolmaster, Kostas Pistolis—the one who came to the cave,' said Eddie. 'By the sound of things, the rest were just pulled out at random.'

'I thought Cairo were going to drop pamphlets and tell them it was us,' said Arthur.

'Yes, well, apparently that never happened,' said Eddie.

'Why bloody not?' I asked.

'We have no idea,' said Eddie. 'But Chris swears he's going to find out. No doubt some operational reason.'

Skoulikaria burnt. Reprisals for Gorgopotamos. Megalochari copped it too, a little later. We walked away each time, but the villagers were helpless targets. You had to ask yourself if it was all worth it.

Not long afterwards a new member of staff arrived from Chris: Thomas Vinson. An escapee from a German prison camp, he had been living with a Greek family in Gardiki. Chris had met up with him in January and insisted he join the mission. He came to me as a cook, but spent half his time very much the worse for ouzo.

I was working on the generators one afternoon a couple of weeks later when the door swung open unexpectedly—and it was Chris himself. He grabbed a stool and sat down. He looked rather strange—black eyebrows, black hair, with red growth showing at the roots. It didn't suit him, and it certainly didn't make him look Greek—nothing could.

'I suppose you've heard about Megalochari?' I said immediately.

'Yes,' he replied. 'I was very sorry to hear it.'

'I've been thinking about a little family there,' I told him. 'I took a photo of them in December, before we left for the coast.' I trusted Chris instinctively—if it had been Denys, say, or even Arthur, I would have kept my mouth shut. 'Father, mother— she didn't look much more than a baby herself—a little girl, the oldest, and two younger boys. The children were barefoot. Mum and Dad had those country shoes. You know, the ones that look like boats? They had a little thatched cottage, not much to look at. A lovely family, so friendly and hospitable. I wonder what will happen to them now.'

'Eddie and I have been talking about that,' said Chris. 'Now that more of us are staying, we think we'll be able to provide some compensation for refugees from the villages. Anyone who's been affected by reprisals.'

'It's the least we can do,' I said. 'Dr Papachristou—he's one. He looked after Eddie when he was sick, and his house was burnt down. How soon could we get it going?'

'I don't know yet,' he said. 'It'll have to be sorted out with Cairo.'

Chris had quite a story to tell. A courier, Thanasis, had accompanied him to Athens, courtesy of Zervas, and Aris had given him a pass asking all EAM/ELAS members to look after him. He'd been disguised as an operator on the black market with cigarettes and razor blades to sell.

'We decided to get a bus to Athens,' Chris told me. 'Thanasis said the enemy never stopped the buses. But we were out of luck.'

'Germans or Italians?'

'Germans, with an interpreter. They seemed more suspicious of two Italian soldiers than anyone else, but they checked everyone's papers.'

'What did you do?'

'Thanasis got into an argument with one of the Germans via the interpreter,' said Chris. 'Everyone else joined in—they must've realised I needed help. I slipped past while it was going on.'

'You were lucky.'

'The passengers must've thought I was an escaped British POW,' said Chris. 'There are still lots around. When we got to Omonia Square in Athens, the driver offered to put me up— under his breath, of course.'

'Nice of him,' I said.

'Yes, but Thanasis and I had other arrangements, so I said no.'

Chris had had one hell of a time in Athens. He had met with Prometheus and with EAM, but the Six Colonels hadn't shown. Then the Italians had trapped one of the agents working with Prometheus—maybe he had been betrayed, or maybe they'd traced his wireless—and killed him in a gunfight. Next the Germans had caught Prometheus in the middle of a transmission. And Prometheus knew Chris's location.

Chris had been sitting tight, expecting the Germans to knock at his door any minute. But when the knock came, it was for his second meeting with the EAM leadership.

'I suggested that they should come out to the mountains and lead from there,' Chris said. 'They didn't seem to take it seriously, although one of them, Tzimas, said he would come and have a look. Anyway, it was a useful meeting. But when it was over I had to admit to my situation. My contacts in Athens were all gone, either dead or captured. In fact they'd warned me at our previous meeting that I was courting disaster by being in Athens.

'One interesting thing came out of our meeting, although I didn't realise it at the time. Tzimas made some comment that our agents were amateurs compared to EAM. They'd all been outlaws for years and knew how to play the game.'

'What do you think he meant?'

'He can only have meant that they were all members of the Communist Party, the KKE. It was outlawed under Metaxas in 1936. Of course I already knew that Aris was.'

'Did you? How?'

'Well, while you people were on your way back from the coast, Aris and Zervas were sniping at one another and I managed to get them together for a conference. I thought there was some chance that they might agree to joint action, but in fact we got stuck because Zervas said Aris was a communist and Aris said Zervas was a potential fascist dictator. Later, Aris told me he'd been a member of the Communist Party for twenty-two years. So that part was true.'

'You said to me once that you thought Aris and Zervas were more alike than different.'

'I remember,' said Chris. 'We were at that café at Gardiki, sitting in the sun. I still think they're very similar, in many ways. They're both against the king, they're both natural leaders. Where they're different is in their attitude to us.'

'I've noticed Zervas is very eager to please,' I said. 'And Aris couldn't care less.'

'I wouldn't put it quite like that,' said Chris. 'I've seen a fair bit of Aris now. What I would say is that his agenda is entirely different from ours. He's in for the long haul—Zervas isn't. This chapter will be over for Zervas when the war finishes. He'll move on to something else. Although if he does well, it'll give him a leg-up. For Aris, things will be only just beginning.'

'So do you think Zervas is a potential dictator?'

'It's hard to say how someone might end up. I'm not sure anyone would've predicted that Metaxas would become a dictator, either.'

In the end, it was only thanks to EAM that Chris got away safely from Athens. They gave him an identity card belonging to someone his age who had just died—they just changed the photo.

'Before I left,' Chris said, 'I heard that the Germans had surrendered at Stalingrad.'

'Yes, we heard too,' I said. 'I can't help feeling hopeful that everything might be over before too long.' If Cairo were planning to leave us dangling indefinitely, the end of the war couldn't come too soon.

I remembered that I had something to ask him. 'Those songs that Zervas sings. You know, the ones they all dance to. Denys says they're called klephtic ballads. Said you might know more about them.'

'I know a bit,' he said. 'The Klephts were from the Epiros region. When the Turks conquered Constantinople, the Klephts took themselves off to the mountains and stayed there for a few hundred years, opposing the Turkish occupation. Went on doing it until liberation.'

'When was that? The New Zealand curriculum wasn't big on Greek history.'

'It didn't come to Epiros until 1832. That's what Lord Byron was all about. He came to Greece in 1823 to try to spearhead a campaign against the Turks—representing interests in Europe, of course. He died a few months later, but his death really put the seal on it. Everyone decided it would be a grand romantic gesture to liberate Greece.'

'So those Klephts were a bit like our *andartes* now?'

'I suppose so. Part brigand, like old Karalivanos, part guerrilla fighter. But they left some great songs. One's about a group of women who were cut off by the Turks and threw their children off the cliff rather than let the Turks get them.'

'Just the children?' I asked.

'No. After the children were gone, the women started dancing, and at the end of every chorus the one on the end threw herself over.'

Resistance at any cost. And now the Italians had put a price on Zervas's head: 350 million drachmas, or 100 million for information leading to his capture. What cost resistance now, I couldn't help but wonder.

At the beginning of March, Eddie called all the officers together. It had been over two months since the submarine had failed to come, and we were impatient for news.

'What I am going to tell you probably won't please many of you,' he said. 'You have now been ordered to stay in Greece for an indefinite number of months.'

'Doing what, sir?' I asked.

'Organising supplies and sabotage,' he replied.

'That is distasteful to a number of us,' I said. 'As you know. I think we've made it pretty clear that we are not happy that our voluntary service has become compulsory. I don't speak for Arthur, of course, or Nat, or the others who always knew they would be staying.'

'I appreciate your position,' said Eddie. 'And I have represented it to Cairo in the strongest terms. At this point I'm afraid I cannot do anything more.'

'We're always hungry, sir,' said Inder. 'The food is bad and there's not enough. We've been able to rest up a bit, it's true, but it's hardly good for your health trying to sleep in your greatcoat by the signal fires, frozen stiff half the time, never knowing whether the Lib will be over or not.'

'All I can say is that I'll keep your position under consideration,' Eddie replied. 'Now that Chris is back from Athens, things should be clearer. We certainly won't be under the direction of the Six Colonels, so that part of Cairo's plan will have to be amended. And another piece of news, which you may or may not have heard: three men dropped onto Mount Olympus just over a month ago. Lieutenant-Colonel Rufus Sheppard, with a Greek officer and W/T operator. I'm sorry to say the W/T operator was killed in the jump.'

'I'm not surprised,' said Denys. 'It could easily have been me, or Bill here, when we jumped.'

'Yes, most unfortunate,' said Eddie. 'And the Greek officer broke his leg. It was a leg he'd already damaged, so he's been out of action too.'

'Mount Olympus,' said Denys. 'That's well into ELAS territory.'

'Yes, that's correct. Lieutenant-Colonel Sheppard will be working with ELAS there.'

'I hope his Greek is good,' muttered Denys. 'He'll want it to be.'

Eddie continued. 'Another officer, Lieutenant-Colonel Nicholas Hammond, was dropped onto Mount Kissavos last month for liaison duties.'

'We're growing,' I said. 'It's not our little Harling party anymore.'

'No, that's right. Harling is over,' said Eddie. 'From now on, the operation is "Keelrow".'

Eddie also had news of events on a larger canvas. ELAS had struck suddenly and unexpectedly against a rival resistance group, a group led by one Colonel Sarafis, and were holding Sarafis and his officers captive. Sarafis was a republican who in 1935 had played an important part in an anti-royalist revolution. He had come to visit Eddie a month before to discuss the cooperation of his independent band with Zervas and to ask for a share of the British supplies, which everyone seemed to have heard about. But tensions between ELAS and Sarafis's group had since flared. When twenty-five ELAS *andartes* who had fought bravely at Gorgopotamos deserted to a group allied with Sarafis, ELAS retaliated swiftly: four men identified as 'leaders' of the deserters were put on trial and executed. Of the rest, those who refused to join ELAS were disarmed by force and sent home to their villages.

None of us was sure what to make of the news. We still didn't know who ELAS really were. Zervas maintained that they were led by communists, but Eddie and Chris were both suspicious of this claim. ELAS had, after all, helped Chris to escape from Athens. Yet it seemed clear that ELAS's leaders were prepared to go to extreme lengths to cement their position in the mountains. Would Zervas be their next target? And could the British mission trust them enough to cooperate with them?

The last day or two of Eddie's visit brought better news: we had all been assigned as liaison officers to local resistance groups in different areas of Greece. I was off to Epiros in the north-west to work with Zervas.

My brief was to recce all potential sapper targets west of the Pindos, from the Albanian border to the Gulf of Patras, for a new set of ops. We would leave the next day, with Captain Myridakis as an escort.

Now our group was really breaking up. Chris would become Eddie's full-time 2IC. Inder was assigned to north-west Thessaly, and John to Albania to liaise with the resistance there. Nat had already gone to Roumeli and Arthur would follow to liaise with Aris. Lieutenant-Colonel Sheppard, when he reached us, would come under Eddie's command, and Lieutenant-Colonel Hammond would go to Macedonia. Denys would try to intercept a supply drop planned for Sarafis.

I didn't know what was ahead of me in Epiros, but I knew things could be difficult. Both Zervas and ELAS had a presence on the ground there; given the situation with Sarafis, things could be delicate. But another full-scale sabotage operation—that was exciting. At last, I had a reason for staying in Greece.

TWELVE

The village of Vourgareli, home to EDES HQ, scrambled up a slope in the southern foothills of the Jumerka mountains. Evening had already fallen when Captain Myridakis and I arrived at the house of the local bishop, where the EDES area commander and leader of their 3/40 regiment, Georgios Agoros, was staying with his family. Inder and Thomas Vinson were with us.

'*Kalos orisate sto spiti mou, Michali,*' said Agoros to Captain Myridakis. Welcome to my house. Under his cap, he had thick, crinkly hair. '*Kalos orisate,* Captain Tom.' He introduced his wife Voula and his sister Toula.

There was a vibrancy and directness in Voula's look that was most attractive. She repeated her husband's welcome.

'*Kalos orisate,*' echoed Toula, coming forward more shyly. Still very young, perhaps fifteen or so, she was already striking. Both Voula and Toula had dark hair. Toula, like her brother, had blue-green eyes.

Bill Jordan was already comfortably ensconced at the table. He was staying at the village doctor's house, but had come over to join us for a real English tea—an unheard of refinement. None of the Agoros family spoke any English, but we managed to keep up a conversation until nearly 1 am.

When I woke the next morning, I went straight to the window. Terraced plots stretched below. To the east were mountains. In spite of my complaints, I was beginning to love those Greek mountains, especially when the morning sun first reached them and the fir trees on the nearer slopes sprang suddenly into solid relief.

Everywhere you went in Vourgareli, you could hear water. It gushed into stone bowls at the water fountains or *vrisi* and bubbled along beside the steep paths as I walked to the large square for a haircut and beard trim. I was starting to feel civilised again.

Now our sapper work began—clambering among rocks and examining bad corners and bridges, looking for promising targets. We were getting ready for a big operation but we didn't yet know what it would be or when it would happen. I met with Zervas's area commander, Major Konstantinides, and eight of his men, who would help with our reconnaissance work. We shared the Greek officers' mess—finally, some decent food. And amid the hard work came the news that Arthur, Denys and I had all been awarded the MC for our efforts at Gorgopotamos.

Eddie must have put all three of us up for decoration in the end, rather than singling just one of us out. I was glad. After all, without the efforts of each of us, the operation wouldn't have come off.

We set up our HQ at Romanon monastery, sleeping seven to a single room with all our kit, and eating eleven to the same room. We had stopped briefly at this monastery on the way to the coast; it was here, according to Denys, that Eddie had brought his pneumonia on himself by declining to rest. That time, we had been so weakened by hunger and fatigue that we'd had little interest in our surroundings. Now I could admire the old church, the muted colours of its weather-worn fresco above the door and the high belfry tower leading the eye upward to the mountains across the valley. Stone buildings below the pleasant refectory housed workrooms for the monks, and the usual stone *vrisi* provided our water.

The monastery must once have been defensible—the narrow arrow slit in the deep stone wall was evidence of that. It wouldn't be too long before we had to give some very serious thought to its defence ourselves.

Following Bill Jordan and the other new arrivals Eddie had told us about—Rufus Sheppard and Nicholas Hammond—other new liaison officers dropped in. John Cook from the Harling party was with us now, and we were expecting a party of British officers and a signaller to drop soon. John would escort them to Albania and then return. Eddie was due to pay us a visit, too.

Among the recent arrivals was my new assistant, Major 'Mick the Miller' (real name Guy) Micklethwait. He was already at Romanon when we arrived. He looked to be in his thirties, closer to my age than many of the others—a man with a strong chin (when you could see it), dark hair and eyes, and one eyebrow perpetually cocked. From the North Somerset Yeomanry, he'd seen service in Ethiopia in 1941 and had a brother who was a POW. I liked him immediately, and we quickly came to a mutually satisfactory division of duties. He was to handle all the supply and liaison work to the *andartes*, while I would look after the sapper work we had underway for future ops. I knew supply would be a highly contentious issue, owing to the rivalries between ELAS and EDES, and I wanted to keep out of it if I could, so as to give as much attention as possible to the sabotage preparations.

One day, after we had been at the monastery for not much more than a week, Mick brought two of the ELAS *andartes*, Georgiades and Anagnostakis, up to our workroom in the square, solid building where we had established our HQ. They had asked to speak to me, he explained, on behalf of their comrades.

In a friendly fashion, Georgiades and Anagnostakis explained that they didn't want any EDES *andartes* in the area. ELAS had organised in the district first and they didn't want to compete with EDES for recruits. It was exactly the sort of problem I'd anticipated, and the reason I'd put Mick in charge of relations with the *andartes*. I had hoped he would be able to handle this kind of situation by himself. After only a few weeks in the country, that was probably too much to expect—but Georgiades and Anagnostakis seemed quite agreeable, and after a brief chat Mick set off to ELAS HQ to discuss things with Georgiades's and Anagnostakis' superiors while they remained behind.

I was tracing plans for the demolitions a few days later when a great racket broke out. The signallers, who had been busy decoding, rushed to the gate with us to see what was happening.

Outside, ELAS forces had surrounded the monastery—perhaps as many as two hundred.

When they saw us appear, Georgiades and Anagnostakis detached themselves from a knot of men and came forward. Their demeanour was no longer relaxed.

'Our demands are simple,' said Anagnostakis. 'All the EDES *andartes* must surrender to us. At once. And unconditionally.'

I wouldn't listen to ultimatums. But I knew I couldn't afford to stand on my dignity, either. Too much was at stake.

'I am happy to consider any reasonable propositions you would like to put to me,' I said through my interpreter, Tony. 'Can I remind you that Major Micklethwait left for your HQ several days ago to discuss your proposals in detail?'

'The time for propositions is over,' said Anagnostakis. 'We are here in force to ensure that the traitor Greeks are handed over.'

'And I refuse to hand anyone over to you,' I said. 'The EDES soldiers are working with the British mission.'

'We are left with no alternative, then.'

'I am sorry you see it that way,' I replied. 'I must warn you that if your forces attack, I will have no hesitation in advising Major Konstantinides to order his men to open fire.'

This was no empty threat, but our numbers were small. I knew we would be in trouble if we had to carry it out.

Georgiades and Anagnostakis went back to their men. We shut the gate and the Major put his forces on high alert. The monastery wall was not high enough to be much use, and the arrow slits were too few to be useful. I hoped the Major could keep his men under control: just one trigger-happy finger could cost all of us our lives.

We went back to our workroom, but there was no point in trying to work. The ELAS forces remained gathered outside, shouting and singing. As the day wore on the racket gradually eased off, but at nightfall it broke out again, as loud as ever but now more threatening.

We could see their fires from the window of our first-floor room. We were well and truly outnumbered. Only the *andartes'* scruples about attacking a monastery stood between us and certain defeat. There was no doubt a clash would mean death for the EDES men—and very likely for us, too.

We didn't sleep. We just waited for the long night to wear itself out, and for morning to reveal what might come next.

Just before dawn, the sentries coming off duty brought good news. The ELAS troops were clearing out. Looking out the window as the sky lightened, we could see only a few knots of men outside, talking together. Soon they too had gone.

The relief practically knocked me off my feet. It was my first real political test, and I'd come through OK. I suddenly felt the need of a substantial breakfast—two, even—but had to make do with several cups of hot tea. Rations were short, as usual.

Eddie, when he arrived a day or two later, was most annoyed. He wanted to get hold of Georgiades and Anagnostakis and tell them off. Funnily enough, Mick arrived back from ELAS HQ just after we started our conference with Eddie, and reported that his discussions had been very satisfactory. We all burst out laughing—he'd missed the siege completely, and had no idea what had been going on.

Eddie filled us in on the latest from Cairo. Lieutenant-Colonel Sheppard had begun his work in Mount Olympus, and had fallen for the line ELAS was feeding him there: that ELAS had no military aims at all. Sheppard had fed this line back to Cairo and they had swallowed it too, hook, line and sinker. It contradicted everything Eddie had told them so far, but they'd decided Eddie must have got it wrong.

'What an idiot,' was my comment.

'Well, a little naïve,' said Eddie. 'To be kind.'

Why be kind, I thought. One of us being naïve could put us all in danger.

Eddie had insisted to Cairo that we had to take a firm line with the resistance groups. Otherwise there could be civil war. We needed a functional relationship with ELAS over the long term, but there had to be boundaries and they had to be respected.

Eddie and Chris had put a new proposal to Cairo. Some time back, Sarafis had suggested the idea of 'national bands'. Now, Eddie and Chris had devised a plan along similar lines. Their proposal would make all the *andarte* organisations 'national bands' as far as Allied military purposes were concerned. Greece would be divided into areas, each with a mutually agreed military commander, with Eddie in ultimate command under the control of Allied GHQ in Cairo. Bands couldn't go into one another's areas without the agreement of the area commander, but they would go to one another's aid if requested to. *Andartes* could transfer to a different band if they wanted to. No resistance fighter would discuss politics in public, but they would be free to have their own political views.

Best of all, no band would receive supply drops if they didn't sign up to the agreement. I was impressed.

'You really think they'll stick to it?' I asked.

'I think it's our only hope,' Eddie said.

'It's got teeth,' said John. 'They don't get supplies if they break the agreement.'

'The beauty of it,' said Eddie, 'is that it provides a measure of central control over a decentralised system. The bands keep their independence. But via a British liaison officer they're answerable to me, on behalf of GHQ Middle East.'

Zervas had already signed up. So had Psarros, the leader of a smaller and weaker band called EKKA that was based in the Parnassus Mountains. Zervas himself had only about a thousand men, compared to ELAS's four or five thousand. But Zervas was firmly entrenched in his own area, and was well up to holding off the Italian attacks that came regularly with each full moon.

While Eddie was explaining all this, my interpreter arrived with a message from ELAS. They wanted Eddie to speak at a gathering the next day.

'Good,' he said. 'I'll clear everything up. I'll reassure them that all the bands have British support. The leaders have heard it plenty of times, but I think the message gets a bit scrambled on the way through to the rank and file.' He was being rather too optimistic, I thought, but I agreed it was too good an opportunity to miss.

Next afternoon, Eddie and Mick departed for the gathering with Eddie's interpreter, Tommy. Tommy had come on Zervas's recommendation, but I'd already heard about his shortcomings as an interpreter. I hoped everything would be all right.

I stayed behind. The party bound for Albania had dropped during the night, and we were busy getting them ready to leave. I lost track of time, and when I looked at my watch I realised

Eddie had been gone a long time—too long. I thought I'd better go and see what was going on.

I found Eddie in the schoolyard, stranded on a small platform in front of a crowd of *andartes*—perhaps 250 altogether. Some hecklers in the front few rows were giving him a hard time. I couldn't make out what they were saying, and Tommy's translation seemed to be arduously slow. Mick was standing behind Eddie.

It was a cold day, but Eddie was wiping his forehead with a handkerchief. When he saw me, his relief was palpable. He immediately stepped down and came over to me. The crowd raised a small and reluctant cheer.

As we headed back to the monastery, we passed Georgiades and Anagnostakis. Eddie stopped and gestured for Tommy to translate.

'I will be leaving Romanon within an hour for your HQ,' he told them. 'I want an assurance from you that your men are under control.'

'Naturally our men are under control,' said Georgiades.

'Well, I hope you're right. Because otherwise I will be asking your colonel to relieve you of your command. Immediately.' They acted nonchalant. But Eddie's threat was a real one, and they must have known it.

Once they were out of earshot, I asked Eddie what had happened. Tommy was ahead of us and couldn't hear.

'We started off pretty well, didn't we, Mick? We had a kind of mock inspection—although they didn't take me round the rear ranks. Anyway, I'd already noticed that only the front rows had weapons. Then we went off to talk to the leaders.'

The leaders had said the usual things. We were giving EDES favoured treatment. The men were so angry that the leaders wouldn't be able to stop them attacking the monastery. They wanted the EDES forces gone within two days.

'I told them the British wanted to support all the resistance bands,' said Eddie, 'but that they needed to sign our agreement. They said they couldn't do that without orders.'

The leaders were still insisting that they couldn't control their men, and that there would be bloodshed if we didn't comply with their demands. They went on and on, until Eddie decided to address the men directly.

This, I knew, was a big mistake. He'd tried to keep the leaders separate from the men by having them stand behind him, but the hecklers in the ranks were getting the best of him. And Tommy was far too slow to allow him to keep control of the situation.

Although Eddie as the leader of the mission had far more clout than I did, he had dangerously undermined his own authority. As we went over the day's events at dinner that night, squeezed tightly around the table, I realised we were all going to need new skills. Not just diplomacy—Eddie had demonstrated plenty of that, although as a regular soldier he mightn't have needed it much before coming to Greece—but how to read the mood of a group and respond accordingly.

The conversation turned to Sarafis and his capture by ELAS. Zervas, I knew, had wanted to go north and rescue Sarafis himself, but Eddie had instructed him not to. We didn't want Greeks attacking Greeks. Instead, Eddie had gone down to the Thessaly plain with Themis to try and negotiate Sarafis's release. While he was there, he tried to persuade the ELAS leadership to sign the Natbands agreement. But everyone he spoke to said they didn't have the authority to sign it. Finally, however, Sarafis had been released; Eddie told him to go back to his own area and re-form his bands.

'And is that what he's going to do?' I asked.

'No. Not at all. He's joining ELAS.' Eddie was relishing the story now.

'What?' said Mick. 'After they took him prisoner and threatened his life?'

'Yes. He told me Greece would soon be invaded by the Allies. There wasn't time to set up a new band. And ELAS is already well organised.'

'What did you say?' said Mick.

'I asked him what his role would be in ELAS. Guess what he said.'

'We can't guess,' said Mick. 'Tell us.'

'Commander in Chief in the field.'

There was silence around the table for a minute or so as we struggled with disbelief. How could Sarafis, a highly respected republican, have so willingly allied himself with the party who had taken him prisoner and executed some of his associates—not to mention their association with the KKE?

British insistence on supporting the Greek king—now in exile in London—was at the heart of the problem, Eddie told us. On the ground, people hated the king because he had appointed the dictator Metaxas, and they were afraid that the British would foist him on them against their will when the Nazis were driven out of Greece. Eddie had advised Cairo that they should announce that there would be free and constitutional elections as soon as possible after Greece was liberated, and that the Allies wouldn't enforce the return of the king.

'Eddie,' I said, 'is it true that Zervas sent a message of support to the king?'

'Yes,' said Eddie. 'For the Greek National Day.'

This was hard to swallow. Zervas was a vocal republican.

'Why?' I said. 'What's behind it?'

'It was Chris's idea. He thought it would help Zervas's case for support from GHQ. He talked Zervas into it.'

'How unfortunate,' I said. 'You know I don't like politics, and I try to keep out of it as much as I can. But blind Freddie can see that this will just weaken Zervas's appeal to the Greeks. They'll think he has no principles.'

'Expediency,' said Eddie. 'It was just a matter of expediency.'

'Well, I think it's dangerous,' I said, 'and I'm disappointed that Zervas agreed. In the long term, it's going to get us all into trouble.'

The next day, bags of mail arrived. We'd had a dribble of letters before this, but now there was a flood. Lots from Beth and Mother, and from friends, too. I devoured them, one after the other, out of date as they were. Feelings that had been submerged for seven months surged up again.

Greek Easter was approaching, and this year it happened to fall on 25 April—Anzac Day. As I watched the villagers preparing their Easter feast, I thought of Beth and her mother, who would be attending the Anzac remembrance ceremony down by the river in Deloraine.

For once we didn't go hungry. There was plenty of lamb—cooked on spits outdoors, filling the whole village with its irresistible aroma—and hardboiled eggs dyed red for Easter. As the local representative of the British Military Mission, I was invited to make a speech through my interpreter. One day perhaps I would be able to make a speech in Greek—but not just yet. I could understand a lot by now but my sentences were halting and my vocabulary limited.

After Easter we left for the far north, heading towards the Albanian border, reconnoitring sapper targets for future sabotage ops as we went. I met with the major from ELAS, and we came to a friendly arrangement about the recces for the demolitions of three bridges. Our work was going well, and we turned back towards our HQ at Romanon.

Then we heard the news. The monastery had been bombed the day after Easter. We had to go like hairy dogs to make the new HQ at another monastery before midnight. When we arrived, I found that a signal had come in to say I had a promotion to acting Lieutenant-Colonel. I was too tired to feel pleased.

A week later a Hun plane came over, dropping leaflets signed by Ioannis Rallis, the acting prime minister under the occupation. Captain Myridakis translated them for us.

'It says, "Villagers, you have until 20 May to surrender your arms to the Italian forces."'

I studied the leaflet. I had a fair handle on the Greek script by now and could write the letters as well as read them. It hadn't been too hard, in the end.

'How are they supposed to surrender their arms?' I asked.

'Go to the nearest Italian garrison,' said Captain Myridakis.

'They'd have to go all the way down to the plains, wouldn't they?' said Mick. 'And those towns must be bristling with Italian soldiers.'

'Yes,' I said. 'They probably think the villagers will go in under a white flag. I can just imagine it, can't you? Then what does it say, Captain?'

'Anyone harbouring arms or communist rebels after that period will be shot.'

'They must be worried about us,' said Mick. 'Good.'

The leaflets were only the beginning. Next to arrive was a warning signal from Eddie. The Axis were gearing up for an all-out offensive. The starting date, according to our intelligence, would be 21 May. Just a few weeks away.

THIRTEEN

From now on, our ops would be far more risky. That's what the German push meant.

We had to believe the warning. The *andartes'* intelligence system wasn't quite foolproof, but it was close to it. They generally knew when the Germans were coming after them. Greek workers operated as spies in German camps and offices, and villagers passed on anything they saw or heard. And of course, dust clouds would advertise troop movements well ahead of their actual arrival.

Until now, the resistance had been able to do their work pretty well unimpeded. The single road winding up the coast that the Germans used to transport supplies was full of likely targets—blind corners, small bridges—for a quick attack and a fast getaway. Like a horde of mosquitoes, the *andartes* must have been making things intolerable. It was hardly surprising that the Germans wanted to take a swipe at them.

Now we would be prime targets and the Germans would be going all out after our intelligence. And no matter how often we warned them, the *andartes* frequently sent their messages unencrypted, freely giving away critical information. There were Axis spies about, too—the *andartes* had tried a girl for espionage only recently. She was found guilty and sent back to her village to be executed.

We'd done Gorgopotamos under fire and got away with it, I reassured myself. Now, on a bigger scale, we would have to bring off the same thing.

We'd already recced the targets—although we still didn't know when the operations would happen. I determined that each officer in charge of a demolition would have to do another recce himself, to make the plans his own. Back-up from the *andartes* would be critical. In particular, I wanted Agoros at my back for the critical target—the Kaloyirou bridge—that I was going to blow myself.

It was the only way to ensure success. We'd take out all the enemy's means of transport and communication—the roads, the railway, the telephone—and then, when the Germans were most vulnerable, Allied troops would land, right there on the Epiros coast. Greece would be liberated, and we could return to Egypt or wherever else we were needed.

German airstrikes on the villages began almost immediately after the leaflets were dropped. Vourgareli was heavily bombed on 5 May. At once, I thought of Agoros and his family. Voula and Toula—were they safe? I pictured them in that comfortable house in their village of bubbling waters, and wondered if it was still standing.

Eddie had set up a new GHQ at Theodoriana, and now I was summoned there for a conference. We stopped at Vourgareli on the way. It was nearly deserted, a few wisps of smoke still rising from the debris. A number of unexploded bombs lay among the ruins, and we kept well away from them as we made our way towards the house behind the church. Would it still be there? As we turned the corner, I almost collapsed with relief as I realised it was intact. Voula and Toula were inside, looking after an assortment of villagers.

Fifteen people had been killed in the bombing, mostly women and children, and about fifty houses destroyed. The house where Zervas had his HQ had been spared, but Dr Anagnostou's house behind it had gone, taking with it the doctor's nineteen-year-old niece.

The first planes had flown over at 6 am and then had come and gone, come and gone, over a hellish twelve hours. Voula and Toula had hidden under the stairs at first, before making a run for the forest.

We barely had time to take in the worst of the damage before we had to move on: Eddie was waiting for us. But those unexploded bombs would be our top priority when we returned. We would make sure of that.

Theodoriana was north-east of Vourgareli and higher up the mountain. I could see immediately why Eddie had chosen it for his GHQ. It was quite large and modern—it even had electric light, powered by a water turbine. And it was completely surrounded by mountains, except for the deep gorge of the Acheloos River nearby.

Mick, my offsider, was there already. He introduced me to some of the new members of the mission. Eddie had been promoted to Brigadier and now had an adjutant, Ross Bower. A new wireless officer, Tom Brown, had also arrived. The signallers occupied the upper storey of a large house. Eddie was in another comfortable house with a balcony that looked out across the steep valley to the mountains opposite. He had the top floor; the family lived downstairs.

It was good to see the old hands again—Eddie and Chris, Themis and Bill. General Zervas was there, too, and a bit later Major Konstantinides arrived. And at last I met the much-discussed Sheppard—known to everyone by his nickname, 'Hills'.

We ate outside in the sunshine. Ross had managed to add some luxuries to the normally Spartan menu—chocolate and raisins, and that delicious Greek sweet called *halva*, traditionally eaten on 'Clean Monday' at the beginning of Lent.

'Tell Tom about the women, Ross,' said Chris. The others sniggered.

Ross looked a little disconcerted. 'You tell him,' he said. 'It's not something I'm very proud of.'

'But you handled it well,' said Chris. 'That's the main thing.'

'Come on, out with it, one of you,' I said. 'I don't care who.'

'Well,' said Chris, 'Ross has been buying this chocolate and so on through the black market, from a pedlar. And one day the pedlar arrived with some luxuries of a different kind.'

I wondered where this was going.

'Three luxuries of a female kind, to be precise,' Chris went on. 'For the British officers. What was it, Ross?'

'For R and R,' said Ross.

Just as well these British officers were a bit more relaxed than some of the ones I had met in Egypt, I thought.

'So what did you do, Ross?' I asked.

'Well, I ordered them out of the village quick smart,' he said. 'And then Chris said no, we'd better lock them up.'

'Just as well I did,' said Chris. 'Because a deputation from the village arrived on my doorstep shortly after to complain. So I said the pedlar had been labouring under a misapprehension.'

'Where are they now?' I asked.

'We looked into their backgrounds,' said Chris. 'One of them was a spy for the Italians. She was shot. The other two had also been consorting with the Italians—but in a different way. We sent them off to the mountains for a sort of enforced leave of absence from work.'

After our meal, we assembled on the school benches to talk business.

'These German drives,' said General Zervas. 'The enemy will be trying to break the resistance movement. The bombing of Vourgareli is probably just the beginning.'

I'd already told them what I'd seen at Vourgareli as I'd come through.

'We can expect more of that,' said Eddie. 'And ground drives, now that the snow has melted. What this means is that all final reconnaissance of sabotage targets will have to be completed as a matter of utmost urgency. You'll get extra sorties of supplies. And those who don't have enough guerrilla support will get extra arms and equipment to make up for it.'

The operation would be code-named 'Animals'. We would all be given a secret code word. When that word was transmitted, it would be the signal for Animals to commence. Coordinated right across Greece.

I was delighted. That signal, I thought to myself, wouldn't just mean the start of the ops. It would signal the beginning of the liberation of Greece—and the liberation of us.

When our conference was finished, I headed off to the signallers' cottage to see Len. He always had a story on tap, each more dramatic than the last. This time he told me about a Stuka they'd watched come down near Theodoriana, hit by a Savona divebomber. They'd picked up the crew and handed them over to the *andartes*. Two had escaped, but no one gave them much chance of getting back to their units. The villagers would hardly befriend them. Not after all they'd been suffering.

'What do you think about the operation, Len?' I knew he would know all about it—he must have been decoding the signals.

'The sooner the better, I say,' he replied. 'Everyone's expecting an Allied landing. I can't wait.'

'Me neither,' I said. 'As long as I get my demolitions in first.'

'Yes, soften up the Hun. Then in we come and out they go. In coffins, preferably.'

* * *

Themis and I were back in Vourgareli with work to do.

Two bombs of a thousand kilos, as long as a man is tall and further around the belly than he can reach, lay among the charred joists in the shell of a bombed building, trying to look innocuous. Three more of five hundred kilos looked small in comparison. One was broken and explosive was washing out in the rain. Then there were the smaller ones—probably fifty kilos each. We didn't know how many there were but the villagers who remained thought there were a lot. They were right. In the end the tally came to ninety-five.

Bomb disposal wasn't really anyone's forte, although I'd had a bit of training in the desert, a lifetime ago. We unscrewed the base caps of the large bombs and took the contents out, hoping they wouldn't go off as we did so. We wanted the precious explosive for ourselves.

The fifty-kilo bombs we took down to the river and blew up. We thought we would train a team of locals to finish the job, but had indifferent success getting one together. We only had a couple of days to spare in the village before heading south to deal with some trouble between ELAS and EDES; we'd have to hope the work would continue after we'd gone.

A week later I was back by myself, having left Themis to deal with more problems further to the south. Now I heard that the Axis had published notices in the local newspapers giving the *andartes* another fifteen days to hand in their weapons. Further airstrikes would come if the new deadline wasn't met.

A Greek civil engineer called Palamyridis had led the bomb disposal party in my absence and had dealt with fifty bombs. We had quite a yarn over dinner at his house. He was interested in the role of engineers in our sabotage work and wanted to help.

'Take Preveza Harbour,' he said. 'I know it very well—I've worked there. I've often thought those ships are just asking to be sabotaged.'

'That's an excellent idea,' I said. 'Just the job for limpets.'

'What are limpets?' he asked.

'They're magnetised mines for ships in harbour. The Greeks call them "tortoises". You pack in the plastic explosive by hand, and then you stick them on, five or six feet below the waterline. You use a time-delay fuse that activates when the ship has sailed out into open waters. They're small, but I believe they can blow quite a sizeable hole.'

Palamyridis was excited about getting involved, and I agreed to get some limpets dropped. He was already familiar with explosives—I got out the time-delay fuses to demonstrate the next day, but there was nothing he didn't already know.

The next day Chris arrived from GHQ at Theodoriana.

'You look tired,' he said at once.

'I am,' I replied. 'Themis and I visited fourteen villages in a week. Soaking wet most of the time—rain and sweat. One lot of villagers couldn't be bothered drying our clothes and we had to put them back on wet the next day. One mountain in the morning, up and down, and two more in the afternoon. And we had to cross the Acheloos in the dark.'

The water had been thigh-deep and swift-running—no one would have been the wiser if we'd been washed away.

'And your meetings?' Chris asked.

'They went all right,' I said. 'I wasn't too impressed with either EDES or ELAS, I have to say. But we had some success with ELAS. I don't believe they'll attack EDES. And we got them to release some EDES runners that they'd captured.'

Chris smiled. 'Your strategy to stay out of all the political stuff isn't working too well, is it? And now you've been promoted, it'll be even harder to avoid.'

'Well, I'm only a buckshee Lieutenant-Colonel for now,' I said. 'Have to wait for the paperwork to go through up on Bludgers' Hill in Maadi to make it official.'

He asked about the progress of the sabotage plans, and immediately I felt less tired. 'They're going well. We've recced all the Epiros targets—with the help of the *andartes*. Everything's pretty well taped. We've got a good intelligence service going now.'

'And the *andartes*?'

'I have to say, they've been quite friendly and cooperative. Both groups. And Mick deals with the political side of things. Mostly.'

When I'd finished with Chris, I went up the hillside to see Georgios Agoros. Since the bombing, he had moved the *andartes* and some of the villagers out of Vourgareli and up to Omali Hill, where they had a clear view of the countryside in almost every direction. On the rocky outcrop they were piling up rock walls, digging slit trenches and dugouts. Later on there would be emplacements for field guns, too.

Agoros greeted me warmly. 'Thank you for your bomb disposal work,' he said. 'It's because of you that we didn't have many more casualties.'

'I wish I could have stayed until the job was finished,' I said. 'How is morale among the villagers now?'

'Very good immediately after the bombing,' he replied. 'I think everyone was spurred on by their hatred of the Germans. But now people are finding it harder to come to terms with. They're afraid of another bombing.'

'Was it us?' I asked him. 'Was that why the Germans chose your village?'

'Not at all,' he said. 'It was an attack on the *andartes*. The Germans hadn't got anywhere with ground operations and they were determined to paralyse the resistance somehow. Vourgareli is the biggest centre for the *andartes* in the region. I'd say we had five hundred there at the time of the bombings—if you count campaign committees from other villages as well as officers and armed men.'

'And how many villagers?' I asked.

'Another fifteen hundred probably. It could have been much worse—the sheer volume of Jumerka protected us. We're grateful for that.'

Agoros told me he was drafting a report on the bombing for General Zervas. And he needed help from the English mission—tents, blankets, medicines.

'For the homeless,' he told me, 'and the children who are orphans now. The poor who've lost the last of their grain. Dr Anagnostou has been in the thick of it, not just as a doctor but as a compatriot, too. But without medicine things are very difficult.'

In the end I think defusing the bombs was the only British contribution. I suppose there must have been gold sovereigns later, but nothing in the way of tents or blankets. They had to rely on each other, as they must have been accustomed to do far into the past, whenever catastrophe overtook them.

Agoros and I discussed the deployment of troops for the demolition of the two big targets, the Kaloyirou and Stravinas bridges on the road from Arta to Yannina, the main centre to the north-west. I confirmed that he would hold the reserve, in case the Italians ventured out of Arta—only two and a half miles away—to attack.

He seemed to be right on the ball, and it didn't take long to line up arrangements to our mutual satisfaction. Later, working with other *andarte* officers, I realised how unusual this was. And he was fun, too, good for a joke and immensely popular with his men—they would do anything for him. If the Germans got wind of our plans and were waiting for us, I'd have the best possible support.

When we first came to Greece, the officers and men of the resistance had seemed like an indistinguishable mass—apart from Zervas himself, who had always stood out, not only for his role but for his compelling presence. Now, just as when I was in Egypt, people were sorting themselves out in my head. Some would become friends—Agoros, I already felt, amongst them.

And then we were off again, up to the north. It was the end of May and the countryside was glorious—red poppies everywhere among the green, and blue cornflowers with their intricate petals. We tasted the first cherries of the season and I made a wish for wee Beth. I'd finally got a letter off to her just recently, but still there was little I could actually say.

A day or two later, two new lieutenants dropped in—'Spike' Moran and Ian Anderson. Somehow we still enjoyed the joke—'dropped in'. It took the sting out of the whole parachute experience—theirs, ours and everyone else's. It was nothing more than a spur-of-the-moment visit to a few friends, really.

Ian Anderson was tall and blond. Spike had a roundish face, not yet bearded. GHQ Cairo had sent them to help with the sabotage ops. We would have plenty of work for them.

We carried on with our preparations, so that we would be ready to go the moment the code word came through. Even Eddie didn't know when that would be.

My team would be working in pairs, each with its own targets on the main roads running out of Yannina, its own *andarte* support to cover the demolitions, and its own dumps of explosive.

I took the team up north in the first week of June to check the intelligence we had received. We made recces of our three targets on the Yannina–Igoumenitsa road—the bridges at Soulopoulon, Tyria and Vrousina.

In one village, we went to visit the school children. As we came into the schoolhouse we heard a chorus of little voices.

They were sitting tidily on their benches, repeating their lesson, but the minute they saw us all order vanished.

'*Kalimera, paidia*,' I said.

'*Kalimera*,' they replied. 'What is your name?'

'Colonel Tom,' I replied.

'*Kyrie Tom*,' they said, 'Where do you come from?'

'From New Zealand,' I replied.

In Greece even the children want to know everything about you. But I felt a surge of satisfaction—I could carry on a conversation. With children, granted. After a fashion. But I could understand a lot, much more than I could say.

Many of the children were obviously ill-nourished, their faces pinched, their stomachs protruding, so I asked their teacher if we might leave some money to feed them. We handed over six sovereigns, and they waved us goodbye.

While I was away up north, a critical signal had arrived from Cairo.

'For your eyes only. Destroy immediately after reading.' Operation number two, code name 'Animals', was about to begin.

By 6 June, everyone knew what the code word would be for the start of Operation Animals, and was on alert for that code word to arrive. My teams had already left for their final recces. I was recovering from an attack of malaria but couldn't allow that to hold us back. I set off with Tony, my interpreter, to our first rendezvous.

There was one frustration after another as we made our way towards the target. My contact at the first rendezvous, one Captain Chalimas, showed up late. At the next village, it was the runner who was delayed. When we finally arrived at the target for the recce at 1 am, we found that our plan of the bridge, which I'd received from a Greek officer, was utterly and completely useless.

We did nine miles of road recces in the dark. Then off again early the next morning to a mountaintop for breakfast, and over the mountain and down the other side to Elafos village, where we found many of the others already assembled. Elafos was to be the *andartes'* new HQ. This region, known as Lakka-Souli, was where those heroic last stands by the Souliots and their women had taken place, as described in the Klephtic ballads General Zervas loved.

Palamyridis the engineer was waiting for me in Elafos. He had news. He and a team of *andartes* had limpeted a 5000-tonner crowded with reserve officers in Preveza Harbour, and got away clear. He didn't know yet whether the explosives had worked—but later the ship was reported sunk, and we were elated. Unfortunately, however, Preveza was a small town. Everyone knew everyone else's business and no one trusted anyone else. We set up a second limpeting team, but as it turned out this was our sole success.

Finally the final recces were complete, and everything was ready to go. All we had to do was wait for the signal.

One night we heard a plane go over. Everyone tumbled out of bed. A few short sharp bursts of machine-gun fire sounded in the direction of our dropping ground. Then we heard the thud of bombs falling. Spike went out to investigate.

He came back looking green.

'Butterfly bombs,' he said. 'They must be. I've heard of them—I've never seen one before, though.'

Butterfly bombs were quite small—only three or four pounds each. They consisted of a metal cylinder with ends that flipped open like wings to arm the fuse.

'Did they all explode?'

'That was the thing. No, they didn't. And the duds are lethal. One of the Greek chaps with me—he just barely touched one. Got blown to kingdom come.'

Now I knew why he was looking so pale.

'How many duds, Spike?'

'A few. We cleared as many as we could find, but you'd best warn everyone. They're no joke. No joke at all.'

Two other villages had been bombed as well.

Off at 10 am to the north next day with Spike and Tony, through pouring rain, nearly running most of the way. I arranged with Major Konstantinides for the cutting of the telephone lines and poles along the Germans' main supply roads for the next day. He wasn't keen. He knew there would be reprisals, and it would be the villagers who would cop it. Nevertheless, he did the job.

Back in Vourgareli village next day, I sought out Agoros.

'Konstantinides did a good job with the telephone wires yesterday,' I said.

'Yes, it all went well,' Agoros replied. 'No thanks to ELAS.' ELAS's promised help hadn't eventuated.

'No,' I said. 'They were waiting for orders from on high. Probably still are. What happened to the wires?'

'Our men cut up some of them,' he replied. 'The rest they brought away. They'll be very useful up here in the mountains. A telephone system of our own—that's what we'll have.'

'And reprisals? What have you heard?'

'Nothing yet.' His face was solemn. He knew they would come.

'Spike,' I said, shaking him awake a few nights later, 'there's the Liberator. Better get up.' We were expecting a drop.

Almost immediately we heard another plane overhead. We weren't expecting two planes—something was wrong.

'A Stuka,' said Spike. 'That's a Stuka. Got to be.'

'Yes,' I said, 'right on the tail of the Lib.'

We didn't know what to do. So we waited. Not for long—we could hear the bombs landing. On the dropping ground, by the sound of things.

Suddenly there was uproar in the village. Everyone was clearing out. Families, children.

We spent most of the night outside. By 4 am everything seemed to be clear and we went back to bed. There were more Stukas in the morning, heading further up the mountain towards Theodoriana. And in the afternoon, worryingly, a recce plane appeared.

Theodoriana had copped it. Eddie's adjutant Ross Bower came to tell us.

'Are you all right?' I asked. 'How bad is it?'

'We're all right,' he said. 'But it was bad enough. Eddie and I dived out of bed and straight out the window when we heard the planes screaming overhead.' As they were on the upper floor, that must have been a sight. 'The house was shaking. Broken glass everywhere. Fortunately we'd dug slit trenches outside after Vourgareli.'

'Just as well,' I said. 'So you made it into the trenches?'

'Yes. But we were only there about ten minutes. Once the Stukas were gone we stood up and looked around. A few places had gone up in smoke. People were trapped and wounded. We sent word to Vourgareli for Dr Anagnostou. Eddie says he's never going to have his HQ in a village again.'

'Did they blame us?' I asked. 'The villagers?'

'No,' said Ross. 'They were so gracious. They said it was the quislings in Athens.'

Later, news came through of further enemy reprisals on the villages near the road.

This was always the worst part of any operation. Later it became a common sight—a row of village men in ordinary pants and jackets strung up in some public spot. Somebody's husband or father or friend. It sickened me—it sickened all of us. It was something we could never get used to, never accept. Some of us couldn't cope with it at all. Others just wanted revenge. Was the operation worth it? If you wanted to keep going, you simply couldn't afford to think too hard about that.

Not long after the bombings two more staff arrived, Captains Fred Wright and Harry Evans. Fred brought in a new wireless operator, Don Mappley, to meet me.

'Hello, Don,' I said. 'You've just dropped in?'

'Yes, the other day.'

'No problems with the drop?'

'No, we landed right on target.'

'I hope you've kept your parachute safe,' I said.

'Why? Might I need it again?' he asked.

I thought about telling him he'd have to drop back into Cairo with the same chute, but then thought better of it.

'Parachute silk is better than gold around here. It's a very poor area. But parachute silk—they'll pay for that.'

'How much?' asked Fred.

'We call it the golden exchange. Panayiotis the Cypriot established the rate. He was one of the original Harling party— joined us soon after we arrived. One panel of silk for a hen, or an "oke" of honey, or a dozen eggs. We trade silk for flour, too, so that we can get some bread baked.'

'I'll remember that,' said Don. 'I'll make sure I don't lose my chute.'

'Good man,' I said. 'By the way, it's a bit crazy round here at the moment. You've probably noticed.'

'Yes,' said Fred. 'He has. We ran right into a scrap.'

'Really?' I asked. 'Why didn't you tell me right away?'

'I think he was being polite,' said Don. 'The parachutes and everything.'

'Never mind that,' I said. 'Did we seem to be holding our own?'

'Hard to tell,' said Fred. 'We didn't stop to ask. Cleared out of there in a hurry.'

No more recces. Our code word came by signal—this time it was the real thing. Four of us—Harry and Don Mappley, Tony and myself—and a load of explosives for the two bridges. It was now 1 July.

When we reached our first stop at Nikolitsi village, it was already 9.30 pm. Stukas had hit the village only that morning and things were still in turmoil. The next morning, we found we had work to do—an unexploded fifty-kilo bomb.

'Good,' said Harry. 'We could do with some more explosive.' We defused it and took it along with us on a mule. I loved the thought of attacking the Germans with their own bombs, even if they'd never know we'd done it.

We trekked on to Papadates, where a team of twelve *andartes* was waiting to join us. We checked our gear and set up our operational base, all in the utmost secrecy.

At 4 am we headed to the rear rendezvous, only an hour and a half from our target, the Kaloyirou bridge. We slept on the ground outside a monastery.

Around midday we heard voices. Another scrap? Perhaps not—there was no firing.

Then a group of men appeared. They began talking urgently to our *andartes*. Tony and I went over to find out what was going on.

'This is the village committee from Thesprotikon village,' said the *andartes'* leader. 'They have a request to make.'

How did they know we were there, I wondered. This was supposed to be a secret hideout.

'Go ahead,' I said.

'You are going to attack the Kaloyirou bridge,' said the village president, a man with greying hair. It was a statement, not a question. 'We have come to ask you—to beg you—not to continue. Please go back where you came from.'

'I am sorry you are frightened,' I said. 'I understand.'

'It is the reprisals,' he said with dignity. 'You come, you blow the bridge, you go. But for us, we cannot escape. We stay—we suffer. Or we die.'

FOURTEEN

The villagers didn't just know the target. They knew the details. This despite the fact that no one was supposed to be in on our plans.

We could do nothing about the reprisals. We knew that, and we had to go ahead anyway. It was our duty. But now we realised that there was effectively no security in the mountains. What the *andartes* knew, everyone would know soon enough.

We left for the Kaloyirou op after night had fallen, Harry Evans and I, with a train of mules carrying our explosives, prime among them our German bomb. All the time we were looking over our shoulder in case the enemy knew our plans and was watching for us.

I was thinking about the descent to Gorgopotamos as I went. How dark it had been, how we had slipped and slithered in the mud, how scared I'd felt, but how full of anticipation at the same time. How nothing turned out the way we thought it would, but how we scraped through anyway. Then, I hadn't known what to expect. This time wasn't a whole lot better, except that I had faith in Agoros and his men. At Gorgopotamos, the *andartes* had been an unknown quantity.

The enemy used the Arta–Filippiada road day and night. The farming area we had to cross to reach our destination was uncomfortably close to the road, and we had to steal along.

Without warning, a flurry of clucking broke out from a henhouse. We were badly startled. Nothing doing, though. We kept going.

The two bridges, Kaloyirou and Stravinas, had to be attacked simultaneously—we couldn't afford to have one attack give the other away. Neither bridge had a permanent guard. By night they were the responsibility of sentries from the military unit stationed in Filippiada, less than half a mile away, with a few machine guns and a couple of tanks. Arta, where there was a larger military presence, was two miles away. We should be able to get away with the preparatory explosions but there would be no hiding the big one, and we could expect a quick response from the Italians.

Zero hour was 11.30 pm. We met Captain Chalimas on the job—everything was in order. He went to his post on the first hills to the west. 11.10. Time to lay the first charges.

Agoros, I knew, would be in position on the mountain immediately above us. One of his officers was in the farmland between the two bridges. Another was in Arta. HQ was a mountain peak about half a mile to the north-east of Stravinas.

Our own target, the Kaloyirou bridge, was on the Louros River.

Harry and I crept forward to lay the first of the charges in absolute silence. Nothing from Filippiada nearby. Not a single glimmer from a cigarette to betray the presence of the waiting *andartes*.

We laid beehive charges first, in the abutment that supported the bridge from the side. Beehives could blast more than two feet into reinforced concrete, leaving a two and a half inch hole into which we would pack the main charges.

We fired the charges, inspected the results, then laid the 120-pound bomb and ninety pounds of plastic explosive in ten minutes. We fired again.

The plain of Arta lit up as bright as day, while the sound of the explosion ricocheted off the hills to the west. Cheering broke out from the *andartes* all around. The abutment was gone— completely demolished—along with part of the bridge.

We held our breath, waiting for all hell to break loose. The Italians must have been taken by surprise. But shots soon broke out—to the west of Filippiada, by the sound of them. We left that to Chalimas and the others to deal with and cleared out in a hurry.

We made it back to our forward rendezvous without any Italians following us—perhaps they were too scared, not knowing how big a force they might encounter. After hasty farewells to the *andartes* we rushed back to the monastery, then across the mountain towards the village of Papadates. But we were too tired to make it. We dropped where we were at 4.30 am and slept.

By 8.30 am we were off again, back to where we had left Don with his wireless set. No messages. Then down to Papadates, too tired to celebrate.

Fred arrived, with good news about the other demolitions. He'd been with Ian on the Bodari bridge, which had been a crashing success. The *andartes* had blown the Stravinas bridge at the same time as we'd done Kaloyirou. And Preveza had copped it from the sea the same night, either bombed or shelled.

'The poor old Wops must be having one hell of a time,' said Ian when he came in with the mules hours later.

'I feel so sorry for them,' said Fred.

'Don't we all?'

We all slept the good sleep that night. When I woke the next morning, Fred had already gone. Shortly afterwards he came back into the room where we'd all been sleeping.

'Bad news from Kaloyirou, Tom,' he said. 'Heavy fighting.'

'Chalimas?' I asked.

'Chalimas,' he said. 'The Wops were shelling from Filippiada—and had a plane over, spotting for them, apparently.'

'Bad?' asked Harry.

'Bad enough. Five *andartes* killed and a mortar lost. But worse for the Wops. Much worse, according to our lot.'

'How many?'

'They reckon 160 casualties.'

'Even discounting for exaggeration, that sounds promising,' said Spike.

'Balls,' I said. 'I bet there were none.'

Our next target was the Asprochaliko bridge on the main Arta–Yannina road. This one was easy. We booby-trapped it and it went up nicely. But the *andartes* behaved like a lot of clowns as we were coming down from the mountains, blowing trumpets and making a hell of a racket. There was no one around to hear—this time. But there could have been. And after what we'd been up to, the Italians would've shot us without a qualm.

Later, we realised that the Italians were largely at our mercy. There were constructions everywhere—bridges, causeways—that lent themselves to mines and booby traps. There was no way they could have garrisoned every potential target. But that didn't mean we could abandon all caution.

When we got back to Don, we set about making up the charges for the next job, at Agios Georgios. It seemed hard to believe that we'd spent six weeks or more on the charges for Gorgopotamos. Now we had it down pat.

It was daylight before we got to Agios Georgios. A letter arrived from Agoros. He sent congratulations on our success and an assurance that he was patrolling the area between Agios Georgios and Kaloyirou to prevent any enemy movements along the Yannina–Arta road. It was good to know he was there.

We blew the rock face down onto the road at Agios Georgios. We put in some time-pencils, too, in what was left of the rock face. These were delayed-firing fuses that came in a box of five and looked just like real pencils—if you didn't look too closely. They came in a variety of time periods, from minutes to days, colour-coded to show which was which, but you had to allow for the temperature. On a hot day, they would go off faster.

Now we walked six miles up to the Kerasovon bridge, where we'd arranged to meet our force of one hundred *andartes*. Dropping down from the mountains, we could see them already on the bridge. They'd lit a large fire and seemed to be clowning around.

We warned them of the impending explosion and then got stuck into the job of holing the abutments. Then we buzzed off.

Word had come through of enemy patrols on the main roads. The *andartes* were getting nervous, and it was becoming more and more difficult to convince them to give us cover.

Early the next morning, after another brief sleep in the open, I was woken by one of the EDES officers. The Italians were half an hour away and heading our way. Then he took off in a hurry, leaving us to it. I was not impressed, to say the least.

By the time we got back down to Agios Georgios later in the morning, there was no sign of the Italians. We put a lot of time pencils into the rocks above the road, setting the time delays for up to seven days. Then we set as many booby traps as we could: these incorporated a trip wire to a mine, with a concealed release switch. There was a certain satisfaction in imagining these going off and blowing an unsuspecting person sky-high. But that was before the accident.

Early the next morning we returned to the Asprochaliko bridge to set some more booby traps. Don, the signaller, was with us. Our so-called 'guard' had already left.

I set one trap and was fixing another when something exploded practically in my ear. Don had copped it. He must have set off the other trap by accident.

He was in a hell of a mess. Half of his arm gone. Both eyes. And riddled with stones. It was my fault, I thought immediately. I hadn't been careful enough.

'Looks like I've scored an own goal, Tom,' said Don. Blood was spurting out of his arm.

'Let's get this onto you,' I said, pulling a tourniquet from my rucksack.

He had plenty of courage, but I could see his face turning grey around the missing flesh. There were big beads of sweat on his forehead.

We got him back up the hill. He rested there for a little while, struggling to speak.

'My family,' he said. 'Write, Tom. Won't you?'

'Stay with us, Don,' I said. 'Stay with us. We'll get you down to the village. The doc there will look after you.' But he was already unconscious.

Between us we got him down to Papadates and laid him down in the house we were using. The doctor said there was nothing he could do. A group of villagers gathered outside and waited to hear the news. Don died at 2 pm.

I had to keep reminding myself that it was an accident. But I couldn't help going over things in my head. If I had done things differently somehow—set the traps in a different order, or warned Don better—it wouldn't have happened.

Mick arrived, looking sombre.

'He was a good scout, Mick,' I said. 'A real good sort.'

'I didn't even meet him,' said Mick. 'He had barely arrived, and now he's gone. You must be feeling terrible.'

I was.

'You know, up to now we've been leading a charmed life,' I said. 'None of our lot had copped it. And the *andartes* haven't done too badly either.'

'Yes,' he said. 'The ops have been going really well. In spite of all the politics.'

We were both silent for a moment.

'I heard that charges have been going off all day in the cliffs above Agios Georgios,' Mick finally ventured.

'Our time pencils,' I said. I chuckled briefly. Then I caught myself. 'I shouldn't be laughing.'

'Tom, it's natural,' Mick said. 'Life goes on.' That night I slept inside for the first time in I don't know how long.

The next morning, the village priest gave Don a Greek funeral service. The villagers came in their good pants and jackets, the men with their hats on, the women in headscarves, and we buried Don in the local cemetery. It felt strange to leave him there in the company of dead Greeks. Particularly as the Greeks don't leave them there for good—after a year they dig up the bones and move them to an ossuary. We weren't sure what would happen to Don's bones. Perhaps his relatives could come and retrieve them after the war was over.

The enemy were now responding in strength to our attacks. They were holding the hills bordering the roads so we could no longer penetrate their lines by stealth. And the *andartes* wouldn't fight. I had a massive row with Chalimas about it, to no avail.

When we made it back to HQ at Elafos, there was big news waiting. Ross showed me a signal from Cairo.

'Sicily invaded. "Animals" completely successful—ops to cease.' It was dated the day before—10 July. The Allies had made a landing on the European mainland. But it hadn't been in Greece.

Animals was over.

'You can sleep the sleep of the just now,' said Ross. 'There'll be a plane over tonight—make sure it doesn't disturb you.'

It didn't.

Between us we had cut all the roads north, south and west from Yannina, the road from Preveza to Paramythia, and all the communications lines. Now the enemy was reacting. Word came in from Yannina that three thousand elite Austrian mountain troops had arrived from Albania. There was fierce fighting in Lakka-Souli but the Huns were getting the worst of it—eight killed and twenty-five wounded. They had managed to reopen the Preveza–Yannina road, but the Kaloyirou bridge was still out, forcing them to use a ferry service—thanks to us. Everyone agreed that the *andartes* under Agoros had put up a good show.

Where did that leave Greece? That was what everyone wondered, what everyone was talking about. We had expected the Allies would land in Greece pretty well straight away. Now, it was clear this had been delayed.

The trouble was, the Greek people had helped us on the understanding that we would liberate their country, and we had made commitments on that basis. I certainly had. And there was nothing I hated more than not keeping my word.

Eddie called a conference at Pertouli for 19 July, code-named Waffles, to mark the end of the Animals ops. We wondered what news he would have for us.

Mick, Tony and I took several days over the trip. In spite of our uncertainty about the future, it felt almost like a holiday. On the way we speculated about the timing of the landing. It must be soon—otherwise what had we been working towards?

Of course I was looking forward to the landings—but I found myself feeling a bit nostalgic, too. For all their difficulties, our sabotage ops had been exhilarating: we had faced and conquered dangers I'd never dreamt of before coming to Greece. It was hard to imagine going back to construction work in Egypt or somewhere else, now that the Allies had made their landings.

Pertouli is in the Pindos range on the western edge of the Thessaly plain. Three thousand feet up with a tiny permanent population, it was a refreshing retreat from the hot Greek summer. Eddie had set up shop in a villa. We found him on his shady verandah, smoking and yarning with old mates from Harling days and new faces I didn't recognise. He stood up when he saw us.

'Good to see you, Tom. Your beard is thriving, I see.'

'That's because I don't let anyone near it with scissors.'

'Afraid they might stunt its growth?'

'Something like that,' I replied.

Eddie introduced me to a new arrival with round glasses and a serious air, David Wallace. He looked to be in his late twenties or early thirties. I had heard his name before—he was supposed to have connections in high places

'I heard about you from Zervas,' Wallace said. 'I thought we might have run into one another at Elafos.'

'We've been pretty busy for the last few weeks,' I said. 'Bridges to blow, you know how it is.'

'Tom has been leading the sapper work in Epiros,' said Eddie.

'Oh, really?' said David. 'We must have a good chat some time.'

'Yes,' I said, 'but will you excuse me for now?' I'd just caught sight of Bill Jordan.

'Tom, old man,' Bill said, nearly yanking my arm off.

'Bill. How are things? Animals ops go well?'

'No thanks to ELAS,' said Bill. 'They made all kinds of trouble.'

'I've just met David Wallace,' I said. 'What do you know about him?'

'David?' said Bill. 'I ran into him on my way here. Wearing a slouch hat—he looked like an Australian. We came on to Pertouli together. He seems OK. Reporting directly to Eden, you know.' Anthony Eden was the British Secretary of State for Foreign Affairs.

'Yes, I've heard a rumour about that.'

'Oh, well, his father's Euan Wallace.'

'Who's that?'

'Transport Minister at the beginning of the war. Friend of Eden's.'

'How do you pick up all this stuff? No one tells me these things.'

'I'm a journalist, Tom. It's in the blood. But how are you?'

'Pretty well,' I replied.

'Pretty well exhausted, by the look of you. A bit like me.'

'Well, yes,' I said. 'But I've had a few days to recover now, coming across from Elafos.'

'Just the odd mountain to cross,' said Bill. 'A walk in the park, really.'

'Very restful after what we've been doing. What about you?'

'Between you and me, I got so tired I collapsed not that long ago.'

'Really? What happened?'

'We had to keep rushing off to villages where our *andartes* were being threatened by ELAS. No sooner had we sorted out one lot than there was another call. And the food situation was very grim. Too much energy going out and not enough coming in. I had to stay put for a night. Got over it all right in the end.'

Denys pulled me away.

'How it's going, Denys?' I said. 'I hardly recognised you without your beard.' He had quite a round face—I'd never noticed that before.

'Things are going exceptionally well,' he said. 'Although they weren't until recently. I'm getting out.'

'Getting out of what?'

'Greece, of course. Getting out of Greece. And not before time.'

'How, man?' I asked. 'We tried pretty hard before, and it all came to nothing.'

'I'm building an airfield. When it's finished, I'm going to be on the first plane out. Eddie has agreed. You should think about it, too.'

'I saw the signal asking for proposals to build one,' I said. 'And I heard you'd got the guernsey, but I didn't see how it could be true. Aren't you up in the mountains?'

'Yes,' he said, 'at Neraida Karditsas. But we've got a long plateau. Orientated just right for the prevailing winds. Only trouble is, a bloody great stream runs straight across it. And at our height above sea-level, the airfield will have to be nearly a mile long.'

'But you're really building it?'

'Absolutely,' said Denys.

He told me how he stood on his balcony every morning and watched the workers beavering away on the plateau. Seven hundred men he had, in two shifts, one starting at dawn and the other at midday. He reckoned with binoculars he could pick out the slackers, and he came down on them like a ton of bricks.

They were filling the stream in with rocks and stones, although Denys was worried it might still be too soft for the plane. Still, he'd had some road engineers over to have a look, and was feeling fairly confident.

'There's just one problem,' he told us. 'When I looked out my window yesterday I realised we're doing too good a job. Anyone flying over will see straight away what it is.'

'I imagine so,' I said. 'What will you do?'

'We'll have to camouflage it,' said Denys, 'but I'm not sure how. I've sent a message to Cairo to ask for advice.'

'When's it due to be finished?' I asked.

'Soon. Early August. It'll have taken us about a month altogether.'

'Wow,' I said. 'That's good going.'

'Too right,' he said. 'I can't wait to get away, that's why. You should definitely speak to Eddie about getting out too. I can tell you now he won't let you go on the first flight. I had the work of the world to get him to let me go. But you might convince him to let you go later.'

'It depends,' I said. 'We always said we wanted to get out of Greece after Gorgopotamos. And it's hard to communicate with Beth here. But I've enjoyed the sabotage work—apart from the reprisals. It's real work, and it uses my expertise. If I went back to Egypt they might put me on building roads again. It's different for you. You're a real commando. You won't be building roads.'

It was something to think about. Either way, it was good news. An airfield behind enemy lines would mean letters. Letters from Beth and from my family. Letters out, too. What a difference that would make. I felt closer to Beth just thinking about it.

Mick came over. 'Want to hear about Asopos?' he said. 'Arthur's going to give us the good oil.' The conference proper wasn't due to start until the afternoon, so there was plenty of time.

I knew that a group had finally blown the Asopos bridge, one of the targets we'd considered for the Harling mission. When we'd first looked at it way back then, Eddie and Denys had declared it impossible. But Arthur had had it in his sights ever since, and now it was in his area of command. I wondered how he had brought it off. As an engineer and as a fellow Kiwi, I have to admit I was a bit jealous.

All I'd heard was that our Palestinian, Mirhail Khouri, had taken part. Our early suspicions of him had turned out to be utterly unfounded. He'd been awarded the Military Medal for the Gorgopotamos operation and now it sounded as though he had distinguished himself again. He might be up for a bar to that medal by the sound of things.

Now, Arthur had everyone's attention as he promised to explain how they'd done it.

'Remember how we used to call Asopos "The Soapy One"?' he began.

'Oh yes,' I said. 'Gorgopotamos was "The George One". And ...'

'I remember,' said John quietly. 'The Priest One.'

'That's it,' I said. 'Papadia.'

'Anyway,' said Arthur, 'I got a signal from Eddie just after Easter. It was time to do Asopos. Code name "Washing". My HQ was still at Gardiki, and when I got back, there was a message saying I was getting three more sapper officers for the op. They arrived in May. We had quite a few Kiwis with us, too, Tom.'

'Anyone I know?'

'Do you remember Don Stott? I met him at Kibrit. He was doing the full parachute training when we did our couple of days. Long, lean chap with a thin face.'

I barely remembered Don from Kibrit. I may have been introduced to him briefly but that was all. He had quite a story, Arthur told us. He'd been captured in Crete and taken back to a prison camp on the mainland. Not wishing to stay there, he and his Kiwi mate Bob Morton pole-vaulted over the perimeter wire in broad daylight and got clean away, back to Cairo. Bob ended up in the Asopos op, too, along with Charlie Mutch, a driver who'd been on the run in Greece since the occupation began. And there was a South African captain, Geoff Gordon-Creed, who'd been with the SAS out in the desert. He'd won a Military Cross while he was there, on a raid to Benghazi.

Arthur had moved his HQ to be closer to ELAS and further from main roads. Then he did a recce of Asopos. Practically speaking, the demolition was impossible. The railway line disappeared into tunnels at each end, with only 600 feet between the openings of the two tunnels—just the span itself, 400 feet long and 320 feet above the gorge. The whole thing was made of steel. Leading up to the tunnels, the railway tracks were in full view of the garrison, and lit by searchlights at night. And the Italian garrison had just been replaced by Germans.

But still Arthur thought there was a chance—and it was urgent. The Germans were preparing to reinforce the base with concrete.

'In the end you didn't do the open attack, did you?' said Denys.

'Hold on, Denys,' said Arthur. 'Hold on. Don't jump the gun, all right? We went off to Mavrolithari village, Eddie and I, to arrange it all with Aris. We were hoping Psarros's lot from EKKA would be in the show too. But when we got there, we discovered ELAS was holding Psarros prisoner.'

'Like Sarafis,' said Mick.

'Yes, we heard about Sarafis,' said Arthur. 'But Psarros is a different kettle of fish. He wasn't going to capitulate. So it went on and on. Three days we waited, to see what would happen. Finally Aris agreed. But then he got orders from on high. ELAS wouldn't take part.'

'How frustrating,' said Mick.

'So Geoff and Don went to see Eddie. They told him they thought we could do it on our own. With stealth instead of force of arms. Eddie sent a signal asking me what I thought. I knew the Germans hadn't taken any precautions for an attack from the gorge. So I said I thought it could succeed.'

'What happened to Psarros?' said Denys.

'No, no,' said Mick. 'Psarros can wait. Keep going. We're all on the edge of our seats now.'

'So Geoff Gordon-Creed led Stott and Georgios Karadopoulos on a recce. I wanted to lead myself but Eddie said I was too valuable. I would have to stay at my HQ and coordinate from there.'

When Gordon-Creed got back he was pretty optimistic. They'd got as far as a big waterfall about forty yards down the gorge. With plenty of rope, he thought, they could probably do it. But they would have to think of a way to keep the water out of the explosive.

They got all the parachute rigging lines they could lay their hands on and plaited them together for strength—fifty-six fathoms' worth of rope. This time they had a party of eight, again with Gordon-Creed in command and Stott as guide. They took the supplies from Mavrolithari up to the top of the gorge by mule. Then they wrapped the explosives in pieces of waterproof cape. They got quite a distance before they ran out of rope and had to go back.

There were sheer walls a thousand feet high, they reported. The water was chest-high and freezing cold; no sunlight ever touched it. There were waterfalls with sheer drops up to forty feet. They'd had to lower the explosives down with ropes. The waterfall that stopped them in the end was seventy feet. But they reckoned they'd got two-thirds of the way down to the bridge.

They needed more equipment. Rope, climbing equipment, packs that could be carried on the head, through the deep water. They would have to wait for them to be dropped by parachute.

And they needed axes. The only way they could think of to get down the big waterfall was to fell a tree down it. And that's what they did.

'Stott, Mutch and Khouri the Palestinian went back to the gorge,' said Arthur. 'The plan was for them to send for the others when it was time.'

'Khouri,' I said. 'He came up trumps in the end.'

'Yes,' said Arthur. 'Remember how suspicious we were of him?'

'And how his rank kept changing?' I said. 'When Eddie made him acting lance-corporal, that was the making of him.'

Arthur got a message from Don to say that Khouri had carried the explosives safely through neck-high water. They'd got down the big waterfall and found it was the last one. They'd arrived at 'Mrs Washing' and she was ready to be hung out to dry. By a stroke of luck the Germans had erected scaffolding all over the bridge, including ladders in convenient places. They were strengthening it so that it could carry heavier loads.

'So they sent for the others,' said Arthur. 'They met up in the gorge, six of them this time. There was only one dry flat spot suitable for camping, back near the start of the descent, so they had to carry everything down and then climb back up the gorge again to sleep.

'The next morning they got everything ready, down near the viaduct. Then they waited. After nightfall they started carrying the stuff up to the base of the steel arch, and discovered that the barbed wire had been conveniently folded back to let the workmen through, and there were ladders up to a platform where they could stand to lay the charges.'

'What about the garrison?' said Mick. 'What were they doing?'

'There was a sentry above them,' said Arthur. 'They could see his cigarette. And there were about fifty more Germans in the guardhouse. But the worst was when a guard came by on his round while they were carting the explosives up to the platform. Geoff was standing watch while the sappers were doing their work, and he motioned them to freeze. As the Hun came past, Geoff took him out with his cosh. He went straight over the cliff.'

'Didn't they hear him fall?' asked Mick.

'No, the roar of the water covered everything,' said Arthur. 'Just as well, because someone accidentally kicked a rivet and it went bouncing down the scaffolding, clanging every time it hit something. And just about this time the searchlight came on for the first time and started sweeping towards them. They waited for the shouting to start, but nothing happened.'

'It must have been terrifying,' said Mick.

'It doesn't bear thinking about,' said Arthur. 'Anyway, they laid their charges. Everything was ready. They had put in five time pencils just to make sure. They crushed them at midnight, so they had about an hour and a half to get away before the charges would go off.'

'And the sentry?' said Mick.

'Nothing. He seemed to be bored. But they knew that soon he'd be for it.'

'So then they had to get back up the gorge in a hurry,' said Denys. 'That must've been tough. They would've been exhausted.'

'The waterfalls were almost too much for them,' said Arthur. 'Their hands kept slipping off the ropes and in the end they had to go up through the water. Charlie Mutch was the strongest of them and he was the last to go up. But he slipped off and knocked himself out on the rocks. The others were too weak to go down and help him.'

'So what happened?' asked Mick.

'Khouri was calling out to him. He did an amazing job helping the others. But it took ten minutes for Charlie to come to. Then he had to climb up through the water as well.'

'Did it go off when it was supposed to?' I asked. I remembered waiting under Gorgopotamos and looking at my watch over and over again.

'No. It took nearly two hours,' said Arthur.

'The time pencils,' I said. 'It must've been pretty cold up there.'

'Eventually they saw the flash,' said Arthur. 'Couldn't hear anything over the water, though. Then Don got himself up to a spot looking over the bridge. At dawn there was just a gap where the bridge should've been.'

'What a story,' said Mick. 'Must be one of the all-time greats. Congratulations, Arthur.'

We all thumped Arthur on the back.

In our excitement, none of us remembered to ask what had happened to Psarros. Later we heard that ELAS had released him. For now.

FIFTEEN

Chris turned up, and the conference began. Pretty well all the senior British officers were there.

'First and foremost,' said Eddie, 'congratulations. I can see you're all pretty happy about Animals—and rightly so. In fact, I have to say I'm proud to be your commander. I know things haven't been easy with the *andartes* …'

'You're telling me,' said Bill.

'But you've delivered the goods in spite of it all. Well done.'

It was good to have all the old hands—and the new ones—together to share in the satisfaction.

Now, at last, Eddie explained to us the real purpose of Animals. The plan had been to divert Axis troops to Greece to get them out of the way of the real target: Sicily. We'd made the Germans believe that the Allies were about to invade Greece. The west coast, our area, had been critical, beause that was where the Germans would expect the invasion to come.

The trouble was, only two people in Greece had known that this was a feint—Eddie and Chris. Everyone else—the rest of us, the Greeks—had believed it would signal the beginning of Allied landings and the liberation of Greece. I couldn't help feeling that I'd betrayed the Greek people who had worked alongside us in the Animals ops. And from now on it meant that for an indefinite period of time—perhaps many months—we would have to keep EDES and ELAS from each other's throats, while trying to assuage the disappointment of all the ordinary Greek villagers who had been hoping for something very different. In the big scheme of things, these factors may have seemed insignificant. To us on the ground, they were far from it.

Eddie did have some good news: ELAS had finally signed the Natbands agreement. One of their conditions was the establishment of a joint GHQ in Pertouli, to be known as 'Workroom'. They insisted on having three representatives on it, in view of their triple control system and their greater numbers. EDES would have only one. Zervas had been most reluctant to agree, but had eventually conceded. Eddie would represent the Commander in Chief in Cairo.

Hearing of these arrangements, I was doubtful that they could be made to work effectively. But EDES and ELAS had promised to cooperate against the enemy, and both were to receive arms and ammunition. Previously, EDES had received the lion's share of supplies.

'We've established four separate areas for military and administrative purposes,' Eddie told us. 'The commanders of each area will be responsible for executing the orders from joint GHQ.'

I was to stay in the west as Area Commander of Epiros and Agrinion. I would lose Mick to Western Macedonia. Themis was to move to Zervas's HQ, and Bill Jordan would replace him in Agrinion.

'We need better communications,' said Arthur. 'It's too slow channelling everything through Cairo.'

'I agree,' said Eddie. 'From now on we'll be using runners. That will be a priority when you each get to your new area.'

'Do you know when Greece will be liberated?' Mick posed the question that was on everyone's mind. 'The Greeks are expecting it any minute. They all think Animals was the prelude.'

'That's a very good question,' said Eddie. 'We've been instructed to keep a low profile until the invasion, but it isn't imminent. Not before winter, they told me. Possibly early next year.'

'So it could be six months,' said John.

'Exactly,' said Eddie. 'And if it's after the winter, we've got major problems on our hands. Refugees from burnt villages to look after, a whole population in the mountains to feed. There's going to be a lot of civil work to take on.'

This all put Denys's proposal in a new light. I determined to raise it with Eddie myself.

Denys cleared off by car not long after the briefing. Places to go, airfields to build. He seemed to be on a wonderful wicket. Comfortable house with a bath, good food, a bed with sheets, even a horse called Freddie. And if his plan worked, he'd soon be out of the place for good. I wondered if I would see him again.

The rest of us made ourselves comfortable in Pertouli. There were plenty of empty summer houses to choose from, even with all the *andartes* in town. There was a strong EDES and EKKA presence, and ELAS had set up its HQ in Pertouli the day before we arrived. Much to our amusement, Aris turned up wearing a British army shirt dyed red.

After a couple of days, Eddie left with Themis for a conference with EAM. He told us that Lieutenant-Colonel Nicholas Hammond, who had been posted to Macedonia, would be arriving in his absence. Hammond answered to the nickname 'Eggs', Eddie told us, and we would recognise him by his handlebar moustache.

The moustache, when it showed up, was huge. Must be to compensate for the receding hair, I thought.

'You must be Eggs,' I said, getting up as he came out onto the verandah where we were sitting over a quiet ouzo. 'Tom Barnes.'

'Let's dispense with nicknames, shall we?' he replied. 'It's Hammond. Nick Hammond.'

'Nick, eh?' I said. 'A nickname.' I admit it wasn't my best.

'I've been hearing that joke since I was at school,' he said. 'Along with Eggs. Ham and eggs.'

'Yes,' I said. 'Quite weak, really. How did you get here? On foot like us hoi polloi, or in a car like the lucky bastards?'

'Well, if you put it like that,' said Nick, 'I suppose I'm one of the lucky bastards.'

'I won't hold it against you this time.'

'We brought the Bishop of Kozani along with us,' said Nick. 'So we had to have a car.'

'Who's we?'

'ELAS. We all piled into a butcher's van. Degutted.'

'It would want to be,' I said. 'The smell would have been quite something, otherwise.'

He laughed. 'Yes. No seats in the back. We rattled around in there for hours.'

'Good road for it?'

'Naturally. Potholes. The radiator kept boiling over. And we had to get out and push the car up the riverbanks.'

'The Bishop too?'

'Of course not. He stayed inside with the driver. Very dignified. Except when the car turned upside down. When he scrambled out he looked as though he'd taken a bath in sump oil—with all his clothes on.'

'And what did he have to say about that?' I asked.

'I wouldn't like to repeat it,' said Nick. 'Let's just say it was most unorthodox.'

David Wallace joined us and I introduced him to Nick.

'Been in Greece before, Wallace?' asked Nick.

'Yes, actually,' replied David. 'On a research trip before the war, with my wife.'

'You speak Greek, then.' It was a statement, not a question.

'Yes, of course,' David replied.

'Oxford or Cambridge?' said Nick.

'Oxford. Balliol. Merton most recently.'

'Cambridge,' said Nick. 'Gonville and Caius.'

And so they were away. I beat a hasty retreat to Bill Jordan.

'Tom Barnes,' I said. 'University of Canterbury.'

'Bill Jordan, school of hard knocks,' he replied without turning a hair. He looked across at Nick and David. 'Narrow escape?'

'One of my narrowest ever,' I said.

Rufus Sheppard—he of the blind faith in ELAS—had turned up with Nick. He'd been letting his ELAS troops make trouble in Bill's area, according to Bill.

'How was your "Animals"?' I asked Sheppard when I saw him.

'Pretty good,' he said.

'Were the *andartes* cooperative?'

Bad question.

'They are always cooperative,' he said. 'ELAS are a superb military resistance movement.'

'So you haven't had any political problems to sort out?' I asked. 'That's how we spend most of our time in the west.'

'Well, you've got EDES there,' he replied. 'I'm not surprised you have problems. They don't have the best interests of Greece at heart.'

'We've had some outstanding support from EDES,' I said. 'Zervas has a couple of excellent commanders in the field.'

'But you've just said they waste your time with political squabbles.'

'That's not exactly what I said. EDES have their problems and I think all the liaison officers here who work with them have had their frustrations. But more usually, it's ELAS who initiate the problems. One time in Romanon, ELAS laid siege to our HQ. We had a hell of a job getting them to lay off.'

'You have to know how to talk to them. Half the problem is British policy. We shouldn't be supporting a whole lot of independent bands. It weakens the struggle, and in the long run we'll get civil war.'

British policy—now that was a can of worms. We'd already figured out that arming two groups who didn't get on might not be the best long-term strategy. But I wasn't going to say so to Sheppard. And I wasn't going to ask his advice about how to talk to ELAS, either. I let the conversation drop.

At dinner that night, conversation turned to our old Harling exploits. Our difficulties getting in touch with Cairo, recalculating the explosive at the last moment, the satisfaction of seeing the tangle of wreckage in the river. We didn't want the Asopos op to entirely eclipse our efforts.

'Of course, Tom already knew all about working in tough conditions,' said Denys.

'I did?'

'From New Guinea,' he said.

'Were you serving in New Guinea, Tom?' asked General Zervas, puzzled. 'I thought you were in Egypt before you came to Greece.'

'I was. New Guinea was before the war. Surveying for an oil development company.'

'Very different from here,' the General remarked.

'You'd be surprised,' I said. 'Malaria and problems with radio transmitters. We had both of them in New Guinea, and then more of the same here. I was constantly having to take generators and wireless sets apart and put them back together so we could communicate with our bosses. Oh, and outboard motors. Not too many of them around here.'

'Did you get malaria there?' asked Zervas.

'I did. Big muscular chaps, those New Guinea mosquitoes. Some camps had mosquito-proof huts but that wasn't any use in the daytime, slashing tracks through the jungle. One fellow working for my company died of the fever. I had it until I got treated in Egypt. I thought it was gone for good but then I came here.'

'And the crocodiles, Tom,' said Denys. 'Tell the General about those.'

'Yes, the wildlife is a bit different from here,' I said. 'We spent quite a lot of time shooting crocodiles from the boat. One day I got a sixteen-footer with a.32 rifle. And the spiders—I was in the jungle one day and I got pulled up by a really strong spiderweb. I backed off and looked for the spider itself and it was as big as my hand—and all the joints of his legs standing out.' I was enjoying myself now.

The General shuddered dramatically. 'Go on, Tom,' he said.

'Cockroaches that move like greased lightning,' I said, 'as big as mice. Leeches. One day I was crossing a creek on a log and I slipped off into the water. I got back to camp and didn't think any more about it until I looked down. Dozens of leeches, fastened on me wherever they could find skin to hang on to. Already getting nice and fat on my blood. Lots of snakes—we were always shooting those. A twelve-foot python one day.'

'Vipers,' said the General. 'We have those in Greece. Around Gorgopotamos, too.'

With such an appreciative audience, I had to keep going. 'Then there are the sago prickles. The palms that produce sago grow in swamps and they're full of prickles that get into your skin. Sometimes we had to work in four feet of water in sago swamps. You'd have to spend days getting the prickles out before they got infected.'

'Well, Tom,' said the General, an amused twinkle in his eye. 'It's no wonder you're so tough. If you can survive all that, you can survive anything. Even working with me!'

A few days later, Chris called us all together.

'Mussolini has resigned,' he said. 'Much to the delight of our Wop deserters.'

There was much cheering and patting of backs.

'The other news is not so good,' he went on. 'A big Hun drive from Yannina and West Macedonia.' Hardly a surprise, after the Sicily landings. The Hun would need a safe route out of Greece north from the Peloponnese when they finally withdrew. But it would mean more work for those of us in Epiros and Macedonia.

When Eddie got back from Denys's airfield, now known as Featherbed—by car—after four or five days, he and David Wallace had some long and serious conversations with General Zervas. I wondered how Wallace would assess Zervas when he reported back to London. Positively, I hoped.

Eddie called us together for the final briefing of the conference.

'Denys has done an amazing job with the airfield,' he told us.

'What about camouflage?' I asked. 'He was worried about that. Did Cairo have any good ideas?'

'No,' he said. 'But Denys did.'

'What?' asked Arthur.

'He got the locals to fell trees for him. They cut down a whole lot of fir trees in the forests and brought them down by cart. Hundreds of cartloads. Then they planted them in the soil. Scattered about in groups so they look quite natural. Broke up the lines along the length of the clearing, too.'

'How does it look?' asked Arthur.

'Good,' said Eddie. 'Wonderful. We'll be able to get the plane in on schedule.'

As we heard later, the camouflage was so good that it fooled Cairo. Without telling Denys, they sent a high-flying aircraft over to take photos of the airfield. The report came back that the landing ground was still encumbered with shrubbery and other obstacles and that everything must be cleared. I wondered if they'd apologised when they found out the truth.

'When's the plane due?' asked Nick.

'The 8th of August,' said Eddie. 'And I'll be on it.'

'You're leaving us?' Mick asked.

'Only for a short time,' said Eddie. 'Chris and I have concerns about what the *andartes* will do with all the arms we're supplying them with, once the occupation is over. I need to speak with Cairo to sort out future policy. Chris will take over as leader of the mission while I'm away. I'll be taking a delegation of *andartes* with me, representing the major groups.'

'Who is Zervas sending?' I asked.

'His 2IC, Komninos Pyromaglou.'

'Why doesn't he go himself?' I asked. 'Pyromaglou is too much of a politician. Zervas would make a much better impression.'

'I suppose he doesn't want to leave Pyromaglou in charge,' said Eddie.

'And now to a bigger issue,' said Chris. 'The Italians. Some Italian garrison commanders have already approached us, putting out feelers about surrender. Each of you is authorised to negotiate with them to obtain the surrender of as many as possible.'

'Under what conditions?' asked Arthur.

'Only formed bodies of troops. Those are our orders. And it has to be unconditional surrender.'

We took a minute or two to digest this. Further questions would come later.

'We believe we have good grounds for optimism,' said Chris. 'The reality is this—there are two Greeces now. They're laid on top of each other like tracing paper on top of a map. There's enemy-occupied Greece. They've got the main towns and the communications between them—by and large. Then there's Free Greece. We've got the main mountain ranges and the communications between. It's true that the communications lines intersect at many points. But the fact that some of you arrived here by car speaks for itself. We can all move about freely in perhaps two-thirds of the country.

'Free Greece.' I was unexpectedly thrilled when I heard it. I don't know why—a lot of it was rhetoric. But it was real, too, and we'd helped create it. And we'd thumbed our noses at the Germans in the process.

'Now that we've got Karditsa,' Chris went on, 'we can even go on leave. There's a cinema there, a cookie shop and a hotel.'

'And we're about to have an airfield behind enemy lines,' said John.

'That's right,' said Chris, 'and that will make all sorts of things easier. Now, it looks as though joint GHQ here will be able to manage the high-level administrative side of things. We all know that ELAS are very good administrators.'

They were. They had a telephone and wireless system of their own, police and law courts too, even taxation. They had set up an officer training school, and workshops for boots and clothes. Effectively, they had a state of their own within occupied Greece.

'As long as it's to their advantage to cooperate with us,' Chris continued, 'the war effort will benefit. But as far as carrying out the decisions of joint GHQ on the ground, that will be up to you.'

It would be a lot of work; that was my first thought. Not just ops, which were dangerous but exciting, but masses of paperwork—bumph.

'What's the plan for keeping the *andartes* occupied?' asked Arthur. 'We've done Gorgopotamos and Asopos. We've done Animals. What will we do with them while we're lying low?'

'Military training,' replied Eddie. 'A serious program of military training. Get them ready for the invasion, whenever it happens. With more frequent supply drops, there'll be plenty of weapons. Not like the old days. Remember when they'd never even laid eyes on a Sten gun?'

'And those old Mannlicher rifles they had,' said Arthur. 'Greek army issue. And no ammunition.'

'And we kept asking Cairo for ammo, and none ever came,' said John.

'Now,' said Eddie, 'all that remains is for me to say good luck with your new responsibilities. I'll be looking forward to seeing you all when I return.'

That night I sat down to write to Beth. There was an opportunity to send letters out to Cairo with Eddie and I didn't want to miss it.

So much had happened, it was hard to know where to start.

My dearest wee kid,
I have had two lots of mail since I have been here and a whole lot of letters from you and lots of people—my biggest regret is that I have been unable to answer them. I think mail will start coming pretty regularly now and I'm looking forward to it.

Now to tell you something of how I am—I'm afraid I can say a little less than usual. When I first came here I expected to be back in two or three months but it turned out to be impossible.

I am about as fit as I have ever been and am extremely busy and flat out most of the time. I am doing some real good towards putting the Axis back where we reckon they belong. I feel like talking to you for hours about this country and its people but the subject matter I am allowed to include is so limited that I'm afraid I won't be able to let myself go.

The photos you sent were great. You are looking very well in them. I was able to bring only a very few small photos of you so please send any that you can, won't you?

I have just received some photos I took some time ago—I hope they will be able to go to you. One of my mates used to say I looked the grimmest thing he'd ever seen, and I believe him now I've seen the snaps. When you get them you will probably want to reconsider your decision of that memorable Christmas Day, but you've no idea what a good polish up will do.

You will be in midwinter now, and it will be pretty cold and wet. We have the hottest part to come as yet.

Kid, I have never felt quite right since I left you. There is always something missing—I will never be complete until I have you with me again and then I think we shall know such happiness as very few people ever experience. Our time is coming.

Yours as always, dearest kid,

Tom

I thought about that Christmas in 1938 when we'd decided to get married—it had been Beth's birthday as well, of course. I had flown down post-haste from New Guinea as soon as I'd heard about her engagement to Ron Ware, cursing myself for not having had the guts to ask her myself. I thought I'd buggered everything. But her engagement to Ron wasn't official—that gave me a little bit of hope. So after a day or two of feeling I wanted to kick the tripe out of everything, I decided to go home and give him a run for it if there seemed to be even the least chance.

It took me a month to make it to Moresby. Then a plane to Townsville, then down to Launceston via Brisbane, Sydney and Melbourne. A bus to Deloraine.

Then it was three days before I found the right time to raise it with Beth. But when I did, I discovered something wonderful. And three days later it was Christmas, the best of my life. Ron Ware was nothing now—the girl I always called 'kid' was going to marry me instead. Christmas in Fingal, north-east Tasmania. A long way from the Papua Oil Development Company. And an even longer way from Greece.

Each of us had his own private discussion with Eddie before he left.

'I'm telling everyone,' he told me, 'that there will be an opportunity to leave Greece for those who want it.'

'From Denys's airfield?' I said.

'Exactly. I can't promise when it will be.'

Until I started to speak, I didn't know what I was going to say. Now I found that I'd made up my mind.

'Denys mentioned it to me already,' I said. 'But I think what I'm doing here might be more worthwhile than what I would be going back to. I never thought I'd say this, but I'll stay.'

SIXTEEN

Eddie was delighted. He was looking forward to working with me as area commander, he said, when he returned from Cairo. In fact it looked as though everyone from the original Harling group had decided to stay on, apart from Nat Barker—and Denys, of course. Things would be tough between now and the British invasion, and Eddie would be glad of the support of the old hands.

I was pleased, too. Somehow, without my realising it, the balance in my mind had shifted away from Cairo in favour of Greece. I thought of my friends in Egypt—my Kiwi mates, the Greek wine-grower Pierrakis from Gianaclis, my Arab friends from Aqaba. I'd already made the break with Aqaba before I'd even heard of Harling or Gorgopotamos. I wasn't likely to see Pierrakis again, either. And God knew where the Kiwis I'd known would be posted now.

But now that I was confirmed in a senior role in Epiros, no doubt I would be working closely with Georgios Agoros and his fine officers and men—as well as Voula and Toula, who now had uniforms and trained with the others. I admired Zervas and enjoyed his company, too. And then there was Chris—when I'd said goodbye to him the last time, I'd hoped to run into him again. Now I counted him as a friend, and he would be my commander until Eddie came back.

There were new responsibilities to take on, of a kind I hadn't envisaged at all when I signed up for that first operation. My first task would be to establish a network of stations of the British Military Mission in my large mountainous area. Much of the work would be administration—never my favourite thing. Much of it would be political, sorting out squabbles between ELAS and EDES. I wasn't too keen on that, either, especially now I was losing Mick, although I'd learnt a few skills over my three months or so in Epiros. But much of it would be doing a job of work with people I liked and respected. And that was always satisfying.

The Germans had brought up their big guns against the *andartes* in Epiros. While we were away at the conference, General Hubert von Lanz and his XXII Mountain Corps— three thousand of them—had arrived in Yannina and had set about reopening the main supply routes. They drove the EDES bands under Konstantinides out of the Lakka-Souli area—only temporarily, we hoped. Zervas had to set up a new HQ at Skiadades.

Now, the Germans were really digging in. Their next step after clearing the main roads would be to establish a network of garrisoned strong points from which the area could be kept under surveillance, protected by barbed wire and minefields, with bulletproof shelters and good communications. As well as foot patrols on the roads between the bases, they set up motorised patrols with searchlights, truck-mounted machine guns and 20-millimetre anti-aircraft artillery.

Already the ill effects of British secrecy were being felt in Epiros. The Germans had been burning villages in retaliation for Animals, and the villagers were blaming EDES and us. They'd supported our sabotage efforts in the belief the British invasion was imminent. Now there was no invasion, only more suffering, and they were angry. It made me angry, too. I felt we'd let them down badly.

My new Area HQ, code-named Watermelon, was in Agnanda village, to the north of Zervas's HQ. The village was built around a deep ravine. The sides and bottom of the ravine were thick with shrubs and trees, so you could hear the water rushing away below but never see it. On the way down, the stream ran a water mill, feeding through a narrow stone channel then tumbling down the ravine once it had done its work.

EDES had arranged three houses for us, and Spike had everything fitted up for us when we arrived, including two girls to do the washing up and other odd jobs. It was a great improvement on anything I'd had before and we had an enormous meal on the first night. No doubt Denys had been enjoying even better for months. He would be gone by now—he was probably right back into the good life in Cairo, dining at Shepheard's Hotel or his club. Not the Kiwi Club, though—he would need me to get him in there.

The new GHQ in Pertouli, meanwhile, seemed to be working well. EDES and ELAS had agreed on combined action against the enemy, and British plans to build both groups of *andartes* into a permanent attacking force were going ahead. The day after I set up my HQ, Zervas and Aris arrived for a joint tour.

The village was crowded with *andartes* of both flavours. A wooden dais was set up in the square, complete with a rostrum draped with two flags sewn together: the Greek flag and the Union Jack. When I was invited to make a speech, I knew I couldn't afford to refuse.

I collected Tony and we both waited on the dais for proceedings to begin. We'd been over my speech carefully to make sure there were no liabilities in the translation that could be seized upon and used to our disadvantage.

Zervas and Aris showed up shortly afterwards, arm in arm, chatting and laughing at each other's jokes. I found it a little hard to swallow, but I seemed to be in a minority. There was wave after wave of cheers as they mounted the dais, took the salute, and sat down side by side. Two short men, one fatter than the other. Tony and I sat too, alongside various other dignitaries— the mayor, the village priest, the local *andarte* leaders.

Then it started. Aris went first.

'Greece for the Greeks!' A pause for cheers from the crowd.

'Freedom and self-determination—that's what we're fighting for. Freedom from the occupiers. Freedom from the enemies of the people, the collaborators, the traitors. Freedom from the Glücksburg tyrant and his cronies, who cheated the Greek people of their freedom.'

The 'Glücksburg tyrant' referred to the Greek king and his predecessors. The Greek royal family were not Greeks at all but descendants of the Danish royal line, foisted on the Greek people in 1863 by European monarchies with their own stake in a stable future for Greece. Many Greeks—not only the communists— resented the power of the king to make decisions that Greeks wanted to make for themselves.

'We fight for the right of our generation to determine our own future, our own government,' Aris continued. 'We embrace everyone who will join us in the struggle.

'Here in the mountains of Greece we know what freedom is. And together we will fight until we prevail, as we prevailed against the Persians in ancient times, as we prevailed against the Turks.

'Today on this dais you see the heart of Greek resistance. My compatriot Zervas is by my side in amity and cooperation. ELAS and EDES together, fighting alongside the British until the enemy departs from our beloved Greece forever.'

There was much more of the same. Then Zervas got up to speak.

'Freedom from the invader!' he began. 'We've had enough of hunger and starvation. We've had enough of burnt villages and innocent victims. From our joint headquarters we will direct operations across the mainland until hunger and starvation are nothing but a distant memory, until we can honour the memory of our dead in our villages in peace and tranquillity. Together we will do this, EDES and ELAS, two bands of *andartes* acting as one.'

When Aris and Zervas had finished it was my turn. Through Tony, I spoke of Britain's intention to support both parties with weapons and other supplies as long as they kept to the terms of the Natbands agreement. I emphasised that the Germans were our common enemy and that all our efforts should be concentrated on them. I spoke of civil organisation and relief for the burnt villages. I said nothing about the date of the Allied liberation of Greece—that was a minefield to avoid at all costs.

It all went remarkably well. The crowd was bubbling over with brotherly love and I got my fair share.

The meeting continued from five in the afternoon until ten at night, and concluded with a promise to kick off again the next morning. They were welcome to it, but I wouldn't be joining them for another round. I couldn't help but wonder how long this show of friendliness between Zervas and Aris would last. For now, however, all appeared to be sweetness and light.

Our situation as British officers behind enemy lines in Greece was precarious, and we knew it. We were utterly dependent on the goodwill of the Greek people. If their trust and respect turned to suspicion or hostility, we would be lucky to get away with our lives. As I gradually became accustomed to my new responsibilities, I realised that maintaining the reputation of Britain more generally was going to be critical. And it wasn't long before I had to face my first test.

An American Greek named Kostas Lawrence had been going from village to village spreading anti-British propaganda—

wearing British battledress. He was said to be an agent of British Military Intelligence, although it seemed hard to believe.

As Lawrence was formally attached to our mission, it was my job to rein him in. No matter how hard I tried, he continued to be a loose cannon, and it had become widely known that two of his 'agents' in Yannina were actually German spies.

Now, further to our spirit of cooperation, ELAS had agreed to arrest him for us. I sent Spike off to escort him back to HQ. If he tried to escape, Spike was to shoot him.

Less than a week later, Spike returned alone.

'Bad news, Tom,' he said as soon as he saw me.

'He's dead?'

'He's dead.'

'How?' I asked.

'ELAS handed him over to me. We were on our way back when he said he was tired and sat down for a rest. I went on a bit, then turned around to see what he was doing. He was flashing his torch across the valley to the Germans. They were answering. I could see their flashes.'

'He was betraying your position.'

'Yes. I asked him what the hell he thought he was doing. He got flustered and tried to deny it. But I saw it with my own eyes. So I shot him.'

'Very unfortunate,' I said. 'But you did everything correctly. You were obeying orders.'

'Yes,' he said.

I could see he needed to wind down.

'Go and see who's outside in the sun having a smoke, Spike,' I said. 'Just go and join them for a while. You can write up your report tomorrow.'

I'd done Gorgopotamos and Kaloyirou. I would have preferred to do either of those again than to see Spike arrive back alone. Perhaps if I'd shot Lawrence myself it might have been easier than commanding Spike to do it. But there was no getting away from it—it had to be done. I had no misgivings about that. Lawrence had been endangering us all.

Local traitors were only one of my worries. There were also doubters within our own ranks. Major Paul Bathgate was one. Paul had dropped in in June, and I'd put him in charge of Shepshed station in Lakka-Souli. Before coming to Greece, he'd seen service in the Abyssinian campaign. He didn't like the Greeks and made no secret of it. One day he said to me that Zervas was more like a company director than a soldier.

'You know the type,' he said, 'the director of a local company, doing pretty well for himself, even though there's a cloud over the company's future.'

'Oily and unctuous?' I said. 'Is that what you think of him?'

'Not quite,' Paul said. 'But bland and easy-going, yes.'

'Bland?' I replied. 'Zervas? You've got to be joking.'

Paul must have realised I was getting annoyed. He tried to steer the conversation in a more positive direction.

'Zervas thinks highly of Spike,' he said. 'Anyone can see that.'

'All the Greeks like Spike,' I said. Stories about Spike's exploits were constantly doing the rounds of the villages. He was fun and eminently trustworthy and the Greeks liked him for it. He'd picked up Greek in no time—largely in bed, or so he claimed. There was something about his eyes that women found irresistible—so I was told. And from the men, he'd learnt invaluable on-the-ground knowledge—no one could put anything over him.

'Oh, the Greeks,' Paul said. 'Our *andartes*. I don't know who's more ineffectual—them or the Ethiopians. It's a real toss-up.'

'Paul,' I said. 'You've been here how long now?'

'A couple of months,' he said.

'If you've been here that long and still think that about the Greeks,' I said, 'I don't know what you're doing here. I really don't.'

* * *

And then there was the episode of Tommy Vinson. That was by far the worst.

It began when Major John Gwynne dropped in towards the end of August. He seemed a good sort—around my own age, give or take a year or two. I sent him off to Vourgareli to take over responsibility for Litton station. Leo Pilkington had been running it up until then. Tommy Vinson, that old soak, had been serving there for some time—if you could call it that. When I went over to Vourgareli a few days later for a meeting, things seemed to be going well. I left them to it, well satisfied. But it wasn't long before I received a disturbing report. About an hour after I'd left, Gwynne had shot Vinson dead. Taking Themis with me, I headed back to Vourgareli to make a summary of evidence.

I knew Vinson was disaffected, and had been for some time. He had never found a role that suited him and had moved from station to station until he wound up in Vourgareli.

'He was drunk,' Gwynne told me as soon as he saw me. 'And we were under fire from the Germans. He was behaving erratically, refusing to obey orders. Putting everyone's lives in danger. I had to shoot him. I had no choice.'

'Could you not have arrested him?'

'Everything happened too quickly,' said Gwynne. 'Obviously I would have done things differently if I could. Regrettably, only one course of action was possible. I've signalled you my statement. And Leo's.'

'I haven't seen them yet,' I said. 'Best give them to me now. Have you given details of the Hun attack?'

'Yes. They had light artillery and mortars trained on the village. Of course we had advance warning, but the Germans meant business.'

Gwynne was right to be worried about a German attack. In mid-August, just when Zervas and Aris had been making fulsome protestations of brotherly love, the Germans had attacked the village of Kommeno, south of Arta, and shot or burnt to death children, women, even the village priest. People in Jumerka had seen the smoke from the burning houses, and gradually survivors had made the horrific story known. The threat of further atrocities was one we had to take seriously.

I went down to have a chat with Len in the signallers' cottage.

'How's it going, old man?' he said. 'Come to see what happened to Tommy Vinson?'

'Yes,' I said. 'Were you a witness?'

'Well, no,' he said. 'But he wasn't all that useful. Liked his ouzo rather too much. But he wasn't a bad bloke. I heard that Gwynne is saying it was insubordination. But Gwynne's a nasty piece of work. Bit of a Nazi himself if you ask me.'

The story came out gradually, largely thanks to Themis's investigations in the village.

'Vinson spent a lot of time drinking with the locals,' he reported. 'He got in good with them by praising the Greeks to the skies and putting down the British. His Greek wasn't wonderful, but he'd picked up a lot of coarse language. Helped out by rude gestures.'

'So what happened?'

'Gwynne shot Vinson in the back.'

'Really?' That put a different complexion on things.

'Sounds as though Johnny Stavridis was the main witness.'

Johnny was an interpreter at Litton station. But he was away—he had left with Leo Pilkington for the south. I would have to get both of them back again.

'I wonder if Gwynne's story will hold up,' I said.

Themis hesitated. 'Not wanting to speak against him,' he said, 'but I'm not sure Gwynne was a good person to be managing Vinson. He takes quite a hard line, I believe.'

'That's what Len said,' I replied. 'I haven't seen it myself.'

'He seems rather rigid,' Themis went on. 'Puts a lot of store by discipline. And he doesn't approve of people getting drunk—a bit of a prig. That can't have helped.'

Gwynne was adamant—he'd done the only thing possible. When I managed to speak to Johnny Stavridis, he told me that Vinson had sworn at Gwynne and then refused to apologise. Gwynne had started beating Vinson with a crook. Leo Pilkington had joined in. Then Gwynne had pulled out his pistol. Johnny had tried to persuade them to send him to a court-martial and they agreed, but on their way to the gaol Gwynne pulled out his pistol again and shot him.

It was hard not to believe the worst. I trusted Johnny's evidence, and it was in line with what I kept hearing about Gwynne. I would have to write to Chris—and he would have the unpleasant task of investigating further. At times like these, my new responsibilities felt heavy. It was certainly a long way from building highways.

On 8 September, Italy capitulated.

The way the Greeks carried on at the news, anyone would have thought they were personally responsible. Of course, they'd reserved a particular hatred for the Italians since 1941. They had beaten the Italians in Albania in 1941, and then when Greece had fallen so swiftly to the Nazis, the conquered Italians had swaggered in like conquerors after all.

When we got word that the Italians in Arta wanted to surrender, both EDES and ELAS took off down there like a shot. It was the Italians' weapons they wanted. So much for cooperation—that was wearing rather thin. The Italians asked for a British officer, but by the time we got there it was too late.

Agoros had tried to get the Italians to surrender to EDES, but they had been understandably nervous. And then the Germans offered them a passage to Italy on a ship that was already in harbour at Preveza.

A wasted trip. A wasted opportunity. Eighteen hundred disarmed Italians marched away towards Preveza.

Meanwhile, the EDES and ELAS representatives came back from Cairo disgruntled and angry. It seemed the delegation had got nowhere. Again, the future of the Greek monarchy had been one of the main stumbling blocks. All the representatives had signed an agreement that the king should not return until a plebiscite was held to determine the shape of post-war government in Greece—exactly what Eddie had been telling Cairo to do all along. But that was the last thing the British government and its representatives wanted to hear, and they'd refused to consider it.

To add insult to injury, Cairo hadn't provided a reception appropriate to the rank of the delegates when they landed, and had treated them as troublemakers rather than as senior representatives of a government in waiting.

Cairo had also decided not to send Eddie and David Wallace back just yet. Instead, they'd been sent on to London to report.

With the return of the disappointed delegates, the atmosphere at joint HQ changed. Cooperation evaporated, replaced by suspicion and mistrust.

On 10 October, without warning, civil war broke out between ELAS and EDES.

I was furious. The British had a lot to answer for—their stubborn insistence on supporting the king, their deception of the Greek people about the timing of liberation, their failure to treat the representatives of the *andartes* with respect. Not that anyone could say it was all Britain's fault. But the potential for it had been obvious, for anyone paying attention—Eddie and Chris had been saying the same thing from the start.

It seemed that British investment in Greece had brought a dangerous dividend to the Greek people. And Britain had recklessly put its own personnel on the ground—us—in peril of our lives.

PART III

OPERATION
'NOAH'S ARK'

SEVENTEEN

The civil war changed everything. Supply drops to ELAS were discontinued—as far as we were concerned, they had started the war. The style of negotiation with ELAS *politikos* that we'd become accustomed to—warily circling around the objectives while maintaining an aura of genial cooperation—would cut no ice now. New tactics would be needed. Moving around in Free Mountain Greece would become far harder, except in the relatively small areas that Zervas held. And I knew that von Lanz and his elite troops in Yannina, if they had any sense, would exploit the enmity between resistance parties for all they were worth.

Set against all this, I had the calibre of my staff.

Some of them had already proved their worth in the Animals ops. Spike, for instance. On the first night of the ops, he blew the Soulei bridge south of Yannina, then walked six hours past Yannina to the north and blew another bridge. Then he returned to Soulei to find only three *andartes* left there—all the others had cleared out. Together they'd held off forty Germans for five hours—an amazing feat.

Fred Wright and Harry Evans had been with me since June. Both were in their late twenties. Harry and I had done the

269

Kaloyirou bridge op together. Fred had successfully undertaken three bridge and two road demolitions, his energy seemingly never flagging as more and more sleepless nights mounted up.

Peter Musson was already an experienced SOE operator when he dropped to me in August, after the Pertouli conference. He looked tough, and he was tough, with a square face and strong cheekbones. His hair was receding but, like him, made up for it in sheer stubborn resilience. Originally Royal Artillery, he spoke Spanish fluently and although he didn't talk about it, I gathered he'd been working in occupied Spain.

Dennis Nicholson, Border Regiment, had arrived in mid-September. Before the war he'd been an articled clerk in accountancy, and he'd been trained in industrial sabotage and demolitions before coming to Greece. He was one of the young ones, only twenty-two, with a propensity to fall in love with the Greek women. He had dark eyes and black wavy hair that, like Peter's, could become unruly. Shunning the fashion for profuse facial hair, he preferred a neat moustache. If his chin was unshaven, you knew things were tough.

In spite of his youth, Dennis maintained focus and stability under the most trying of circumstances. His work as adjutant to my HQ eventually brought him an MBE.

Company Quartermaster Sergeant Frank Hernen, Royal Corps of Signals, was in charge of our wireless transmissions. The demanding and thankless task of deciphering coded signals from Cairo—and later, sending operational orders to our outstations as well—then encoding our responses ready for scheduled transmission times ('skeds') kept the signals staff flat out. Sometimes we had more than forty signals in at once, and then it was all hands on deck. Coding mistakes had to be kept to an absolute minimum if our messages were to be decipherable at the other end; the substitution of 'Pera Kapsi' for 'Sakaretsi' when we were first dropped into Greece was still fresh in my mind.

When not on duty, Frank had another remarkable skill—his capacity to let his hair down. He could outstay the entire mission staff at any party. It was not unknown for him to stay out until it was too late to go to bed before his next shift began.

Then there were our Greek colleagues. My friendship with Georgios Agoros had flourished since his magnificent support for Animals, and the three of them—Georgios, Voula and Toula—had become my Greek family.

Other EDES officers also stood high in my estimation. Major Galanis, commander of the 2nd Cretan Independent HQ Battalion, was one. He had striking eyes above a thick fringe of beard and a moustache always coaxed upwards at the tips. I had no patience myself for such niceties, but I was fascinated by others' attention to them. Captain Myridakis was another I had thought highly of since our trek across Greece after the Harling op. And Colonel Zorbalas, commander of the EDES 39 regiment and the proud owner of what was surely the largest, blackest and bushiest beard of them all, was a third.

My admiration for General Zervas had grown too, as I worked more closely with him in my new role. And with admiration had come regard, and with regard had come friendship. We enjoyed working together, and we enjoyed drinking together after the work was over—whisky if we could get it, otherwise ouzo. Zervas had an endless supply of funny stories. My Greek was much better now, and he'd developed a certain respect for my stories of New Guinea and Aqaba Bay.

Like senior mission staff—Eddie when he was there, Chris, Nick Hammond—our interpreters, by the nature of their role, were there at the most critical moments. 'Boulis' Metaxas, solid, round-faced and clean-shaven, his hair always neatly parted in the middle, found himself right in the midst of events as the civil war progressed.

Two rivers, the Arachthos and the Acheloos, defined the territory in Epiros that everyone was fighting over.

Zervas wanted it because it was his heartland. The villages were full of his supporters: Megalochari, Vourgareli, Agnanda. The Germans wanted it for exactly the same reason. They knew who'd provided the support for the Animals ops. And ELAS wanted Zervas out.

I was intimately acquainted with both rivers.

The Acheloos separated Epiros from Thessaly, and had marked the limits of Zervas's fiefdom when we forded it on our trek to the west coast, heading for Megalochari village. In summer it was a river of wide meanders and gravelly beaches. In winter it was a different story.

And the Arachthos—we'd crossed it in that crazy little ferry, in the pitch dark, hoping desperately we wouldn't end up in the freezing water. We'd been lucky then: it had been too early for the snowmelt, which in spring would rush down from the mountains through the canyons, turning the river into an uncrossable torrent.

Soon we would all get to know those rivers a whole lot better.

Normally we could move around in the mountains with more or less complete freedom, except for a handful of passport documents signed by ELAS or EDES, depending on who held the area you wanted to cross. Now, with the civil war, travelling became dangerous.

We first encountered the *andartes* fighting each other on our way north-east to Alteration station at Gotista, in the foothills to the east of Yannina, close to the Arachthos river. Then, travelling back to our HQ at Agnanda, we had to cross a battlefield—if you could call it that. ELAS and EDES men were playing at war with

Stens and sub-machine guns—firing from a range of 3000 yards. But as we got closer to Agnanda it was all EDES, and we got a warm welcome.

Dennis Nicholson greeted us, looking dapper as usual with his neat moustache.

'The Red Cross committee called in while you were away,' he told me. 'A Swede, name of Bickel. Had the mayor of Yannina with him. A representative of the archbishop, too, and one or two others.'

I was immediately suspicious. What were they up to?

'They were supposed to be looking into the food situation for the villagers,' Dennis went on. 'But they seemed to have another agenda as well. Collaboration with the Hun. Not us, of course. Zervas. The Red Cross wanted to broker a short-term truce. A month, they said, to get supplies into Preveza. The Germans wouldn't come to the party unless the ops on the road stopped.'

'So what did you do?'

'Well, Zervas wasn't here. I sent them off to his HQ. But he refused to have anything to do with it.'

The Hun were quick to take advantage of the civil war. They mounted four simultaneous drives over a vast swathe of country. The big drive through Epiros came in early October, southwards from Gotista and northwards from Arta towards Jumerka and Vourgareli. ELAS took advantage of the attack to mount their own. Zervas was faced with two enemies at once, ELAS and the Germans.

The cosy days of Free Mountain Greece, when we could move around in a vast area of the country in complete safety from the enemy, were gone for good. The Germans weren't playing games. They would try to encircle us, leaving no gaps for us to escape through. All they had to do then was pull the ring tight.

* * *

These were days of utter misery for me. Just a few days before the civil war started, nasty boils had broken out at the base of my spine.

They started out as hard, painful red lumps. That was bad enough. But then a disc of whitish-yellow pus would make its appearance at each site, with a hard core of dead tissue. At that point the pain became almost unbearable.

The doc offered to lance them for me.

'Anything would be better than this,' I said. 'What's causing them? Is it poor nutrition?' In fact Cairo had been dropping us some supplies—dried meat and vegetables, cheese, that kind of thing—so we were messing better.

'More likely poor hygiene,' he said. 'Although fatigue and poor diet probably don't help. How long is it since you had a bath?'

'Let's see. Months and months.'

'And how often do you wash your clothes?'

'When I'm at HQ,' I said. 'But a lot of the time I'm on the move. You know how it is.'

'Yes,' he said, 'and the bugs get a nice little trip in the seams of your clothes. You just get over one boil and another breaks out. Isn't that right?'

'I thought it was just bad luck.'

'Luck doesn't come into it,' he said. 'Now, let's see what we can do with this one.' He dug the core out of it and as usual there was instant relief. It would heal now—until the next one came along.

The odds of us staying in one spot and getting a chance to wash our clothes properly were getting slimmer and slimmer. The Germans were moving down from Gotista and up from Agrinion. Seven hundred ELAS men had shoved off without fighting. EDES had managed to drive the Hun back, but now the Germans were moving purposefully towards Metsovo with wide flanking parties. Vourgareli was threatened. Aris had got hold of two light field guns—I wondered where from.

Garbled information kept arriving. Zervas reported that ELAS had shot Leo Pilkington. Then he said no, they had killed John Cook and captured Bill Jordan, but Leo was all right.

This was what we had feared all along. While the Natbands agreement was in place, ELAS had to respect our authority as representatives of British GHQ. Once it had been abandoned, we became their enemies, and therefore fair game. In the new context of civil war, where all the old operating rules came under question, reports of ELAS attacks on our personnel had to be given credence. With Zervas, of course, things were different. His respect for the British was ingrained.

We were expecting a new British Liaison Officer, Hamish Torrance of the Highland Light Infantry, and hoped he would bring reliable information from Chris's HQ at Pertouli. I was looking forward to his arrival. But time passed and still he didn't show up.

I was finishing a late breakfast and looking at the signals that had been deciphered overnight when finally Torrance appeared, grimy and untidy. We all looked like that much of the time, it was true—but he seemed even more so than usual.

'Sorry I'm late,' he said, sitting down and helping himself to bread and cheese. 'I got a bit held up.'

'What happened?'

'ELAS. They arrested me three days ago. First of all they said we couldn't move without a pass. I had a wireless operator with me, too, and a runner. Chris asked them to give us a pass, but they said no.'

'So you went anyway?'

He nodded, his mouth full of bread and cheese.

'We ran into some of Aris's bodyguard on horses,' he went on after a few more large bites. 'They tried to turn us back. I wasn't having any of it and in the end they said we could go on to Mesochora, with an escort of Aris's men. I enjoyed that bit.'

'How's that?'

He laughed. 'We gave them a hard time. We walked slowly on the easy bits and fast where it was hard going. Eventually one of them fell off his horse. Then they got really mad and the Tommy guns came out.'

All the bread and cheese was gone. I wished I had more to give him, but our supplies still weren't exactly princely.

'When we got to Mesochora,' he continued, 'they locked us in a garret. On top of the local store. Put a guard on the building. We could hear firing from down in the Acheloos gorge. Then Lefteris, the commander of Aris's bodyguards, appeared and was very rude. Finally—grudgingly—they gave us a bit of food, and a lousy blanket each.' I knew those louse-ridden blankets all too well. 'Lefteris said he would ask Aris what to do with us. When he came back we had a big argument. I said I had to follow orders and go to Epiros. He said he had to follow orders and stop me. He went off saying he was going to increase the guard on the building.'

'But you got away, obviously,' I said. 'How did you manage that?'

'An old woman,' he said. 'The one who delivered our meals. She told us where the guards were. And she sent a little boy round the hills to find the ELAS outposts, so that we could keep clear of them. Then Lefteris came back and said we had to go back to Pertouli. I pretended to agree and asked for a pass. The wireless operator did go back to Pertouli, but the runner and I had different plans. There was a convenient balcony at the back of the house and we made our escape that way early the next morning, then scrambled down to the river. Once we got to Vourgareli we were fine. No, before that, really—as soon as we got into Zervas's territory.'

'Thank God you managed to escape,' I said.

'Yes. Not like poor Hubbard.'

'Arthur Hubbard?' I asked. 'The Kiwi? Why, what happened to him?' I had met Hubbard briefly on one occasion. He was a big, cheerful man whom we had taken to straight away; he came from the same town as Bill Jordan and had gone to school with him.

'Haven't you heard? ELAS shot him.'

'He's dead?' I couldn't believe it.

'Yes, unfortunately.'

'So it's true what Zervas said. And Cook? Him too? And Bill Jordan captured?'

'As far as I know John is OK. But ELAS attacked Bill's station on October 13th. Bill was captured briefly. But he's all right.'

'And Hubbard?'

'We know very little. Chris was waiting for more news when I left. But he's confirmed killed.'

It was hard to believe things had changed so much. Clearly, the friendliness of the previous few months had been superseded by something very much more sinister.

'What has Chris had you doing over there?' I asked, 'now that Eddie hasn't come back?'

'We did an attack on Larissa airport. With the Italians. I planned it with Sheppard.'

'How did it go?'

'A fizzer. First of all the RAF withdrew their cooperation. Then ELAS tricked the Italians.'

ELAS had agreed to give General Infante, the Italian commander, a section of his own to be responsible for. General Infante led the Italian Pinerolo division, the sole formed body of Italians that we'd managed to get to surrender to us. Then, the same day as ELAS had made the offer, they disarmed the lot of them, saying it was a precaution against the fascists. That explained how Aris had got hold of the field guns he'd brought up against EDES.

'What's he like, Infante?' I asked.

'Chris played bridge with him one night. Apparently he's very pro-British. Not a dyed-in-the-wool fascist like some of the others.'

'And Gwynne?' I asked. 'I heard Chris charged him with murder.'

'It's true. He's getting repatriated to Cairo on the next flight out of Featherbed. Leo Pilkington, too.'

I longed to see Chris. Communicating by signal wasn't the same. I wanted to ask him if he'd had as much trouble believing the evidence about Vinson's death as I had. I wanted to know when Eddie would be coming back. Above all, I wanted to talk over the civil war and how to handle Aris if it came to a confrontation. When Aris was getting an advantage out of being nice to us, he could be charming. But Cairo had cut off his supplies since the civil war had started, and there was every chance we would now see a very different side of him.

But ELAS were between Chris and us.

The Hun were closing in.

I briefed Hamish on the Vourgareli situation post-Gwynne and sent him down there to take charge of Litton station.

Two days after Hamish arrived, just as the Germans were getting stuck into EDES with bombs and machine guns, Aris launched an attack—not on the Hun, but on EDES, at Pramanda. I tried to broker some kind of reconciliation between EDES and ELAS by telephone from Agnanda, but ELAS weren't interested.

We started to move our stores, getting ready for a quick getaway. Then Pramanda fell to ELAS. With the Hun only two hours away, we evacuated Watermelon station.

We headed south-east, fortunately with a battalion of surrendered Italians, who carried most of our gear. It meant a massive climb over the Jumerka Mountain—nearly 2,400 feet. Even with extra mules, the men and animals were all in; we simply couldn't manage the last 500 feet. A couple of men went on ahead up the mountain, but the rest of us made camp in the open.

We woke covered in frost. From our lookout we watched as the Huns shelled and burnt a substantial portion of Agnanda.

Up the last 500 feet with almost everything we owned, including the charging engine, then down to Theodoriana village, Eddie's old GHQ, still held by EDES. There we were pretty well surrounded. It started to rain. Almost everyone was sick by now. Many of us had malaria, and the regular attacks— the shakes at the start, the slamming headache, and then the drenching sweats when the fever broke—had weakened us all.

In Theodoriana, I caught up with Zervas. He'd come east with his own battalion to take over personal command.

'Tom, I'm delighted to see you,' he said immediately.

'And I'm delighted to see you,' I replied. 'I've got good news. We got a drop of ammunition and clothes for you last night.'

'That's wonderful,' he said. 'We were down to almost nothing. And I suppose you know how well equipped ELAS are now.' He spoke bitterly and I knew why. ELAS had helped themselves to all the supplies of the Italian Pinerolo division and were taking every advantage of their strengthened position.

EDES pushed back two Hun attacks. Agoros was harrying the German column coming up from Arta in the flanks and rear— brilliant work. But the pressure from the Hun was increasing and Hamish made the decision to evacuate the Litton station W/T equipment to Theodoriana. Then he withdrew with his staff to the high ground behind Vourgareli before coming on to me at Theodoriana for a situation report.

While he was there, wonderful news arrived. Agoros had routed the Hun—driven him back towards Arta, forcing him to leave a lot of matériel behind. Torrance, who was now ill, sent part of the station stores back to Vourgareli and remained with me to wait out the illness.

But the following day we could hear fighting below Vourgareli and Zervas said it was the Germans. We couldn't understand it.

We weren't in the dark for long. Hamish's staff arrived, retreating from a renewed attack. Fresh German troops—the First Mountain Division no less—had made a forced march overnight from Arta. Zervas's sentries must have been asleep after fourteen days fighting in the rain.

After another day's fighting, the Hun forced their way to Vourgareli. Theodoriana would be next.

Hamish and I had a quick discussion with Zervas's staff. ELAS, we knew, were only two hours from Neraida, but there was nowhere else to go.

Our first and only priority was to keep our staff safe from the Germans. Falling into their hands would mean torture, then death. That was certain.

We made Neraida in the evening of 30 October—Hamish's staff and mine.

Behind us, the Germans took Theodoriana. Neraida would be next. We couldn't think of staying.

Wedged now between two German drives and ELAS, we fled before dawn across a ridge to the east of Neraida.

German shelling broke out shortly afterwards. We'd barely got out of Neraida in time.

And now we were separated from Zervas.

We needed to make contact with Cairo. Hamish stopped to set up his W/T. They were just putting up the aerial when a volley of firing broke out. It was ELAS. EDES replied across the valley.

We got that set packed up and on the move in record time.

Following a small creek bed, we made our way to a tiny settlement, hardly a village. We were holed up in the buildings, trying to set up the W/T again, when ELAS redoubled their fire.

Almost immediately we heard mortars and machine guns from the other side of the hamlet.

It was the Germans.

A hurried conference—Hamish and myself. We had to get out. We would make for Mesochora.

We packed up the cumbersome equipment again. Through ELAS lines—that was what it meant. But there was no alternative. Stay, and the Germans would have had us.

We set off. ELAS bullets snapped past our heads.

It was no good. But then a civilian offered to go forward with a white flag. These are British personnel, he warned. Leave them alone.

We made it to the cliffs above Mesochora village. Those positions are virtually unassailable, we thought. We'll be safe there.

In Mesochora we found Aris. He had defeated Zervas, and he was jubilant. He confiscated our W/T—a disaster for us now that we were separated from Zervas.

But he had no idea that the Germans were so close behind us. When we passed on the bad news, he and General Sarafis looked very sick and surprised and rushed off to make their arrangements.

Now the Hun were bursting through that 'unassailable' gorge. Unchecked, in spite of Aris's 3000 men.

We escaped from Mesochora with a crowd of refugees as the Germans approached. Most of Aris's men had already bolted and we brought up the rear.

A hell of a walk, fourteen hours and raining all the time. Two of our Italians and a mule fell beside the path and died. It was

Dennis Nicholson's turn now with the fever, and he was delirious for most of the journey.

All uphill—or should I say 'up mountain'—to the next village the following day, and to the village after that. ELAS were fleeing before the Hun, and now that we were separated from Zervas we were unavoidably caught up with them. Often we formed their rearguard.

By all reports, Featherbed was clear. We headed off there over the mountain through the rain.

We arrived tired and fed up and our inhospitable reception by Sheppard—clearly well under the thumb of ELAS—didn't improve our mood. Our mission staff were living in luxury there—which was only what I expected after Denys's stories at the Pertouli conference—but there seemed to be no blankets for us even though we were wet through.

Sheppard was a refugee himself. His station had been very close to the Metsovo road to the north, where hordes of Germans were now ensconced and likely to remain. He had been forced to move further and further south until he ended up at Featherbed.

Between us, Hamish and I had managed to keep one W/T set intact although the batteries needed charging. We'd been out of contact with Cairo for more than a week.

We were alive, at least. I'd pulled my station out intact from under the double threat: German and ELAS. It had been by the skin of our teeth, that was true—under fire at times, often having to change direction at a moment's notice. And who knew what we would face when we had to return to Agnanda. But for the moment, we were safe.

At last we had a chance to catch our breath. The food was good, and I had my first bath in more than thirteen months. We were all at the end of our tether and needed a bit of luxury—a few days to rest and re-equip.

* * *

On 12 November Chris turned up to see me.

He parked himself on a stool. I couldn't sit down owing to a fresh crop of boils—six this time—so I leant against the window sill.

'Hasn't it been wet?' I said. 'We're so tired of it. Especially when we're always on the run.'

'Yes,' said Chris. 'There was one day—the wettest I've ever known in Greece. That's what I thought. I walked through a river without even noticing the difference. I was wrong, though. The next day was even wetter. By the way, we've got another Kiwi liaison officer. Name of Mulgan. Major John Mulgan.'

'Don't know him,' I said. 'Where's he from?'

'Christchurch, I believe,' said Chris, 'but he's British army, so it's probably not surprising you don't know him. I've left him in charge of my HQ.'

'How old?' I asked. I thought we might have coincided at school.

'A bit younger than you, perhaps,' said Chris. 'I don't know exactly.'

'I'll look forward to meeting him. Maybe at another conference. And Gwynne? I wasn't surprised to hear you charged him with murder, on the evidence, but what a terrible thing.'

'Gwynne was absolutely incredulous,' said Chris. 'Polite, but incredulous. Just said, "I beg your pardon?" when I read out the charge. I had to read it again and he still couldn't believe it. To be honest, Tom, charging him with murder was one of the hardest things I've ever had to do.'

'At first I thought he'd probably done the right thing,' I said. 'In the circumstances. But Johnny Stavridis' testimony put things in a different light.'

'Gwynne's a bit strange,' said Chris. 'Rather eccentric, don't you think?'

'I got on quite well with him before all this,' I said. 'But I didn't have to work closely with him. So what will happen to him in Cairo?'

'Court-martial, I suppose,' said Chris. 'Have to be, now.'

'What else has been going on?' I said. 'We've been too busy running away from the Hun to get any real news. Or to get the big picture. But I did hear that you've been elevated to Eddie's job. Congratulations.'

Chris explained to me that the big German drive from Trikala had taken Kalambaka quickly—more or less unopposed—and moved on. Meanwhile the drive across from Yannina had taken Mctsovo, where Rufus Sheppard had been, and fanned out. By the end of October three columns of Germans had been converging on Pertouli.

'Where were you?' I asked.

'Not in Pertouli, thankfully. We'd made an emergency evacuation by truck with ELAS. By the time the Hun arrived I was at Karpenisi. By 5 November we heard that Pertouli had fallen. Obviously they knew we had our joint HQ there.'

Then Karpenisi fell. Chris and the others had just made it out. When they went back to try to get some things they found it was already too late—the Hun had torched it.

'So the joint HQ is finished,' I said. 'What with the Germans and ELAS.'

'I suppose it is,' said Chris. 'A shame. In spite of everything it was going quite well. Eddie had done a good job getting everything set up.'

'When's he coming back, Chris?'

'A very good question. We keep getting conflicting signals from Cairo. First they said I had to take over full command because Eddie wasn't returning. Then they hinted that they might be evacuating the whole mission.'

'Really? And leave Zervas to sink or swim?'

'I don't know if that's how they see it,' he said. 'But anyway, then that message was cancelled.'

'Dithering around,' I said. 'They can't make up their minds.'

'Apparently. Because then I got a message from Eddie to say he might be coming back soon.'

'I can't believe they would think of replacing him,' I said. 'Even with you.'

'It's no surprise to me,' said Chris. 'They don't want to hear anything to suggest that the king isn't wanted. Remember when Wallace was here?'

'Yes, I met him at the Waffles conference.'

'Yes, well, he was with the Foreign Office, remember?'

'I do remember. Connections in high places.'

'Exactly. I sensed that there might be some personal criticism of Eddie, so I refused to talk to David except when Eddie was there. But of course the message Eddie was sending wasn't the one they wanted to hear.'

'Chris, there's been a lot of rumours about collaboration,' I said. 'That Red Cross representative, Bickel, was trying to get Zervas to sign up to an armistice.'

'Yes, I know. The Germans used him to negotiate for a truce in Epiros. They told ELAS that Zervas had already signed it.'

'Well, I'm sure he didn't,' I said.

'But ELAS did,' said Chris. 'Their Colonel Petroulakis showed me something he shouldn't have.'

What Chris had seen was a report from the ELAS commander in northern Epiros, Colonel Nassis. It said that he'd agreed to a fourteen-day armistice because the Red Cross said Zervas had made one.

'Stupid of him to show you,' I said.

'He's like that,' said Chris. 'Always doing the wrong thing. Amiable little man, though. Of course it's my word against theirs.

Anyway, ELAS had to cover it up by running with the German rumours that Zervas was collaborating.'

'Well,' I said, 'the rumour about Zervas can't be true, anyway. Because he was fighting the Germans then. On two sides. Fourteen days of it. And ELAS as well. On his flank.'

'Zervas had the Germans on two sides and ELAS on his flank at the same time?' asked Chris.

'Exactly. And Aris told me himself that EDES was their first enemy and the Hun came second.'

'Did he indeed? Doesn't surprise me. He's been acting pretty crazy recently.'

"That's what's worrying me,' I said. 'Aris is extremely dangerous when he's like that. You never know what he might do. You have to second-guess him. And I'm no good at diplomacy. Not like you.'

'Sometimes you just have to bluff, Tom,' said Chris, 'and hope it works out.'

Bluffing was something I had never been particularly good at. I've always found it hard to dissimulate; it suits me better to be direct.

We had two days at Featherbed, and then we were on our way. No more luxury for us. We had to get back to the west and Zervas—my job was with him, after all. We set out for Theodoriana, where we were due to meet Themis and Sergeant Tom Brown, the wireless operator.

We arrived in Theodoriana through belting rain to find Aris ensconced, somewhat to my surprise. He was extremely angry with the British and delighted to take it out on me. He railed for quite some time. Finally he quietened down and we got settled into three poor houses by 2 am. There was no sign of Themis or Tom Brown. Everything was soaked.

In the morning I went up to Aris's HQ with my interpreter, 'Angelo' Angelopoulos. Seeing as Aris was there, we might be able to have some useful discussions. But first I had a question.

Aris was holding court among his inner circle with their Cossack hats.

'Aris,' I said, 'I was expecting to meet Themis Marinos here. Is it possible that you came to Theodoriana because you knew that Themis and I had arranged to meet here?'

Aris seemed to have calmed down since the previous night. He was smooth and reassuring.

'Themis Marinos? No, I had my own reasons for coming— nothing to do with your comings and goings. I'm afraid I can't give you any information about Marinos. No one has seen him.'

That puzzled me, but I took him at his word. We went on to other topics. After a while Angelo and I left Aris and returned to our house.

After lunch I had an unexpected visitor. Among the mission staff was a local called Mitsos. This was his sister Spiridoula.

Spiridoula stole into my room looking around anxiously and saying nothing. As soon as she saw me, she put her finger into her mouth, picked out a small piece of paper, and passed it to me.

My heart thumped in my throat. The damp paper was sticking together and I struggled to unfold it.

The message was short. 'Aris is holding me. Come at once or it will be too late.'

It was from Themis.

Spiridoula knew where to go. She told me Aris had two others as well, but as a Greek working for our mission, I knew Themis was most in danger. I left at a run.

Arriving at the house, I dashed upstairs, pushed aside the sentry, and kicked in the door.

Themis was still there.

He was in a bad way. His face was mottled with bruises.

'They attacked me,' he gasped. 'Thrashed me for being a collaborator. Then they threatened me. Aris tried to get information out of me about the mission. I didn't give them anything.'

'Who attacked you?'

'Aris, and four of his men. Slapped me in the face and punched me. Kicked me. Then Aris had a go at me with his whip. One of his colonels spat in my face.'

'They called you a traitor, I suppose?'

'And worse. They said I had sold myself to the British and the Greek king. They said no one would ever find out where I was—and then they started talking about EAM policy in front of me. That was the most frightening thing of all. In their eyes I was already dead.'

They had told him the usual stuff. The real war was between proletarians and capitalists. England was weak and decaying. Unless Churchill guaranteed that the Greek king would not return, ELAS would attack any British forces that might arrive in Greece. The Germans were less of a danger to Greece than the bourgeoisie, and EAM would turn against the bourgeoisie when the war was over. Members of our mission were interfering in Greek politics without understanding them and should get the hell out.

Themis knew he was lucky to be alive and was extremely grateful to me for stepping in. I got the others released as well. One was Tom Brown, the signaller I was supposed to meet. He was probably in less immediate danger than Themis, but after what had happened to Hubbard, you couldn't count on anything.

I was as relieved as they were—and also deeply satisfied. For all my worries about how I might handle a conflict with Aris, I had snatched his prey from under his nose.

Aris was more conciliatory after this. We got our wireless transmitter back, with apologies. But I wasn't fooled. Aris would see me as a threat from now on. And sure enough, before too long, I heard through the grapevine that I'd moved to the top of his list of people who must be done away with.

EIGHTEEN

Only a week after we'd extricated Themis from his clutches, Aris played a trick on Zervas. A planted 'German' document—a fake, engineered by ELAS—convinced Zervas that the Germans were evacuating Yannina and Arta. Zervas rushed across with all his forces, abandoning his stronghold between the two rivers. Immediately, ELAS took up strategic positions in the mountains of Jumerka and Valtos, preventing his return. Now he was stuck in the west.

Aris and his band had left for Pramanda with instructions for us to follow. To hell with his instructions, I thought. Shocking weather kept us in Theodoriana anyway. At night, rain and hail blew in under the roof tiles and we had to wear our greatcoats inside the house. Bridges and tracks were washed away all over the place.

The runner brought a letter from Beth among the other messages. So normal—boring even—but so desirable.

My own Tom,
I wish I could imagine what you are doing now. When you were in Egypt it was easier because you could tell me more.
    You asked me about clothes rationing. Each adult gets 112 coupons a year, and when we're dressing the shop

window we have to put labels on everything, showing
how many coupons you need for each item.

Rationing can be quite funny at times. For instance,
men's underpants are almost impossible to get hold of.
But babies' nappies aren't rationed. So women are buying
nappies to make underpants for their menfolk.

I couldn't help laughing when I read that. I thought of the men
around Deloraine having to hitch up saggy towelling underpants
every few minutes as they went about their work.

I do miss your parcels. Mother and I are reduced to
wearing rayon and lisle stockings since you left Cairo.
They wear well, but they don't do anything for your
legs.

I can't wait for you to get home. I don't care how grim
and ragged you look. When you get here everything will
be right again.
Your very own Beth.

Recently I had felt very close to Beth—almost close enough to
touch her—and now my spirits soared. The war in Europe was
going well for the Allies. Surely it wouldn't be long until we
were together again. As long as I survived the civil war, that is.

Now, as our mission staff returned to Agnanda to re-establish our
HQ, we passed through Vourgareli. First it had been bombed;
then it had been burnt. This was the worst thing about the war,
especially when it happened to villages I had come to love, tucked
up on their hillsides beneath the great bulk of the mountains. I
thought of Toula and Voula. I knew they'd evacuated in a hurry
and hoped that when we were finally able to join Zervas we
would find them safe with him.

We got a great welcome at Agnanda. The villagers were terrified of ELAS and relieved to see us return. We declined another 'invitation' to join Aris at his HQ in Pramanda and fixed up a comfortable house in Agnanda as our HQ.

My orders were to reunite with Zervas, who had set up his HQ in Kalenzi, to the west of the Arachthos River, with about 3000 men. Spike Moran was with him. Joining Zervas meant crossing the Arachthos at Plaka, where I knew a battle was raging. I couldn't risk taking all the staff of Watermelon, so my plan was that Boulis and I would go on alone.

In early December we went up to Pramanda for talks with Aris. Relations were now ostensibly cordial.

'I am concerned that you have not obeyed my orders to join us here in Pramanda,' said Aris. 'It is very much in your interests to do so as soon as possible.'

'That doesn't accord with my own instructions,' I said.

'And what are they?'

'To rejoin Zervas.'

'Zervas is a traitor,' he replied.

'Zervas has been fighting the Germans,' I said firmly.

'Zervas has never fought the Germans. Zervas has signed a treaty with the Germans.'

'I have seen Zervas fighting the Germans with my own eyes,' I said. 'I can only believe what I have seen.'

'So can I,' he replied. 'Zervas is the first enemy of ELAS. The Germans are second.'

'So you are fighting EDES rather than the Hun.'

'When the traitor has been wiped out, we will fight the Germans. Meanwhile you are to stay away from him.'

'No. I'm going across the river to join him.'

I had managed to get hold of a pass from ELAS. The telephone wires were down, so Aris was unable to cancel it in his usual manner. I'd left Dennis Nicholson in command at Agnanda—a most unenviable task—and went on west with my interpreter, Boulis.

We lost no time in making our way to Plaka. The bridge arched high above the gravelled river bed. Above, on the mountaintops, there was already snow. Below, on either side of the river, there was a battle going on. ELAS and EDES were hard at it, and this time they weren't playing games.

The bridge would afford us no protection. A flight of shallow steps followed its curve, the parapet barely a foot high. The higher you went, the more exposed you were. Up the steps we crept, over the arch and down the other side—but no shots came.

Once back in Zervas's area of control—a much reduced area, now—we could count on protection.

Spike was already there, and Fred Wright, who'd had a close shave himself, getting his staff out when Aris had captured his station at Gotista. And we found Voula and Toula there with Agoros, safe and sound.

Cairo ordered us not to return to Agnanda. Watermelon station would remain on the east side of the river, but without us.

Zervas, when I finally saw him, seemed confident but not quite sure what my game was. He had never been able to count on Cairo absolutely—although he was often more sanguine about their good intentions than he should have been—and now that I was separated from our GHQ, Cairo's instructions were coming straight to me. We knew that when the Germans finally left we would be engaged in harassing their withdrawal—we just didn't know when. But without the *andartes* there could be no useful operations, and at the present all their energy was engaged against each other.

Many villages had been burnt as the Huns tried to root out the *andartes* and secure their supply lines, and the villagers had lost their supplies of winter food, destroyed or captured. Most suspiciously to my mind, the Germans had burnt every single village that the Red Cross committee had seen *andartes* in just at the start of the civil war. How had the Hun got the intelligence, if not from that committee?

The Germans had had the Yannina–Kalambaka road open and garrisoned since late October—they had taken it virtually without opposition. I felt bitterly towards ELAS over this. I was convinced the *andartes* could have held that road if they'd put their minds to it. Now the Germans were busy instituting no-go zones around railway lines, making our operations potentially far more difficult. Meanwhile ELAS had been slaughtering innocent villagers, so everyone was terrified.

It was hard to see how we could keep doing our job, let alone achieve the long-term plan to weld the two groups into a guerrilla army. All my time was taken up with politics instead of sabotage.

On Wednesday, 8 December, ELAS attacked across the Arachthos River. We had to evacuate in a hurry. From Kalenzi we fled via Dodoni to the village of Tseritsana, where a runner from Zervas caught up with us.

'*Kala nea*,' called the runner as soon as he was within earshot. '*Kala nea*.' Good news.

'What good news?' we shouted back.

'Colonel Agoros,' he panted. 'He's chased ELAS out of Kalenzi, right back over the Arachthos River.' We gave a cheer of relief.

The *tsipouro* flowed freely that night. There were no toasts the next day, however, when Boulis and I went over to see Zervas in his camp at Lipso village. Colonel Agoros and a few others aside, his officers had been letting him down, and I told him so. I convinced him to sack a couple of his colonels. It was a pity nothing could be done about Komninos, his 2IC, but he was far too well ensconced.

A day or two later, still in Tseritsana, we heard planes overhead.

'Liberators!' yelled Spike. 'Ours! On their way to Athens. Come and look.'

We all rushed outside. It was a great sight. Right behind the Liberators, less familiar planes appeared.

'More Yank planes,' said Paul. 'Flying Fortresses.' Having been in Greece for so long, I had never seen one, although they must have been a common sight for most of our troops by now.

We watched and counted until they had all disappeared. A hundred and twenty bombers, escorted by fighters. Two hours later they came over again, returning to their base in liberated Italy.

Things were changing. Now that the Allies held airfields in southern Italy, they were within range of the Greek mainland. Surely the liberation of Greece couldn't be far away. Always hoped for, endlessly postponed, it had to happen eventually. Airstrikes would change the balance in our favour, making the Allied invasion that much easier.

In another sign of the times, General Infante, commander of the Italian Pinerolo division, came through about a week before Christmas. Chris had engineered an escape route for him via Albania, where a liaison officer was to put him on a small boat across the Adriatic to Italy. Glad of an excuse to celebrate, we entertained him and his small staff to dinner.

This was what I loved. People coming through with stories to tell, sitting together around the table over dishes of lamb or pork with the sharp scent of oregano in our noses—the black-scarved Greek grandmothers gathered it wild off the mountain slopes— and its savour in our mouths, walnuts perhaps to follow or apples cooked with a little sugar, then lingering, yarning, over whisky and cigarettes. They'd been dropping us cigarettes for a while now—that crumbly old tobacco we'd had to make do with in the Stromi cave before Gorgopotamos, using whatever we could get hold of to roll it in, was a distant memory, unregretted.

General Infante might have been in his early fifties. A shortish, cultured man who spoke good English, he had a neatly trimmed beard and no superfluous weight about him—unlike our General Zervas.

'How did you leave Colonel Chris?' asked Harry Evans.

'Well,' said the General. 'Very well. All the better for my spaghetti.'

'Really?' asked Harry. 'Did he eat with you often?'

'Yes,' said the General. 'Often. For lunch. We had excellent stocks of spaghetti.'

'Spaghetti,' I said. 'That sounds good.'

'It was,' said the General. 'Whenever Colonel Chris was expected for lunch, I would send my ADC, Villaresi, up to a hill where he could see Chris's house. When Chris came out of his door, Villaresi would signal to our cook, who would have the water already boiling. In the spaghetti went, and just as Chris walked in the door it would be ready to serve.'

'Chris has plenty of worries, though,' the General went on. 'There are many mouths to feed. Our Italians, of course. And the escapees—Russians, Poles, British.'

The escapees were former prisoners of war, who'd evaded the Germans' clutches and made their way to Chris's HQ. At first, ELAS had armed some of them, so that they could help fight the enemy. But when the enemy turned out to be other Greeks, the escapees had declined and ELAS had stepped back. Now Chris had all of them on his hands.

It should have been ELAS's problem, I thought. They'd disarmed the Italians and made them useless to everyone including themselves, and now winter was coming on. At least Zervas treated the Italians in Epiros pretty kindly. And the Greek villagers, who had loathed and detested the Italians when they were occupiers, had done everything they could to help them once they were vulnerable and in need.

Just a few days before Christmas, Fred Wright arrived with a newcomer, Jim Russell. He was young, fresh-faced, beardless—and utterly exhausted. They had walked all night so that they could make the dangerous crossing of the Yannina–Arta road under cover of darkness.

Fred got Jim straight into bed, then came to find me.

'Jim's not used to the walking,' he said. 'Fell asleep as soon as he got his boots off. Still in his clothes.'

'So who is he?' I asked. 'Not one of ours?'

'Seems to be the new Kostas Lawrence,' Fred said quietly. 'SIS.' Secret Intelligence Service—my curiosity was piqued. 'I think he's a little unsure of his welcome here,' Fred continued. 'Wonders if we might shoot him if he steps out of line. Like Kostas.'

'Understandably,' I said. 'I wonder what kind of briefing he's had.'

'Not much, I'd say. We've had a few discussions since he landed the other day. I thought he would have known all about the Gorgopotamos op, but I got the impression he knew very little.'

When Jim was back in the land of the living, Fred brought him in. He was obviously embarrassed by his lack of fitness. But I cut short his apology to ask him to clarify his role. As I had hoped, he was there to gather information about German troop movements.

'We'll be glad to help you,' I said.

'Of course, it's a different ...' he started.

'Different organisation?' I said. 'Doesn't matter. That's Cairo's problem. Here we just get on with the job. I'll be delighted if you want to take over intelligence. It's not my area of interest at all.'

Jim was visibly relieved. 'Thank you,' he said. 'To be honest, I wasn't sure what kind of reception I'd get from SOE on the ground.'

'I don't know what briefing you had in Cairo,' I said, 'but whatever you've heard against Zervas, forget it. He's much more useful to us than the other side. He's got more regular officers working with him than ELAS have and some of them are first-rate. Not all of them, though, eh Fred?'

Fred laughed.

General Infante departed on Christmas Eve. Spike was taking him and his party on to Albania.

'Safe journey, General,' I said. 'Think of us now and again when you eat spaghetti, back in Italy.'

'I will, Colonel Tom,' he replied. 'I will.'

Christmas Day, 1943. My second Christmas in Greece. Another missed birthday for Beth. The previous Christmas, waiting for the submarine, had been our lowest point. This year wasn't much better: Cairo had sent some filthy South African brandy, undrinkable stuff. When the W/T operator on duty in Cairo came on the line to wish us the season's greetings, he was drunk. No doubt he'd got hold of something more palatable. But on New Year's Eve we had one hell of a party at Agoros's place with Voula and Toula. Wine, singing, dancing—everything I most loved about Greek parties. Not that it stopped me hoping that next year I'd be celebrating with Beth in Deloraine.

NINETEEN

As 1944 began, Greece was still mired in civil war. ELAS was nicely ensconced in Jumerka and Zervas was still stuck west of the Arachthos.

If we were to get cracking against the Hun again, Zervas would have to do something about ELAS, and he knew it. He toured his area, making some changes in command, getting rid of some (never enough) of his weaker officers, the ones I was always having a go at him about.

On 4 January, Zervas's forces under Agoros crossed the Arachthos in five places to recontest Jumerka. After heavy fighting, ELAS started to give ground. In just four days, Agoros drove them out of Jumerka and Epiros.

Our return to Jumerka was like a triumphal procession. Crowds turned out in all the villages to welcome Zervas back—even the priests in their long black robes and tall black hats like smokestacks, their long beards dangling in front and their long hair behind. There was music and dancing in one village square after another. And the joy wasn't just for Zervas—we got our share, too. After the nightmare of our escape it was good to be among friends and we made the most of it. Back in Agnanda, we christened our new station: Renovation.

It seemed that ELAS had been thoroughly cleaned up and was asking for an armistice. Aris, so I heard, blamed his defeat on my influence on Zervas, and was going to cut pieces off me and fry them in oil in front of me—if he caught me. But I'd learnt something about bluffing now, and I took his posturing with a grain of salt.

Things were going well. Boulis and I took a day to walk south to Zervas's HQ, where he was entertaining some Americans who had just arrived. The British Military Mission had now become the Allied Military Mission.

Five aircraft came over that night. One of them dropped Captain Derek Dodson, who brought with him a voluminous brief from Cairo. A new operation, code-named 'Noah's Ark'.

There had been talk of this operation for some time. Originally it had been purely and simply a plan to harass the Germans as they withdrew from Greece—an event which had seemed to exist only in some uncertain future. But now that was only Phase 3. Phases 1 and 2 were to keep the *andartes* out of mischief until Phase 3 actually eventuated.

The target date for the German withdrawal was set for the beginning of April 1944. On what basis this date was determined I was never sure, but it would certainly put all kinds of pressure on the *andartes*—perhaps not always the kind of pressure that Cairo anticipated. Each side simply accelerated their efforts to emerge as top dog before the British marched back into Greece.

Chris would head the new Allied Military Mission with a mobile HQ. Under him would be two senior officers, one liaising with ELAS and one with Zervas. Nick Hammond would be one. For my sins, I would be the other. My zone of command was 'Area 4', that portion of Greece west of the Pindos range all the way from the Albanian border in the north to the Gulf of Patras in the south. For the first time I would have direct wireless communication with my subordinate officers.

As both EDES and ELAS had a stake in Area 4, there would be fun and games ahead. That was assuming Chris was able to bring off some kind of armistice so that we could get on with the job—sabotage of road and rail communications.

Dodson and I put the new brief to Zervas in his office a few days later. He cut immediately to the point.

'What level of support will I be getting? Assuming an armistice with ELAS—which is not looking highly likely just now.'

I swallowed hard. 'For support and payment purposes, the relative numbers of men have been calculated at three thousand to seven thousand.' In reality, the ratios had been set at Zervas's three thousand to ELAS's eleven and a half thousand—but I knew he would hit the roof if I told him that straight off.

'Their seven to my three?' he said. 'Is that what you're saying?'

'It is,' I replied. 'Based purely on numbers.'

'Based purely on numbers?' he repeated. 'Why? Their numbers are numbers of communists. Is that what you want? A whole lot of communists that you've armed and equipped for when the Germans leave?'

'We just want people who are prepared to do the ops,' I replied. 'That's the beginning and the end of it.'

'I thought Allied GHQ was more strategic than that,' he said. 'I thought they were supporting me to keep the communists in check.'

I had tried to disabuse him of this notion before, never with any great success. He was convinced that GHQ saw him as a defender of his country against a threat greater than that of the Nazi occupiers. As it was clear by now that the German withdrawal would certainly take place eventually, he assumed that his role as the champion of freedom and democracy would be more important than ever.

Now, finally, the real situation was getting through to him and his shock was obvious.

'Then I must rethink my whole position,' he said, turning away from me to the papers on his desk.

That afternoon we moved our HQ to Skiadades, even closer to Vourgareli. We could hear the sounds of fighting from the east—mortars and medium machine guns—as ELAS made repeated attacks across the river.

Zervas was in a hole. Cairo had forbidden him to exploit his military advantage by crossing the Acheloos River himself, and now we were getting word of a Hun drive up our way. Zervas left for Vourgareli and we went over to visit the forward units and see Agoros. It was so cold up where he was that only the Bren guns would work.

There was to be a conference in Thessaly for senior mission staff. I was keen to see Chris—but it would require a trip through ELAS territory, and no pass was forthcoming for me; Aris would not allow it. Chris decided it was too risky for me to make the trip without a pass, and so Dodson went on my behalf, with a one-way pass: he would not be returning. From now on, Aris told Chris, the only way for British officers to reach Zervas would be by parachute.

Less than a week later, just as EDES was completing an encircling movement of all ELAS forward bases, Cairo signalled that ELAS wanted to come to terms. Zervas was ordered to take no further offensive action. Within three hours, Zervas had ordered all his units to withdraw across the Acheloos. Militarily, it was insanity, but Zervas scrupulously did what he was told. Hostilities ceased at 11 pm.

Next morning, ELAS attacked through heavy fog along the whole east front with much increased firepower, including many Spandaus. Withdrawing, EDES troops were caught out of position and there was fierce fighting just below our HQ—as well as news of a German drive up from Kato Kalendine to our rear. All this was horribly familiar.

At 10 pm we had to clear out, heading west. Boulis and I took off after Zervas with the two wireless transmitters—ours, familiarly known as 'Tommy' or 'Lord Tommy'—and Zervas's. We caught up with Zervas at Plaka on the Arachthos and pressed on together. After a bloody journey we made Plaisia at 7 am to find forty-three signals waiting for us. All hands were flat out decoding.

EDES were forced back to the line of the Arachthos— accompanied by a good proportion of the civil population of Jumerka, fleeing before ELAS. We'd seen it all before, when we'd escaped over the Jumerka Mountain to Thessaly. A woman with a heavy load strapped to her back. A small girl in a calf-length dress piggy-backing her smaller brother, barefoot in spite of the cold. A baby strapped in a kind of papoose. Mules laden with household goods and food for the journey. Water wasn't a problem—every village had its row of *vrisi* where the refugees could help themselves.

By now EDES were completely out of ammunition. ELAS had plenty, even though they'd suffered heavy casualties at the hand of EDES, and plenty of machine guns. Fortunately we were expecting a drop. After a poor sortie one night, we got five planes and five beautiful drops the next—bags of Breda MMGs and mortar bombs, plus 7,600 sovereigns.

Just in time. Reliable information was coming in that the Huns were coming to Kalenzi and Plaisia. We got away just ahead of them, one group for Shepshed station at Tseritsana and ourselves for Sklivani to establish our new HQ. There we heard that an armistice for the civil war had been negotiated for 4 February.

The Hun were driving down from the north by the truckload. There was heavy fighting towards Gotista, so we sent Voula and Toula away to safety with Spike. We heard that the Hun had been enquiring about 'Lord Tommy', not realising it was the name of our wireless transmitter; they wanted to know if we had a real English lord with us.

With the armistice in place, we should have been able to take joint action with ELAS against the Germans. But no—ELAS wouldn't hear of EDES crossing the river.

The Germans had operation 'Sperber' in full swing now, driving west from Porta and north from Agrinion in an encircling movement designed to trap large numbers of *andartes* in a ring that was pulled gradually tighter and tighter. The Germans would take any towns within the circle with heavy artillery, often burning them to the ground.

This time, however, the cold weather got the better of the Hun, and we were able to return to Plaisia within a few days.

On 9 February Hamish Torrance arrived. Chris had sent him as my 2IC, replacing Bathgate, who was going across to Nick Hammond.

I liked Hamish, and I was delighted to have him with me. He had just been promoted to lieutenant-colonel—well deserved, I had no doubt. Like Chris, he'd had previous experience in this game—as a captain he'd been in Narvik before the British had made their abortive attempt to hold Norway against the Germans. He wasn't able to tell me much, but I knew he'd been there twice, remaining the second time after the Hun occupied the town, having no idea how he was going to get out. I knew he had an MBE and I assumed that was what it was for.

The new year also brought some new excitement, as we started to feel the effects of the Allied progress in the war. On 11 February we made contact with the new Allied base at Bari, on the east coast of Italy, for the first time. A new operation, 'Glasshouse', was to commence in March—sea sorties from Italy to our west coast to bring in supplies and exfiltrate personnel and prisoners behind the Huns' backs. We had high hopes. You couldn't drop trucks by parachute, but with a big enough ship all kinds of things were possible.

Chris had now established his HQ in Viniani. I remembered him telling us the story of his first visit there on his way to find Zervas, and the American Greek who was so frightened of ELAS. I wondered if he was still there.

Chris was arranging a conference to negotiate the armistice, but finding a mutually acceptable place to meet was proving a sticking-point. And then there were the terms that ELAS was putting forward. They wanted a united army and government, something Zervas would never agree to. But he might have to agree to another of their terms: that he would denounce the known collaborators within the ranks of his own party, of whom apparently there were a number.

I would travel to the armistice conference with a party of men, leaving Hamish in charge of Renovation station and our reconnaissance work for Noah's Ark.

The conference had already been going on for the best part of a month. It had started out in Merokovo on the east bank of the Acheloos River, but although Zervas had already sent Komninos Pyromaglou and his chief of staff, he would not agree to come himself unless it moved further west, nearer to his own area. Eventually it settled at Plaka on the east bank of the Arachthos River, where Boulis and I had crossed the high arched bridge while ELAS and EDES shot at each other below us.

Plaka was bristling with machine guns, and in the meeting room the faces were sour. There were senior officers from all three resistance groups, with Kartalis from EKKA in the chair. Chris had the new US representative, Major Wines, with him, and the two of them seemed to have decided to let discussion run on as long as possible. Zervas was entertaining himself by throwing the odd spanner into the works.

There was much acrimonious bickering—who would command a combined resistance army, and what would it be like? It was the usual political bullshit, and as usual I found myself getting impatient and angry. After not much more than a day, I cleared out and headed back to Plaisia, unconvinced that they would resolve anything at all. Zervas was only a day behind me, leaving Komninos Pyromaglou to see the proceedings through to the end. That kind of thing was right up his alley.

At the end of February, when the conference finished, the various delegations started to turn up at our station—the reps from EDES and EKKA first, then Chris and Major Wines. They were there for a big event—the presentation of British awards to General Zervas and Captain Myridakis.

The conference had ended in success, with the signing of an agreement—the Plaka Agreement, as it later came to be called. In terms of boundaries, the status quo would be maintained. Zervas had agreed to denounce certain infamous members of his organisation in Athens who were known collaborators—a good thing, too.

The next day was the EDES parade. The senior officers took the salute as the various formations marched past. Chris decorated Zervas with the OBE and Myridakis with the MC. Aris, too, had been recommended for a decoration after Gorgopotamos, but the recommendation had been rescinded because of his role in the civil war. Only Barba Niko was missing. He'd won the MBE for his contribution to Gorgopotamos. But he was far away.

Watching the ceremony, I started to wonder. If someone had told me, way back at Mavrolithari, when we'd done Gorgopotamos and were saying goodbye to Barba Niko, everything that would happen—that we would have to flee for our lives ahead of ELAS and the Hun not once but twice—would

I have decided differently back in July when Eddie had offered me the chance to get out of Greece?

Maybe it's the kind of question you shouldn't ever ask yourself—perhaps it's pointless speculation. But I knew the answer. I wouldn't have changed my decision. Zervas and I now had a good working relationship based on mutual respect, and a growing friendship based on being able to put away a lot of whisky together without falling under the table. I had come to think of him as 'Old Zed', although I never would have said it to his face. Agoros, too, was a wonderful leader and a real friend. I could laugh and joke with Voula and Toula like one of the family. And my own staff were good mates and good soldiers. Allowing for circumstances I was content. Now I just had to stay alive until I could get home to Beth.

A couple of days after the award ceremony, Chris and I found ourselves alone, enjoying the relative warmth inside the house. Outisde it was wet and miserable. The BBC had recently announced the Plaka Agreement, which seemed to have gone down well with the British. And we had just heard that Noah's Ark had been postponed: no operations were imminent, we'd been told, and we should relax the tempo of our preparations.

'At least Zervas has his area to himself now,' said Chris. 'It's not ideal, strategically or probably in any other way. But he's got rid of ELAS and that must make things easier.'

'It certainly makes things easier for me,' I replied. 'Although we'll still need to keep the *andartes* out of mischief.'

'You'll be busy with the Glasshouse ops,' he said. 'You're going to need a hell of a lot of mules to get the supplies away into the mountains in a hurry.'

'That's right,' I said, 'they're coming from all over Greece. And they'll all have to be fed. Defence is complex, too, of course. We're working on that with Zervas.'

'Right under the Germans' noses. It'll be a real coup if we can bring it off.'

It was good to have Chris to myself for a little while. Agoros had paraded his men in the morning but now there was little to do, so we lingered and chatted.

'I had a letter from Beth in the drop the other day,' I said. 'Among others.'

'I hope you'll write to me after the war,' said Chris.

'Of course. I'll let you know when my first son is born.'

'Or daughter.'

'A son first,' I said. 'A son called Chris. You can be godfather.'

'Well, when I have a son, I'll return the favour,' he said. 'I haven't got a mother lined up yet, though, so it might take a little while. And a daughter would be fine with me, too. Emma. Then we would have our own Emma Woodhouse.'

'You'd better get on with it, then.'

'Ross has managed it,' he replied. 'Although he didn't seem to think it necessary to tell me before the event.' His adjutant, Ross Bower, had married a Greek girl at Karpenisi in December.

'And what will you do with yourself after the war?' If he had to do anything, that is. It was hard to remember that Chris's father was the third Baron Terrington, although Chris was the second son. Perhaps that meant he would have to earn his own living. I didn't like to ask.

'I always imagined myself as an academic,' he replied. 'A fellowship at All Souls, something like that. Lecturing on Greek philosophy, perhaps. But a funny thing happened to me. An old woman read my palm. Told me I would stop my studies forever when I was twenty-three.'

'And was she right?'

'So far. Hitler attacked Belgium and Holland the day before my twenty-third birthday.'

I'm a bit of a sceptic, I have to say, but I could see this had made an impression on Chris, in spite of his customary practical attitude. I also suspected he didn't tell that particular story to too many people.

A few days later, we moved our headquarters across the Preveza–Yannina road from Plaisia to Derviziana. The day we were leaving, a Junkers transport aircraft circled twice within 200 feet of the ground. We were getting out just in time.

TWENTY

I was glad to be moving to Derviziana. The village climbed the lower slopes of the mountains on one side of the Lakka-Souli valley. The most beautiful valley in the world, I thought to myself as I looked out early on my first morning there.

Spike had gone on ahead to get everything ready as only he knew how. Zervas was already there, having decided that Derviziana was more centrally placed for operations, and Fred Wright and Harry Evans were not far away, just across the valley at Tseritsiana.

There were only two suitable houses in the village—*archonda spitia*, as they called them—belonging to those sufficiently well-to-do or distinguished to afford, or to have once been able to afford, a larger and better house. Spike had arranged for us to have the doctor's house. Zervas had the other.

Dr Rossis had died in 1938, leaving his widow with four children. The oldest, Koula, was about twenty-one. Nikos, the youngest, was about fourteen. Mrs Rossis rented the top two rooms to us. There we slept and worked, squeezing a table against the wall in the only space that wasn't taken up by beds. A staircase led to the flat concrete roof, where they dried the oats they used to make *trachanas* for the winter.

On the ground floor was the doctor's surgery, kept just as he'd left it with the door firmly locked. There was a tiny kitchen, barely large enough to get into, where they did the washing up. Apart from that there was one other downstairs room. Here the family usually lived (although they were now dispersed throughout the village for sleeping) and our Italian cook, Spiro, prepared our meals in a cauldron hanging from chains in the fireplace. When the weather was bad we ate there, too. No bathroom: the toilet was a hole in the ground behind the house—but of course we were used to that. The villagers used the forest.

The windows on two sides of our sleeping room looked to mountains to the north, and to more mountains across the valley to the west—they were white with snow when we arrived. The valley was hilly, with gentle ranges rising from flat ground. The position was excellent—no one could creep up on that village unobserved.

Five minutes away was the village square, built around a giant plane tree twelve yards around the trunk—750 years old, according to the locals. The local *kafenion* was actually inside it, with a panel of parachute silk nailed up to a wooden frame for a door.

They seemed to find new uses for those parachute panels every day. We did, too—they made a great outdoor shower curtain, with the water bucketed in from above. Our habit of showering daily when we were at HQ was a source of great amusement to the villagers, but we didn't care. It kept the boils at bay.

A few days after arriving in Derviziana, we met Chris in Tseritsana to discuss plans. Jim Russell, the young intelligence agent, took me up to the village president's house where he was staying, high up on a hill. The house looked down on Tseritsiana's *vrisi*, where the village women gathered every morning to gossip as they drew water for their homes. Jim had got himself well set up, with a good supply of eggs and cheese from the president's chickens and goats.

He told me about the intelligence activities he was coordinating. Since January he had co-opted informants in Yannina, Corfu and Lefkas Island and instituted a traffic watch on the Yannina–Trikala road to collect information on German troop dispositions. As we were in the throes of recces for Noah's Ark, whenever it might eventuate, his intel was invaluable.

We were sitting over breakfast one morning when a runner arrived from Zervas's HQ. Zervas wanted to see me. I took Boulis with me to interpret. Although my Greek was now serviceable, it was always worthwhile using an interpreter. It gave you more time to think.

Just five or six minutes took us down the hill to the stone house where Zervas had the bottom floor for his offices and sleeping quarters; the family had kept the upper floor for themselves. The house was bigger than ours, and the accommodation for the family more satisfactory, but I preferred our view.

'Our preparations for Glasshouse are going well,' Zervas told me. We had fixed on Alonaki Bay, a quiet bay about six miles south of Parga, for the op. 'All the caïques for the seaward side have been organised. Quite a lot of captured German craft as well as Greek. And troops to cordon off the area by road.'

'Let's hope it goes well,' I replied. I always expected something to go wrong at the last minute—based on long experience—but I usually tried to keep that expectation to myself.

'Yes,' said Zervas. 'Let's hope. Because we have problems with ELAS again.'

'What kind of problems?'

'Truce-breaking problems.'

ELAS, it seemed, had been trying to establish a base in one of Zervas's areas and had brought in 120 men over the last month. He was very angry. I was annoyed, too. This was trouble that we could do without.

'Best cable Cairo,' I said. 'Let them bring pressure to bear.' What with the two ops to prepare for simultaneously, Glasshouse and Noah's Ark, the last thing we needed were boundary disputes.

It was mid-March by now, and the weather was vile. Rain, sometimes snow, and no fire in our room. We'd finally got everyone away for Glasshouse, and I was lying low with one hell of a cold.

Outside the window, the mountains had disappeared in swirling snow. I heard two people chatting as they climbed the creaky wooden stairs—Zervas and someone whose voice I didn't know. They came into our crowded room steaming and still loud with talk. Zervas introduced his companion—a tall man in a suit and tie, one Professor Christos Sgouritsas.

Sgouritsas looked to be around fifty. The anti-left-wing parties in Athens who supported the EDES cause had sent him up to the mountains to be their liaison officer with Zervas and to keep in contact with the Allied Military Mission. Cairo had told me he might be coming, and had asked me to check up on him.

I wasn't feeling up to much that afternoon, but over the next few days I found out a bit more about Sgouritsas, although he seemed a little surprised at my questions. He told me the Germans had put him in prison a few months earlier for harbouring British officers. He assured me that it wasn't Zervas who had sought the support of the parties in Athens—in other words, Zervas wasn't politicking—but vice versa, and that he himself didn't have any political ambitions, either. I sent this information off to Cairo. Was he after political power in post-war Greece? I thought not.

A few days later, everyone in the village turned out to see the mule train coming back up from the valley with three tons of stores: the first Glasshouse op had been a success. A naval lieutenant had landed to do coastal recces for further sea ops, and several of our sick personnel had been evacuated. Seventeen British and American aircrew who had been forced down in

Greece had also got away on the ship. Before the op, we'd had intel that two columns of ELAS were on their way to the coast and another was en route, preparing to attack the returning mule trains, so we had sent Agoros off with his 3/40 regiment and Hamish to protect the column.

I was constantly being summoned to Zervas's HQ to hear complaints about ELAS incursions. Many cables went back and forth between us and Cairo. Sometimes the facts proved to be rather different from the initial reports. One turned out to be more than a little embarrassing. One hundred and twenty men rumoured to have infiltrated one of Zervas's areas turned out to be twenty-one men and two mules.

One day I was down at Zervas's HQ hearing about yet another complaint. When we'd finished talking business, the General broke out the whisky.

'Agoros thinks highly of you, *paidi mou*—my friend,' he said.

'It's mutual,' I replied.

'Apparently you're the only one of the British who can hold your liquor,' he went on, grinning. 'He says the others are barbarians when they're drunk—he had to reprimand his sister Toula for laughing at them. And when they're sober they're inscrutable. You're neither one nor the other.'

'Well, I'm not British.'

'That's his explanation, too. You're a New Zealander—so you're not like the rest of them.'

Following the success of the first Glasshouse op, bringing in large quantities of equipment for Noah's Ark, training of the *andartes* became top priority. Our instructions from GHQ Middle East dictated that the sea ops were to take priority over action against the Germans, which would have endangered the continuation of supplies.

We posted Allied liaison officers to units to assist with training the *andartes* in preparation for Noah's Ark. Dennis Nicholson and I went up to see Agoros's Brens at Georgani, where his independent 3/40 regiment, one of the best striking forces of Zervas's organisation, was based. Thanks to its excellent officers it was well disciplined, and we found it to be well equipped as well—a first-class fighting formation that had successfully taken part in almost every action. Old Zed had some other excellent units, too—the Cherovouni independent regiment and the Pentolakkos independent battalion, for instance. Major Galanis as commander of the 2nd Independent HQ battalion was another who stamped his strength and energy on the men under his command—and offered me his friendship.

Early one morning, I took my camera down to Agoros's training ground. Stripped to the waist, the men were already well into their PT. Some were running and grappling, others doing crawl-throughs. Later, when the soldiers were dressed again, there was drill and marching for men and women alike, then weapons training. Favourites were the British army weapons— Vickers, Brens, 3-inch and 4-inch mortars. More British officers meant better weapons training, but getting all units up to the required standard was a big challenge.

We had become accustomed to the sight of women in uniform, although they were kept out of the scrapping itself. Voula and Toula travelled everywhere with Agoros and took part in the training, well turned out in their khaki skirts, military shirts and serviceable boots. And word had started coming through from Athens of a young woman who was engaged against the Germans in another capacity, running resistance activities for the British—her code name was Patricia or Pat. She must have been running incredible risks, I thought, right under the Germans' noses in Athens.

In the evening, everyone went to the *kafenion* in and around the plane tree to wind down. There was much loud discussion of the day's exercises, and many appeals to Major Galanis for his opinion. The rigorous program was engendering a sense of common purpose and achievement that was good to see. We would need it in the action against the Germans that lay ahead.

Invariably, the conversation would turn to the Allied invasion of Greece.

'It's got to be soon,' a chorus of Greek voices would say. 'You must have the date, Tom.'

Their faith in what we could do was exaggerated. In their minds, if we didn't invade, it would be because we didn't want to, rather than because we couldn't. But Noah's Ark was continually being postponed. I knew what would happen to their hopes and expectations if time kept passing and no invasion happened. They would be let down badly, and they would be bitter.

Greek Easter in 1944 fell in mid-April. We went to the church service in Derviziana on Good Friday, and on Saturday watched as the villagers prepared the spitted lamb for the festivities that would begin after the midnight service. It was hard to keep our eyes open at the service—three planes had been over at 1 am— but we went off to Zervas's house afterwards in good spirits for the celebration.

We found Old Zed and the others sitting outside, genial and relaxed around a small table decorated with flowers. Plenty of food and drink, and dancing, naturally—it was Greece.

Next day, the general after-Easter gloom set in—Zervas had it particularly badly. But we had work to do. Both inside and outside Greece, the situation had changed materially. At the end of March, a new body had declared itself in Free Mountain Greece: the Political Committee of National Liberation, or PEEA. Its establishment had more or less coincided with a serious mutiny of the Greek armed forces in the Middle East. Although the mutiny was instigated by EAM, the members of PEEA were not all communists by any means; the dissent could claim to be broadly representative of the Greeks in Greece. Needless to say, EDES and EKKA refused to join.

A signal came in from Bari in Italy. The next sea op would take place just a week after Easter—Glasshouse 2—and I would be on the ship out. Cairo had called an all-party conference in the Middle East. I was to escort Zervas's representatives and make my own report to GHQ.

I was excited. It wasn't the end of my time in Greece: I knew I would be coming back—unlike Eddie, who had still not been allowed to return. But apart from the odd day here and there, I'd had no time off since Harling. ELAS and EDES had played ping-pong with the Jumerka area and I'd felt like one of the balls, helplessly batted from one side to the other and back again. A spell in Cairo would be a holiday in comparison. It would be good to find out what was really going on, too, not just in Greece but in the wider war. Was it likely that I'd be back with Beth before next Christmas came around?

I determined to have a good time in Cairo. I hoped some of my mates would be around, and I was looking forward to the food—Shepheard's Hotel beckoned—and comfortable living quarters. Then I could return to my friends in Greece to see this thing through to the end.

Zervas summoned me by runner while I was finishing my breakfast porridge the day after Easter Monday.

'I'm thinking of sending Colonel Metaxas to the conference,' he said. Colonel Stavros Metaxas, father of Boulis, had arrived with a painful broken arm the day before. He was a retired Reserve Army officer.

I was horrified. 'But he's only just come. He doesn't know anything about what's going on.'

'What does that matter?'

'This conference is important,' I said. 'They'll be deciding on representation to the national government in exile. You don't want to be dealing yourself out.'

'Politics,' said Zervas, 'just politics. I have no interest in it. Nothing will be achieved with EAM present.'

'But you won't have any credibility unless you send good representatives. Who else are you thinking of?'

'Komninos,' he replied. 'I don't know about the third one yet. What about Boulis here?'

I looked across at Boulis, who had come with me as interpreter. Boulis knew what was going on, true, but he wouldn't have much credibility. Komninos Pyromaglou knew the politics inside out, but his lack of military understanding was embarrassing, and he was so verbose that people lost patience with him.

'Perhaps we can discuss this later,' I said. 'But in my opinion you need a good military officer. Someone who will emphasise the military character of your organisation.'

The next day I was back in Zervas's office again, this time with another interpreter in case Boulis's name was put forward again.

Zervas wasn't beating about the bush. 'I've settled on my three representatives,' he said. 'Stavros and Boulis, and Komninos.'

My heart sank.

'General,' I said. 'You have to reconsider. These representatives are unsuitable. They won't make a good impression in Cairo.'

'Enough,' he said. 'Why should I waste valuable officers on such affairs? They are needed in the field. God knows we have few enough of them, and so much to do.' He turned back to the papers on his desk as he always did when he was cross. I knew I had been dismissed.

I was more than a little annoyed. Usually I could talk him around—in fact I prided myself on my ability to do so. But he certainly had a tendency to drop his bundle sometimes, and rarely to his own advantage.

Hamish Torrance was to take over command while I was in Cairo. But first, we had Glasshouse 2 to prepare for. The sea ops would be bringing in military supplies for the whole of Greece. An infantry landing craft was due to Alonaki Bay on 22 April.

Between the bay and the mountains ran the Preveza–Paramythia Road, where the Germans moved freely. We would need several thousand *andartes*, working with British saboteurs, to prepare bridges on this road for demolition and to provide a ring of defences while the op was on. All the mules from Zervas's entire area had to be assembled to carry the anticipated supplies, some coming from as far as six or seven days' journey away. I was glad to have Dennis to look after logistics.

We left on 21 April, Hamish and Dennis and the rest of us, plus Zervas's representatives, of course.

Five hundred mules were waiting at the pinpoint. There was no moon—sea ops were always scheduled for a dark night.

At 11 pm the ship appeared. There was pandemonium for a time. All around the sweep of the beach, working frantically, the *andartes* piled up cases of ammunition and bundles of weapons. Mules stood by quietly, waiting for their loads. Before first light, as long as everything went according to plan, the bay would be empty and five hundred mules would be heading inland, their safe passage secured by sabotage ops to keep the enemy out of the way.

By 2.30 am I was away—my first time out of Greece in over eighteen months.

TWENTY-ONE

We headed out between the two islands that stand off the coast, Paxos and Antipaxos, and made good time to Bari. After a couple of days in Bari we flew down to Cairo via Malta and a car picked us up at the drome to drive into the city—the Greek delegation and myself.

Cairo was just coming into its long, hot summer. In the Greek mountains the summers were coolish, which was why in peacetime people from Athens took their summer vacations up there, at places like Pertouli, or on one of the islands. The heat struck me in the face as I left the plane, and I knew immediately that my beard would have to come off. Not yet, though—I wanted a few people I knew to see it first, so they would wonder who I was. That would be fun.

It was the time of year when the *khamsin* wind blows in off the desert. I hadn't given it a thought all the time I was in Greece, but now something in me started to anticipate one. I thought about the day I'd collected a dust storm smack in the face, just as I was heading out of Gianaclis on a motorcycle—must've been in 1941. Instantly I'd been choked by reddish-yellow sand. I'd had no goggles, and had barely been able to see fifty yards, when I could look up at all. It had been impossible to keep going. I wasn't looking forward to more of those.

I'd forgotten how noisy it was in a big city. In the mountains where I'd been, you could hear the goats clonking the bells around their necks as they pottered about on the slopes. Here it was bedlam. It would take a little bit of getting used to, but only a little bit. The night life, and parties with my mates—that was what I was looking forward to most.

Since our victory at El Alamein, I found, Cairo had pretty well emptied of troops. While we'd been carrying out the Animals ops, the Sicily landings were going ahead, and as civil war was breaking out in Greece, the Kiwi division had embarked for Italy—almost to the day. There were hardly any Kiwis left in Cairo.

The Greek king had arrived in Cairo on 12 April. The following day, the Prime Minister in exile, Emmanouil Tsouderos, had resigned and been replaced by Sofoklis Venizelos. Venizelos, I knew, was a very famous name: his father had been a hero of the Greek independence movement and had twice served as prime minister before the war. Sofoklis Venizelos would serve as prime minister again, in peacetime, but for now he didn't last long in the job: just ten days. On 23 April, while we were on our way from Bari, Georgios Papandreou, a leading liberal and republican, arrived in Cairo from Athens and the king asked him to become prime minister in Venizelos's place. Papandreou had agreed.

Now the responsibility for the all-party conference with the delegates I'd brought from Greece lay on Papandreou.

Political activities in Athens had seemed very remote to us in the mountains, and these leaders were just names to me. None of them had much to do with resistance activities in Free Mountain Greece. But the arrival of the king and the resignation of Tsouderos had pushed Greek events to the fore in Cairo. On my very first morning there, I was invited to lunch with Brigadier Barker-Benfield, a tall chap who looked to be in his fifties, now in command of SOE, or Force 133 as it now seemed to be called.

He was universally known as 'B.B.'. He seemed like a nice old boy, although I don't think he thought too highly of my beard.

I gave the Brigadier an overview of things from Zervas's side, and he asked me to brief the General Operations Committee that afternoon.

I duly arrived for the committee meeting and reported to someone called Bickham Sweet-Escott. What a name, I thought, but he was an interesting chap with some stories to tell. It seemed he'd been trying to get into the Greek show himself for some time but it had never happened. He knew about Gorgopotamos, of course, and I think he was a bit envious. When I told him I'd had lunch with Barker-Benfield, Sweet-Escott said the Brigadier knew nothing whatever about 'our kind of work'. I couldn't help wondering how much Sweet-Escott knew about it himself.

I think I gave them a bit of a shock when I went into the meeting. I suppose my appearance wasn't quite what they were used to. I thought I had better wear my MC, but my battledress was filthy and my beard could probably have supplied the whole clean-shaven crew with a respectable moustache apiece.

They had been discussing Epiros, they told me, and they wanted my opinion. Was it worth continuing to support Zervas? What did I think of his character?

I told them what I thought. I didn't gloss over Zervas's failings—his love of good living, his reluctance to cut the dead wood from his command—but I also told them of his absolute loyalty to Britain, and how I'd seen him put joint HQ commands ahead of his own interests. I told them about ELAS, too—that they were absolutely disciplined and much more numerous than Zervas's lot, but that the Epirot villagers hated them for their ruthlessness and you couldn't rely on them in action.

What did I think of the likelihood of civil war after liberation? I didn't pull any punches. ELAS had the weapons we'd been supplying them with, plus everything they'd scored from the

Italians. The Plaka Agreement had stopped the fighting for now, but the civil war had plainly revealed ELAS's intention to be on top when Greece was liberated. Now they'd set up the PEEA, designed as an alternative government, which I understood laid some claim to represent all of Greece. In effect they were laying their cards on the table.

The talk went round and round. The thing was, they were the ones making the decisions. They sat in their committee room asking questions and then, based on no personal knowledge of their own, made choices that affected the lives of everyone on the ground—ours, Zervas's, the villagers', the *andartes'*. Had they ever seen a villager hanged from a branch of the plane tree in the square, a sign around his neck warning his neighbours that this would happen to them, too, if they supported the *andartes*? Had they returned to a village they loved to find that the Germans had burnt the houses just as winter was coming on? Would it have made a difference if they had?

On my way through Italy, at the New Zealand Forces Club in Bari, I'd heard that two of my Kiwi mates were dead. Now, at the New Zealand Forces Club in the Sharia Malika Farida, I got the details.

Colin Hornig had lasted until March. He'd been commanding a Kiwi road construction party in the hills to the north-west of Cassino, in Italy. Apparently there was a mountain there with a monastery on top that we couldn't get around in the push for Rome—it was hard to get a good idea of it all because everyone at the club had lived through the whole sequence of events and didn't feel inclined to go back over what seemed to them like ancient history. They stared at me in astonishment when they found out I had barely heard of the campaign.

It was no surprise that Colin was dead. They'd been working within enemy range, widening a road with precipitous grades into a tank track. On the exposed sections they had to operate the D6 dozers at night, without lights. Colin copped it after only two days.

Arthur Allen, another old friend, had been killed in the same area a couple of weeks before Colin. He'd been on mine-lifting work—which the forward troops were supposed to do for themselves, but tended to leave to the engineers. The Maori Battalion had been trying to take the railway station, and Arthur's group had been clearing the way for support vehicles. Their position was completely exposed. Arthur and another couple of sappers were killed almost immediately.

I remembered Arthur trotting down the gangway of the *Nieuw Amsterdam* beside me when we'd docked at Fremantle in Western Australia on our way to the war from Wellington early in 1941, looking for a good time. The last time I could remember seeing him and Colin was in Egypt, at Arthur's camp at Sidi Heneish—nearly two years ago now.

Another old mate, Charlie Bowie, was still in Cairo as head of the Kiwi Club, and we arranged to meet there a few days after I arrived. Charlie had been with me on that leave I'd taken in Palestine and Lebanon—the trip when the desert sore on my toe was giving me hell and I had to keep stopping off at the forces hospitals to get it dressed.

The club was just the same. That meant it was just as good. One of the things that set the Kiwi clubs apart was that they were for all ranks—General Freyberg was supposed to have said that you couldn't expect a man to fight like a gladiator if you treated him like a butler. Another big attraction was that all the Allied nursing sisters could use it, too.

'Tom?' said Charlie when he found me at the bar. 'I hardly recognised you with that forest on your face.'

That was the response I was after. Now I could get a photo taken and shave the thing off. I'd give it a day or two, perhaps—no more.

We went to sit at one of the round tables in the lounge.

'What have you been up to?' said Charlie. 'I haven't seen you in forever.'

'Can't say.' That was the best way to answer that particular question—it shut people up pretty quickly. Charlie was no exception. I could see him scouting about in his head for a safer topic of conversation.

'Remember those Lebanese women?' he said. 'Beautiful, eh?'

'How could I forget?'

'There are some very nice girls in Cairo at the moment,' said Charlie. 'There's one I like called Marie Innes—and she's got a friend called Jean. Want to come out with us one night?'

I was up for it. Charlie took us to the Auberge des Pyramides, a new nightclub on the Mena road—new to me, at least—with an outside dance floor. We danced under the stars.

'Have you been to the Continental roof garden, Tom?' asked Marie as we sat over beers and gin slings during a pause in the music. 'It's a bit like this—great fun.'

'No, never,' I said, 'but I heard about it last time I was in Cairo. Do you like it there?'

'It's wonderful,' she said. 'There's a dance floor and a cabaret. Belly-dancers and magicians. You should go.'

'We should look out for the king,' said Charlie. 'He comes here a lot.'

'Which king?' I asked.

'King Farouk, of course,' he said. 'The Egyptian king. Who else?'

I had the Greek king on my mind, but stopped myself from saying so just in time.

Denys Hamson was also in Cairo, heading up the Islands desk at SOE HQ. We greeted each other with great enthusiasm. He had sometimes irked me in Greece with his easy cynicism, but now he seemed like an old friend.

'Bill Jordan's here,' he told me.

'Good old Bill,' I said. I knew his health had given way, and he'd been evacuated in March, but I hadn't actually seen him since before the civil war began. 'We should all get together.'

'Let's,' he said. 'How long are you here for, Tom?'

'I don't know yet,' I replied. 'I've been having interviews with this person and that. Report to write and so on.'

'Bill, too, I think,' he said. 'I'll get hold of him and see what we can do.'

My Greek friend Pierrakis from the days in Gianaclis—before Aqaba—was in Cairo. We had dinner together at the Greek Club in Talaat Harb square.

'*Yia sou*,' I said when I met him. '*Ti kaneis?*' Hello, how are you?

'*Kala, kyrie Tom*,' he said. 'Do you speak Greek now?'

'*Etsi ki etsi*,' I said. Well enough.

He was tickled pink. Of course he wanted to know how I had learnt and of course I couldn't tell him much at all. But we had a lot of fun in a combination of Greek and English over our village salad and our strong black coffee, the two of us and one of his friends.

Exhaustion hit me after about four days in Cairo. They put me into the 15 Scottish Hospital for a check-up. That was a big mistake on my part—I was fed up within a day. There was absolutely nothing to do and I was afraid of getting stuck there. But after a chest x-ray came back clear, I managed to get a series of day passes. I escaped from the hospital to the convalescent depot for a few more days, then back to my flat.

While I had been in hospital, the delegation of EAM and EDES that I had escorted from Greece had gone off to the Lebanon. The British had called a conference there—the location chosen, no doubt, to get away from Greek politics, Cairo style.

* * *

I had been in Cairo almost a month by the time Denys, Bill and I finally managed to get together.

'Sandwiches, Denys?' I said as our food arrived. 'Not quite the lunch we planned, that day in the mountains.'

'When was that?' he asked.

'On the way to the submarine,' I said. 'Remember? When we imagined it all? The Nubian waiters at Shepheard's Hotel? Asparagus for you and bacon for me?' But I could see he had no idea what I was talking about.

'So what have you been up to, Tom?' asked Bill. 'I haven't seen you around the office.'

'Hospital,' I said. 'Then the Number 3 Rest Home.'

'You OK?' he asked.

'Fine,' I said. 'Just a bit tired.'

'I got stuck in hospital too,' Bill said, 'almost as soon as I got here.'

'I'm not surprised,' I said. 'You'd already collapsed once when I saw you at the Pertouli conference.'

'Yes, well,' he said. 'At first I thought it was just the usual bout of fever.' Malaria—we all knew about that. 'But then the fever didn't go off. It turned out to be pneumonia. They thought I was going to kick the bucket—the doc stayed with me most of one night. Exhaustion and malnutrition—that was the real problem. At least that's what they said later.'

'But you're OK now?' I asked.

'Pretty good,' he said. 'Can't complain.'

'What about you, Denys?' I asked. 'How do you like your office job?'

'Can't wait to get out,' he replied. 'I'm a trained commando. Not like you lot. I'm hoping for another posting. France would be good.'

I bet you fall on your feet there, too, Denys, I thought.

No one worked in the afternoons in Cairo. From one until about six, everyone was free to hang about, eat, drink and gossip. Denys had other fish to fry and excused himself when we'd finished eating, but Bill and I settled in with cups of tea and cigarettes. There was something I wanted to ask him.

'Arthur Hubbard, Bill,' I said. 'I never got a chance to ask you. What really happened there? All we heard was that ELAS shot him. Is it true?'

Bill said nothing for a long minute. Then, 'You really want to know?'

'I heard a bit from Hamish Torrance,' I said, 'but he didn't know much, either.'

'It's a long story,' Bill said, 'but all right.' He stubbed out his cigarette and lit another one, taking his time about it.

'Everything should've been OK. Choutas was supposed to be looking after us.' Choutas was Zervas's commander in south-west Epiros where Bill had been stationed at Triklinos, a doctor by profession. Like Bill, I didn't trust him and had put pressure on Zervas to get rid of him.

'They were supposed to be defending the west bank of the Acheloos River. Choutas and Colonel Pantelidis. We'd planned the troop dispositions together. But then Choutas changed the plans. Only sent a small force. Overruled Pantelidis when he protested. Next thing we knew, the communists had crossed the river.'

'ELAS?' I said.

'Yes,' he said. He always called them 'the communists'. 'A thousand of them.'

'Who was with you? Besides Arthur?'

'Joe Abbots and Chris Carratt.' Joe Abbots had been Bill's signaller, and Chris Carratt, a Greek-American, his interpreter. 'Just the four of us,' Bill went on. 'It was getting dark and we were nervous. Chris thinks he hears a noise, and we're telling him he's imagining things when someone bangs on the door. Joe goes to open it and Chris goes to help because they're speaking in Greek. Chris opens the door into the hall from my room, so I can see. Two communists. One with a rifle and one with a Tommy gun.

'Next thing we know the guy with the Tommy gun is firing straight into the room, at Chris. I yell "Get your guns" and we dive for cover. Chris has a Luger but I tell him to give it to Arthur because Arthur doesn't have his weapon, even though I warned them earlier to be ready. And Joe has left his down at the house where we eat.

'When the dust clears, the communists seem to have disappeared. We check all around the house. Nothing. So we make everything secure and go back inside. Then Arthur thinks he hears something. "I'll just go and check," he says.

'I shout to him to come back but he ignores me. He disappears round the house to the right. Suddenly firing breaks out—rifle, machine gun, sub-machine gun. They were waiting for him. I think I hear Arthur fire a shot immediately afterwards but I can't be sure. The firing goes on and on. Then it stops. I yell to Arthur to come back inside.

'"I can't, Bill," he says. "I've been shot."

'"Can you just get inside?" I call out. But he can't. He can't even crawl.'

Bill lit another cigarette and inhaled.

'I open the door and the firing starts up again,' he went on. 'I shut it. I know I'm for it if I go out. But I can't leave Arthur out there helpless.

'We're yelling out that we're the Allied Military Mission. Doesn't cut any ice with them, either in English or in Greek. There are grenades in my desk drawer, but if I throw one outside Arthur will die for sure.

'Then suddenly I realise Johnny Stavridis has arrived from the other house.' Johnny was another interpreter—he was the one who'd given evidence in the killing of Tommy Vinson.

'Chris yells to the Reds again. "They want us to go outside with our hands up," he tells me.

'Just then Arthur groans again. That's it. We have to do it. I hide my weapon under a pile of wood in the house. As I come out I can see the row of rifles poking across a stone wall just a few yards away.

'The reds are yelling at me. *"Fasistes. Prodotes."'* Fascists and traitors.

'The usual stuff,' I said.

'They get stuck into me and I nearly go down,' Bill went on. 'I know they'll kick me to death if they get me off my feet, so I straighten up as quick as I can. Then an ELAS officer appears. Major so and so. I say I'm a British major and ask what's going on.

'They knock me down again. I get up. Then three young guerrillas push to the front. One points his rifle at my head. I can't understand what he's saying. Chris tells me they want me to go down the path. Joe's with me.

'Chris tries to follow us, but they don't let him. They were beating him up, I find out later. "Where did you learn Greek?" they ask him. "From my mother," he says. More beating. "Where are the other British officers?" they ask. "There aren't any others," he says. "You've got the lot here."'

'And Arthur?' I said. 'What was happening to Arthur all this time?'

'He was just lying there. There was no way for me to get to him.'

We needed more tea. I called the waiter over and ordered another pot, and some cake to go with it.

'We're lined up against a bank, me and Joe. I try to play for time. "A doctor," I say, "for the wounded man." They say the doctor is coming. One of the young bloods sees my watch. He snatches at it and the strap breaks.

'They throw Chris into a ditch. Then they push Joe and me in after him. We all think we're done for. We're going to be dead before Arthur. They raise their rifles and take aim.

'We have one chance left. I keep talking. "What will Churchill do when he finds out the Reds are murdering his officers?" I ask. "This New Zealand officer will die if you don't get a doctor."

'Suddenly someone new appears—a fellow in a long coat and a fur hat. He looks like a Russian. It's *Politikos* Fotis of the ELAS "death battalion"—the one we equipped and trained in June '43. He asks for Major Bill and I tell him what's going on.

'"Stop!" he yells to the three guerrillas. "You're shooting British officers. Come up here and bring the officers with you."

'"Thank God, one of the good ones," says Chris.

'"A misunderstanding," says Fotis.

'They hurry to give our guns and watches back.

'"Not now," I say. "The doctor. Get the doctor."

'I get them to help carry Arthur inside. Then they all crowd around. I can't get rid of them.

'Arthur has the cut-down top of his flying suit over his tunic. We take it off. There are two bullet holes over his heart.'

Bill paused. He looked around the terrace where we were sitting, and then down at the street. He poured himself another cup of tea, put some cake on his plate, picked it up and then put it down again without tasting it.

'The doctor arrives at last. I demand an explanation for the attack. Fotis says we fired first. I say we were sitting at the table when they started shooting at us from the door. He says we attacked his men with a machine gun.

'"Where is it, then?" I ask. "How come no one has found this supposed machine gun? But this isn't the time to argue. Arthur is my friend. We went to school together. Now he's dying. Murdered."

'"Murder is a strong word," says Fotis. "An accident. It was all an accident." A few minutes before, it was self-defence. You know how it is.'

'Yes, Bill,' I said. I thought about all the times we'd been at the mercy of ELAS. With a good dose of luck, we'd always been OK. Sometimes by guile, sometimes simply by decamping before things got worse. Sometimes by bluster, like when I rescued Themis.

'The doctor finishes. He asks me to come outside with him. Chris Carratt comes too. "He'll die before morning," the doctor says. I go back inside to Arthur. I manage to get Fotis to give us a couple of guards to keep people out of the room.

'"The doctor says you're going to die, Arthur," I say. I can see in his eyes that he knows.'

Bill's chin was trembling. He paused again, steadied himself, drew hard on his cigarette.

'You know what he says, Tom? He says, "I understand. I'm a soldier."

'Then he asks me why they would want to shoot him.

'"They're saying you fired first," I say. He's sinking, but he opens his eyes and says, "They fired first." Then he says, "Tell mother." I say a few prayers. Then he's gone.'

Bill took a deep breath, got out his handkerchief and wiped his face roughly.

'And the investigation?' I asked. 'The finding that it was an accident?'

'That was Ramseyer.' Major Norman Ramseyer had succeeded Bill at Tingewick station in Agrinion. 'He and I didn't get on—religious differences, mainly. He wanted to cover everything up. The only person they interviewed was Joe Abbots. Well, how would he know anything? He didn't speak Greek. All he knew was that he'd been thrown into the ditch along with the rest of us.'

'What, they didn't speak to you or Chris?'

'Ramseyer didn't go any higher than Joe. He just wanted to be able to say that it was all a mistake. Of course I don't suppose ELAS was actively looking for British officers to shoot. They were after EDES. They were the real enemy.'

There was a moment's pause, then he said, 'I'm just glad I'm out of there.' Then, jerking himself back to the present with an obvious effort, he asked, 'What have you been up to?'

I was glad to change the subject to something more mundane. I told him about my excursions to the Muski, poking around in the shops. The Muski was the European quarter of Cairo, named after the Muski Bridge over the canal that some relative of the sultan Saladin had built. Cairo had been in existence in one form or another for more than a thousand years, and its past was always in evidence in the midst of its noisy, smelly present.

I had been wanting to hear the story of Arthur Hubbard's death for a long time—and from Bill himself, because I knew he wouldn't give me a load of bullshit. Maybe it was cruel to have asked him—it was hard to know whether talking about it would make him feel better, or worse.

I didn't see eye to eye with Bill about everything, but I had great respect for him as a human being. Like me with Aris, he'd had to assert and maintain his authority as a British officer just at the moment when that authority was no longer accepted by ELAS. And in doing so, he'd saved the lives of the others—Joe Abbots and Chris Carratt—as well as his own. I hoped he didn't feel that, in losing Arthur, he'd failed.

We went out again that evening. Somehow the conversation kept coming back to the situation in Greece. In his head, Bill hadn't left at all.

'When the war's over I'm going to make sure people know the truth,' he said. 'What the communists are really like. They're murderers. And it wasn't just Arthur. There was a runner from my HQ, too. He'd been a member of ELAS.'

'He'd sworn the oath, then,' I said. When people joined ELAS, or its political arm EAM, they had to swear never to leave. The penalty for breaking the oath was death.

'He was murdered in a field,' said Bill. 'The body just left lying. And he was young, with a family to look after.'

Over the next few weeks, I had more interviews with senior military officers, and another lunch with Brigadier Barker-Benfield. The question of collaboration kept coming up. Was Zervas collaborating with the enemy? The press started asking, too. Greece was big news, especially now the king was in town. Not just in Cairo, either. I had an interview with two pressmen, from the *Sunday Times* and the *Daily Telegraph*. Next day they showed me what they'd written—an account of our conversation, embellished with plenty of additions of their own. I had to tell them to cut about two-thirds of it.

It was as hot as blazes in Cairo and I was very tired. Too many parties in Charlie Bowie's flat, perhaps, and too many evenings at Shepheard's Hotel. I got a pass to Alexandria and went down by train through the delta. Waking up every now and again, I watched buffalos pulling wooden water wheels around on an endless circuit. They looked bored.

Alexandria was boring, too, but in just the way I needed. A swim before breakfast. A swim before and after lunch. Steady drinking in between—unfortunately the beer was rather weak.

The news came through that we had invaded France. Surely the liberation of Greece must be just around the corner.

Suddenly Alexandria and Cairo seemed like scenes in a play I'd lost interest in. The real action was in Greece and I couldn't wait to get back. But I still didn't know when that would be.

Back in Cairo, I heard Chris was coming out. The day he arrived, I was invited out to Mena House to have lunch with the Greek king's brother, Prince Paul, and his wife Princess

Frederica. Prince Paul was heir to the throne, as King George didn't have any children.

Mena House sat more or less at the foot of the pyramids, with a stunning stepped façade from the end of last century. As I walked up the steps at the front, past the glassed-in terrace, I was silently practising how to address the Crown Prince and Princess—'Your Royal Highness'. I would have to bow, too. I could already hear myself reporting the whole thing to Beth later. She was rather keen on royalty. For myself, I thought the whole question was fraught with problems in Greece. I agreed with Chris—they should hold a plebiscite to decide the king's future before he returned, not when it was a *fait accompli*. We all knew most Greeks didn't want the king back. The British insistence on foisting him on the country again had already cost a lot of lives. If it brought civil war again, who could tell how many more lives would be lost, and how many people would suffer.

The interior of Mena House was Islamic in style, and sumptuous. Princess Frederica, I knew, was German, but when I was introduced to her I found her most attractive. We chatted briefly about Epiros. She said she would like to see the mountains there. She had heard Jumerka was very beautiful and hoped she might take her children there one day. I mentioned that there were no roads to most of the villages, so travel might be difficult. She said that would need to be remedied when the war was over.

That evening I finally caught up with Chris. Although in Epiros we'd been in touch by cable, I hadn't seen him for a long time. We went to a meeting with the Commander in Chief together. They'd gone through a few Cs in C since we'd first been recruited for Harling. Alexander had been succeeded by 'Jumbo' Wilson, and now it was General Sir Bernard Paget.

Afterwards, Chris and I went to Shepheard's and ordered drinks from 'Saint' Joe the bartender. We chatted in a desultory fashion about Zervas's finances—the main topic of the meeting with the C in C.

'They seem to be dead against Zervas,' I said. 'I reckon they've missed the boat.'

'It would do them good to meet him,' said Chris. 'He's a lot more impressive in person.'

'Yes. But sometimes he doesn't think strategically at all. His representatives, now—I tried to persuade him to send a better calibre of officer but he said he couldn't spare them.'

'You've been with him for a long time now,' said Chris. 'You should know him if anyone does. It's obvious how much you admire him—Agoros was telling me so. Love him, even. That's what Agoros said. He reckons you've become a real philhellene.'

It was true, I had to admit. And if a moment were to come when I had to choose between Greek and British interests, I was no longer sure what I might find myself doing.

TWENTY-TWO

First they hadn't believed Eddie. Then they hadn't believed the Greek delegates who'd come over on that first flight out from Featherbed. Now, it was hard to know whether or not they were believing what I said. Meanwhile the BBC and the newspapers pushed their own version of events, often to Zervas's detriment in favour of ELAS.

It wasn't that we wanted Cairo—or London—to abandon ELAS in favour of Zervas. If they didn't keep ELAS on side, most likely we British personnel in the field would come to a sudden and sticky end, just like Arthur Hubbard. That was the reality. But I wanted Zervas to get his due for his support of the Allied effort against the occupying forces, and we all wanted— desperately wanted—the British to send a sizeable force to occupy Greece when the Nazis cleared out, to keep the Greek people safe from another civil war.

Now our best hope lay in an unexpected direction. David Wallace, the round-spectacled young man I'd met at the Pertouli conference a year earlier, dropped with me into Derviziana when I returned to Greece on 18 July 1944. He'd been sent to provide first-hand reports to the Foreign Office and specifically to Anthony Eden. And, unlike Eddie and the EDES and ELAS delegates, and perhaps unlike me—as all of us could be considered to be too close to things to take an objective view—he had the cachet to get the truth across to those who really counted in the British war ministry.

Our first night back in Greece, we stayed up all night talking, David and I, Hamish Torrance and Dennis Nicholson, and our interpreter 'Angelo' Angelopoulos. Everyone else was away on ops. Even the Rossis family were staying somewhere else by this time, so there was no one to disturb.

There was a lot to talk about. While I'd been away, Zervas had snatched the airfield at Paramythia from the Germans. Peter Musson and Agoros had jointly commanded the attacks on the German positions—Hamish told me of Peter's courage when the HQ came under heavy artillery fire. Now the airfield was under repair. Our position was strengthened to the same degree as the Germans' was weakened—we would be able to launch air attacks against them from Greek soil.

Our staff had recced the targets for Noah's Ark ops and cached the stores. The training of the *andartes* was going well—I soon saw for myself the improvement in Zervas's forces. They were well armed and looked smart, and morale was high. But we were vulnerable. The airfield was within shelling range of the Hun garrison at Menina. Something would have to be done about that.

Relations between EDES and ELAS had deteriorated again. The longer the Noah's Ark ops were delayed, I knew, the worse it was likely to get. It didn't help that both sides seemed to put their worst officers on their common frontiers. On the EDES side it was probably because the better officers, who were non-political and heartily sick of squabbling with their fellow Greeks, refused to serve at those potential clash points. When disagreements did arise, Zervas's officers rarely knew the text of the agreements between the two groups as well as the ELAS officers did, which put them at a disadvantage.

The Glasshouse operations, now renamed 'Bracing', continued, and were still supplying the whole of Greece from that little bay south of Parga. We were now the proud possessors of four 75 mm pack guns, and couldn't wait to use them against the Hun. There were various heavy weapons and motor transport, too. Some changes had been made after the May op, when one of the gangways had washed away and the ship had had to leave with some stores still aboard. Now, they were clearing 100 tons an hour, from two ships instead of one. Each ship dropped off an American operations group consisting of two officers and twenty men, who, once established, were deployed attacking German convoys. Raiding support regiments were coming in too, although in no time they were suffering badly with malaria and all had to be evacuated after only four months in the field.

Together the *andartes* and the mission staffs had built a road to the pinpoint so they could use old lorries and horses and carts to clear the beach more quickly—usually by 2 o'clock the afternoon after the drop-off, with the whole plain cleared by evening. On almost every op, the ELAS 24 regiment had caused an incident, attacking the ring of defences keeping the Germans out of the area. As it was threatening the security of the operations, Hamish had asked General Zervas to clear them out of the area by force. Zervas had been happy to oblige.

Of everything that had happened while I was away, the most unexpected and bizarre was the plot Cairo had hatched to capture General von Lanz, commander of the XXII Mountain Corps in western Greece and Albania. The policy of leaving the Germans alone had been suddenly reversed, and Hamish had received orders to make a diversionary attack on Yannina (the Germans were attacking the partisans in southern Albania at the time)—and, while he was at it, to take von Lanz prisoner.

Hamish and Zervas had made all the preparations for the attack and everything was ready to go. But two days before zero hour, it fell through.

It was no fault of theirs—the Germans had reinforced the Yannina garrison, and von Lanz left for the Albanian border. Although Zervas was still willing to go ahead, Hamish decided there was no point. It would only come to street fighting—never the guerrillas' strong suit—and without von Lanz to capture it seemed pointless.

I loved looking out the window of my Derviziana HQ first thing in the morning. I would watch while the wisps and pockets of mist merged into a long white ribbon along the low hills, gradually dropping towards the depths of the valley and trailing cobwebs on the lower slopes as it descended. I loved that moment when the high mountains behind took on definition, the white walls of the villages on their slopes gleaming in the early light.

With the hot summer weather, we ate all our meals outside. We had breakfast early, and lunch about 2 pm. I had got used to the Greek time system by now—2 pm was still midday. Appointments for the 'afternoon' were for 5 or 6 pm. In between was the siesta, and there was no point trying to get anything out of anyone then, not in the villages.

We were sitting eating breakfast one morning when Nick Hammond arrived. We'd been expecting him; he was here for a meeting with Zervas.

'Come and join us, Nick,' I said. The food situation in the mountains was grim and we were glad of our drops of dried food.

He sat down, looking disapproving.

'Bit dirty around here, Tom, isn't it?' he said.

I was annoyed. I'd been back from Cairo less than a week. But I said nothing. I didn't see Nick very often but we got on. I didn't particularly want to disturb that—especially as he was in command while Chris was away.

He turned to Hamish.

'Von Lanz,' he said. 'Pity that didn't come off. Would've been a bit of action.'

'A wee bit,' said Hamish.

'Of course, you were with the commandos, weren't you, Hamish?' Nick went on. 'You must've seen a fair bit of action there.'

'Yes,' said Hamish. 'Up north.'

'He's got the languages for it,' I said. Hamish had told me that he'd worked for a timber company in Glasgow before the war, and spoke fluent Swedish and Finnish, as well as a fair bit of Norwegian.

I poured Nick a cup of tea. These days we had real tea with dried milk to put in it, unlike that yellow mountain tea we used to drink, which had looked like nothing so much as piss although fortunately it tasted better.

Nick pushed his chair back and stretched.

'How did you find things in Vourgareli?' I asked.

'Rather sad,' he said. 'They never liked ELAS and they like them a lot less now. I heard a lot of stories. Beatings, executions. I used to go there before the war and the difference is quite upsetting.'

'What exactly were you doing before the war?' asked Hamish.

'Research,' replied Nick. 'I was a university lecturer at Cambridge. Ancient Greek remains, especially in Epiros. When the war's over I'd like to write a book. Not just the archaeological sites. Something about this place here, the mountains and the valleys, the villages near the remains—perhaps even the people.'

Nick and I had a good talk that morning. I told him how I managed Old Zed, trying to keep him on the straight and narrow with Cairo. I didn't want Nick disturbing our working relationship and I told him so—politely of course. Later I wasn't quite so polite. Nick told me the further adventures of Mick the Miller, who had been infiltrated into Thrace. Nick had decided

Mick was a dead ringer for a Greek priest, with his wild black eyes and black moustache and beard, and had disguised him accordingly to get him through Salonika safely. Mick had taken to it like a natural.

When the time came for Nick's talk with Zervas, he asked me to come with him. He wanted me to know he wasn't doing anything behind my back, he told me. The conversation went OK—Old Zed was his usual self. But as we came away, I could see Nick wasn't satisfied. I told him if he stirred Zed up it would take me ten days to get him back on side. But he said he had to know what Zed thought would happen after the Germans left— the truth, not what Zed thought we wanted to hear.

'Do you ever think old Zervas might be pulling the wool over your eyes?' he asked me.

'No, I don't,' I said. 'He's easy to work with and he invariably tells me the truth. He's very pro-British and absolutely loyal.'

'Yes,' said Nick, 'but he's also Greek. Things aren't likely to be quite as straightforward as you're making out. If he's a patriot he must have Greek interests at heart as well as British.'

'To him it's the same thing,' I said. 'He thinks that the future of Greece depends on a continuing relationship with the British.' But Nick seemed unconvinced.

The second conference with Zervas, a couple of days later in the presence of Komninos Pyromaglou, progressed badly. Eventually it wound up entirely in Greek as the topic shifted to politics. I left them to it and headed off on horseback to do some recces around the German strong point at Menina.

When I returned, David Wallace was back. We all sat over our shepherd's pie that night—it was made with dried potatoes and preserved meat—and discussed what was going to happen next.

'What I want to know,' said David, 'is what do you think would have happened if we'd left everything as it was?'

'When do you mean?' asked Hamish. 'Right back at the start?'

'After Gorgopotamos, say,' David replied. 'What if we hadn't supplied anyone, but we'd left Zervas free to do as he liked?'

'Instead of what we tell him to do?' I said.

'Exactly,' said David.

Nick, Hamish and I exchanged glances.

'It's obvious,' said Nick. 'ELAS would have wiped him out. Their forces were far stronger and better disciplined.'

'And then what?' David asked.

'All those years in prison or exile under Metaxas,' said Nick. 'ELAS had the whole underground organisation in place. They would've been the only armed group in Greece. No doubt about it.'

'So in a sense,' said David, 'Zervas is a creation of the British?'

I thought I could see where he was going.

'So you're saying that even though he has a lot of support,' said Nick, 'he represents a reality that wasn't intrinsic to Greece?'

'In a way,' said David. 'But now he's in a very strong position. What did you say he has, Tom? Ten thousand men?'

'Ten thousand,' I said. 'Well trained and well equipped.'

'Probably better trained and equipped than ELAS now,' said Nick.

'And he managed to clear ELAS's 24th without much trouble,' said Hamish. 'Thanks to his independent units and his excellent commanders.'

'With a bit of help from you,' I said.

'Do you think he could take on ELAS?' asked David.

'I think that's going a bit far,' said Nick. 'He's very confident, old Zervas, and he's wily, but he could overstretch himself.'

'I wonder,' said David. 'I think he could clear the Germans out of Epiros if he set his mind to it. And it's only our policy that's restricting the amount of supplies he can bring inland from the coast.'

'So he's an asset,' I said.

David nodded. 'Could be a good idea to start thinking that way. Especially as he's holding an area that could easily be used for an Allied invasion.'

This was encouraging. We needed to be sure of the *andartes'* complete cooperation in the ops against the Germans as they withdrew. We could count on Zervas's cooperation, but ELAS had different loyalties and their own goals to pursue. David was leaving us with the hope that he could get that message through to London. Then things might start going better for all of us.

For myself, what I wanted for Zervas was recognition for his service to the Allied cause, often at great cost to his own interests. I didn't want them to ignore what he'd done, or to denigrate it. And for the Greek people, I simply wanted them to be able to enjoy their liberation, free from the fear of another civil war.

Next time he came, a couple of weeks later, David was angry. We had just lost a great opportunity, he told us. Harry Evans had blown up the first truck in a German convoy, but then the EDES *andartes* had shot through, leaving the whole convoy of twenty-nine trucks stuck on the road all night long, with no one to finish them off.

I sent off a signal to Zervas, and gave him one hell of a rocket. I said we couldn't get any cooperation from the *andartes* against the Huns. Zervas had repeatedly promised to get on with ops, I reminded him, but there was no action. And we were now in a position to attack Menina, having cleared the Turko-Albanians out of the fertile coastal strip where they had been ensconced, in a relatively easy five-day operation. The EDES commander had attacked too soon, unfortunately, before Galanis and Agoros were in position, letting the enemy get away with most of the food and stock that we so badly needed, but the strategic outcome was excellent. If we were to take advantage of this and attack Menina, we would need Zervas's full support.

The next day I got a message back. Zervas was offended by my signal. He was running short of food for his men, he said. Because the land in Epiros was unproductive, we had to buy in food from outside, and when our ops against the Germans were on we could get nothing through. His men were living hand to mouth. It didn't help that Cairo had been tardy paying Zervas the money they had promised to support his troops—but even when that had finally arrived, it hadn't solved everything. However, he acknowledged that feeding the troops would be easier now that we had access to the coast, and agreed to do the op against the garrison at Menina.

It wouldn't be easy, we knew. The Germans had turned Menina into a fortress, with a number of fortified ammunition stores and well-sited artillery outposted in pillboxes on the surrounding hills. Manpower was 240 Germans and about a hundred Turko-Albanians.

Derviziana was soon full of *andartes* preparing for the attack. Mules, too—Zervas had his own units of muleteers. Without them, logistics to and from the mountain villages, where there were no roads suitable for motor transport at all, would have been completely impossible. Then, just as suddenly as they'd appeared, the *andartes* were gone, at 6 o'clock on the morning of 16 August. David Wallace went with them as an observer. Good, I thought. He would see Zervas's troops in action.

A few of us from the Allied Military Mission followed later on horseback. By 2 pm we were at Narkissos, where Peter Musson was in charge. The Americans under Captain Andy Rogers were fighting with us, doing a great job. Already we'd captured a lot of materiel, and had turned a captured 50 mm German anti-tank gun against the pillboxes.

In the early morning we attacked again. A few Germans escaped, but we had killed seventy-nine and taken 101 prisoners.

At 4.30 in the afternoon, with everything going exceptionally well, we took off for the coast to meet the ship from the 'Bracing' op. The landing craft was in at midnight, and in an hour and twenty minutes we had unloaded seventy-five tons of supplies. We saw the ship off in good time. In the afternoon we travelled on to Parga in a caïque, meeting another large caïque on the way which we thought was a Hun boat—it was a great relief to find ourselves mistaken. Parga, with its curving beach, was another nice little benefit of clearing the coastal strip.

The news reached us in Parga. David Wallace was dead.

Somehow he'd got caught up in the action and a sniper had taken him out.

I was stunned. I'd just been getting to know him, and now he was gone.

And then it hit me, a sudden blow to the guts. All those hopes we'd had riding on David's reports—gone. Who would stand up for us to the war ministry now? We'd be at the mercy of people who thought we knew nothing, and who had their own agenda for Greece. And so, that meant, would the Greeks.

By late August, Noah's Ark preparations were complete. It was evident that the date for the operation was approaching fast—withdrawing German units were moving up from the Peloponnese and Agrinion, mostly by sea to Preveza, then to Yannina and on eastwards to Thessaly. A few were moving north from Yannina to Albania.

The order was that full-scale attacks against the enemy would only begin when we received the code word 'Smash'em'. Before this, only minor targets were to be blown. Hamish left to take charge of the ops east of the Arta–Yannina road. By this time he and Agoros were firm friends and worked well together.

And then, at the end of the month, General von Lanz approached me via a Greek emissary: he wanted to discuss terms of honourable surrender. On 30 August, the envoy told me, the commanders of Crete, Albania and Salonika had met at Yannina. Recent RAF and guerrilla activities had badly shaken their morale. Von Lanz had authority from High Command to proceed with a meeting.

I drafted a cable to Cairo stating the terms von Lanz's envoy had brought, and my response: I was submitting all points to a higher authority and had asked the envoy to return on 4 September.

Meanwhile, pressure on the Germans continued to mount. On 1 September, with Hun units streaming up from the south in large daily convoys, Zervas issued an order for full-scale attacks against the enemy, to continue until they were destroyed or driven from Epiros. He fondly believed that an Allied invasion would now take place. This belief, I knew, was still shared by practically every Greek in Epiros. Whether their faith was misplaced or not remained to be seen. Our Noah's Ark attacks on minor targets began on 2 September—but long term, I still didn't know what Cairo had planned.

Cairo's instructions about von Lanz didn't come until 7 September. I was authorised to see him, but only unconditional surrender was on the table. There was to be no discussion of terms. He could prove his bona fides by sending a senior German officer to Allied Forces Headquarters, to be picked up at Paramythia to travel to Italy. I sent a letter to von Lanz conveying this news.

Then I got another message, an informal one this time, via one of the EDES spies in the German HQ. When von Lanz had received my letter, he had flown into a rage, threatening to order a general attack to wipe out Zervas and let ELAS take Epiros. He would open the door for the Russians to enter Greece instead of the British. He did indeed order a general attack on Zervas, 'Operation Treachery', but it was shortlived.

* * *

The German convoys travelling northwards to Yannina made excellent targets. In the first two days we took out five hundred killed, ninety-two prisoners and an unknown number of wounded. Our casualties were light. Our 75 mm guns were now ten in number—eight American pack-guns had been infiltrated by infantry landing craft and two captured. They were impressively accurate in a practice shoot—we thought it must be good luck, but the new engagement proved otherwise. In their first attack, seven trucks were knocked out in almost as many minutes, as the gunners got straight onto their targets.

Morale had never been higher, while low German morale led to needless heavy casualties. Many strong point garrisons were desperate to surrender, but we could accept no surrenders of less than a whole division.

My job was to send signals and messages over the whole area and to Cairo. Just as well I wasn't in the thick of it, as I had boils again and was feeling vile. The M&B tablets I was taking didn't help, either.

There was fighting around the clock. For a couple of nights in early September the guns were firing nearly all night. Roads were closed and the *andartes* were performing magnificently.

Nick Hammond had been holding the fort while Chris was away in Cairo and then in London. On the night of 9 September, Chris arrived back in Greece. I hadn't seen him since my trip to Cairo. A day or two later he arrived at my station.

We went down to the *kafenion* after dinner for a *tsipouro* with the villagers. No one else was left. Then we went home and broke out the whisky. I had a Distinguished Service Order to celebrate—it had gone through at the end of August.

Chris had been in London. He'd met the king of Greece and talked to the Foreign Office. And he'd met Churchill himself.

'Very few people knew who I was,' he told me. 'My father introduced me to the First Lord of the Admiralty. Just as his son, you know, and told him I'd been in Greece. And the First Lord said, "Ah, you must be working with Chris Woodhouse." He only knew my father as Lord Terrington, so I suppose that explains it.'

I laughed. But I couldn't quite imagine it.

'The real purpose of Noah's Ark isn't what we thought,' he went on. 'I think it must've changed since it was first mooted.'

'Isn't it just to harass the German withdrawal?'

'Well, that's what we all thought,' he said. 'But no. It's actually to prevent the Germans leaving Greece, so that the Russians can cut them off as they come through.'

'Well, that's good to know,' I said. 'Nice of them to tell us. And how was Churchill?'

'Strange,' he said. 'And small.'

'Compared to you.'

'Compared to anyone. I heard he wanted to cut EAM off completely. They'd vetted the brief I'd sent through—the PM's adviser on secret operations had already told me Churchill wouldn't like my point of view. They seemed to think of me as on the left.' Of course, Churchill himself was absolutely pro-monarchy in Greece, so he was most unlikely to support EAM.

'So did you get anywhere with Churchill?'

'In the end,' Chris said, 'an appeal to his feelings was the only thing that worked. He kept getting sidetracked onto Yugoslavia. I think it interests him more because his son Randolph is there. Anyway, we weren't getting anywhere, so I told him if we cut EAM off I didn't think many of our mission would survive.'

'And did that work?' I asked.

'He put a hand on my shoulder and said he understood. And I think that must have clinched it, because I didn't hear any more about breaking with EAM.'

'And the Greek king? How did you get on with him?'

'A social visit, nothing more. He was chatty and told a lot of stories. But nothing controversial. Nothing at all.'

I wanted to know what Chris thought would happen when the Germans left. I knew Zervas's fears and I shared them.

'People in England have funny ideas,' Chris said. 'Some of them are great EAM enthusiasts. I met Aneurin Bevan—you know, the Labour MP—and that was his position. Barker-Benfield seems to have similarly naïve views. And then there are those who share Churchill's views. Neither is particularly helpful.'

'The BBC seems to have been rather mindlessly pro-EAM recently,' I said. 'Zervas is doing great work and not getting any coverage.'

'I'm not surprised,' he said. 'The thing is, Tom, things have moved on here. That's what I learnt from being in Cairo and in England. We're the men of 1940s Greece, right here. And I'd far rather talk to Aris Velouchiotis or Napoleon Zervas about the future of Greece than all those people outside Greece who are stuck in the 1930s.'

'Do you mean the government in exile?' I asked.

'Them and others,' said Chris. 'Here we talk the same language. We've been through the same things and we understand each other even when we disagree. Not just the mission. The people of EAM and EKKA and EDES. The ordinary people in the villages who have suffered under the occupation.'

'Well, there's no more EKKA,' I said. EKKA had been attacked back in April, and Colonel Psarros had been killed under circumstances which remained unclear. 'But after the occupation? What then?' That question was always in my mind, no matter how busy we were with operational plans and logistics and signals in and out. A question and a fear. 'I think it's going to be bad. I see ELAS positioning themselves to move into the towns as the Germans move out. If we're not careful it's going to be a *fait accompli*. I told them when I was in Cairo that we had to have an Allied invasion. Even a small one would be better than nothing. And that's what the Greeks are expecting.'

Nick Hammond had similar concerns, I knew. His idea was that both EDES and ELAS should become part of the Greek national forces, with senior Greek officers from the Middle East infiltrated to sit on ELAS and EDES HQ as equals with their own officers. And he wanted picked units of the Greek national army brought in to cooperate in ops, to help unite the two groups in a common purpose. It was already too late for a large force to come from the Middle East.

'Everything depends on how the political situation is resolved,' said Chris.

'If it can be resolved,' I said. I was pretty cynical about that. There was already a string of agreements behind us—Natbands, Plaka, the agrecments of the Lebanon conference, which had been conducted while I was in Cairo—and none had achieved anything permanent.

'You know they didn't want to send me back?' Chris said suddenly.

I shook my head.

'It was B.B. He thought we'd got the wrong end of the stick— Nick Hammond and myself. And you, too.'

I was surprised. B.B. had seemed genial enough, during those lunches in Cairo where I'd told him what I thought. I hadn't pulled any punches, of course. That wasn't my style.

'We're too close to things, so we can't be objective,' said Chris. 'So we've misjudged ELAS. He was impressed with them and unimpressed with reports of Zervas's collaboration.'

'But those stories aren't true,' I said. 'And all those cables we kept getting saying that Zervas wasn't engaging the enemy and did he have a secret truce—they didn't seem to remember that it was their policy, not his.'

'You've got to be careful about Zervas, Tom,' he said. 'You're very close to him. I know you think highly of him. But just keep an open mind.'

I changed the subject. 'What will there be for us to do when the Germans have left? We've been looking forward to it for so long. But at some point it's going to be all over, for good or ill.'

'Go back home,' he said. 'You can marry Beth and settle down. Have that son you've always wanted. It's going to be like *Henry V.*'

'How do you mean?' I asked.

'You know, the band of brothers.'

Shakespeare wasn't exactly my strong suit. 'Go on,' I said cautiously.

'Well, Henry tells his men what it's going to be like after they've won the decisive battle. They're going to go home and show their wounds and boast. And they're going to "remember with advantages" what they did in the battle. You know, talk it up.'

'I suppose I can imagine that,' I replied. 'At the Returned Services League in Australia. "My experiences with the Greek resistance", something like that. But I'm not at all sure that we are going to win here. Against the Germans, yes, of course. But what kind of victory will it be for the Greeks?'

'I wish I knew,' said Chris. 'I've asked Cairo to warn ELAS off attempting to enter the towns in Zervas's area but to no avail, I'm afraid.'

The time for 'Operation Smash'em' seemed to have arrived. That's what we gathered, anyway.

Chris explained the details to Zervas. One detail was the bitter fact that no British or American troops would be used in Epiros.

Zervas would get no help to defend the towns he'd fought so hard for against ELAS, and no recompense for his service and his sacrifices.

He was deeply disappointed. I was ashamed.

Unsurprisingly, he decided to redeploy his forces. Agoros's 3/40 regiment moved to Dodoni near Yannina, Zorbalas's 39 regiment moved south near Arta and Galanis's 2nd Independent battalion towards Preveza. Old Zed wanted his best units near the towns where ELAS was concentrating. Rightly, he was determined to get into the towns for which his troops had fought so well. What else could we expect with such a lousy British policy in Greece? If Cairo would have let us accept the overtures for surrender from the German garrisons the main towns would have been isolated and so fallen to us.

There were now twenty to thirty thousand Huns in the Arta–Preveza plain, their casualties mounting despite a desperate drive from Filippiada. Our casualties were heavier now, too.

I finally got away from issuing operational orders for twenty-four hours. I went down to an op near Pentolakkos then down to the road to have a look—dead Huns and burnt trucks all the way along. We couldn't get anywhere near our main targets for 'Smash'em'—the concentration of German guns was too heavy. We blocked the Yannina–Igoumenitsa road with two major demolitions, but the Huns were moving up, shelling day and night. They had 155 mm guns up near Derviziana and we shifted our HQ to Romanon, fearing we would be cut off. We were just in time—they occupied the heights and shelled Derviziana.

Villages changed hands and changed hands again. Spitfires came over and destroyed fourteen trucks. There was heavy fighting and shelling around Preveza and Paramythia airfield. Zervas was waiting at Paramythia to go out to a conference in Caserta, Italy, but eventually had to leave from Bovington station up north because of the fighting around Paramythia. Sarafis was representing ELAS at the conference, whose aim was to bring all resistance fighters together under Allied command.

Unmolested by ELAS, Huns were pouring up the Arta–Yannina road. They had all the passes guarded with 155 mm guns and were giving the *andartes* hell, and we couldn't get air support. EDES and ELAS were fighting each other in Preveza.

We couldn't get near the main roads because of heavy shelling, so we shifted to night sabotage of roads with mines and tyre bursters.

EDES managed to dislodge the Huns from the hills above Derviziana, so we shifted our HQ back again. Hamish and Papadopoulos with the Cherovouni regiment were putting in some good attacks on the Hun rear. *Andartes* from the 39 regiment under Colonel Zorbalas were driving the Hun off the high ground overlooking Kanetta just as a large convoy arrived. Our mortars stopped the convoy and at the exact same moment several Hurricane fighter bombers—known as 'hurri-bombers'—arrived. The Hurricanes and the mortars from the *andartes* mauled the whole convoy—most satisfactory.

Zervas and his chief of staff, Colonel Nikolopoulos, arrived back from Caserta full of jubilation.

'First I travelled in the Commander in Chief's private plane,' Zervas said as soon as I walked into his office, 'with an escort of seven spitfires. And then in my own private car.'

'Good,' I said. I could see the beneficial effects of all the attention—he was buoyant. I only hoped it would all be borne out by later events.

'Sarafis brought Despotopoulos, his political adviser, along,' Zervas went on. 'He was very conciliatory—surprisingly so.'

'So there was an agreement?'

'Indeed there was. Both parties agreed to cooperate under the command of General Scobie.' General Scobie was now General Officer Commanding in Greece.

'We defined areas of operation for both resistance groups,' said Nikolopoulos. 'And both groups agreed not to enter the capital.'

'And how did His Majesty's Government treat you?' I asked Zervas.

'I have their full confidence and trust,' he said. 'I'm sure of it.'

I couldn't help but feel hopeful. Zervas's right to the Epiros area was confirmed, as boundaries had stood at the Plaka conference. If these terms were adhered to, things might yet be salvaged.

The horde of Germans retreating to the north was dwindling. Zervas was positioning himself to take control of the area that was his sphere of influence according to the Caserta Agreement. The city of Yannina, still under evacuation, was one prize. The island of Lefkas was another. Scobie had decided it was to go to ELAS, but my intelligence was that the islanders largely supported EDES.

Then there was Corfu. It too was supposed to be in Zervas's sphere of influence, but if he'd waited for the British as instructed it would have fallen to ELAS, so Zervas got in first with his 10 division troops.

At 6 am on 14 October, Papadopoulos entered Yannina with his Cherovouni independent regiment to clean up ahead of Zervas's triumphant entry. On 18 October the last of the German rearguard crossed into Albania.

All fighting in Epiros was now over and I was off to join Zervas at his new HQ in Yannina. Zervas staged a ceremonial entry to the city, with a horseback parade watched by thousands of people crowding the balconies and streets.

Immediately afterwards, however, something odd happened.

A few weeks earlier, Zervas had been asked to supply ELAS in Macedonia with approximately three tons of small arms ammunition and grenades. He had agreed, even though it was clearly against his own interests to be supplying ammunition to ELAS. After the ELAS attack a week or two earlier, I was concerned that this was bad policy and asked for confirmation via a direct order from the Commander, Force 133. This came on 20 September.

As soon as the Germans were clear of Epiros, an ELAS representative turned up with 150 mules. Owing to a mistake, he was expecting nine tons of equipment rather than three. Cairo asked us to supply this larger quantity.

It would take all of Zervas's surplus ammunition, leaving him vulnerable. But Zervas agreed. He thought it was a good opportunity to demonstrate his good faith. Besides, we were now under the operational command of General Scobie and 3 Corps, and had to obey orders.

It was a time for celebration. One evening in early November we had a tremendous party at Agoros's *spiti*. They'd done pretty well with food for once—the tables weren't quite groaning under its weight, as I knew was customary in more plentiful times, but the spread was a definite improvement on what we'd encountered over the last couple of years. And my tastes had changed too. I'd come to love the big broad beans cooked with olive oil and oregano, for example—the ones we'd so loathed when (minus the olive oil) they'd been the only item on the menu during those first difficult months before Gorgopotamos.

I spied Toula with a young EDES fighter who'd lost an arm in one of the EDES attacks on the German defences at Preveza in June. Her cheeky grin didn't seem to be doing her any harm in that direction. She was deep into an account of her escape from Vourgareli with Voula and a few others, that time when I'd had to take my mission staff up and over Jumerka to get away.

'Voula and I were on foot,' she was saying. 'My brother Georgios had given me a bag of documents and a box of matches. If we were in danger, I was to burn the documents.'

'Narrow escapes,' I said. 'Lucky you didn't have to use the matchbox.'

'Yes,' she replied. 'Oh, and *Kyrie* Tom, that reminds me—did you hear about Georgios's escape in Dodoni?'

'We've been so busy,' I said.

'It's a great story,' she said. 'But look, there's Georgios. He'll tell you all about it.'

She pulled him over to our group.

'I hear you've got a story to tell,' I said, 'about an escape at Dodoni.'

His eyes were dancing. 'Yes, it happened on *tou Stavrou*'—the festival honouring the Holy Cross, celebrated on 14 September—'just a few days before the Germans left. We were holed up in a little country chapel—just three of us.'

I could picture the chapel, perched up on a slope outside of the village, a winding path among the trees, stone decorations on the low walls leading up to the little building.

'Someone had betrayed our position after a big battle,' he said, 'and the Germans were heading straight for us with tracker dogs. We all had our weapons out—for ourselves. But the dogs got distracted by a dead sheep at the last minute and went the wrong way. We were safe—a miracle.'

'On *tou Stavrou*,' I said. 'You must have been very happy.'

Now his eyes were quiet. 'I will never forget it,' he said. 'Every year I will fast on *tou Stavrou*. It was so close ...'

General Zervas's organisation took over civil administration of the whole area, but EAM/ELAS had their own offices, a newspaper, and full rights to hold political meetings and so on.

Gradually, strife between EDES and ELAS intensified. Food was very short and we had thousands of refugees from ELAS as well as Italians to feed. It was a disheartening and difficult time.

Now that operations were completed, 3 Corps seemed to have lost interest in Zervas's *andartes*. No one was supplying them.

They could get no petrol for their captured and requisitioned vehicles. They managed to obtain food by devious means but it was never enough. Payment at the rate of £10 per man per month until demobilisation had been promised by 3 Corps but didn't eventuate, causing widespread dissatisfaction.

General Scobie called a conference with Zervas and Sarafis in Athens in mid-November to discuss demobilisation of the *andarte* forces.

I attended only part of that conference. For me, the trip was memorable for other reasons. General Scobie, when I saw him, was very interested and fair-minded. I saw Spike and Chris Woodhouse, attended various parties and sometimes couldn't find my way home. I shaved off my beard, which had grown back more unruly than ever. I shared the Athenians' joy at their liberation, its emblem, the blue and white national flag, at every house front. And at lunch at Angelo Angelopoulos's home in Kolonaki I met Miss Sylvia Apostolides—who had led a sabotage and resistance group in Athens for the British since just before the civil war. She struck me immediately as most attractive—a good height, with wonderful dark wavy hair, twenty or twenty-one years old.

Over lunch, the conversation turned to Sylvia's activities in Athens during the occupation. Don Stott had recruited her to Force 133—in Athens, after he'd covered himself in glory in the spectacular Asopos bridge op that Arthur had told us about at that conference in Pertouli so long ago.

'I wanted to run away to the mountains,' Sylvia explained. 'I was twenty, and I thought I could be an interpreter or a runner, something like that.' Her mother was English and Sylvia spoke English as well as she spoke Greek. 'But I wanted to make sure I went to the Greek National Organisation, to General Zervas, and I was worried that I might get caught up with ELAS instead. So I asked for Don Stott's help. He's an extremely nice man— tall, thin, good-looking. But he was very much against it.'

'Why?' I asked. 'We had girls with us—Georgios Agoros's wife Voula and his sister Toula, and others. ELAS had girls too, of course.'

'I don't know,' she replied. 'But he said if I really wanted to work for the British he could get me into the Allied Military Mission and I could work for him. I accepted immediately.'

Sylvia worked for Don for only a week. He passed her on to his mate Bob Morton, who introduced her to the people she was to collect intelligence from and give further orders to. But soon Bob got busy with other things and she had to see everyone herself and report back to him, and before too long he left for the mountains. She was left in charge, by herself.

'Then it got difficult,' she said. 'I was supposed to get 300 sovereigns from someone to pay all my contacts. "Tomorrow," he kept saying. "I'll pay you tomorrow." But of course tomorrow never came. I had to borrow the money from my father and a friend, until eventually Bob sent down some money and I was able to pay it back.'

Sylvia received all the ammunition and arms sent down from the mountains and took it by taxi to the ammunition dump she was in charge of. This was in addition to translating reports, which she and her mother had to do every day.

'One night,' she said, 'some Germans of the *Feldpolizei* called on us to stop at a checkpoint. But the car was stinking of ammunition and it was too dangerous. We went straight through under fire. My lucky shamrock helped me'—she meant her Girl Guides badge. 'Oh, and I had two boys from the gang with me, too.'

'You were pretty lucky,' I said.

'I know,' she said. 'Another time I had to go out and show the gang how to use a time bomb to blow up parachute dumps at the aerodrome at Hassani.'

'You knew how to use a time bomb?' I was astonished.

'No, of course not,' she said. 'But Bob Morton came down from the mountains and showed me how to do it. And he offered to pay me for my work—five sovereigns a month. I refused—I was much happier working as a volunteer.'

After lunch that day, we all went for a drive to look at some of the sights of Athens—Angelo and his wife, Sylvia and myself. It was cold. I had my greatcoat and Sylvia was wearing a coat with a broad fur collar.

I'd barely had a taste of her stories when it was time for us to leave Athens. I wondered if I would ever see her again.

Chris and I went back to Epiros in a Douglas Fairchild, a very nice bus with a great view of the whole countryside. General Zervas returned to Yannina delighted with his reception in Athens. He was confident that in the event of trouble with ELAS he would receive British support, including air support.

Arrangements for the demobilisation of the *andartes* had already begun when ELAS began to fight again. Zervas asked Scobie for precise orders. 'Trust me,' Scobie replied. Zervas was disappointed. He had hoped EDES would be recognised as a Greek national army to fight alongside British troops against ELAS.

The Caserta Agreement had left Zervas vulnerable. Although he held Yannina and Arta, the hills north of Yannina and east of Arta were in ELAS territory. Preveza was within mortar range of ELAS-held Fort Aktion on the south side of the Ambracian gulf. Zervas had asked permission to occupy these positions while it was within his capacity to do so, but permission was refused—he was not to take any offensive action.

On Monday 4 December we heard that all the EAM ministers in the government had resigned. Fighting had broken out in Athens the day before, with ELAS fighting first the Greek police and gendarmerie, then British troops. Casualties on all sides were mounting. I thought about Angelo Angelopoulos and his wife.

I thought about Sylvia. It was hard to imagine battles in the streets of the city that I'd visited so recently, where people had been so happy at their liberation—and hard to know how safe ordinary people would be in their homes. At least they'd learnt how to keep their heads down since the Nazis had first flown the swastika from the Akropolis—those who'd survived.

In Epiros, ELAS was concentrating their forces around Yannina and Arta in a show of strength meant to intimidate. Zervas's situation was grim. On 16 December all British troops except Force 133 were ordered to leave Preveza. Hamish Torrance, Peter Musson and Dennis Nicholson had already been evacuated from Preveza and would go on from Italy to Cairo.

On 18 and 19 December, ELAS attacked outposts near Yannina. General Scobie again refused permission for EDES to improve their positions. And General Zervas was still anxious to obey Scobie's every order to the letter.

On 20 December, ELAS went on the attack in Yannina and Arta. My third Christmas in Greece—and we were at war again.

TWENTY-THREE

EDES troops were losing faith in Britain. Scobie had promised he would look after them if they obeyed his orders. They'd done so, to their own loss. Now Scobie had shoved them in a hole and was leaving them to climb out of it all by themselves.

On 22 December, Arta fell to ELAS with 550 EDES casualties.

Chris and I arrived back in Yannina only to find we had to pack up and leave. EDES and our mission were evacuating south to Preveza.

The road to Preveza was choked with military transport, mules and refugees on foot carrying all their gear with them. We met Spike and Fred Wright at Filiates, blew up and burnt Kaloyirou bridge behind us and went on to Preveza. But Zervas knew he couldn't hold Preveza if ELAS brought guns to Fort Aktion opposite.

Bitter and defeatist, Zervas decided to go to Corfu and make a stand there. He asked Scobie for shipping. The Hunt class destroyer *Cleveland* with Brigadier Mainwaring and Captain Turner arrived to take charge of the evacuation.

A stiff easterly was blowing, making it difficult to handle the ships and too rough for the caïques. We had three destroyers, three support landing craft, three sweepers and numerous small craft in the harbour and were loading nearly all night. We held a conference to coordinate the evacuation with the timetable of the ships' arrival. Zervas was not feeling cooperative, and Mainwaring and Turner had no idea how to deal with *andartiko* leaders.

EDES had by now fallen back to a very strong line nine miles north of Preveza that might hold for several days. Agoros and Major Galanis with the EDES 3/40 regiment and the 2nd Cretan Independent HQ Battalion were fighting the rearguard, cheerful and confident.

Agoros was waiting for the promised British air support.

'It's not coming,' I told him. 'Don't sacrifice your men waiting.'

'How do you know?' he asked me.

'I know,' I said.

'Then you're telling me something you shouldn't. Why are you doing that?'

What could I tell him? It was almost two years since that March evening when we'd first met at the Bishop's house in Vourgareli. We'd been fellow-fighters ever since, sharing the struggle as I laid the explosives and he held my back, at Kaloyirou bridge and so many times after. I trusted him with my life. As he'd put it himself more than once, we were brother-friends.

My disappointment, my shame, my frustration at British policy and the representatives the British wheeled in to implement it— Scobie now topping the list—had gone beyond anger into a quiet determination. This time I would choose Greece. And at that moment, as I stood there in the uniform that spoke of duty and obedience to orders, Greece was embodied in this friend who had shared everything with me.

'Because I love Greece, *paidi mou*,' I told him, 'and I love the Greeks. I don't want to see your men dying because of British bloody-mindedness. Don't wait, I tell you.'

'Just a little longer,' he said, 'otherwise it will look bad.'

No planes came. Orders for withdrawal were given, then rescinded. In the process the line was broken.

Like Zervas, Agoros still thought that one day the British would come to a fairer estimation of EDES' contribution to the war. Both of them were waiting for the time when those in Cairo would finally realise that Zervas had been their only faithful ally. And they both hoped that I would be able to make this happen— far overestimating my real influence.

The final stand was made along a line that ran through Nikopoulos, four miles north of Preveza. Galanis and Papadopoulos were confident of holding this shortened line for several days. A British destroyer was shelling ELAS north of the line.

The day for final evacuation arrived. The navy had already set alight 200,000 gallons of petrol. On the beach it was chaos— mules, civilians, *andartes*, none of them under control. Eventually we got the 260 mules loaded. Agoros's regiment had already left on the *Prince Henry*.

Chris and I went up to Galanis on the line for the last time. Galanis knew he could have held the line another day. The weather had moderated and with another twelve hours we could have loaded the remaining thirty vehicles. Instead we had to set fire to them, and the rest of our petrol. For us, those fires were consuming nearly three years of work, the *andartes'* and then ours.

The last ships left Preveza at 3.30 pm on 30 December. We had opened the remaining food stores, let the animals loose, and invited the civilians to help themselves. We'd evacuated between five and six thousand cilivian refugees and six thousand *andartes*, plus six hundred Italians, the 11th Greek battalion who had taken no part in the fight, and a number of pieces of military transport. Except for the best-disciplined units, Zervas's officers made no attempt to control their men in the final evacuation.

It was windy and cold when we arrived in Corfu. We were short of labour and transport to unload and dispose of the stores, and in the interim enterprising locals and the crew of one of the Greek destroyers looted large quantities, which they later sold on the black market. I'd been in Corfu briefly in early November and made a speech there in Greek. My return was dispiriting to say the least.

Chris was leaving soon for Italy. A day or two after we arrived, a few of us went across to Doukades village. Chris and I rode together in the back of a jeep.

He spoke to me quietly. 'I wanted to let you know that there was some credible evidence about Zervas in the end—about dealings with the Germans, I mean.'

'What did you see?' I asked.

'Not something I saw,' he said. 'Something I heard. From Captain von Schenk when he deserted to us.' Captain von Schenk had been ADC to General Loehr in Salonika. 'There was some kind of liaison going on with General von Lanz in Yannina. Remote—via intermediaries only. Not to the extent of personal collusion. But dangerous all the same. And of course that period of enforced inactivity before Noah's Ark lent credence to the reports.'

'That was most unfortunate,' I said. 'But Zervas's contribution to Noah's Ark should have put the lie to all that. He was terrific against the Germans—he wouldn't have done that if he'd been collaborating.'

'I agree it should've tipped the balance of opinion,' said Chris, 'but it didn't. Zervas's contribution isn't being valued as it should be.'

'I know,' I said. 'I noticed that when I was in Athens in November. The BBC just didn't seem to be reporting Noah's Ark ops in Zervas's area. But EDES fought magnificently. Their gunnery in particular—and their close fighting. I wrote a letter to Special Forces Unit about it.'

'Their final operational order from His Majesty's Government,' said Chris. 'I know. They really excelled themselves.'

That trip in the jeep was the last real chance we had to talk. Chris and Spike were leaving the next day for Italy on LCI 260. Chris was expecting to return shortly so I didn't worry about a farewell, but it was time to say goodbye to Spike. He had been utterly dependable, unfailingly courageous and a lot of fun.

'You've got so many friends in Greece, Spike,' I said. 'I reckon you'll be back after the war.'

'So have you, Tom,' he said. 'Maybe we'll meet up here.'

On 9 January the 40 Commando Royal Marines arrived in strength in Corfu with Colonel Sankey in charge. Pretty soon they got themselves ensconced in Mon Repos, the beautiful villa south of Corfu Town which the Greek kings had as a summer residence. In theory, defence of the island was the Commando's responsibility, but it was clear that if anything happened, it would actually fall to the seven thousand EDES troops to defend the island as the Commando numbered only 450.

The threat was real—the Albanian coast is not much more than a mile from Corfu at one point. Fortunately there seemed to be no concentration of ELAS there. Nevertheless the defence of Corfu was a critical issue. EDES troops took up position over the whole island, from Lefkimi in the south to Cape Cassiopi in the north.

Renovation station was still not entirely depleted. One of my interpreters, Allen Sotiracopoulos, was still with me and our three wireless operators were keeping our station open. Later my other interpreter, Dimi Papaioannou, came back to us from Athens.

The weather was shocking. If it wasn't raining like blazes there were terrific storms. Once our windows got blown in. Occasionally there was light snow. In the midst of this we had several thousand refugees to feed and clothe, and accommodation was strained to the uttermost.

The EDES troops were in a sorry plight. No clothes had arrived for months and they were in rags, pretty much as they had been when the first of them joined us for the Gorgopotamos op. They couldn't wash because they got no soap, and they had no clothes to change, so they were mostly dirty. They weren't given any olive oil, either—in fact they got barely enough food to live on. And they were still expected to man the outposts in all weathers. In these circumstances looting on a large scale wouldn't have been surprising, but there was remarkably little of it. Eventually 3 Corps reluctantly agreed to feed them.

The trouble was that Zervas was not receiving the pay for his men that Scobie had promised. The agreement with 3 Corps was £10 per man per month for ten thousand men. For November and December EDES were due for £140,000.

Early in January a field cashier arrived with £125,000. The next day we got a signal saying this must be paid over to Zervas in amounts of £10,000 at a time to prevent inflation.

When I made the first payment, Zervas was not at all pleased. The following day he returned it, saying it was of no use to him.

Then he was unexpectedly summoned to Athens, no reason given. The street battles were over, EAM/ELAS had lost their attempt to take Athens, and the British were in control.

Zervas's creditors took to pestering us instead. Many of them had given their all for Zervas, and he had been unable to pay them. It seemed so unlikely to them that the British weren't paying him that they concluded he was lying to them. Zervas's prestige suffered badly—as did ours.

General Zervas returned to Corfu on the *King George V* at the end of January and was greeted with a guard of honour. He was to be retired and his forces disbanded. Those who were suitable would be offered the opportunity to join the *Ethnofylaki*, the National Guard.

I went around to see Zervas the next day. He was going to visit all the outposts and farewell his troops.

It was still a pleasure to see him, in spite of the recent difficulties.

'What happened in Athens?' I asked.

'Nothing much,' he said. 'I shaved my beard.'

'I noticed,' I said. He didn't look nearly so impressive without it. 'And the money?'

'Nothing resolved,' he said. 'And I never found out who sent for me in the first place—British or Greek.'

So, I thought, his creditors will continue to hound us.

'Tom,' he went on, 'you know I have become very unhappy.'

'I know,' I answered. Over the last weeks his mood had been difficult.

'Britain has let me down,' he said. 'I thought if I did everything General Scobie asked me to do, he would support me. He didn't. I thought he would keep his promise to pay my men. He didn't. Now I find out that the appointments I have made—promotions and commissions—will not be recognised.'

He was speaking of the officers and NCOs who had gone to the mountains to join EDES in 1942. Many of their contemporaries, I knew, had been commissioned in Cairo for no greater feat than attending an officer cadet training unit. They had probably spent their war sitting in coffee shops.

'I'm sorry to hear that,' I replied. Some of Old Zed's officers, I knew, were undeserving, but many were excellent soldiers who had distinguished themselves as leaders of bands. 'And I'm sorry there's nothing I can do about it.'

'If you do get the chance, put in a good word for them,' he said.

I accompanied Old Zed up to Ipsos, north of Corfu Town, to 1 Brigade. Corfu had had a change of heart, it seemed, and put on a string of beautiful days. The sea was quiet beside the pebbled beach that ran along the road. The mountains behind were quiet too.

Zervas used a microphone to speak to his troops.

'I am here to say goodbye,' he said, 'and thank you. We started out for Gorgopotamos with shining eyes and the belief of victory in our hearts. We had no boots, we were hungry, our weapons were pitiful. Many of us were far from home. But we succeeded that night.

'When the Allies were landing in Sicily we made the Germans keep strong forces here, thinking that the landing would take place on Greek soil. When Italy fell to the Allies we brought in hundreds of tons of supplies right under the noses of the enemy— supplies for the whole of Greece. When at last the Germans were withdrawing, we mauled them as they tried at the last to escape from Greece.

'Our job is complete. Soon we will be going home to our families in the knowledge that we have done what we could— all we could—for Greece. Until then,' he smiled, 'orders are orders—as usual!'

Number 1 Brigade put on a great dinner for us afterwards. As we headed towards 2 Brigade at Skripero to put on the show again, we were all slightly tight.

The following morning there was a parade of the 40 Commando in the big square in Corfu Town, near the Venetian fort. Zervas took the salute. Then we went out to Mon Repos for a party in honour of those leaving and the *andartes*. We took our drinks out through the French doors and chatted on the balcony, looking out across the darkening water to the silhouettes of the mountains of what was once Free Greece.

Over to 3 Brigade in Potamos with Old Zed the next day, then to Lefkimi and 4 Brigade the following morning for an open-air church service and speeches. The mission was holding a farewell dinner for Zervas that night—he 'ordered' the ladies from Lefkimi to attend, and they all hopped into cars and came.

Finally there was another large farewell dinner at Zed's house. Our last chance to talk.

'I wouldn't like to think there was any chance you would forget us, Tom,' he said. 'All the struggles and sacrifices we went through together.'

I shook my head. For a moment I couldn't speak.

'It's been a turning point for Greece,' he went on. 'No matter what happens now. A critical moment in our history. And you were there beside us. When you're back in Australia you can think of us, sitting over our whisky and telling the old stories. And speaking of you.'

'I will,' I said. 'Often. Until I come back. And then we can tell the old stories all over again.'

We all went off to the port at 2.30 am to see him away on the *King George III*. I embraced Voula and Toula who were leaving with him, Dimi my interpreter, and Old Zed himself. Then I watched as the ship cleared the harbour.

On 2 February a letter came from Chris. I opened it eagerly. All around me the world that had been my home, my work, my family, too, ever since I followed Eddie through the hatch of the Liberator above Mount Giona, was disintegrating. I needed the thread of continuity that Chris's friendship gave me.

Dear Tom,
Very disappointed to leave without seeing you, but hope to return from UK in a few weeks. Future uncertain. Your best bet obviously to go back to NZEF.

Feel your way carefully here. Zervas still regarded with suspicion and even contempt within our own HQ. Very odd but can't be helped. I saw your list of names for gongs and made a few minor adjustments to conform with other areas: hope you will accept these. Have tried to do all for best, and on the whole not disappointed.

<u>Must</u> see you again one day.

So he was back in Britain. There'd been a change of plans, and now I'd missed saying goodbye. But in taking up our conversation where it had left off, Chris's note spoke of continuity as well as loss. He would always understand, even if no one else did. Why I loved Zervas (even if what Chris said about his dealings with the Germans was true, which I doubted). What we had tried to do in Greece. Why things had worked out as they did.

In the sadness of one parting after another, I had one consolation. I loved writing letters. As people left, I had been adding their addresses to a list in the back of my diary, and I was going to make very sure I used them.

But first, I had work to do. I couldn't get clearance to pay Zervas's troops the money due to them, so I decided to pay the money owing for January—£35,000—on my own authority. After that 3 Corps refused to allow the Field Cashier to pay EDES anything further.

One hundred and ten Greek officers had arrived with Lieutenant-Colonel Dauban towards the end of January to form the nucleus of the National Guard. Some were quislings. Many were unfit—while the *andartes* were fighting in the mountains they had been sitting pretty in Athens or Cairo, it seemed. Zervas's regular officers didn't like it and most of them refused to join. Fortunately for everyone, Major Hutchinson, who had been Liaison Officer to the Governor of the Ionian Islands, knew how to handle the situation and the successful formation of the National Guard was largely due to him, in the end.

The first day of the National Guard call-up was 12 February. Everything went smoothly on a rainy morning and a large number of EDES troops joined up over the next couple of days.

The *Corinthia* came into port to embark eleven hundred *andartes* and their families who were returning to Athens. Georgios Agoros and all his lads were on board. The rest of the EDES troops for Athens would embark when the *Corinthia* returned.

On 16 February, the day the *Corinthia* sailed for Athens, EDES was officially dissolved. The wireless link between Renovation and Cairo was closed the same day. Everything we had been doing on Corfu had been leading towards this day, but when it arrived I felt nothing but sadness.

The clothing of the National Guard continued. They were a very mixed bag but their first parade on 24 February was surprisingly satisfactory.

Meanwhile, we had some time for leisure. I went out to Paleokastritsa with the families of a number of Zed's officers, scrambling around the rocks and generally having a good time. We got to Doukades on the way back just in time to catch a wedding party as it spilled from the church door onto the square where the tables for the guests were laid out under the trees. Food first, dancing afterwards—white blouses and headscarves for the women, a wedding wreath for the bride, a suit and tie for the groom. Sundry children joined in, ducking and chasing around the trees, breaking into a dance step or two every now and again—big boys and smaller girls, mostly. Behind were the mountains where the British mission, we were told, had conducted training exercises with ropes on the sheer cliffs, watched by the villagers to whom it was a strange and entertaining spectacle. One time *andartes* of both flavours had put out a fire in one of the village buildings.

The stories—that was what the villagers would remember long after the British soldiers and *andartes* alike had gone.

Now that the war was over, the hospitable Corfiots were trying to get things back to normal. Some of the old families were inviting foreign officers like us who had been fighting on their side to their homes. One day Mrs Ventoura invited us to afternoon tea.

The big town house had survived the war. We were an excited lot coming up the steps from the entry with its columns and niches to the first-floor apartment. Mrs Ventoura welcomed us into the sitting room, comfortably furnished with a wood fire glowing in the fireplace below an antique mirror, and the table laid out ready with fine porcelain cups and saucers.

I crossed immediately to one of the full-length windows looking across the sea. Now we could count the number of days we had left in Corfu—that morning we'd been given the date, although of course in the end we left on another day—I was beginning to feel nostalgic, as though our departure was in the past instead of the future. The island was taking on a glamour it hadn't had while we were struggling with Zed's finances and anticipating trouble from disgruntled *andartes*—the narrow streets of the old town, the park where the *andartes* had paraded and I had taken the salute with Zervas on that earlier trip to Corfu before the civil war had broken out, the esplanade winding round towards the fort from Mon Repos.

I was standing near Mrs Ventoura as she poured the tea from a brown English teapot. I noticed the teapot cover, embroidered with orange flowers to match the pattern on the teacups. I'd had an eye for embroidered linen since I'd arrived in Egypt and started collecting it for our home, Beth's and mine. Since then I had seen much more in modest Greek homes in Epiros.

'Is the embroidery yours, *Kyria* Ventoura?' I asked her.

'It is,' she said.

'It's beautiful. And that portrait on the wall there? One of your ancestors?'

'My husband's great-grandfather,' she said, 'Count Antonio Theotoki Kalokardari. A very distinguished Corfiot. He was Governor of the Island of Ithaka, and the leading member of the committee of three who travelled to England to present the Viceroy with the papers for the unification of the Ionian Islands with the rest of Greece.'

'And your house must be old,' I said, 'and in such a wonderful position, so close to the palace and the water.'

'It is old,' she agreed. 'It was built in 1840 by a very well-known architect of the time. Please help yourself to cake, Colonel Barnes.'

It was orange cake, plain and delicious. For one moment I thought of asking for the recipe to take home to Beth. Then I thought better of it.

We saw the rest of the EDES men off on the *Princess Kathleen*. Then I put in a day or two of work with Zervas's creditors, who were getting frantic when they saw everyone leaving. The 3 Corps had proposed to settle affairs with Zervas in Athens. As far as I know that was the end of it. Yes, some of the money that had been supplied had been misappropriated. But not nearly on the scale that was generally believed and used as an excuse for non-payment of the rest.

On 27 February I left Corfu for the last time with all that remained of the staff from Renovation station.

I was ten days in Italy. There was work to do at HQ in Mola, winding up Corfu affairs and handing back our remaining gold sovereigns—ninety-three in all. From Mola three of us drove via Bari and Caserta to Rome for our flight to Greece.

Back in Athens I called in to see John Mulgan at Advanced Force 133. I had heard about him constantly from Chris and

Nick Hammond—he was one of the best liaison officers, hugely successful at getting ELAS to go on ops—but as he had been in Thessaly I had never met him. Now we made up for it.

'Cairo are screaming for you, Tom,' he said with an engaging grin.

'Really?' I said. 'Why?'

'Beats me,' he said. 'But you'd better get cracking.' John himself was working on relief for Greeks who had contributed to the Allied war effort. Among them was Yannis Peltekis, the famous face of the 'Apollo' organisation who had worked in Athens during the occupation, evacuating Greek and Allied personnel wanted by the Germans to the Middle East.

'I've got to stay a few days,' I said. 'Then I'll be off.'

'Come for lunch then,' he said. 'We've got the most amazing house, all black and white marble. Belongs to Sofia Vembo—you know, the singer.' Sofia Vembo had been the 'Victory Voice' of the war against the Italians in 1940 and had fled to the Middle East after the German invasion.

I went to lunch with John the next day. Then Old Zed saw me in the street as he passed in his car and took me back to his house. I kept missing Georgios Agoros but finally made it to tea at his house with Voula, Toula and some of Georgios's officers. I managed to see Spike again, too, before clearing out by plane for Cairo.

In Cairo I found Sylvia Apostolidou. My memory had served me well—she was a stunner with that dark wavy hair and her strongly marked features. Everything had changed since we'd last seen each other, but I hadn't forgotten her.

Once again, we hit it off. I took her to what we jokingly called the Auberge du Turf, really the Turf Club, where I discovered she was an exceptionally good dancer. Not every girl can tango—many try who shouldn't—but she certainly could.

We made a pact. It was my idea. We were both in Cairo by ourselves, writing reports and looking for a good time. We were both engaged to be married—to people we didn't want to hurt. Everything would be perfectly proper. We would go out together and enjoy ourselves, have a real friendship—and leave it at that.

We often went dancing at the Auberge des Pyramides. The rule there was no alcohol after 10 pm, so after 8 pm they served 'tea'. One night somebody arrived late.

'I'll bring some tea,' said the waiter.

'I don't want tea,' the latecomer replied.

'It's very nice tea,' said Sylvia.

'But I don't drink tea.'

'Try it. You might like it.'

After his first taste, his lifelong aversion to tea miraculously disappeared.

I could see I wasn't the only one to find Sylvia attractive. King Farouk started holding parties for the British and one night Sylvia received an invitation, along with her sister's husband (a British general with the RAF) and her sister. Farouk wanted to dance with Sylvia. His large belly got in the way, so he held her off to one side for the whole dance. When it was over, her brother-in-law, who didn't like Farouk, suggested they leave. But no one must see them going—that would have been dangerous.

Over the evenings we spent together at the Auberge des Pyramides or the Turf Club or the Continental Roof Garden, Sylvia told me some more about the British resistance in Athens and Bob Morton.

In early 1944, Bob had come down from the mountains with orders to dismiss the gang who had been working for them. 'It was very hard on the men,' Sylvia said, 'because they'd abandoned their other jobs to work for us, so they didn't have any other income at all. And with inflation the way it was by then, you needed millions of drachmas just to exist.'

Sylvia herself had about fifteen days off before she got news that four British soldiers were hiding out in a village. The

Germans had caught them and put them on a train to Leros, but they'd escaped. One had pneumonia. She borrowed a car and a chauffeur from a friend who had a *passe partout* permit because the German admiral was staying at his house.

'I had to walk a long way up a side path,' she said. 'Some Germans were in the village for some reason, and they would have noticed me. And I couldn't put too many of the soldiers in the car at once—that would've looked suspicious. As we were stopped at one German block after another—there were three of them—the boys became more and more frightened, until they saw the salutes the Germans gave us when they saw the car's papers.'

'I suppose you had a code name, did you?' I asked jokingly. 'Like Apollo?' Even then I had no idea who she was.

She didn't say anything for a moment. Then she said, 'I suppose I can say it now. Even though it nearly got me killed. It was Patricia. Or Pat—mostly Pat.'

So it was Sylvia all along—that 'Patricia' we'd heard so much about while we were in the mountains.

A few days later we went out riding around the pyramids and the sphinx—just one of a string of wonderful days we had together, a kind of Indian summer before we had to take up the threads of our regular lives again. We had lunch on the verandah of Mena House, where I'd met Princess Frederica that time I went to Cairo to report. Back at Sylvia's house for dinner that night, I had something to ask her.

'You said you nearly got killed. Was it the Germans?'

'Yes,' she said. 'Someone working in the GFP, the Secret Military Police, told me they were on the track of a girl named Pat. If they got her they would be able to arrest the British Mission in Athens.'

'What did you do? You must have been terrified.'

'I went straight to Bob Morton and Colonel Sheppard.' This was the Colonel Sheppard who'd been so well persuaded by ELAS propaganda when he first came to Greece. Sylvia had started working with him after he arrived outside Athens late one night in April 1944. Later, keeping her out too late at night on mission business, he had been responsible for her arrest by the Security Battalions, and she had had to swallow an incriminating letter before a friend of her father's got her released.

Sylvia told them what she'd heard and asked them to evacuate her to the Middle East. They didn't believe the story was true, but they sent a signal to Cairo anyway. A month went by. Then Sheppard told Sylvia that Cairo wasn't interested in her. If she wanted to leave without their help she could, and he offered to pay her expenses. But when she needed ten sovereigns for her trip, he was annoyed and said he could only give her two. She told him he could keep his money.

'What a louse,' I said.

Sylvia agreed. 'When Bob Morton heard, he was very upset. Said he was going away too with three other runners and if I could organise things for all of us he would pay. We were supposed to leave on 24 June.'

But at 4.30 am on the very day of her departure, she was arrested by the GFP, along with her parents and the maid's husband, who had helped Sylvia with a lot of her work.

'They questioned me continuously for twenty-one hours with no food or water,' she told me. 'When I asked for water what they gave me was black and muddy. They took us to the Averoff'—I knew the name; we all did; it was the most notorious prison in occupied Athens—'then they put us in the men's prison, all in solitary confinement. My mother and I were the only women there. I was questioned nearly every day for a month.'

Sylvia told me they had found incriminating items belonging

to Bob Morton in a cupboard in her mother's room. They had been there for a long time and Sylvia had forgotten about them.

'And the charges?' I asked.

'Being Pat, being an interpreter for the British, being the British contact with the Greeks. Belonging to a sabotage group collecting information on German movements, taking ammunition to the camp—and so it went on. Different men kept appearing to identify me—some said I was Pat, some said I wasn't. There was a whole list of names they kept asking me about. I knew most of them, of course, but I denied every single one. They didn't like that and the Komissar of the GFP beat me for it.'

'After two months the others—my parents and the maid's husband—were let out. They had to pay 150 sovereigns. Then my brother found out I could get out too if they paid 300 sovereigns.'

'Did you get it from the mission?' I asked.

'Well, they authorised him to borrow it,' she said. 'He paid 150 to the GFP and twenty to the SS. The SS were meant to collect the rest after I was released. Then I was court-martialled. They wanted another 100 sovereigns. My mother refused to pay. I was sentenced to death.'

I had stopped eating long before. Now I poured more wine for both of us.

'Go on,' I said.

'They brought me down and put me in a truck with another nine women. They were going to shoot all of us. At the very last minute the interrogator took my name off the list and I was let down from the truck.'

'And the others?' I asked.

Sylvia shook her head.

'They transferred me to the women's prison. I was there for three months. Then they let me out—it was the end of September.'

I understood. For me it had been the horrors of the civil war, wedged between ELAS and the Germans, constantly on the run. Bill Jordan struggling to speak of Arthur Hubbard's death. Danger shared with my Greek friends—Agoros, Zervas, Toula, Voula. My love for them, and its poignancy, with my departure for Australia now so close.

And Sylvia understood. She'd been living the life we'd imagined for ourselves, back in Cairo, when we were first recruited at the 'spy house'. While we were in Epiros blowing up bridges and attacking convoys as the Germans withdrew, Sylvia had been in prison facing death by firing squad every single day.

Would Beth understand? All that time in the mountains, I'd built my whole future around her, our home, the little boy we would name after Chris. How far could I expect Beth to comprehend my life here, my Greek friends, my job with Zervas? I suspected it would always be something I couldn't fully share with her. With Sylvia, who knew what war was, it was easy. It was just as well we'd made that pact back at the beginning of our time in Cairo not to stray beyond friendship—and kept to it.

After I'd been in Cairo a few weeks, I heard John Mulgan was back in town. Then, a few days later, I was shocked to hear he was dead. An overdose of morphine, apparently. It seemed impossible to believe.

A letter came from his wife. Was there anything I could tell her about his death? I went up to the office to see if they had any information, but there was nothing further to put in my reply. He had seemed perfectly OK when I saw him last. I couldn't understand why he would want to take his own life.

On June 19 I read in the papers that Aris Velouchiotis was dead in the Agrafa mountains, apparently by his own hand. After how he'd treated us during the civil war—Themis particularly—it was hard to feel upset.

Everything was changing.

* * *

Word came through on 11 July—we would be leaving in about two weeks. 'I sincerely hope not,' I said to myself. My own beautiful Beth and marriage were waiting for me in Tasmania, but I wasn't ready to leave Cairo. Perhaps we can come back after the war, I thought, live here for a while.

We went out riding again at Mena House, Sylvia and I. We went to a dance, me in civvies and she in a white evening dress. She looked smashing. I had a studio photo taken—some copies to take home, and one for Sylvia to keep. "To my dear and true friend Sylvia with all my heart. Tom, Cairo, 3 August '45." I meant every word.

Arthur Edmonds came through Cairo. He was to marry a Greek girl and work with the United Nations on the island of Chios. I gave him a letter for Chris, who was back in Greece— we had kept on missing each other since he left Corfu in January.

By early August, we were on six hours' notice to depart. Sylvia and I went to an open-air dance at Helmeh, and didn't get home till 1.30 am.

August 6. I was leaving by road the next day. I had dinner with Sylvia—the last time. She promised to write, and suggested it would be best for her to write to Beth first, so that everything was above board. I agreed.

Then I was off to Alexandria in a staff car, and on board the *Strathaird*. It had taken considerable effort to get permission to disembark in Melbourne rather than going on to New Zealand, but it had finally come through. Now I was away, watching my life in Egypt shrink before my eyes as we pulled out of the harbour.

I'd made it through alive.

Leaning over the railing, I thought about Beth. She would be there to turn to every morning when we woke beside one another, to laugh and have fun with, to bring our children into the world together and build our love for each other around them as well. But the morning outside our window wouldn't be a Greek morning. I wouldn't be able to watch the first rays of the sun striking the fir trees on the mountains or the white walls of villages across the way. There would be no more Sylvia, who had brought Greece with her to Cairo for me.

Beth hadn't lived through what I lived through, and no doubt she wouldn't understand it all. But gradually a new thought was forming. My life in Greece was threaded through with memories of Beth. The photo of her in the blue dress with white spots that I looked at every night before I went to bed. Thoughts of her dancing in a white frock as I waited in the dark and cold, signalling for the submarine that never came. Poppies and blue cornflowers up near the Albanian border as I bit into the juicy redness of a cherry and made a wish for her. Giggling over the thought of Deloraine men wearing underpants made of towelling nappies. And whenever I thought of my good friend Chris, of Zervas with his generous beard, now sadly gone, of Agoros and his crinkly hair or Toula with her cheeky grin, shy and mischievous at the same time, whenever I thought further back to Barba Niko with his cauldron or grumpy old Denys Hamson as we softened and moulded the explosives for Gorgopotamos, or more recently to the glowing days with Sylvia in Cairo, Beth would be part of the fabric.

We'd have an ordinary suburban house, in Hobart perhaps or Melbourne, growing vegetables and fruit trees in our yard or keeping chickens, fixing the car on a Saturday afternoon. Around us our neighbours would be doing the same ordinary things. I would record in my diary the comings and goings of D8 bulldozers and Tournapull excavators rather than *andartes* and mission staff. But whenever my thoughts turned to Greece, thoughts of Beth would be there too—as I'd longed for her during the days and months and years of our separation.

Afterword

Tom disembarked from the *Strathaird* in Melbourne on 31 August 1945. He and Beth were married in Tasmania the following October. A daughter, Deborah (Debbi), was born in Launceston in 1947 and a son, Christopher (Chris—my husband), in Melbourne in 1950. Between the two living babies there was a stillborn son.

Chris and I still have movies of Tom and Beth's wedding and of Beth as a beautiful young mother with the two small children, Debbi with large bows in her hair and Chris as a toddler in a red dressing-gown.

Tom continued to keep up his diaries through the following years as he worked for the Tasmanian Hydro-Electric Commission, first in Hobart and then in Waddamana, later as a contractor and finally for the State Electricity Commission in Morwell, Victoria. He continued to work with his beloved heavy machinery, bulldozers and scoops from Lorain and Le Tourneau and Caterpillar, as a civil engineer.

The diaries finish abruptly in June 1952. Tom drove a Humber Super Snipe at the time. On the bonnet was a little silver snipe with a black rubber beak, which Debbi was allowed to polish when she helped Tom work on the car, sporting a blue boiler suit with studs just like her father's. Driving home to Morwell late one night from a Returned Services League meeting in Melbourne, Tom crashed the car and was killed instantly. Beth gave birth to their third child, Rosalind (Roz), three months later.

Debbi remembers her mother coming down the stairs in the Morwell house to tell her and Chris that their father had been killed in a car crash. Debbi asked what had happened to the little bird on the bonnet of the car. Afterwards she used to dream of seeing him in a busy city: he would tell her he was coming home. It was only when she came on her mother sitting on the grass behind the chicken house and crying quietly that Debbi finally realised he was dead. Chris, not yet two at the time, has no memories of his father.

Not long after Roz was born, Beth moved the family back to Deloraine to be with her mother and went back to managing the family business, which she continued to do into her seventies.

Bill Jordan came to Australia, first to Melbourne and later to Sydney, and he and Tom remained friends. After Tom's death Bill proposed to Beth and they were briefly engaged. Later Beth married Bob Thomas from Deloraine and her second son, Robert, was born in 1959. (After a period pursuing journalism, Bill Jordan became a lay teacher at St Ignatius College Riverview in Sydney before finally becoming a Catholic priest in Auckland at the age of sixty.)

Tom and Beth's children grew up without their father. Chris inherited his father's ability with mathematics but had no one in the family to share it with. As a young woman, Roz moved to New Zealand, and later developed strong connections with Greece.

Tom's notes on Denys Hamson's book *We Fell among Greeks* are still in a copy from the New Zealand National Library Service that he had in his possession at the time of his death. His

1947 diary records, 'Read Denys Hamson's book *We Fell among Greeks* through and didn't like it.'

Sylvia found out about Tom's death when she read the report in an Athens newspaper. She kept and treasured the studio photo Tom had given her in Cairo until she gave it to us in 2010.

Tom's diaries show that he kept in touch with many of the friends he made in Greece, both Greek and non-Greek.

Tom and 'Chris' (Monty) Woodhouse exchanged letters and occasionally telegrams on special occasions. Monty married and he and his wife had a son, Christopher, in September 1946, and later a second son Nicholas and daughter Emma. Monty asked Tom to be one of Christopher's godfathers and Tom asked Monty to return the favour for his son Chris. Monty sent Tom the draft of his 'History of the Allied Military Mission in Greece', also in 1946, and asked Tom to read it and make corrections. But they never met again.

We visited the Woodhouses in 1977. In his autobiography *Something Ventured*, mentioning our visit, Monty recorded that 'all of them who survived remained close to me in later years, but the closest of all was Tom Barnes, though he was one of the first to die'. Monty served two terms as the Member of Parliament for Oxford in the 1960s and '70s; he published a number of books about modern Greece. He died in 2001, aged eighty-three.

When General Zervas heard of Tom's death, he sent a condolence letter to Beth in English:

> With great grief I was informed of the sudden death of our dear Tom and was deeply touched from the terrible news. Please accept dear Mrs Barnes the expression of my sincere sympathy to your mourning.
>
> The doleful news came to me through a letter of my friend and fellow-combatant Major W.S. Jordan who has described to me the circumstances of the accident.

I never thought that our dear Tom who went through all he did should meet such a simple death and so young.

Tom wasn't only a brave fellow-combatant and valuable counsellor for me but also was a precious friend with a rare character. He was an outstanding figure for all of us and we feel that Tom is not dead. He lives as a symbol of the ideal man and brave soldier.

Tom Barnes was for Greece a second Lord Byron and the whole Nation has admired his heroism and is grateful for his love to our country.

His name will be written among the names of the heroes of the II World War.

His death has classified him among the immortals and you must be proud.

To you, dear Mrs Barnes, and our dear Tom's children myself and all the fellow-combatants of the National Resistance Army and all the Greek patriots we wish that God gives his comfort, and remain,

Sincerely Yours

General Nap. Zervas

Acknowledgements

This book was written while I was a Visiting Fellow in the School of Literature, Languages and Linguistics (formerly the School of Cultural Inquiry) at the Australian National University, and I am grateful to the School for their support.

Thanks are due to the following people and organisations for permission to use unpublished material in this book: Sylvia Apostolidou–Ioannidou for her 'Report on activities in Athens during the period 1943–1944'; Ioannis Agoros for the diary of his father, General Georgios Agoros; Jason Chandrinos for his 2005 interview with Stergios Voulgaris; Christopher Terrington for the note from his father, Christopher Montague Woodhouse; Deborah Barnes, Chris Barnes and Rosalind Stephens for materials belonging to them; Eva Zervas for letters written by her father, General Napoleon Zervas, to Tom and Beth Barnes; the Trustees of the Liddell Hart Centre for Military Archives for extracts from the Woodhouse papers held in the archive. I am also grateful to the Alexander Turnbull Library in Wellington, New Zealand, for permission to use a photograph from their collection; to Christopher Terrington for permission to reproduce the group photograph of the Harling party in his possession; and to Jason Chandrinos for permission to reproduce several photographs in his possession.

I am indebted to those who took part in informal interviews or discussions, or took me to visit places as part of the research for this book: Ioannis and Anthi Agoros, Sylvia Apostolidou–Ioannidou, Chris Carratt,

Gregory Jordan SJ, Nikos Manousis, Themis Marinos, Vangelis Petsotas, General Nikolaos Rossis, Susie Rossi, Dimitris Sgouros, Giorgos Sofis, Vasilis Tembelis, Eleftherias Trypas, Dimitra (Toula) Tsitsika, Lambrini Velogammi, Marilla Ventoura-Dantou. Many thanks to villagers from Derviziana, Theodoriana and Vourgareli in Epiros, and Doukades and Skripero in Corfu, who shared stories of the years of the Nazi occupation.

I am grateful to others whom I consulted for advice about various aspects of the research: Martyn Browne, Frank Cain, Jason Chandrinos, James Cotton, Hagen Fleischer, Eleanor Hancock, Megan Hutching, Richard Mulgan, Matthew Ricketson, Craig Stockings and Vangelis Tzoukas. Thanks to Susan Cowan and Stephen Smith for superb assistance with my research. Alan Cowan advised on medical matters. Thanks also to those who read and commented on some or all of the manuscript: Chris Barnes, Debbi Barnes, Rosemary Barnes (who also drove us around Epiros in September 2013), Jason Chandrinos, Hugh Crago, Maureen Crago, Konstantinos Dragatsis, Meg Evans, Themis Marinos, Ben O'Cianain, George Serras, Rosalind Stephens and Marilla Ventoura-Dantou.

I am grateful to Glenn Baker for help at the very beginning of the project and Jeremy Barnes at the end.

Many thanks to my publisher HarperCollins, especially Catherine Milne and Shona Martyn, for their interest and support and advice along the way. Special thanks to my editor Denise O'Dea.

Lastly, several people need special mention. One is my husband, Chris, for whom in many ways I wrote this book and without whom I certainly could not have written it. My Greek teachers at the Hellenic Club in Canberra, Yiota Eleftheriou and Michael Kazan, gave me insights into Greek language, culture and ways of thinking that have enriched my story, and without their help in translation this book would have had a much more limited point of view. And finally there is Verona Burgess, whose enthusiasm, advice and encouragement have sustained me from start to finish.

Notes

Chapter one

Material for this chapter is drawn from the following sources: C.E. Barnes diary entries, September 22–23 1942; C.E. Barnes, 'Notes and dates from diaries'; C.E. Barnes, 'Final report on activities and observations in Greece, period 1 October 1942–27 February 1945', p. 3; C.E. Barnes, manuscript speech notes; J.F. Cody, *New Zealand Engineers, Middle East* (part of the *Official History of New Zealand in the Second World War 1939–45*), Wellington: Department of Internal Affairs New Zealand, 1961, pp. 18–19, 318; Arthur Edmonds, *With Greek Guerrillas*, n.p.: Times Print, 1998, p. 1–2; Alex Hedley with Megan Hutching, *Fernleaf Cairo: New Zealanders at Maadi Camp*, Auckland: HarperCollins, 2009, pp. 38, 140; Themistocles Marinos, *Harling Mission—1942*, Athens: Papazisis, 1993, p. 27; E.C.W. Myers, *Greek Entanglement*, London: Hart-Davis, 1955, p. 24; David Stafford, *Secret Agent: The True Story of the Special Operations Executive*, London: BBC, 2000, pp. 92–94.

Details about life in Egypt in chapters one, two and twenty-one are drawn from: Artemis Cooper, *Cairo in the War, 1939–1945*, London: Penguin, 1995 (1989); W.D. Dawson, *18 Battalion and Armoured Regiment* (part of the *Official History of New Zealand in the Second World War 1939–45*), Wellington: Historical Publications Branch, 1961, Chapter 3, Maadi Camp, p. 8, New Zealand Electronic Text Centre; Denys Hamson, *We Fell among Greeks*, London: Cape, 1946; Megan Hutching, ed., *The Desert Road: New Zealanders Remember the North African Campaign*, Auckland:

HarperCollins, 2005; Harold Macmillan, *War Diaries: The Mediterranean 1943–45*, New York: St Martin's Press, 1984; Alan Moorehead, *African Trilogy*, London: Hamish Hamilton, 1944; and W.G. Stevens, *Problems of 2 NZEF, Official History of New Zealand in the Second World War 1939–1945*, Wellington: Historical Publications Branch, 1958, Chapter 2, p. 11, New Zealand Electronic Text Centre.

Details of Tom's conversation with Brigadier Stevens are drawn from M.B. McGlynn, *Special Service in Greece*, Wellington: Department of Internal Affairs, 1953, p. 3. Information about Brigadier Stevens himself is taken from 'Stevens, William George', http://www.teara.govt.nz/en/biographies/4s43/1, accessed 1 January 2012.

Chapter two

Material for this chapter is drawn from the following sources: C.E. Barnes diary entries, September 23–October 1 1942; C.E. Barnes, 'Notes and dates from diaries'; C.E. Barnes, 'Final report on activities and observations in Greece', p. 3; C.E. Barnes, manuscript speech notes; Cooper, *Cairo in the War*, p. 262; Edmonds, *With Greek Guerrillas*, pp. 4–9, 60; Hamson, *We Fell among Greeks*, pp. 15–33; James Ladd and Keith Melton, *Clandestine Warfare: Weapons and Equipment of the SOE and OSS*, London: Book Club Associates 1988, pp. 27, 33, 44; Liddell Hart Military Archives, Brig. Edmund Charles Wolf Myers Collection, http://www.kingscollections.org/catalogues/lhcma/collection/m/my30-001/?searchterms=myers, accessed 4 August 2014; Marinos, *Harling Mission*, pp. 23–24; Themis Marinos (Θέμης Μαρίνος), *O Efialtis tis Ethnikis Antistasis (Ο Εφιάλτης της Εθνικής Αντίστασης)* (The nightmare of the national resistance), Vol. 1, Athens: Papazisi, 2003, pp. 13, 113–15; S. Muthiah, *Born to Dare: The Life of Lt. Gen. Inderjit Singh Gill PVSM, MC*, New Delhi: Penguin, 2008, pp. 8, 15; Myers, *Greek Entanglement*, pp. 14–27; C.M. Woodhouse, 'Early British Contacts with the Greek Resistance in 1942', *Balkan Studies*, Vol. 12, No. 2, 1971, pp. 349–51, 354; C.M. Woodhouse, *Something Ventured*, London: Granada, 1982, p. 25.

Chapter three

Material for this chapter is drawn from the following sources: C.E. Barnes diary entries, 4 January 1938 and 1–16 and 27–31 October 1942; C.E. Barnes, manuscript speech notes; C.E. Barnes, 'Final report on activities and observations in Greece', p. 3; C.E. Barnes, 'Notes and dates from diaries'; Edmonds, *With Greek Guerrillas,* pp. 8–20; Hamson, *We Fell among Greeks*, pp. 38–54; Hedley and Hutching, *Fernleaf Cairo*, p. 111; Myers, *Greek Entanglement*, pp. 28–48; John Simpson and Mark Adkin, *The Quiet Operator: Special Forces Signaller Extraordinary*, London: Cooper, 1993, pp. 54–55; C.M. Woodhouse, 'History of the Allied Military Mission in Greece (September 1942 to December 1944)', unpublished manuscript, p. 8.

Chapter four

Material for this chapter is drawn from the following sources: C.E. Barnes diary entries, 16 October–1 November 1942; C.E. Barnes, 'Notes and dates from diaries'; 'Final report on activities and observations in Greece', p. 3; C.E. Barnes Egypt notebook; Edmonds, *With Greek Guerrillas*, pp. 21–31; Hamson, *We Fell among Greeks*, pp. 55–58; McGlynn, *Special Service in Greece*, p. 25; Myers, *Greek Entanglement*, pp. 23, 41, 49–61; Simpson and Adkin, *The Quiet Operator*, pp. 56–58; Woodhouse, 'History of the Allied Military Mission in Greece', p. 9; Woodhouse, *Something Ventured*, pp. 8, 22, 35–37.

Chapter five

Material for this chapter is drawn from the following sources: C.E. Barnes diary entries, 2–15 November 1942; C.E. Barnes, 'Notes and dates from diaries'; C.E. Barnes, 'Final report on activities and observations in Greece', pp. 3–4; Edmonds, *With Greek Guerrillas,* pp. 31–33, 64; Hamson, *We Fell among Greeks*, pp. 60, 63, 83; Marinos, *Harling Mission*, pp. 64–66, 71–76, 84–88; Themis Marinos, personal communication to the author, August 2009; Mark Mazower, *Inside Hitler's Greece: The Experience of Occupation, 1941–44*, New Haven: Yale University Press, 2001 (1993), pp. 37–41; Muthiah, *Born to Dare*, p. 22; Myers, *Greek Entanglement*, pp. 58–64; Stefanos Sarafis, *ELAS: Greek Resistance Army*, trans. Sylvia Moody, London: Merlin, 1951, p. 154; Woodhouse, *Something Ventured*, pp. 37–38, 42–43; C.M. Woodhouse, *The Struggle for Greece: 1941–1949*, London: Hurst, 2002 (1976), pp. 21–25.

Chapter six

Material for this chapter is drawn from the following sources: C.E. Barnes diary entries, 29 August, 6–7 September, 9 October, 12 October and 16–25 November 1941; C.E. Barnes, 'Notes and dates from diaries';

Edmonds, *With Greek Guerrillas*, pp. 36–43; Hamson, *We Fell among Greeks*, pp. 79, 97–101; Marinos, *Harling Mission*, pp. 90–112; Themis Marinos, personal communication to the author, August 2012; Myers, *Greek Entanglement*, pp. 66–73; Simpson and Adkin, *The Quiet Operator*, pp. 61–63; Woodhouse, 'History of the Allied Military Mission in Greece', p. 14; Woodhouse, *Something Ventured*, pp. 38–47.

Chapter seven
Material for this chapter is drawn from the following sources: C.E. Barnes diary entries, 25–28 November; C.E. Barnes manuscript notes, 'Guerrilla warfare 1942–5'; C.E. Barnes manuscript speech notes; C.E. Barnes, 'Final report on activities and observations in Greece', p. 4; Edmonds, *With Greek Guerrillas*, pp. 41–51, 86; Hamson, *We Fell among Greeks*, pp. 107–121, 124–125; Marinos, *Harling Mission*, pp. 113–137; Themis Marinos, personal communication to the author August 2012; Simpson and Adkin, *The Quiet Operator*, pp. 63, 66; Stergios Voulgaris, unpublished interview by Jason Chandrinos, 7 April 2005, Athens; Woodhouse, *Something Ventured*, pp. 48–49.

Chapter eight
Material for this chapter is drawn from the following sources: C.E. Barnes diary entries, June–August 1941 and 28 November–2 December 1942; 'Notes and dates from diaries'; 'Final report on activities and observations in Greece', pp. 4–5; Edmonds, *With Greek Guerrillas*, pp. 31, 53–54; Hamson, *We Fell among Greeks*, pp. 88, 126–132; Marinos, *Harling Mission*, pp. 141–42; Mazower, *Inside Hitler's Greece*, p. 273; L.S. Stavrianos, 'The Greek National Front (EAM): A Study in Resistance Organisation and Administration', *Journal of Modern History* 24.1, 1952, pp. 42–55; Woodhouse, *Something Ventured*, pp. 47, 52.

Chris Woodhouse's assessment of Zervas and Aris is adapted from his 'History of the Allied Military Mission', p. 13.

Chapter nine
Material for this chapter is drawn from the following sources: C.E. Barnes diary entries, 3–25 December 1942; C.E. Barnes, 'Notes and dates from diaries'; C.E. Barnes, 'Final report on activities and observations in Greece', p. 5; Edmonds, *With Greek Guerrillas*, pp. 54–59; Hamson, *We Fell among Greeks*, pp. 133, 135–39; Marinos, *Harling Mission*, p. 142; Themis Marinos,

personal communication with the author, August 2012; Myers, *Greek Entanglement*, pp. 89–95; Simpson and Adkin, *The Quiet Operator*, p. 81.

Details of Shepheard's Hotel, Cairo, in this chapter are drawn from Andrew Humphries, *Grand Hotels of Egypt in the Golden Age of Travel*, Cairo: American University in Cairo, 2011, pp. 93–96.

Chapter ten

Material for this chapter is drawn from the following sources: C.E. Barnes diary entries, 25 December 1942–17 January 1943; C.E. Barnes, 'Notes and dates from diaries'; C.E. Barnes, 'Final report on activities and observations in Greece', p. 5; Chris Carratt (interpreter with the Allied Military Mission), informal telephone discussion with the author, September 2013; Hamson, *We Fell among Greeks*, pp. 142, 144; William Jordan, *Conquest without Victory: A New Zealander in the Greek and French Resistance*, Bedford: Little Hills Press, 1989 (1969), pp. 70, 75; Marinos, *Harling Mission,* pp. 145, 149–50; Marinos, *O Efialtis tis Ethnikis Antistasis (Ο Εφιάλτης της Εθνικής Αντίστασης)* (The nightmare of the national resistance), Vol. 2, pp. 16–17, 24–5; Myers, *Greek Entanglement*, pp. 97–9, 110, 113–14; Woodhouse, 'History of the Allied Military Mission', pp. 16–19; Woodhouse, *Something Ventured*, pp. 53–4.

Chapter eleven

Material for this chapter is drawn from the following sources: C.E. Barnes diary entries, 17 January–11 March 1943; C.E. Barnes, 'Notes and dates from diaries'; C.E. Barnes, 'Final report on activities and observations in Greece', p. 5; C.E. Barnes, 'Guerrilla warfare 1942–5'; Edmonds, *With Greek Guerrillas*, pp. 51, 62; Hamson, *We Fell among Greeks*, p. 150; Marinos, *O Efialtis tis Ethnikis Antistasis (Ο Εφιάλτης της Εθνικής Αντίστασης)* (The nightmare of the national resistance), Vol. 2, p. 24; Myers, *Greek Entanglement*, pp. 112–14, 124–29, 169; Woodhouse, 'History of the Allied Military Mission in Greece', pp. 21, 38, 175; Woodhouse, *Something Ventured*, pp. 50, 55–60.

Details of how the *andartes* carried out ambushes are drawn from D.M. Condit, *Case Study in Guerrilla War: Greece During World War II*, n.p.: American University, 1961, pp. 207–9.

Chris Woodhouse's account of his meeting with Aris and Zervas, and his assessment of their differences, are adapted from his 'History of the Allied Mission,' pp. 20–21.

Information about klephtic ballads is drawn from Rodney Gallop, 'Folk-songs of Modern Greece', *The Musical Quarterly*, 21.1, pp. 89–91.

Chapter twelve
Material for this chapter is drawn from the following sources: C.E. Barnes diary entries, 12 March–12 May 1943; C.E. Barnes, 'Notes and dates from diaries'; C.E. Barnes, 'Final report on activities and observations in Greece', p. 5; Guy Micklethwait, personnel file, HS 9/1030/6, Special Operations Executive Personnel Files (PF series), 1939–1946, The National Archives, UK; Myers, *Greek Entanglement*, pp. 115, 144, 154–59, 164; Woodhouse, 'History of the Allied Military Mission in Greece', pp. 25, 29, 32, 34, 38, 45, 47.

Chapter thirteen
Material for this chapter is drawn from the following sources: C.E. Barnes diary entries, 12 May–4 July 1943; C.E. Barnes, 'Notes and dates from diaries'; C.E. Barnes, 'Final report on activities and observations in Greece', pp. 5–8; Nigel Clive, *A Greek Experience 1943–1948*, Wilton: Michael Russell, 1985, p. 66; Edmonds, *With Greek Guerrillas*, p. 63; Nicholas Gage, *Eleni*, London: Vintage, 1997 (Kindle edition) (1983); Ladd and Melton, *Clandestine Warfare*, p. 137; Lanz, *Partisan Warfare in the Balkans*, p. 37; Marinos, *O Efialtis tis Ethnikis Antistasis* (Ο Εφιάλτης της Εθνικής Αντίστασης) (The nightmare of the national resistance), Vol. 2, p. 39; Myers, *Greek Entanglement*, pp. 162–63, 197; Simpson and Adkin, *The Quiet Operator*, pp. 77–78; Dimitra (Toula) Tsitsika, informal discussion with the author, Voulgareli, September 2013; Woodhouse, *Something Ventured*, p. 63; reminiscences of men from Theodhoriana village, as told to the author, September 2013.

Chapter fourteen
Material for this chapter is drawn from the following sources: C.E. Barnes diary entries, 4–31 July 1943; C.E. Barnes, 'Notes and dates from diaries'; C.E. Barnes, 'Final report on activities and observations in Greece', pp. 7–9; Lars Bærentzen (ed.), *British Reports on Greece 1943–1944*, Copenhagen: Museum Tusculanum Press, 1982, pp. xxxi, xxxiii; Ladd and Melton, *Clandestine Warfare*, pp. 16, 20; Lanz, *Partisan Warfare in the Balkans*, pp. 73–76, 109; Woodhouse, *Something Ventured*, p. 65.

Some details of the attack on the Kaloyirou Bridge are drawn from an unpublished diary entry by Georgios Agoros, 4 July 1943.

The account of the Asopos operation is drawn from the following sources: Citation for Mirhail Khalil Shibli Khouri, bar to Military Medal;

Citation for Geoffrey Gordon-Creed, DSO; Edmonds, *With Greek Guerrillas*, pp. 93–111; McGlynn, *Special Service in Greece*, pp. 23–29; Myers, *Greek Entanglement*, pp. 169–185.

Chapter fifteen
Material for this chapter is drawn from the following sources: C.E. Barnes diary entries, 15 January, 7 April, 25 April, 3 May, 15 June, 18 July, 27 August, 4 September, 14 November, 21 November, 22 December and 25 December 1938; C.E. Barnes diary entries, 20–27 July 1943; C.E. Barnes, 'Final report on activities and observations in Greece', pp. 9–13; C.E. Barnes, 'Notes and dates from diaries'; C.E. Barnes, letter to Beth Harris, 24 July 1943; Bærentzen (ed.), *British Reports on Greece 1943–1944*, p. xxxi; Nicholas Hammond, *Venture into Greece: With the Guerrillas 1943–44*, London: William Kimber and Co., 1983, pp. 75–77; Hamson, *We Fell among Greeks*, pp. 189–97, 202; Myers, *Greek Entanglement*, pp. 224, 225, 228–35; Sarafis, *ELAS: Greek Resistance Army*, pp. 100, 102, 176–77; 'Weekly progress report No. 6 by SOE for period ending 16 September [1943]', FO 371/37205, National Archives, UK; C.M. Woodhouse diary entries, 20, 25 and 26 July 1943; Woodhouse, 'History of the Allied Military Mission in Greece', p. 88; Woodhouse, *Something Ventured*, p. 65.

Two places called Neraida appear in this book. Denys Hamson built his airfield at Neraida Karditsas on the Nevropoli Plateau, while Neraida Trikalon, where Tom fled with his station from Agnanda village during the first round of the civil war, is on Jumerka Mountain, near Theodoriana. To avoid confusion, the first will be referred to as Featherbed, the name the British mission used for the airfield once the first flight ('Feather 1') took off. The second will be referred to as Neraida.

Chapter sixteen
Material for this chapter is drawn from the following sources: C.E. Barnes diary entries, 26 July–11 October 1943; C.E. Barnes, 'Notes and dates from diaries'; C.E. Barnes, 'Final report on activities and observations in Greece' pp. 9–13; Baerentzen (ed.), *British Reports on Greece 1943–1944*, p. 27; Paul Bathgate, 'The andarte movement in Epiros, Jun 43–Feb 44', March 1944, HS 5/695, The National Archives, UK; Clive, *A Greek Experience*, pp. 56–57; Janet Hart, *New Voices in the Nation: Women and the Greek Resistance 1941–1964*, Ithaca, NY: Cornell University Press, 1996, p. 79; Lanz, *Partisan Warfare in the Balkans*, pp. 77–80; Mazower, *Inside*

Hitler's Greece, pp. 190–95; Myers, *Greek Entanglement*, p. 235; Sarafis, *ELAS: Greek Resistance Army*, pp. 176–77; Simpson and Adkin, *The Quiet Operator*, p. 80; Woodhouse, 'History of the Allied Military Mission in Greece', pp. 122–26.

Johnny Stavridis's account of Thomas Vinson's death is taken from Marinos, *O Efialtis tis Ethnikis Antistasis* (The nightmare of the national resistance), Vol. 2, pp. 189–90.

Chapter seventeen

Material from this chapter is drawn from the following sources: C.E. Barnes diary entries, 26 July–21 November 1943; C.E. Barnes, 'Notes and dates from diaries'; C.E. Barnes, 'Final report on activities and observations in Greece' pp. 13–14; Marinos, *O Efialtis tis Ethnikis Antistasis* (*Ο Εφιάλτης της Εθνικής Αντίστασης*) (The nightmare of the national resistance), Vol. 2, pp. 271–82; John ('Spike') Moran, citation for the Military Cross, WO 373/46/144, The National Archives, UK; Dennis Thomas Holme Nicholson, personnel file, HS9/1099/4, The National Archives, UK; 'Report by Capt D.T.H. Nicholson on past activities etc in Greece', HS5/697, The National Archives, UK, p. 6; J.W. Torrance, 'Report on activities in the field', HS 5/697, The National Archives, UK, pp. 5–10; Woodhouse diary entries, 1–17 October, 26 October, 29–30 October and 7 November 1943.

John Gwynne was completely exonerated in relation to the death of Thomas Vinson. See John Nevile Wake Gwynne, HS 9/640/1, Special Operations Executive Personnel Files (PF series), 1939–1946, The National Archives, UK.

Chapter eighteen

Material for this chapter is drawn from the following sources: C.E. Barnes diary entries, 21 November 1943–25, December 1943; C.E. Barnes, 'Notes and dates from diaries'; C.E. Barnes, 'Final report on activities and observations in Greece', pp. 14–17; C.E. Barnes, 'Guerrilla warfare 1942–5', p. 9; C.E. Barnes, letter to Beth Harris, 24 July 1943; Clive, *A Greek Experience*, p. 29; Condit, *Case Study in Guerrilla War*, 244–55; Torrance, 'Report on activities in the field,' p. 2; Woodhouse, 'History of the Allied Military Mission in Greece', pp. 139–63, 175; Woodhouse, *Something Ventured*, p. 72; Woodhouse diary entries for 9 December and 24 December 1943, 1 and 24 January 1944 and 6 and 26 February 1944.

No letters from Beth to Tom during the war have survived. Beth's letter in this chapter is based on Beth Thomas (née Harris), 'Personal reflections of Deloraine', talk given to Meander Valley School for Seniors, 13 July 1994, and the Australian War Memorial Encyclopedia, 'Rationing of food and clothing during the Second World War', http://www.awm. gov.au/encyclopedia/homefront/rationing.asp, accessed 3 February 2013.

Chapter nineteen

Material for this chapter is drawn from the following sources: C.E. Barnes diary entries, 26 December 1943–2 March 1944; C.E. Barnes, 'Notes and dates from diaries'; C.E. Barnes, 'Final report on activities and observations in Greece', pp. 15–17; C.E. Barnes, 'Guerrilla warfare 1942–5', p. 9; Condit, *Case Study in Guerrilla War*, 244–55; John Louis Hondros, *Occupation and Resistance: The Greek Agony 1941–44*, NY: Pella, 1983, p. 183; J.W. Torrance, citation for MBE, 27 September 1940, WO/373/75/698; Woodhouse diary entries for 9 and 24 December 1943, 1 and 24 January 1944 and 6 and 26 February 1944; Woodhouse, *Something Ventured*, pp. 1, 72.

Tom Barnes' diary offers no further evidence about whether or not Tom encouraged Zervas to cross the Acheloos to the east beyond what is cited by Procopos Papastratis in *British Policy Towards Greece During the Second World War*, Cambridge: Cambridge University Press, 1984, pp. 154–56.

Chapter twenty

Material for this chapter is drawn from the following sources: C.E. Barnes diary entries, 7 March–21 April 1944; C.E. Barnes, 'Notes and dates from diaries'; C.E. Barnes, 'Final report on activities', pp. 17–19; C.E. Barnes, 'Report on Zervas Andarte Movement', 14 August 1944, pp. 1–4; C.E. Barnes, 'Report on observations in Greece from July 1943 to April 1944', FO 371/43688, The National Archives, UK, p. 6; C.E. Barnes, 'Photo diary', including photographs of training in 1944; C.E. Barnes, telegram, 23 March 1944, FO 371/43685, The National Archives, UK; Clive, *A Greek Experience*, pp. 29, 65, 67–68, 89; photographs from Kosta E. Ioannou (Κώστα Ε. Ιωάννου), *Ethnikes Omades Ellinon Andarton* (Εθνικες Ομάδες Ελληνικών Ανδάρτων) (National bands of the Greek resistance fighters), n.p.: Etaireia Meletis Ellinikis Istorias (Εταιρεία Μελέτης Ελληνικής Ιστορίας), p. 75 and *Pos Plastografeitai*

I istoria tis antistasis (Πως Πλαστογραφείται η ιστορία της αντίστασης) (How the history of the resistance is falsified), p. 117; Torrance, 'Report on activities in the field,' p. 12; C.M. Woodhouse, *Apple of Discord: A Survey of Recent Greek Politics in Their International Setting,* London: Hutchinson, 1948, pp. 177, 183.

Details of life in Derviziana are drawn from an informal discussion with Susie Rossis, daughter-in-law of Dr Rossis, conducted at Derviziana by the author in September 2013.

Chapter twenty-one
Material for this chapter is drawn from the following sources: C.E. Barnes diary entries, 1 July 1941, 22 April–18 July 1944; C.E. Barnes, 'Notes and dates from diaries'; C.E. Barnes, 'Final report on activities and observations in Greece', pp. 15–17; C.E. Barnes, 'Report on Zervas Andarte Movement', 14 August 1944, pp. 1–4; James Aldridge, *Cairo: Biography of a City,* London: Macmillan, 1970, p. 178; *Cairo 360,* 'Greek Club: Greek food in Cairo with vintage charm' (review), 6 June 2010, http://www.cairo360.com/article/restaurants/479/greek-club-greek-food-in-cairo-with-vintage-charm; Cody, *New Zealand Engineers, Middle East,* pp. 66, 483, 532, 543–5, 552–3; Cooper, *Cairo in the War,* pp. 251–52; Hammond, *Venture into Greece,* pp. 169–70; Humphries, *Grand Hotels of Egypt,* pp. 107, 129; Jordan, *Conquest without Victory,* pp. 147, 158, 164, 248–50; W.S. Jordan, *The Truth about Greece,* Melbourne: Araluen Publishing: 1946, pp. 26, 31; Reginald Leeper, *When Greek Meets Greek,* London: Chatto and Windus, 1950, pp. 47–49; Macmillan, *War Diaries: The Mediterranean,* p. 35; Marinos, *O Efialtis tis Ethnikis Antistasis* (Ο Εφιάλτης της Εθνικής Αντίστασης) (The nightmare of the national resistance), Vol. 2, pp. 21, 29; Bickham Sweet-Escott, *Baker Street Irregular,* London: Methuen, 1965, pp. 156, 198, 203; Wikipedia, 'New Zealand Forces Club,' http://en.wikipedia.org/wiki/New_Zealand_Forces_Club, accessed 2 May 2013.

Bill Jordan's account of the death of Arthur Hubbard is based on Jordan's books *Conquest without Victory,* pp. 184–97 and *The Truth about Greece,* pp. 29–31, and on personal reminiscences by Chris Carratt (informal telephone discussion with the author, September 2013).

Agoros's observations about Tom's attachment to Zervas and to Greece are drawn from Agoros's diary, entries for 2 September 1943 and 30 January 1944.

Chapter twenty-two

Material for this chapter is drawn from the following sources: C.E. Barnes diary entries, 18 July–20 December 1944; C.E. Barnes, 'Notes and dates from diaries'; C.E. Barnes, 'Final report on activities and observations in Greece', pp. 20–36; C.E. Barnes, 'Report on observations in Greece from July 1943 to April 1944', p. 4; C.E. Barnes, telegram, 'German surrender feelers in Greece', 31 August 1944, FO 371/43692, The National Archives, UK; Sylvia Apostolidou-Ioannidou, 'Report on activities in Athens during period 1943–44', pp. 1–3; Bærentzen (ed.), *British Reports on Greece 1943–44*, pp. xxxiv, 119–21; Chris Carratt, informal telephone discussion with the author, September 2013; 'German surrender feelers', The National Archives, UK, FO 371/43692, telegram from Force 133 dated September 7 1944, FO 371/43693; Hammond, *Venture into Greece*, p. 81; N.G.L. Hammond, 'Report on AMM and Greek situation June 4–Aug 20, 1944', p. 4; Hondros, *Occupation and Resistance*, p. 198; Kosta E. Ioannou (Κώστα Ε. Ιωάννου), *Symantika Gegonota tis Ethnikis Antistasis* (*Σημάντικα Γεγονότα της Εθνικής, Αντίστασης*) (Important events of the national resistance), Athens: Εταιρεία Μελέτης Ελληνικής Ιστορίας, n.d., p. 161; Peter Runciman Musson, HS 9/1080/5, Special Operations Executive Personnel Files (PF series), 1939–1946, The National Archives, UK; 'Report by Capt. D.T.H. Nicholson on past activities etc in Greece', pp. 2, 8; Torrance, 'Report on activities in the field', pp. 13, 14–16, 18–19; Wikipedia, 'Euan Wallace', http://en.wikipedia.org/wiki/Euan_Wallace, accessed 3 October 2013; Woodhouse, 'History of the Allied Military Mission in Greece', pp. 1, 201, 212–13; Woodhouse, *Something Ventured*, pp. 23, 76, 82.

Chris's warning to Tom about Tom's closeness to Zervas is drawn from a telegram dated 19 March 1944, in which Chris warns Cairo about Tom's judgement about Zervas as expressed in Tom's cables (FO 371/43683, The National Archives, UK).

Chapter twenty-three

Material for this chapter is drawn from the following sources: C.E. Barnes diary entries, 21 December 1944–10 August 1945; C.E. Barnes, 'Notes and dates from diaries'; C.E. Barnes, 'Final report on activities and observations in Greece', pp. 36–45; C.E. Barnes, 'Report on observations in Greece from July 1943 to April 1944', p. 4; C.E. Barnes, letter to Comrd SFU, 1 December 1944; 'Apollo' files, Force 133, Benaki Museum,

Athens; Woodhouse diary entry, 1 January 1945; C.M. Woodhouse, letter to C.E. Barnes, 2 February 1944.

Details of Agoros's wait for British air support are based on an anecdote recounted during an informal discussion with Dimitra (Toula) Tsitsika by the author, September 2013, and from Agoros's diary entries for 25 April and 3 September 1944. I have located the anecdote at this historical moment but due to breakdown of recording equipment this may not be absolutely accurate.

Zervas's farewell words to Tom are based on his letter to Tom Barnes, 7 May 1946.

The account of the wedding at Doukades is based on photographs by Tom Barnes and discussions with villagers from Doukades conducted by Dimitris Sgouros on behalf of the author in Doukades, September 2013.

The account of Tom and Sylvia's time together in Cairo is based on an informal discussion with Sylvia Ioannidou conducted by the author in P. Psychiko, September 2013.

Afterword

Material for this chapter is drawn from the following sources: C.E. Barnes diary entries, 25 and 29 September 1946; Gregory Jordan, SJ, Afterword to *Conquest without Victory*, p. 291; Gregory Jordan, SJ, informal email and telephone discussions with the author, July–August 2013; Woodhouse, *Something Ventured*, p. 23.

Bibliography

UNPUBLISHED SOURCES

Diaries

Agoros, Georgios (Αγόρος, Γεώργιος), Unpublished diary 1943–44.

Barnes, C.E., Diaries 1938, 1941, 1942, 1943, 1944, 1945; notebook used as a diary 1 October 1942–8 August 1943.

Barnes, C.E., 'Notes and dates from diaries'.

Woodhouse, C.M., 'Resistance diary', typescript transcript of Christopher Montague Woodhouse's diaries on service with British/Allied Military Mission to Greece, Papers of Col. Hon. Christopher Montague Woodhouse, 5th Baron Terrington (1917–2001), Woodhouse 2/2 1942–1944, Liddell Hart Centre for Military Archives, Kings College, London.

Informal discussions with the author

Apostolidou–Ioannidou, Sylvia (Αποστολίδου-Ιωαννίδου, Σύλβια), June and July 2010, September 2013.

Barnes, Deborah, December 2010.

Carratt, Chris, September 2013.

Jordan, Gregory, SJ, August 2013.

Marinos, Themis (Μαρίνος, Θεμιστοκλής), June 2010; personal communication, 2013.

Rossis, Nikolaos G (Ρώσσης, Νικόλαος Γ), September 2013.

Rossis, Susie, September 2013.

Isitsika, Dimitra (Toula), (Τσιτσικά, Δήμιτρα), September 2013.
Ventoura–Dantou, Marilla, September 2013.
Villagers from Theodoriana, September 2013.
Villagers from Doukades, Corfu, conducted by Dimitris Sgouros on
     behalf of the author, September 2013.

Letters

Barnes, C.E., letter to Beth Harris, 24 July 1943.
Barnes, C.E., letter to Comdr S.F.U., 1 December 1944.
Woodhouse, C.M., letter to Tom Barnes, 2 February 1944.
Zervas, Napoleon, letter to Tom Barnes, 7 May 1946.
Zervas, Napoleon, letter to Beth Barnes, 8 August 1952.

THE NATIONAL ARCHIVES UK
Special Operations Executive Personnel Files (PF series), 1939–1946:

Barnes, Cecil Edward, HS 9/91/2.
Bathgate, Paul, HS 9/103/1.
Gwynne, John Nevile Wake, HS 9/640/1.
Hammond, Nicholas Geoffrey Lempriere, HS 9/652/5.
Jordan, William Sydney, HS 9/812/3.
Micklethwait, Guy, HS9/1030/6.
Musson, Peter Runciman, HS 9/1080/5.
Nicholson, Dennis Thomas Holme, HS 9/1099/4.
Pilkington, Arthur Henry Lionel Alexander, HS 9/1189/1.
Torrance, John Watt, HS 9/1476/3.
Wright, Frederick Percy, HS 9/1623/5.

Citations

Barnes, Cecil Edward, citation for DSO, WO 373/46/168.
Gordon-Creed, Geoffrey Anthony MC, citation for DSO, WO 373/46.
Khouri, Mirhail Khalil Shibli, citation for Bar to Military Medal, WO
     373/46/127.
Moran, John, citation for Military Cross, WO 373/46/144.
Torrance, JW, citation for MBE, 27 September 1940, WO/373/75/698.

Reports

'Weekly progress report No. 6 by SOE for period ending 16 September
     [1943]', FO 371/37205.

Apostolidou-Ioannidou, Sylvia (Αποστολίδου-Ιωαννίδου, Σύλβια), 'Report on activities in Athens during period 1943–44'.

Barnes, C.E., 'Final report on activities and observations in Greece Period 1 October 1942–27 February 1945', April 1945, HS 5/695.

Barnes, C.E., 'Report on observations in Greece from July 1943 to April 1944', FO 371/43688, 1944.

Barnes, C.E., 'Report on Zervas andartes activities during period July–October 1944', HS 5/695.

Bathgate, Paul, 'The andarte movement in Epiros, Jun 43–Feb 44', HS 5/695.

Hammond, N.G.L., 'Report on AMM and Greek situation June 4–Aug 20, 1944', FO 371/43693.

Jordan, William, 'Report on tour of duty in Greece', FO 371/43686, 1944.

Nicholson, D.T.H, 'Report by Capt DTH Nicholson on past activities etc in Greece', HS 5/697.

Torrance, J.W., 'Report on activities in the field', HS 5/697.

Telegrams

Telegram dated 19 March 1944 from a W/T controlled by General Zervas, FO 371/43684.

Addendum II to telegram dated 19 March from a W/T station controlled by General Zervas, FO 371/43684.

Telegram dated 19 March 1944 from Colonel Woodhouse, FO 371/43683.

Telegram dated 23 March 1944 from Lt. Col. Barnes, FO 371/43685.

'German surrender feelers in Greece', telegram from Barnes dated 31 August 1944, FO 371/43692.

'German surrender feelers', telegram from Force 133 dated 7 September 1944, FO 371/43692.

OTHER UNPUBLISHED SOURCES

'Apollo' files, Force 133, Benaki Museum Archives, Athens.

Barnes, C.E., Manuscript speech notes.

Barnes, C.E., Notebook from Egypt.

Barnes, C.E., 'Guerrilla warfare 1942–45'.

Chandrinos, Jason (Χανδρινός Ιάσονας), interview with Stergios Voulgaris (Στέργιος Βούλγαρης), 7 April 2005, Athens.

Thomas, Beth (née Harris). 'Personal reflections of Deloraine', talk given to Meander Valley School for Seniors, 13 July 1994.

Woodhouse, C.M. 'History of the Allied Military Mission in Greece (September 1942 to December 1944)', unpublished manuscript.

PUBLISHED SOURCES
English

'Aiding guerrillas: Work of N.Z. airmen', [Wellington] *Evening Post*, Volume CXXXVIII, Issue 40, 16 August 1944, p. 6.

Aldridge, James, *Cairo: Biography of a City*, London: Macmillan, 1970.

Australian War Memorial, *Encyclopedia*, 'Rationing of food and clothing during the Second World War', http://www.awm.gov.au/encyclopedia/homefront/rationing.asp, accessed 3 February 2013.

Bærentzen, Lars (ed.), *British Reports on Greece 1943–44*, Documents on Modern Greek History 1, Copenhagen: Museum Tusculanum, 1982.

Clive, Nigel, *A Greek Experience 1943–1948*, Wilton: Michael Russell, 1985.

Cody, J.F., *New Zealand Engineers, Middle East, Official History of New Zealand in the Second World War 1939–45*, Wellington: Department of Internal Affairs New Zealand, 1961.

Condit, D.M., *Case Study in Guerrilla War: Greece During World War II*, n.p.: American University, 1961.

Cooper, Artemis, *Cairo in the War, 1939–1945* (1989), London: Penguin, 1995.

Cox, Geoffrey, *The Race for Trieste*, London: William Kimber, 1977.

Dawson, W.D., *18 Battalion and Armoured Regiment, The Official History of New Zealand in the Second World War 1939–45*, Wellington: Historical Publications Branch, 1961, New Zealand Electronic Text Centre.

Edmonds, Arthur, *With Greek Guerrillas*, n.p.: Times Print, 1998.

Fleischer, Hagen, 'Contacts Between German Occupation Authorities and the Major Greek Resistance Organisations: Sound Tactics or Collaboration?' In John O. Iatrides (ed.), *Greece in the 1940s: A Nation in Crisis*, Hanover, NH: University Press of New England, 1981, pp. 347–53.

Fleischer, Hagen, *Im Kreuzschatten der Mächte : Griechenland 1941–1944 (Okkupation, Resistance, Kollaboration)*, Frankfurt am Main: Peter Lang, 1986.

Gage, Nicholas, *Eleni*, London: Vintage, 2010 (1983), Kindle edition.

Gallop, Rodney, 'Folk-songs of Modern Greece', *The Musical Quarterly*, 21.1, pp. 89–91.

'Greek Club: Greek Food in Cairo with Vintage Charm', http://www. cairo360.com/article/restaurants/479/greek-club-greek-food-in-cairo-with-vintage-charm, accessed 18 May 2013.

Hammond, Nicholas, *Venture into Greece: With the Guerrillas 1943–44*, London: William Kimber and Co., 1983.

Hamson, Denys, *We Fell among Greeks*, London: Cape, 1946.

Hart, Janet, *New Voices in the Nation: Women and the Greek Resistance*, Ithaca, NY: Cornell University Press.

Hedley, Alex, with Megan Hutching, *Fernleaf Cairo: New Zealanders at Maadi Camp*, Auckland: HarperCollins, 2009.

Hondros, John Louis, *Occupation and Resistance: The Greek Agony, 1941–1944*, New York, NY: Pella Publishing Co. Inc., 1983.

Hugh H. Gardner, *Guerrilla and Counterguerrilla Warfare in Greece, 1941–1945*, Washington DC: Office of the Chief of Military History, 1962.

Humphries, Andrew, *Grand Hotels of Egypt in the Golden Age of Travel*, Cairo: American University in Cairo, 2011.

Jordan, William, *Conquest without Victory*, Bedford: Little Hills Press, 1989 (1969).

Jordan, William, *The Truth about Greece*, Melbourne: Araluen Publishing, 1946.

Kédros, André, *La Résistance grecque* (The Greek Resistance), *1940–1944*, Paris: R. Laffont, 1966.

Ladd, James and Keith Melton, *Clandestine Warfare: Weapons and Equipment of the SOE and OSS*, London: Book Club Associates, 1988.

Lanz, Hubert, *Partisan Warfare in the Balkans*, US Army, European Command, Historical Division, 1952.

Leeper, Reginald, *When Greek Meets Greek*, London: Chatto and Windus, 1950.

Macmillan, Harold, *War Diaries: The Mediterranean 1943–45*, New York, NY: St Martin's Press, 1984.

Marinos, Themistocles, *Harling Mission – 1942*, Athens: Papazisis, 1993.

Maule, Henry, *Scobie: Hero of Greece: The British Campaign 1944–5*, London: Arthur Barker, 1975.

Mazower, Mark, *Inside Hitler's Greece: The Experience of Occupation, 1941–44*, New Haven: Yale University Press, 2001 (1993).

McGlynn, M.B., *Special Service in Greece*, Wellington: Department of Internal Affairs, 1953.

Moorehead, Alan, *African Trilogy*, London: Hamish Hamilton, 1944.

Mulgan, John, *Report on Experience* [1947], Auckland: Blackwood & Janet Paul, 1967.

Muthiah, S., *Born to Dare: The life of Lt. Gen. Inderjit Singh Gill PVSM, MC*, New Delhi: Penguin, 2008.

Myers, E.C.W., *Greek Entanglement*, London: Hart-Davis, 1955.

NZ official history, http://www.nzetc.org/tm/scholarly/tei-WH2Alam-c32.html

Obituary, Leslie Philip Bliaux, Papua New Guinea Association of Australia (PNGAA), http://www.pngaa.net/Vale/vale_june92.htm, accessed 18 January 2013.

O'Sullivan, Vincent, *Long Journey to the Border: A Life of John Mulgan*, Auckland: Penguin, 2003.

Papastratis Procopis, *British Policy Towards Greece During the Second World War*, Cambridge: Cambridge University Press, 1984.

Sarafis, Stefanos, *ELAS: Greek Resistance Army*, trans. Sylvia Moody, London: Merlin Press, 1980.

Scarfe, A. and W., *All That Grief: Migrant Recollections of Greek Resistance to Fascism, 1941–1949*, Sydney: Hale and Iremonger, 1994.

Simpson, John and Mark Adkin, *The Quiet Operator: Special Forces Signaller Extraordinary*, London: Cooper, 1993.

Stafford, David, *Secret Agent: The True Story of the Special Operations Executive*, London: BBC, 2000.

Stavrianos, L.S., 'The Greek National Front (EAM): A study in Resistance Organisation and Administration', *Journal of Modern History* 24.1, 1952.

Stevens, W.G., *Problems of 2 NZEF, Official History of New Zealand in the Second World War 1939–1945*, Wellington: Historical Publications Branch, 1958, New Zealand Electronic Text Centre.

'Stevens, William George', in *Te Ara: The Encyclopedia of New Zealand*, http://www.teara.govt.nz/en/biographies/4s43/1, accessed 1 January 2012.

Summerville, Donald, *World War II Day by Day*, London: Bison, 1989.

Sweet-Escott, Bickham, *Baker Street Irregular*, London: Methuen, 1965.

Tsatsou, Jeanne (Ioanna), *The Sword's Fierce Edge*, trans. Jean Demos, Nashville, TN: Vanderbilt University Press, 1969.

Van der Kiste, John, *Kings of the Hellenes: The Greek Kings, 1863–1974*, Dover, N.H.: Alan Sutton, 1994.

Wallace, David, 'Conditions in Zervas-held territory' in *British Reports on Greece 1943–44*, ed. Lars Bærentzen, Documents on Modern Greek History 1, Copenhagen: Museum Tusculanum, 1982.

Waugh, Evelyn, *Officers and Gentlemen*, London: Chapman and Hall, 1955.

Woodhouse, C.M., 'Early British Contacts with the Greek Resistance in 1942', *Balkan Studies*, Vol. 12, No. 2, 1971.

Woodhouse, C.M., *Apple of Discord: A Survey of Recent Greek Politics in Their International Setting*, London: Hutchinson, 1948.

Woodhouse, C.M., *Modern Greece: A Short History*, London: Faber, fifth edn, 1991.

Woodhouse, C.M., *Something Ventured*, London: Granada, 1982.

Woodhouse, C.M., *The Struggle for Greece 1941–1949*, London: Hurst, 2002 (1976).

Greek

Charitopoulos, Dionysis (Διονύσης Χαριτόπουλος), *Aris, o Archigos ton Atatkton* (Άρης, ο Αρχηγός των Ατάκτων) [Aris, leader of the irregular forces], Athens: Topos Books, 2009.

Dimos Lakkas Souliou (Δήμος Λάκκας Σουλίου), *Dimos Lakkas Souliou* (Δήμος Λάκκας Σουλίου) [The municipality of Lakka Souli], n.p.: INTERREG III Greece-Italy, 2008.

Marinos, Themis (Θέμης Μαρίνος), *O Efialtis tis Ethnikis Antistasis* (Ο Εφιάλτης της Εθνικής Αντίστασης) [The nightmare of the national resistance], Vols 1 and 2, Athens: Papazisi, 2003.

Ioannou, Kosta E (Ιωάννου, Κώστα Ε), *Ethnikes Omades Ellinon Andarton* (Εθνικές Ομάδες Ελλήνων Ανταρτών) [National groups of Greek resistance fighters], Athens: Εταιρεία Μελέτης Ελληνικής Ιστορίας, n.d.

Ioannou, Kostas (Ιωάννου, Κώστας), *Pos Plastografeitai i Istoria tis Antistasis* (Πώς Πλαστογραφείται η Ιστορία της Αντίστασης) [How the history of the resistance is falsified], [Athens]: Εταιρεία Μελέτης Ελληνικής Ιστορίας, n.d.

Ioannou, Kosta E. (Ιωάννου, Κώστα Ε), *Simantika Gegonota tis Ethnikis Antistatis (Σημάντικα Γεγονότα της Εθνικής Αντίστασης)* [Important events of the national resistance], Athens: Εταιρεία Μελέτης Ελληνικής Ιστορίας, n.d.

Index

Katherine Barnes is the author of *The Higher Self*, about Australian poet Christopher Brennan, which won the Walter McRae Russell award in 2007 and was shortlisted for the NSW Premier's Prize for Literary Scholarship in 2008. She holds a PhD in Australian literature from the Australian National University and formerly lectured at the Australian Defence Force Academy, where she taught creative writing and English literature, including the literature of war. She lives in Canberra.